LARS VON TRIER
BEYOND DEPRESSION

Lars von Trier at work on the set of *Melancholia*, with Kiefer Sutherland,
Manuel Alberto Claro, Kirsten Dunst, Alexander Skarsgård, and Charlotte Gainsbourg.

LARS VON TRIER
BEYOND DEPRESSION

CONTEXTS | AND
COLLABORATIONS

LINDA BADLEY

Wallflower

New York

Wallflower Press is an imprint of
Columbia University Press
Publishers Since 1893
New York   Chichester, West Sussex
cup.columbia.edu
Copyright © 2022 Columbia University Press
All rights reserved

Library of Congress Cataloging-in-Publication Data
Names: Badley, Linda, author.
Title: Lars von Trier beyond depression : contexts and collaborations / Linda Badley.
Description: New York : Wallflower, [2021] | Includes bibliographical references
and index.
Identifiers: LCCN 2021036421 | ISBN 9780231191524 (hardback) |
ISBN 9780231191531 (trade paperback) | ISBN 9780231549448 (ebook)
Subjects: LCSH: Trier, Lars von, 1956—Criticism and interpretation. | Motion
pictures—Denmark—History—21st century. | Motion pictures—Production and
direction—Denmark. | Motion picture producers and directors—Denmark—Biography.
Classification: LCC PN1998.3.T747 B343 2021 | DDC 791.4302/33092—dc23
LC record available at https://lccn.loc.gov/2021036421

Columbia University Press books are printed
on permanent and durable acid-free paper.
Printed in the United States of America

Cover design: Lisa Hamm
Cover image: Film still from *The House That Jack Built*, Zentropa.

CONTENTS

PREFACE

POSTCRITIQUE

This book examines the late work of Lars von Trier, the cycle of four films he made in the decade after his clinical depression of late 2006 through early 2007, through primary-source research (archival materials, interviews, scripts, and official statements), close analysis of the films, and synthesis from a range of cultural contexts. Much has been written about the reception of von Trier's films, which is often skewed by controversies stoked by the director himself, as well as his working methods on set—the imposition of constraints, the handheld camera following the action, the "liberation" of actors by forcing them to try out different interpretations of a scene, and so on. Far less has been written about the brainstorming, incubating, and writing stages, as well as what genetic critics call the "avant-textes"—the author's (or, in this case, the auteur's) notes, statements of intention, sketches, drafts, shooting scripts, consultations, research materials, and hypotexts in general, in addition to a rich array of paratexts.[1] Hence, one of my aims is to shift the understanding of von Trier's work toward a sort of preproduction history: a study of artistic development and the creative processes employed by it, including the inspirations, collaborations, and material conditions of his practice. During the last decade, these have changed considerably. Publicized as the nearly unfiltered product of—and therapy for—his depression, *Antichrist* (2009) epitomized the highly Romantic (even Faustian) approach to the creative process that he claims to have used for years, in which he wrote in self-isolation for a week or two of intoxicated frenzy. Beginning with *Melancholia* (2011), he shifted to a dialogic and dialectical methodology in which he brainstormed and wrote with collaborators, a process reflected in the "digressionist" form of the last two films. My approach shifts accordingly, from textual comparisons of notes and scripts that reveal the development of *Antichrist* to an analysis that liberally interpolates interviews with the various makers of the last three films.

My methodology also concurs with the postcritical turn that attempts to find means of interpretation venturing beyond a "hermeneutics of suspicion" (Paul Ricoeur) or "paranoid" reading (Eve Sedgwick) that informs much of the commentary on von Trier. Sedgwick, for example, points out the value of a "reparative" impulse, one that is "additive and accretive," aiming "to assemble and confer plenitude."[2] Rather than treating archival materials with distrust, or looking for what is concealed, I have chosen to trust my sources, to follow the grain, the visible signs and "watermarks" (Ann Laura Stoler), with the aim of interpreting carefully, commonsensically, and comparatively while attempting to resolve or explain contradictions.[3] Rather than intervention, my aim is elucidation, through description and analysis of the origins, influences, circumstances of production, paratexts, ideas, and affects of the films together with the films themselves. Risking credibility, I quote the eponymous antihero of *The House That Jack Built* (2018), who pontificates that "the material does the work," that it "has a kind of will of its own," and that following that will produces the most efficacious results. While reading in this fashion a large folder consisting of von Trier's notes, fragments, and research materials for *Antichrist*, a fascinating and rich metanarrative emerged: of how a transparently autobiographical psychodrama about a male anxiety patient with an irrational fear of nature developed into the film that shocked, offended, and polarized Cannes in 2009. Along the same lines, the contents of a folder archived at Zentropa with the label "Director's Intentions" I have taken as just that—as manifesto-like statements von Trier wrote prior to each of the films that provide insights into those films, together with commentary from interviews with a range of practitioners including cinematographer Manuel Alberto Claro, cowriter Jenle Hallund, assistant director Anders Refn, story supervisor Vinca Wiedemann, sound designer and composer Kristian Eidnes Andersen, personal assistants Katrine Sahlstrøm and Emilie Spliid Pearce, producer Louise Vesth, and writer-director Lars von Trier. Additionally, I bring a range of critical contexts to the films and these materials, including genre studies, film-philosophy, ecocritical perspectives, and the postcinematic.

From Trilogies to Duologies

This method has yielded revelations that revise several ingrained critical assumptions about the person and practice of Lars von Trier, including my own. My first book on Lars von Trier was organized to reflect his grouping of his films into trilogies, a performative auteurist practice he adapted from Ingmar Bergman, and I originally envisioned this book to focus on the "depression trilogy," the designation that fans, critics, and scholars have given to *Antichrist*, *Melancholia*, and *Nymphomaniac* (2013–2014).[4] Any trilogy is to a greater or lesser extent an auteurist construction, but early in the series of interviews I conducted from June 2018 through fall 2019, it became apparent that the "depression trilogy" was a fantasy created and shared by fans and critics. When I approached von Trier, Claro, Wiedemann, Hallund, and others about the designation, they were bemused, then quickly dismissive. When I asked von Trier what he thought of the notion, he laughingly noted that since he has been depressed much of his life, it "could fit all my films." When I interjected that he had "always made a point of . . . ," he finished my sentence with "of having trilogies," before quipping, in reference to the failure of the third installment of the USA trilogy, "Wasington," to materialize: "But I'm also an expert at making trilogies with only two films."[5] Similarly, Claro, his cinematographer since 2010, observed that von Trier has shifted "from trilogies to two films. To Two-logies."[6] Wiedemann, who has known him since film school and served as his amanuensis and script consultant for *Melancholia* and *Nymphomaniac*, explained that she has "always" seen his movies as "coming in couples, like twins," a pattern that has played out since *Riget* (*The Kingdom*, 1994 and 1997).[7] From this perspective, the Gold Heart "trilogy" is really a pair (*Breaking the Waves*, 1996, and *Dancer in the Dark*, 2000) plus *Idioterne* (*The Idiots*, 1998), which is remembered primarily as something else—as Dogme #2, a radically transgressive, performative ensemble experiment that enacted or perhaps parodied the spirit of Dogme 95 itself, than for its self-sacrificing female protagonist, Karen. "What always happens," in Wiedemann's view,

> is that he takes a theme and he tries to reinvent the theme or expand on it and . . . but also . . . it has to do with the feeling that he's not finished with it. . . . to replicate . . . because it's easier. So you have to get through this crisis before you then invent something completely new. So on *Manderley*, I believe

it was very obvious that, I mean there was not enough new to it. I mean, it was uninspired. And I feel that [von Trier made] *The House That Jack Built* . . . kind of to make two testaments."[8]

Apparently, von Trier has become more comfortable with acknowledging this strategy. Accordingly, *Antichrist* and *Melancholia*, which are similar in their opening prologues, operative elements, and virtuosic cinematic flourishes, constitute a "depression duology." *Nymphomaniac* and *The House That Jack Built*, however, as Claro stressed in my interview with him in June 2018, were born out of a rebellion against what he came to regard as *Melancholia*'s "popcorn film" elements and classical aesthetic flourishes and an urge to experiment with a new transmedial and essayistic form von Trier called "Digressionism." In fact, the developmental process of the two most recent films may have had less to do with his depression than the conditions surrounding his recovery, a pursuit of sobriety, and the joys of reading long philosophical novels (by Marcel Proust, Fyodor Dostoevsky, Thomas Mann, and Hermann Broch, among other classic European authors), together with collaborations at the conception and writing phases. *Antichrist* and *Melancholia* had returned to cinema in the grand style; *Nymphomaniac* and *The House That Jack Built* were deliberately "ugly," talky films about intensely driven characters, compelled by sexuality and violence. And while expressing and reflecting on von Trier's experience of depression and anxiety, *Antichrist* and *Melancholia* were transmedial experiments directly inspired by his work on Wagner's Ring cycle. Alternating Dogme-style realism with a sublime expressionism, both opened with brilliantly stylized prologues or preludes set to classical music. Finally, while *Nymphomaniac* and *The House That Jack Built* were also, arguably, about psychological disorders—sex addiction and psychopathy—they are equally, perhaps chiefly, "testament" films about the female and male principles at their extreme limits, as masochistic hypersexuality and sadistic violence, respectively.

ACKNOWLEDGMENTS

This book was planned as a sequel of sorts to *Lars von Trier*, a volume in the Contemporary Film Directors series from University of Illinois Press (2011). Ending with a short "epilogue" on *Antichrist* that focused primarily on the surrounding contexts—the Cannes 2009 scandal, paratexts, reception, genre, and affect—it felt truncated and impressionistic. Since then, fascinated with the film's intensity and confessional nature along with its departures from von Trier's previous trajectory and intrigued with its dense tapestry of hypotexts, I had been needled with an urge to do the film justice. In 2017, after the successive stirs caused by *Melancholia* and *Nymphomaniac*, I proposed a relatively limited study of the three films that von Trier made following his depression of 2006–2007, by then dubbed his "Depression Trilogy." I originally intended to analyze the films within the context of extreme cinema, but further developments altered the project's contours substantially—in methodology, scope, and length. I thank Yoram Allon and especially Ryan Groendyk at Wallflower Press for their infinite patience, understanding, support, and guidance during what has been a very long haul and for their continuing encouragement. And I thank the three anonymous readers of the typescript for their generous comments and suggestions.

Without Peter Schepelern—his initiative, encouragement, support, assistance, and expertise—this book would most certainly not exist in its current form. In the spring and fall of 2017, while preparing the catalog for a major exhibition at the Brandts Museum of Art and Culture, *Lars von Trier: Det Gode Med Det Onde* (November 8, 2017–July 29, 2018), he encouraged me to expand the relatively limited study I had planned into a quite different, and far more elaborate, undertaking grounded in research into the origins, production, and materials that went into the films, in part, as a way of completing the work already done—most notably his own benchmarks *Lars von Triers Film: Tvang og befrielse* (Rosinante, 2000), *Lars von Triers Elementer: En filminstruktørs arbejde* (Rosinante, 1997), and a host of articles, both in Danish and in English, that he has published since. Offering his time, labor, a treasure trove of materials (including a large file of materials and a draft of his uncompleted manuscript for a book on *Antichrist* originally intended for the Nordic Film Classics series, now discontinued, at the University of Washington Press), and an encyclopedic range of information, Peter has been my guide and translator in situations where I would have been clueless otherwise—for example, when sorting through the Lars von Trier Collection at the Danish Film Institute, or when floundering through a Google translation of Nikoline's rap video *Gourmet* (2020). He has kept me abreast of new materials (interviews, articles, and the like available in Denmark), while carefully reading drafts. Throughout this time, he and his wife, Anne, have been generous and delightful hosts. His assistance and their friendship have meant more than I can say.

I thank Lars von Trier for devoting his time and energy to the June 2018 interview that is quoted and reflected throughout the book, especially in chapter 4, on *The House That Jack Built*. Talking to him was, as before, in 2006 and 2007, a great pleasure, richly entertaining as well as enlightening, as was talking to several of von Trier's collaborators. Von Trier's longtime assistant director Anders Refn provided a generous and delightful June 2018 interview that spanned *Breaking the Waves* and editing *Dogville* through *The House That Jack Built*. Manuel Alberto Claro, von Trier's cinematographer beginning with *Melancholia*, has been unfailingly gracious, helpful, and articulate. Since October and November 2013, when I interviewed him over the phone for what was then a mere conference paper about the cultural, political, and aesthetic significance of *Melancholia*'s version of Tjolöholm Slott, he has granted interviews at regular intervals—on *Nymphomaniac* in 2015, *The House That Jack Built* in 2018, and an assortment of subjects in 2019. Although I met her just in June 2019, interviewing von Trier's brainstorming partner and cowriter Jenle Hallund then and again in October 2020 provided nothing less than a series of revelations about the evolution of *Nymphomaniac* and *The House That Jack Built* especially. I am grateful for her trust, generosity, time, and effort. Making time for a Skype interview during the middle of her July 2019 vacation, Vinca Wiedemann, von Trier's sparring partner and story supervisor during the writing of *Melancholia* and *Nymphomaniac*, offered a thorough, lively, and detailed account of the process. Kristian Eidnes Andersen, von Trier's sound designer and composer since 1996, made time for a substantial two-part interview amid a hectic schedule complicated by the COVID-19 pandemic in early February 2021. Additionally, von Trier's producer Louise Vesth and former assistants Emily Spliid Pearce and Katrine Sahlstrøm provided essential information and illuminating comments during the summer and early fall of 2019.

The staff at Zentropa Productions deserve my gratitude for their patience and energy, notably von Trier's personal assistants Stine Vesterskov, Laura Plummer, and Hugo Dichman for their help in arranging interviews, obtaining scripts and documents, and making it possible for me to obtain information and permissions over these last four years. I owe special thanks to Vesterskov, who set up a special screening of *The House That Jack Built* for me at Zentropa in 2018, and Simon Lytting, Zentropa Post Production, for technical assistance with subsequent screenings. And I am especially grateful to Birgit Granhøj, who oversees the Lars von Trier Collection at the Danish Film Institute and guided me before, during, and after a research trip to Copenhagen in June 2019, while making the research experience a true pleasure.

I am indebted as well to a host of colleagues and others for supporting or assisting aspects of my work on this project in its various stages: Andrew Nestingen, Mette Hjort, Anders Marklund, Elisabet Björklund, Christine Holmlund, Annette Brauerhoch, Mariah Larsson, Doru Pop, Christina Stojanova, Anna Stenport, Scott MacKenzie, Arne Lunde, Carol Vernalis, Lisa Perrott, Holly Rogers, Bodil Marie Stavning Thomsen, Ralph Beliveau, Danny Shipka, William J. Simmons, and Liberty Patterson. I thank Nancy Roche, Lisa Williams, Kirsten Boatwright, and Dawn Hall for our mutual and passionate cinephilia, for their friendship, for countless discussions of film and Trier-related subjects. I thank my niece Lydia Cornett, who has developed in the last few years into a canny and brilliant documentary filmmaker, for our many wide-ranging conversations about filmmaking, women in film, making art, and Lars von Trier. I owe countless former students who screened, discussed, and wrote about von Trier's films in my Horror Film, Contemporary World Cinema, and Women and Film classes, and to whom I am indebted for too many insights to account for. Finally, I thank my husband Bill Badley, who meticulously and with great insight read and critiqued various versions and drafts of these chapters throughout these months of COVID-19 detention, and for his patience, encouragement, and companionship.

Quotations from von Trier's films on DVD as well as from supplementary materials (commentaries, featurettes, interviews, and press conferences) are taken from the (typically definitive) Region 2 DVDs; when the language is other than English, from their subtitles; or, in instances where von Trier's original intentions are especially important, from the shooting scripts, to which Zentropa kindly provided me with access. Figures 1.1, 1.2, and 1.3 are courtesy of the Lars von Trier Collection at the Danish Film Institute. Figures 3.1 and 4.1, publicity posters for *Nymphomaniac* and *The House That Jack Built*, are courtesy of Zentropa Entertainments. All other illustrations are frame enlargements.

As for the book's numerous translations from the Danish, when a specific translator is not mentioned, the translations are mine—assisted considerably by Google Translate. I am fortunate to have Peter Schepelern to thank for a great number of translations, and I have credited him accordingly. Several of these he had already included in his unpublished manuscript "Antichrist I–V (2015)," to which he generously gave me access; many of the others were videos or other texts inaccessible to Google Translate. Especially where archives are concerned, much can be lost in translation. For that reason, in most instances where Danish is the original language, I supplement the English translations in the text with the original Danish in endnotes.

I have presented versions of portions this material at various conferences and as keynotes: from the introduction, for the exhibition opening of *Lars von Trier: Det Gode Med Det Onde* at the Brandts Museum of Art and Visual Culture in Odense, Denmark, on November 8, 2017; from chapter 1, at SASS (the Society for the Advancement of Scandinavian Studies conference) on May 4, 2012; from chapter 2, at PCA (the Popular Culture Conference) on April 12, 2012, and at SASS on May 8, 2015; and from chapter 3, at SCMS (Society for Cinema and Media Studies conference) in March 25, 2015, and at Cinema as Provocation: Ekphrasis Conference in Cinema and Visual Culture, in Cluj, Romania, on May 28, 2015. I thank fellow panelists and audience members for their comments and suggestions.

Additionally, some of the chapters in this book draw on material previously published elsewhere. I thank the publishers and editors for their permission to use material from the following texts:

For the introduction: Linda Badley, *Lars von Trier* (Urbana: University of Illinois Press, 2011); and Linda Badley, "Tag det gode med de onde," in *Lars von*

Trier: Det Gode Med Det Onde, ed. Peter Schepelern, Brandts Museum of Art and Visual Culture (Copenhagen, DK: Strandberg, 2017), 99–110.

For chapter 1: Linda Badley, *Lars von Trier* (Urbana: University of Illinois Press, 2011); and Linda Badley, "*Antichrist*, Misogyny, and Witch Burning: The Nordic Cultural Contexts," *Journal of Scandinavian Cinema* 3, no. 1 (March 2013): 15–33.

For chapter 2: Linda Badley, "Diamonds, Wagner, the *Gesamtkunstwerk*, and Lars von Trier's Depression Films," in *Transmedia Directors: Artistry, Industry, and New Audiovisual Aesthetics*, ed. Carol Vernallis, Holly Rogers, and Lisa Perrott (London: Bloomsbury Academic, 2019), 378–88.

For chapter 3: Linda Badley, " 'Fill All My Holes:' *Nymphomaniac*, Sade, and the (Female) Libertine Body," in "Cinema as Provocation," special issue, *Ekphrasis: Images, Cinema, Media, Theory* 14, no. 2 (2015): 21–38; and Linda Badley, "*Nymphomaniac* as Retro Scandinavian Blue," in "Sexuality and Scandinavian Cinema," special issue, *Journal of Scandinavian Cinema* 5, no. 2 (2015): 191–204.

INTRODUCTION

Is Lars von Trier OK?

On Sunday, August 9, 2020, episode 4 of *ArtyFarty*, a new Danish television magazine-style television show about culture, addressed the question "Er Von Trier Okay?" (Is Von Trier OK?). Prompted by a Facebook post by a worried former von Trier assistant and presented as an odyssey in and around Copenhagen, the hosts approach various associates and experts—including television producer and director of the National Film School of Denmark Poul Nesgaard, von Trier's longtime business partner and producer Peter Aalbæk Jenson, and mentor and scholar Peter Schepelern—in settings and costumes evoking his oeuvre. The episode builds with tremulous anticipation to a confrontation with von Trier himself, as Zissel Astrid Kjertum-Mohr (wearing a slightly tattered bridal gown) approaches the door of his home with *the* question, to which he answers:

> VON TRIER: I'm never OK . . . look, there are always fourteen different
> things wrong with me, so it's piss awkward.
> KJERTUM-MOHR: But you ended up being right—the world is about to
> collapse.
> VON TRIER: Yes, that's nice . . . I can be pleased about that.
> KJERTUM-MOHR: Have you prepared yourself for the end of the world?
> VON TRIER: It must be a mental preparation, you mean? Because I
> mean, it doesn't help to buy a lot of canned ham, it doesn't help [to do]
> anything. . . . unless you expect the water to rise first . . . yes, it will

probably go to hell, it is the only thing we know . . . but it worries me about my kids and my grandchild . . . that they have to cope with this.

KJERTUM-MOHR: Is it serious this time that the world is going under? We have a pandemic, the climate is going downhill, Donald Trump is president—

VON TRIER: I guess he can't stay that all the time . . . maybe he can.

KJERTUM-MOHR: Then it's going to be Kanye West afterwards, maybe—

VON TRIER: America is too stupid for democracy, but it's interesting what kind of government the world is going to have. That's not something I can answer, unfortunately—

KJERTUM-MOHR: What do you hope for?

VON TRIER: Of course, I hope for a giant explosion like . . . when Krypton exploded and Superman was released, fell to Earth . . . ! I hope in my old age to make tolerable films.[1]

If Lars von Trier's most recent, and most tumultuous, decade is any indication, the films of his old age are likely to be both more and less than "tolerable": uncomfortably subjective yet extraordinarily prescient about the doom we have brought and continue to bring upon ourselves. This book is about the cycle of films from 2009 through 2018 that followed and, to a greater or lesser extent, expressed, reflected, or were impacted by his experience of clinical depression in late 2006 through early 2007. Bookended by Cannes controversy, it began with *Antichrist* (2009) and was followed by *Melancholia* (2011), *Nymphomaniac* (2013–2014), and *The House That Jack Built* (2018). I take up where my 2011 volume, *Lars von Trier*, concluded with a short "epilogue" that focused on *Antichrist*'s backstory, marketing, and reception. Ten years later, that film is recognized as having introduced a more defiantly provocative, and difficult-to-decipher, phase in von Trier's career, one that marks a sharp turn from the cultural politics of the period from Dogme 95 through the USA: Land of Opportunities duology and *The Boss of It All*. Von Trier's films from 1998 through 2006 employed an increasingly overt and multileveled critique of American cultural imperialism— his shorthand for late capitalism at its worst—while taking on issues such as the death penalty, the injustices of neoliberalism, hostility to immigrants, gun violence, racism, and the heritage of slavery. *Dogville* was epic and theatrical in a

Brechtian sense, its characters engaging in formal position statements (followed by voting) and philosophical debates, for example, between Grace and her father in the penultimate chapter. *Antichrist*, in contrast, was a primal scream, to the extent that von Trier claims to have been inspired directly by Edvard Munch's iconic expressionist painting *Skrik* (*The Scream*, 1893).

Although *Antichrist*, *Melancholia*, and *The House That Jack Built* are set in America and radiate political commentary for anyone who wishes to see it, these films mark a deeply personal, even narcissistic, turn, while subjecting audiences to what has been described as "extreme" cinema, trauma cinema, or Artaudian cinema of cruelty. Marrying this with film-philosophy in provocative ways, they blended auteurist art cinema with "low" or exploitation genres (horror, science fiction/disaster film, pornography, and the serial killer film) and subordinated narrative to affect on the one hand and essayism on the other. Uniquely overdetermined with mythic resonances and gendered cultural and psychological triggers, *Antichrist* unearthed the ancient fear of and reverence for the chthonic feminine, raising questions without answers, and its sexualized violence produced a precisely calibrated frisson. *Melancholia* was, as advertised widely, an exquisitely "beautiful" movie "about the end of the world" that delivered on its premise with the absolute, if understated, finality of a black screen.[2] Then, in a reaction against its Wagnerian Romanticism, von Trier shifted to a narrative mode he dubbed "Digressionism," which subordinated plot and affect to dialectic and dialogue. Flaunting their pedantry through exceedingly bookish scripts and a digressive structure, *Nymphomaniac* incorporated pornography into the cinematic language, and *The House That Jack Built* cheekily assimilated the serial killer genre to von Trier's public persona. Finally, these films are marked by a profoundly retrospective compulsion, a return—in part nostalgic, in part desperate—to von Trier's earliest influences, efforts, and the controversies raised by them: to the expressionism, and film noir influence, of the Holocaust-haunted Europe trilogy, to his longtime obsession with the Wagnerian aesthetic, and, even further back, to his student films and two unpublished novels.

If von Trier's late films may be seen as a period, roughly a decade from 2009 through 2018, they can also be understood as a cycle, with several characteristics in common that distinguish them from his earlier work. As detailed in the following paragraphs, these films (1) are performatively self-reflexive and feature elaborate paratextual strategies; (2) deploy a strongly polarized gender politics; (3) feature psychologically damaged characters and psycho-dramatic narratives; (4) mark a profound if unconventional philosophical turn; and (5) brandish transmediality as a mark of their auteurism.

Performative Authorship, Provocation as Paratext

As Peter Schepelern put the issue in 2005, Lars von Trier's career aim has been less to make films than "a prototype auteurist initiative . . . to construct Lars *von* Trier, the auteur filmmaker."[3] Moreover, von Trier's "self-made" auteurism is performative in the senses that J. L. Austin, Judith Butler, and Raul Eshelman have used the term. Contingent upon audiences within social and institutional contexts, his films, like his extradiegetic provocations, have performative *illocutionary* functions to accomplish things or bring things about, often becoming *perlocutionary* in inciting controversy, affecting audiences, creating scandals, and effecting changes in the aesthetic, cultural, and political climate.[4] Mixing showmanship, provocation, and scandal, von Trier's performance of Lars von Trier invariably functions as a metacinematic layer or paratext. Coined by Gérard Genette, *paratext* refers to the parts of a text extraneous to the narrative proper but that greatly influence how we interpret it: titles, genres, pseudonyms, blurbs, authorial commentary, prefaces, reviews, chapter headings, illustrations, typography, production design. In visual media culture, paratext overlaps with marketing—especially of "high concept" movies in which trailers, posters, games, toys, and food become hermeneutical devices. To compete with Hollywood's blockbuster remake-and-sequel onslaughts, von Trier issues manifestos and proclamations, proposes anti-genres (Dogme 95, Digressionism) and creates scandals among what are more obvious paratextual strategies such as trailers, teasers, and progress-report-like announcements. Heralded with a ten-commandment-style manifesto on red leaflets that required handheld, on-location filmmaking and prohibited, among other things, genres, weapons, murders, and special effects, Dogme became a paratext for "certified" films along with the Dogme 95 certificate, numbered and signed by the four Dogme "brothers" and displayed at the beginning of each. The USA duology's production design itself functioned as a paratext. Consisting of a soundstage with a chalk map and a few props, resembling a diagram, map, or lecture embellished with spoiler chapter title cards, it alienated the audience, denied a "cinematic" aesthetic, and brought ideological subtexts to the surface.

Von Trier's staging of Cannes press conferences as political and auteurist has been equally if not more impactful. Hence von Trier's explanation, in a Cannes interview in 2003, for making films set in and about America: he claimed to be "60% American" and asserted that the American entertainment industry has "standardized our culture in a most moronic fashion. Entering a country with troops is small change compared to the way we have allowed ourselves to be occupied," an assertion that contributed to an understanding of *Dogville* as a combative, even "anti-American" reversal of Hollywood's global imperialism.[5] Likewise, his response to Baz Bamigboye at the Cannes interview after *Antichrist*'s critics' screening, in which he refused to "justify" what is arguably his most disturbing film, asserting that he made the film for himself and that "you are all my guests, not the other way around," helped to spark discussions of whether a filmmaker's "therapy" could be considered entertainment or even art.[6]

In the last decade, von Trier's most obvious paratexts have played off his auteurist fascination with exploitation genres, beginning with the horror film. A publicity photo for *Antichrist* parodies Hitchcock's deadpan pose with a raven on his shoulder for *The Birds* (1963), which parodied Edgar Allan Poe's signature poem *The Raven* (1845): in a one-up, von Trier sits with a crow splayed dead at his feet. For the science fiction disaster film *Melancholia*, a dour Lars von auteurism Trier stands holding an hourglass next to the caption "no more happy endings"—reminding us that his films have ended with plague, wrongful hanging, and mass murder. Von Trier even used the *Melancholia* press conference fiasco to his advantage—with what the late Thomas Elsaesser defended as a deft strategy of "self-contradiction"—by posing with a duct tape gag over his mouth to protest his enforced silence and defiantly wearing a T-shirt emblazoned with "PERSONA NON GRATA" that turned the denouncement into a badge of distinction.[7] Lacking a voice for his *Nymphomaniac* campaign, Zentropa mounted a poster series that featured its cast members posing in the throes of orgasm. In the first publicity photo for his serial killer film *The House That Jack Built*, von Trier posed as the scythe-bearing Grim Reaper in an iconic frame from Carl Dreyer's *Vampyr* (1932).

In other instances, provocation, paratext, and intertext have intertwined and overlapped with increasingly intricacy and risk. *Nymphomaniac* incorporated an intertextual retrospective of von Trier's paratextual provocations, including arguments that von Trier inadvertently and disastrously raised during *Melancholia*'s Cannes press conference in which he jokingly claimed to be a Nazi—for instance, Seligman's pointed distinction between anti-Semitism and anti-Zionism was an obvious defense of von Trier's reference to Israel as "a pain in the ass."[8] In *The House That Jack Built*, which might be described as a transgressive performance of self-parody, the eponymous protagonist's argument that murder is art is supported by a stream of references to the Nazi aesthetic and the Holocaust that had been raised by those same comments and the Wagnerian sublimity of *Melancholia* itself. Indeed *Jack* is in many ways a retrospective, blurring distinctions between the nihilistic and misogynistic character many believe von Trier to be and the serial killer that the film sends to hell, to the extent that watching it without factoring in the writer-director would mean missing the point.

GENDER AND THE DIALOGIC

Darkly philosophical and aesthetically dazzling, von Trier's films of the last decade are gendered psychodramas with "universal" pretensions. Gender is his "allegory or . . . mythology . . . his tension," Jenle Hallund explains: "For Lars it's definitely been the man and woman conflict, irrespective of what's going on in society. It's what he knows, how he sees himself."[9] And while gender politics have been implicit in his films since at least *Medea* in 1988, the films of the past decade are pointedly dialectical, pared down to Socratic dialogues or debates between gendered characters and elements, the male rational and the female emotional, intuitive, and stronger than the male: "he" is invariably obtuse and obstructive, "she" the truth seer whose torment must be inflicted on the audience.

The protagonists of von Trier's Europe trilogy (1984–1991) were weak and hapless men doomed to catastrophic failure—a failure preordained by "Europe," by the human systems and institutions of Western culture. The Gold Heart films (1996–2000) shifted to "good" but simple women who performed the role of the holy fool. Von Trier's latest antiheroines embody neither binary; they are anything but submissive or self-sacrificing. Nor are they fools, and certainly not holy (whereas their male counterparts have devolved from feckless humanists to self-deceptive hypocrites like He, John, and Seligman). They are transgressive and self-determined, choosing their own agency, pleasure, and pain over the institutions of society, especially marriage, family, and the ideal of love. Like Bess, they are seers, but their "madness" is a product of their clear-sighted comprehension of the chaos at the heart of things. Female madness offers a medium for exploring the problem of evil in a quest that, holding out hope for a glimmer of good, more often offers a darkness edged with the sublime.

Especially in the postdepression psychodramas, gender roles are metaphorical projections in a performative project at whose core is a desperate identity politics. So why does *The House That Jack Built*, which von Trier deems his most "moral" and testamental film, return to a tradition in which his stand-in literally tortures "stupid" women—to the point of nicknaming Jacqueline (Reilly Keough) "Simple"?[10] "I've made quite a lot of films about good women," he explained in a June 2018 interview: "Now I wanted to make a film about a really bad man"—and to send him to hell.[11] Notably Bess, von Trier's ultimate "good girl," ascends to heaven, indicated half-ironically in the film's final moment with digitalized church bells pealing from the sky. In contrast, Jack's journey to hell is already well underway with the film's opening lines against a black screen, uncannily hollow dripping sounds, before an elaborate, darkly sublime, twenty-minute "katabasis" caps von Trier's career.

THERAPEUTIC PSYCHODRAMA AND EXTREME CINEMA

With the "extreme" phase that *Antichrist* introduced, the films' paratexts and performative affects have often overwhelmed the discussion surrounding the films themselves, provoking critics' accusations that von Trier was no longer making films so much as creating provocations to traumatize and polarize audiences. Rather than communicating through manifestos, Brechtian staging, or direct references to American imperialism, however, the postdepression films have embodied and performed von Trier's personal trauma in forms designed to force audiences to experience trauma themselves. And where critics like Bamigboye expressed outrage, others like Roger Ebert suggested that there was something courageous and larger-than-life about this level of risk-taking. After calling *Antichrist* "the most despairing" film he had ever seen, he heralded it as "heroic" art, placing von Trier with the "ecstatic giants" Ingmar Bergman, Akira Kurosawa, and Werner Herzog.[12] "Do I believe his film 'works?' Would I 'recommend' it? Is it a 'good' film?" he asked before placing it beyond such questions: von Trier "had the ideas and feelings, he saw into the pit, he made the film, and here it is."[13]

Antichrist especially was marketed—and often received—as a transparent "performance" or projection of the director's state of mind or soul. In a publicity announcement when shooting began in Germany in August 2008, posed between Willem Dafoe and Charlotte Gainsbourg against a poster emblazoned with the film's title, von Trier invited audiences to a "glimpse behind the curtain, a glimpse into the dark world of my imagination: into the nature of my fears, into the nature of Antichrist."[14] As Stephanie Zacharek, who had disparaged his earlier films as sexist and sadistic projections of pain and suffering onto martyred female protagonists, observed in a *Slate* retrospective on the best films of 2011, "With *Antichrist* and now with *Melancholia*, von Trier finally knows how to lay out his own suffering and fears so baldly that it actually means something; it's as if he's finally opened himself up."[15] Thinking along much the same lines, film-philosophers following Robert Sinnerbrink have begun to approach the postdepression films as "trauma" films.[16]

Further, if von Trier is to be believed, in the case of *Antichrist*, working on the film itself was therapeutic. As expressed in his "Director's Confession" (included in the Cannes press book), the film, the "most important" of his career, "was a kind of therapy, but also a search, a test to see if I would ever make another film."[17] With chapters labeled "Grief," "Pain," and "Despair," the narrative took a form resembling psychoanalytic confession, and critics suggested that von Trier had sublimated his trauma into a kind of Artaudian cinema of cruelty intended as therapy for the audience.[18] Ebert wrote, for example, that von Trier drew on the horror genre's inherent violence "to inflict violence upon us, perhaps as a salutary experience."[19] It is true that, as Caroline Bainbridge has argued from a psychoanalytic perspective, trauma has been von Trier's primary subject and aim from the beginning: his films and initiatives such as Dogme 95 are meant to disturb, to induce productive emotional, ethical, and intellectual distress in audiences, other filmmakers, and himself. If the notion of "therapeutic" trauma has long been attached to his work, however, the films of this recent decade take this to a new, far more extreme level of confessionalism, performativity, and self-construction, to the extent that Lars von Trier the person, provocateur, filmmaker, and oeuvre have become coexistent. Ultimately, as Bainbridge claims, the widespread publicity about his experience of depression and anxiety is associated with the films' traumatic content, allowing audiences "to internalize the projections, and to process them as a form of communication about unspeakable experience."[20]

To put the issue another way, von Trier's recent films are, and have been marketed as, psychodramas, in three common senses. They are films in which psychological elements are a primary interest: a case study in which anxiety develops into psychosis, *Antichrist* is taken up with therapy sessions; the titles of *Melancholia* and *Nymphomaniac* name psychological disorders and likewise pose as case studies; and *The House That Jack Built* is the narrative of a self-aware psychopath. By *psychodrama*, I also mean the psychological concept of projection of a psychological state onto characters and the external world—thus *Melancholia* projects von Trier's condition onto Justine's experience but also onto Melancholia the planet destined to collide with Earth—hence the end of the world and consciousness itself. Finally, I mean *psychodrama* as a form of psychotherapy in which patients enact traumatic events from their past as a means of expressing and understanding themselves.

A key paradigm for the postdepression films is the patient-therapist relationship. While taking up popular if low genres, all four films have little more than what von Trier, speaking of *Antichrist*, described as "the bare necessities" of a plot or, in the case of *Nymphomaniac*, wildly episodic plots, and are framed as dialogues between two characters that von Trier has said allegorize opposing elements in his personality: one rational and "politically correct" and serving in a therapeutic role, and the other perverse and irrational and assuming the role of the "case" studied: He and She, Claire and Justine, Seligman and Joe, Verge and Jack.[21] *Antichrist* is pared down to a "two-hander" between the male therapist and female patient, indicated only by the pronouns "He" and "She." *Melancholia* distills the apocalyptic science fiction/disaster genre into a woman's melodrama that contrasts the reactions of sisters, Gainsbourg's caregiver Claire and Kirsten Dunst's Justine, who embodies von Trier's depression. As von Trier's intellectual "porn" film, *Nymphomaniac* is also equally and unconventionally a case study of female sex addiction, with Seligman an obvious parody of Freud's abstruse interrogations and interpretations. *The House That Jack Built* consists of the confessions of a serial killer to an unseen interlocutor in a replication of the narrative situation of von Trier's first feature, *The Element of Crime* (1984), in which a traumatized cop recovers his memory of a case that revealed he was a murderer.

The four films feature protagonists with dysfunctions that the auteur has publicly owned: anxiety, panic attacks (*Antichrist*), depression (*Melancholia*), addiction (*Nymphomaniac*), and narcissistic, obsessive-compulsive, psychopathic tendencies (*Jack*). Critics and von Trier himself have described *Jack* as a kind of capstone to his recent extreme cinema, if not to his entire career. "When I saw it on screen, I felt that very strongly," von Trier told Xan Brooks. "It looked to me like some kind of last testament."[22]

Viewed in this way, the postdepression films have been seen an amplification of the "film-as-provocation" or "trauma cinema" for which von Trier has long been notorious. In challenging cinema's expressive limits and thrusting audiences beyond reassuring ideologies and familiar modes of reasoning, they are arguably the director's most excessive and risk-taking. Unsurprisingly, they have sealed von Trier's reputation as a (if not *the*) leading figure in the international extreme cinema trend. Also called the "feel-bad film," and boasting international art film auteurs such as Michael Haneke, Gaspar Noë, Catherine Breillat, Yorgos Lanthimos, Claire Denis, Takashi Miike, and Carlos Reygadas, extreme cinema's identifying characteristics are graphic sex and violence whose intense affect is unpleasure or trauma rather than the "visual pleasures" offered by Hollywood horror and soft-core eroticism.[23]

Studies of von Trier's "extreme cinema" argue that being forced into confrontation with the unwatchable or inconceivable, viewers are pushed beyond conventional responses, provoked to feel and think in ways that require both empathy and reflection, forcing them to examine their responses. This process is potentially both creative and ethical, as critics have argued by way of continental philosophy texts—from the writings of Emmanuel Levinas, Jacques Derrida, Jacques Lacan, Slavoj Žižek, Laura Mulvey, Michel Foucault, and Alain Badiou. Von Trier's extreme cinema in particular has resonated in an era of trauma culture and ecological disaster exacerbated by unchecked greed.

FROM FILM-PHILOSOPHY TO ANTI-PHILOSOPHY TO DARK ECOLOGY

Von Trier's late-phase films, among his most philosophical and problematic, are perverse and "psychopathic" (2019), as Jenle Hallund described *The House That Jack Built*: they project contradictions or offer equally offensive alternatives. Yet despite being deeply personal expressions of his state of mind, especially in contrast to the overtly political films that came before them, they have nevertheless often uncannily tapped the zeitgeist and made an impact on the world at large.

Robert Sinnerbrink and Thomas Elsaesser, moreover, have argued von Trier's significance within the trend toward film-[as]-philosophy or "cinematic thinking" that interrogates philosophical concepts or poses a dichotomy or dilemma that pushes audiences toward new ways of understanding experience. As Elsaesser puts the issue more broadly, in an era dominated by blockbusters, franchises, remakes, streaming media, and digitalization and a corresponding decline of national and auteur cinemas, European cinema is confronted with its (and cinema's) "abjection," its marginality and eventual extinction. Yet its current irrelevance has released it from the commercialization that has all but destroyed creativity in Hollywood, freeing European auteurs such as Michael Haneke, the Dardenne brothers, Aki Kaurismäki, Claire Denis, and von Trier to make "thinking" films for small but discriminating international audiences and mapping out a territory for European auteur cinema. Turning their limitations into opportunities for creative mind games and philosophically challenging cinema, they practice cinema as a kind of "thought experiment" based in a "What if?" situation.[24] For Elsaesser, von Trier is the seminal figure in this group. After singling out the Dogme 95 manifesto as a eureka moment, one in which four Danish filmmakers turned economic and cultural limitations into arbitrary "creative constraints," "obstructions," or mind games, Elsaesser turns to *Melancholia* as an epitomizing example of a film that turns the death of cinema—and the end in general—into its hypothesis, creating out of the ultimate impasse a creative opening.[25] Therefore, and however paradoxically amid the continuing disparagement of auteurist notions and approaches, the work of European and global auteurs has become the last bastion of philosophical cinema, of cinematic art, in the twenty-first century.

In his most recent films, von Trier's practice of cinematic thinking often works directly through genres, which he reworks and interrogates. As Lisa Coulthard and Chelsea Birks point out, commenting on *Antichrist*, in contrast to genre horror movies "horror tropes are not so much subverted as they are . . . rendered radically ambiguous: these monstrous incarnations do not re-repress the libidinal energies they foster, but articulate the more fundamental and more terrifying underlying horror of sexual difference in all of its incommensurability."[26] Thus Sinnerbrink has explored von Trier's anticognitivism in *Antichrist* not only in relation to the cognitive exposure therapy He inflicts on She, which ends in psychosis and violence, but also as an inadequate explanation for the aesthetic appeal of horror cinema in claims made by cognitivists such as Noël Carroll.[27] *Melancholia*, moreover, is an extreme variation on the disaster/apocalypse film as a way of confronting the end of philosophy and thought itself.

That said, and revising his own earlier argument as well as Elsaesser's, Sinnerbrink in 2016 reframed von Trier's auteurism, pronouncing it a cinematic "antiphilosophy." Accordingly, through provocation, perversity, game-playing, and satire, *Antichrist*, *Melancholia*, and *Nymphomaniac* employ a Romantic critique or subversion of Enlightenment reason and demonstrate the limitations of philosophy in the classical sense—for instance, in He's disastrous application of therapy, which accelerates his wife's descent into psychosis—or revelation.[28] From such a perspective, as chapters 3 and 4 suggest, *Nymphomaniac* and *The House That Jack Built* satirize and parody the philosophical art film in the classical sense. *Nymphomaniac*'s "philosopher" Seligman turns Joe's narrative of sexuality into a series of pedantic riffs that ultimately add up to nothing, and in the film's final scene, he is exposed as a hypocrite whose crowning act (trying to rape Joe in her sleep) exposes the ethical and emotional emptiness of his "feminist," politically correct defenses of her behavior. Thus the film advances a nihilistic critique of philosophical reason whose antiargument is, nonetheless, intrinsically philosophical. Along the same lines, in *The House That Jack Built*, a misogynistic serial killer employs reason in service of an argument that art is intrinsically destructive, and that, likewise, murder is art, thus glorifying his "work."

From a broader and more existential perspective, however, and as the following chapters explore, von Trier's films of the last decade are nihilistic in a radical and positive philosophical sense, one that is deeply in tune with recent schools such as skeptical realism (Quentin Meillassoux), transcendental nihilism (Ray Brassier), and dark ecology (Timothy Morton). These oppose classical, correlationist, and anthropocentric perspectives with a combination of science-based and "gnostic" (Morton) epistemologies that acknowledge, as Brassier puts it, a "mind-independent reality, which despite the presumptions of human narcissism, is indifferent to our existence and oblivious to the 'values' and 'meanings' which we would drape over it in order to make it more hospitable."[29]

TRANSMEDIAL AUTEURISM

A twelve-carat white double diamond, cut out of two raw stones, sits on a black pedestal in a large white space at the M HKA Museum (Museum of Modern

Art) in Antwerp. Von Trier's most recent completed project, *Melancholia: The Diamond*, an exhibition that ran from February 8 to May 5, 2019, brings together "the oldest material that exists on Earth and an absolutely new material," as the exhibit's coproducer Leonid Ogarev explained.[30] The visitor, wearing a virtual reality helmet, is invited to enter its scintillating center. The first of thirteen such projects planned, one for each of his films, *Melancholia: The Diamond* suggests the 2011 film's apocalyptic conclusion, in which two planets collide, merging into one. Senior curator Anders Kreuger describes the project's goal: to transmute one medium into another, a film into a microscopic crystalline sculpture designed to make us think "about how you can reformulate reality from one form and language into another."[31] *Melancholia: The Diamond* epitomizes the transmedial—and narcissistic—impulse that has driven von Trier's entire career, but most especially the films of this last decade. Brilliantly cut on one side and rough on the other, it further embodies the binary oppositions, both conceptual and stylistic, from which his four most recent films are composed. Constructed as Socratic dialogues between two opposing characters, all juxtapose a raw, handheld camera style with an otherwise highly polished, technically virtuosic aesthetic.

The postdepression films represent a return to cinema as an art form after a career-defining "punk" period devoted to demolishing conventional notions of aesthetic beauty and "elevating the ugly."[32] As Manuel Claro explains from his perspective as von Trier's cinematographer,

> Lars changes a lot from . . . what he was doing in the nineties until *The Boss of it All*, . . . [which was] very much what I call destruction of cinema. And then with *Antichrist* and on, he's been . . .—maybe reinventing is a big word, but he's being very respectful, and he's come back to . . . his big love for cinema. What he was doing earlier was very much like a reaction to the pompousness of cinema. . . . Now he's more trying to create something that is . . . not a reaction to the concept of beauty and classical cinema. . . . he's taking it in and using it in his own way, to create something that both is interesting and beautiful and . . . mixing everything.

"I've been very lucky to work with him in this period where he's reinventing instead of destroying," he adds, "because there's not much space for a cinematographer when you're in the disruption."[33] Claro's comments illuminate what critics have described as von Trier's "post-cinematic atavism" of late, his return to past or archaic cinematic traits that are jeopardized in an era of increasing digitalization.[34] Take, for example, the exaggeratedly cinematic slow-motion, black-and-white, choreographed montage of *Antichrist*'s prologue and epilogue, set to an elegiac Handel aria. In the context of von Trier's oeuvre as a whole, the Dogme-style naturalism of the narrative proper in this film and *Melancholia*, which followed it, starkly set off the darkly impassioned expressionism of what von Trier has called "monumental" sequences. Writing about the vastly different, essayistic *Nymphomaniac*, *Guardian*'s Tom Shone was fascinated by "the tension between its bristling air of art-terrorist provocation, and the clear nostalgia, left over from von Trier's previous film, *Melancholia*, for the older, more humanist forms of centuries gone: the music of Bach, the novels [sic] of Edgar Allen Poe, the penny dreadfuls of the Victorians, which drew readers with promises of lewdness under cover of concern for the nation's youth."[35] In all four films, von Trier has confessed looking both inward and backward to his own previous films and obsessions, in particular the "disreputable" fin de siècle influences and preoccupations of his youth, whether in literature (August Strindberg), painting (Edvard Munch), philosophy (Friedrich Nietzsche, Arthur Schopenhauer), music (Richard Wagner), or architecture (Albert Speer). *Antichrist* and *Melancholia* incorporated elements and themes from his aborted stage production of *Der Ring des Nibelungen* (the Ring cycle, 1876) commissioned for the 2006 Bayreuth festival and, albeit in very different ways, all four films aspire toward Wagner's *Gesamtkunstwerk*, or total work of art. More generally, the postdepression films mark a return to the obsession with Germany that infuses the Europe trilogy, to German locations and motifs, and to fin de siècle German and Scandinavian artists, philosophers, and writers. Nowhere is this Germanic and Nordic transmedialism more apparent than in *Antichrist*, the subject of chapter 1.

1

NATURE AS SATAN'S CHURCH

Antichrist's Dark Ecology

THE GENESIS OF *ANTICHRIST*

Surrounding *Antichrist* is a mythology—perpetrated in part by von Trier himself, in part by the Cannes 2009 critical reaction—that the film was a primal scream emanating from the depths of his depression. His director's statement, dated March 25, 2009, included in the press pack and called a "confession," asserted that the film was made "using about half of my physical and intellectual capacity":

> The work on the script did not follow my usual modus operandi. Scenes were added for no reason. Images were composed free of logic or dramatic thinking. They often came from dreams I was having at the time, or dreams I'd had earlier in my life.
>
> Once again, the subject was "Nature," but in a different and more direct way than before. In a more personal way.
>
> The film does not contain any specific moral code and only has what some might call 'the bare necessities' in the way of a plot.

He added a coy disclaimer:

> I read Strindberg when I was young. I read with enthusiasm the things he wrote before he went to Paris to become an alchemist and during his stay there . . . the period later called his "inferno crisis"—was "Antichrist" my Inferno Crisis? My affinity with Strindberg?

In any case, I can offer no excuse for "Antichrist." Other than my absolute belief in the film—the most important of my entire career.

Before blaming Strindberg, von Trier suggests that he took the project on quite rationally, as "a kind of therapy" in the sense of "a kind of a test to see if I could make another film."[1] This move was consistent with the cognitive therapy he was undergoing, in which the patient is encouraged to take up projects and make a schedule—as he described to biographer Nils Thorsen, "to find out what you like a *tiny* bit more than other things. To solve a crossword puzzle. Play computer games. Then you should place it on certain hours where it *has* to be done so that the day has a content. And it actually *helps*."[2] And so, while marketed as an urgently resuscitative, "emergency" film based on his experience of mental illness, *Antichrist* was a uniquely rational production, a conscious attempt to tap the unconscious.[3]

The project was by no means a new idea. Interested in making his own variations on genre films, von Trier had gravitated toward the horror genre for several years, and in the autumn of 2006, before his depression had become so debilitating that he checked into the psychiatric ward at Rigshospitalet, he had a preliminary script in hand—written by Anders Thomas Jensen from scraps, notes, and plot summaries von Trier had jotted down between 2004 and August 2006.[4]

Indeed, in October 2004, as von Trier was editing *Manderlay*, producer and Zentropa co-owner Peter Aalbæk Jensen had announced that, before completing the USA trilogy, von Trier would make a film "for a wider audience, a horror film . . . in the style of *The Kingdom*," his television series of 1994 and 1997, a rollicking blend of horror, comedy, and grotesque satire that had riveted audiences and made him a household name in Denmark.[5] "As I understand it," Jensen said, "Lars spins a yarn over the big lie that it was God who created the world. In fact, it is Satan himself. . . . The plot in *Antichrist* takes place around an anxiety therapist who gets a biologist in therapy who has become afraid of nature. It is evil, he thinks and seeks help with the therapist to get rid of his delusions—but is he actually right? That is the question in the film that still only exists in the Danish director's head."[6] Jensen had spoken too soon, and a furious von Trier allegedly kicked a hole in his producer's office door, spraining his foot, comparing the disclosure to leaking the shock ending of *The Planet of the Apes*. He pronounced the film canceled and went on to make the "light" office comedy *The Boss of It All* (2006). But *Antichrist* had merely gone underground, and from 2004 through autumn of 2006, he continued working on it—dictating and jotting down notes, writing outlines and summaries, and collecting materials.

Von Trier claims that the original concept was inspired by a television program about European primeval forests envisioned as a "jungle," a brutal battle for survival.[7]

> If I try to imagine the most comforting image in the world, I see a forest lake with a bellowing stag, a waterfall in the background, and some mossy remnants of tree trunks. What's amusing about precisely that image in relation to the jungle is that the latter involves an ongoing struggle for survival, whereas there's hardly any struggle connected with the kind of forest we have here [in Denmark], because we know who the winners and losers are. It's interesting that what we find most soothing is an image that points back to the worst thing of all. Had it been people instead of trees and animals, it would have been a Hieronymus Bosch image, humanity as a battlefield.[8]

The Bosch image would appear near the end of the finished film, just before the epilogue, as a stark, dead tree surrounded by naked corpses in contorted positions.

Von Trier lives in a house perched above a slope down to the Mølleåen (Mill) River and near Ravnholm Skov (Ravnholm Forest). In the neighborhood are the much larger Geels Skov and Denmark's deepest lake, Furesø. He is surrounded by trees, in which he (like Joe's father in *Nymphomaniac*) takes a great interest. The tree outside Eden's cabin, dropping acorns on the roof, may have been suggested in part by the oak in his garden. "If I should mention a place where I would feel most safe in this world and most *happy* to be," von Trier has said, "it is in the forest at the forest lake. And then this is evidently a hell."[9] From this revelation came the the idea of a horror film capped by the disclosure that the world was created by Satan or an Antichrist rather than a loving and righteous Jehovah.

In these earliest stages, as is almost painfully obvious from notes and outlines, the film was a personal/existential ecohorror film. The chaos inherent in natural process is concentrated in the old growth forest adjoining the protagonist's childhood home, named Eden, turning him into a channel through which its evil is manifested. The film was also a psychodrama featuring a patient-therapist relationship that exposes the limitations of therapy in the face of the real. Thirty-something therapist Mary (later Brenda) proposes cognitive exposure therapy or "flooding" to cure her patient Nicklas (eventually Jeremy) and, with the intention of publishing an article based on his case, accompanies him to Eden to help him confront his fears head on. In this environment, his condition deteriorates, he takes on Satanic attributes, and Mary becomes affected as well.

After a hiatus, in autumn 2006, von Trier returned to the 2004 plans. Among several brief notes are the following:

> She [Mary] develops evil and the will to live. And kills Nicklas. Mary goes home. And throws out the notes. . . . She lives a time well but tired. One day she hears the little one crying. But it's not the small [child] inside the playpen. . . . it's the grass on the concrete. She runs in and tears the Bible out [of the bookshelf]. . . . but in all the places where it before said God it now says Satan. . . . Zoom out and up past trees and birds and nature and all the way out into space. Finish the zoom away from the blue planet that screams. "And on the seventh day, Satan saw that everything was good."[10]

In the finished film, the murderous woman, the illusion of the crying child, the cry of nature, and the zoom out and over the canopy of trees would be among the most devastating and iconic moments.

In fact, many "loose ideas" that were there from the beginning would end up as significant elements in the finished film. In various lists, there is a bridge, Nicklas/Jeremy "burns" his feet, the trees "breathe," an oak tree rains down acorns, and the therapist "sleeps with her hand out the window and wakes up with a hundred ticks on it." There are encounters with the deer with the miscarried fetus, the fox that "shreds himself" and "speaks by thought transfer," as well as various birds, including young ones that die. There are human bodies with "fixed bolts through limbs." The forest "screams." It is a place where "evil manifests itself a kind of reverse Eden's garden." Von Trier adds, "Remember a general distortion . . . images stretched out or similar without being directly visible."[11]

Dictation notes describe "the wind as a gigantic breath that goes through the forest,"[12] and remind him to include "the image of naked corpses which are imprisoned like the tree roots that intersect with each other."[13] The note labeled "Anti-x ide 2" sums up the theme, repeated in "Anti-x ide 6":

> There is a place where nature manifests its evil. Where one can hear the grass scream. This is mentally unhealthy because it gives the insight: that the idea of life is evil! That Satan created the world as a sadistic idea. This insight that goodness does not exist and that a good God is not present is forbidden because it

will break down the world . . . the Fall was when this occurred for Adam and Eve . . . That they were going to die . . .[14]

Later these ideas are shaped into a short undated summary of the action:

> Jeremy lives with his father who is a priest and his little sister in great happiness in their idyllic house Eden in the midst of mountains and forest. A winter night, his little sister dies of an acute illness or accident because they cannot come to the doctor because of a snowstorm. Jeremy changes and now sees the nature that before seemed so romantic as evil. His anxiety grows and eventually he escapes from the sound he can now hear from the forest that is screaming.
>
> Many years after, he seeks out an anxiety therapist [Brenda] who takes him back to "Eden" to heal him by a so called "flooding." He must be exposed to the maximum for his fear of nature by being confronted with the "most dangerous" place, namely where the anxiety arose. Slowly she is more and more able to deal with his symptoms until one night he's gone and she gets to see him outside. . . . he's starting to grow Satan. He has divided the building plot into the parts his father's church had down in the city.[15]

By August 15, 2006, von Trier had written a much longer "action sketch" in which the basic patient-therapist relationship (with the patient's madness infecting the cognitive-exposure therapist), situation, and setting that is, except for the genders of the protagonists, very similar to the finished film. (For the full text, see appendix A.)

Yet, in all of these notes and synopses, the gender difference between patient and therapist, which corresponds with von Trier's own experience of anxiety and therapy and of female cognitive therapists, is scarcely noted. They are essentially sexless—except in a few notes that refer to the therapist's "maternal" relation to him and that include Jeremy's mother (whom he resents for giving him life). It is the unstable male patient, with his past trauma involving the death of his younger sister and his paradoxical occupation as a biologist, who becomes the easily influenced medium for the evil of the forest. Several versions suggest that Jeremy becomes a variation on the werewolf archetype. When the therapist awakens, he is gone from the cabin; she goes outdoors and sees him changed in appearance, accompanied by wolves, or having taken on Satanic characteristics, having merged with nature's "evil." (In some versions Jeremy takes his own life.

In others, he kills his father and Brenda kills him at his behest, leaving Brenda in the position of He in the epilogue of the finished film.)

The conflict is between a rational, positive perspective that includes a wholesome "green" ecology, represented in the well-intentioned but deluded therapist, and Nicklas/Jeremy's understanding of nature as chthonic, chaotic, encroaching. Immersing him in nature, exposure therapy becomes fatal, forcing Nicklas/Jeremy into the position of medium for the evil inherent in natural process, much as in the finished film, in which He's therapy browbeats She into a position where she is overcome by "Satan's church."

Juxtaposed against therapy are religion, gnosis, and the irrational. That said, conventional religious elements and their allegory dominate most of the early versions, with the title referring to the common notion of the Antichrist as Christ's nemesis and a variation on Satan, who is revealed to have created an intrinsically "fallen" world. Nicklas/Jeremy's parents are religious, or the father is a priest, and a church is located in the woods near their home, offering a simple opposition of Christianity and demonic "Nature" and suggesting the Puritan fear of the wilderness as harboring Satan. The founding trauma, the death of the child during a blizzard, provokes a reversion from Christianity to a worship of the power inherent in (Satanic) nature. A note dated August 16, 2006, lists arcane symbols usually associated with Judeo-Christian culture, including a tower, a catacomb, a baptismal basin, a pulpit, and a "Sacrifice."[16]

None of the notes or summaries through fall 2006 even hint at the issues that would shock and scandalize audiences, beginning with Cannes in May 2009: the battle of the sexes, grotesque nudity, shockingly explicit sexualized violence, the monstrous feminine, witch burning, and a liberal, feminist, highly educated American couple's reversion to misogyny. Rather than linking female sexuality—or for that matter, sexuality at all—with nature, the film's original ideas associated male irrationality with bestial violence, as suggested in Jeremy's joining the company of wolves. As for sexuality, a single note floats the idea of Jeremy kissing the therapist in a more "grown up" way, and another suggests that "Mary frightened . . . joins Nicklas in animalistic intercourse."[17] These ideas were dropped.

In the fall of 2006, as von Trier's depression deepened, in order to move the project along and to obtain funding von Trier commissioned Anders Thomas Jensen with the task of writing a script from von Trier's notes and synopses, which Schepelern summarizes as follows:

a prologue with an initial traumatic event—two children, a brother and a sister, play in a cave under a tree. Later the sister dies in the winter in spite of the minister-father's attempts to rescue her and the brother is traumatized. As a grownup Jeremy suffers from fear of nature, he is afraid of flowers, grass, and trees. His female therapist (Brenda) takes him back to the childhood nature universe (train trip, two persons alone in a summerhouse), where he grows increasingly ill. He burns his feet. Acorns hit the roof. Deer with unborn foetus, talking fox . . . insects on the hand. . . . Satan will not let something live without that something else must die!" . . . He commits hara-kiri (self-mutilation), so that Brenda can survive. There is a third person, a local middle-aged man Clive who is involved in some occult events in the forest. There are the scream of the forest . . . and crowds of dead people in the end. . . . The religious theme is more explicit here: The father was a minister, he built a church, and in the end Jeremy seems to be obsessed by a kind of religious madness (he—as a nine years old boy who suddenly appears—wants to baptize and sacrifice Brenda). After Jeremy's suicide, Brenda is alone in the cabin. Clive, a middle-aged man who knew the father and the children in their childhood, appears with 9-year-old Jeremy. Then Jeremy the boy and Brenda talk. He warns her that the darkness is approaching. She knows, he says, she should run away . . . "you haven't got much time." . . . She realizes that she should face "it" [evil?]: "Look it in the eyes," she repeats again and again. She turns around and sees a horrifying landscape:

> "Millions of dead bodies lie woven together in chaos. Eroded faces, silent, white, screaming, dead. A chaos of pain.
> The poor human bodies are everywhere, behind the roots of the trees, in the grass, in the reeds, in the mountains. Small new shoots grow up between and through them.
> Everywhere is death.
> Brenda . . . looks directly into evil. She falls down on her knees, in silence, sits there staring, stays in the anxiety forever.
> We move away. Up into the sky, through the apocalyptic inferno, until everything turns white.
> FADE OUT."

The controversial issue is the religious, Satanic theme.[18]

On the surface, the choice of Jensen, a leading screenwriter and director in the new Danish cinema who often teamed with director Susanne Bier, seems counter-intuitive. Piqued that Bier's film had won an Oscar nomination (*Efter Brylluppet/ After the Wedding*, 2006) and an award for Best Foreign Film (*In a Better World*, 2010), von Trier had vilified Bier's and Jensen's collaborations for what he described as mechanical dramaturgy, political correctness, and emotional insincerity, alienating Bier. Jensen, moreover, had scripted *Sprængfarlig bombe* (2006, *Clash of Egos*, directed by Tomas Villum Jensen), a raucous satire on contemporary Danish cinema, with von Trier as a key target. Yet, according to von Trier's producer Meta Louise Foldager, Jensen was tasked with turning out a relatively commercial script to attract financing rather than for creative purposes, which he produced in ten days.[19] Looking back in 2009, von Trier said in an interview:

> What he [Jensen] did was very important to the film. It started with some ideas I had. Then I got the depression and could only mumble some words for Anders Thomas. . . . And then he wrote through the whole story. He made a script so we could move on with the movie. And then I read the script and threw it all away. He also read my script and thought it was a mess. He may have had more influence than I am willing to admit.[20]

POSTDEPRESSION: THE SECOND SCRIPT

As his depression slowly, intermittently, abated in the late spring and summer of 2007, he turned back to the project, now motivated by a desperation to prove he could make another film, and wrote a new version of the script. As his wife Bente explained it, "Suddenly he had an idea for *Antichrist* and began watching horror movies."[21]

Horror films had been on his mind for some time, as on September 19, 2006, when I interviewed von Trier in Copenhagen just before the premiere of his screwball office comedy *The Boss of It All*, at the Copenhagen Film Festival. Interested in adapting the constraints of genre to his own vision, he said he had recently been watching Japanese horror movies, mentioning *Ring* (*Ringu*, 1998) and *Dark Water* (*Honogurai mizu no soko kara*, 2002), his favorite. At the beginning of the interview, after I had mentioned editing a series of books that included a volume on Japanese horror and teaching a horror film class, he asked me to poll my students for suggestions: What were the scariest Asian horror films and the scariest moments in them? What made them scary? For three weeks after the Copenhagen trip, as I followed on von Trier's parting request for students' viewpoints, the class blog raged with debate from J-horror fans showing their chops. *Ôdishon* (*Audition*, 1999), *Jisatsu Sākuru* (*Suicide Club*, 2001), *Juon* (*Ju-on*, 2003), *Janghwa, Hongryeon* (*A Tale of Two Sisters*, 2003), *Dark Water*, and cross-genre films such as *Batoru Rowaiaru* (*Battle Royale*, 2000), were at the top of their lists, which I emailed to von Trier in mid-October with their discussion and class handouts on *Ring* and *Audition*.[22] But, during the next couple of months, he plunged into the depression for which *Antichrist* was to become a form of therapy.

Following a gap in the timeline, probably in the summer of 2007, an undated "Brief om research til *Antichrist*" (Brief about research on *Antichrist*) requests the following: "We need texts that describe the woman as being cruel and dangerous by nature. All material substantiating this thesis. Research as for an article or trial. It can be fiction but preferably expressed in poems, songs, literature, religious texts and manifests, and like both older and newer dates and from all regions of the world."[23] This was per von Trier's usual working method. Throughout 2007 and 2008, assistants and specialists researched various subjects that could be of relevance to the script: his personal assistant Katrine Acheche Sahlstrøm, horror specialist Rikke Schubart, religious history scholar Jens-André P. Herbener, psychologist Lisbet Lassen, Lise Præstgaard Andersen, and Line Holt, who contributed statements, surveys, examples, and bibliographies on misogyny, persecution and abuse of women, evil women and horror films.[24] IMDb lists Heidi Laura on misogyny; Asta Wellejus on mythology and evil; Poul Lübcke on theology; Trine Breum on horror, and several "therapeutic consultants." Most notoriously, as noted in reviews—producer Meta Louise Foldager commissioned Heidi Laura to find arguments to explain She's radical "shift of opinion" from feminism to misogyny and to provide "a broader view of Western misogyny."[25] This research was gathered into a folder labeled "Research—om kvinders ondskab—med oversatte citater" (Research on women's evil with translated quotes), dated August 17, 2007, and consists of twenty-eight pages of double-spaced material. A smoldering five-page treatise, supported with citations from Aristotle's *De Generatione Animalium* (*On the Generation of Animals*, 4th century BC); Hesiod's *Værker og dage* (*Works and Days*, 700); Thomas Kingo's "Far, Verden, far vel" ("Fare, World, Farewell," 1674); Aristotle's' *Politik* (4th century BC); John Knox's *The First Blast of the Trumpet Against the Monstrous Regiment of Women* (1558); Schopenhauer's *Über die Weiber* (*About Women*, 1851); Friedrich Nietzsche's *Also*

Sprach Zarathustra (*Thus Spoke Zarathrustra*, 1883–1891) and *Beyond Good and Evil: Aphorisms and Interludes* (1886); poetry by James Kenneth Stephen (1859–1892); Otto Weininger's *Sex and Character* (1903); William Shakespeare's Sonnet 147; Heinrich Kramer and James Spreyer's *Malleus Maleficarum* (1486); and Camille Paglia's *Sexual Personae* (1990) is followed by lists of famous female temptresses and monsters, violent women, and images of demonic women, together with additional sources.[26] Laura's work is reflected in several of She's lines and scenes, including the husband's discovery of his wife's research in the cabin loft.

When I interviewed him for the second time on October 3, 2007, via Skype, von Trier announced that he had just finished the first draft of the screenplay. It was short, he lamented, only forty-seven pages, whereas most of his films approached two hundred.[27] (The published draft eventually reached seventy-two pages.). He emphasized that he was still "trying" to make a horror film, in spite of people who "tell me that it's not." He attributed his attraction to the genre to "all this anxiety that . . . I deal with every day or do not deal with [and that] is something that I can use in this film," adding that "it's better to use it than to suffer from it."[28] Secondly, horror, especially the Japanese films he had been watching, is "a forgiving genre . . . one of the most open forms of films in the sense that the storytelling is not as important as it is in other films. You know, actually, if you changed the music to non-horror film music then they could be seen as art films [as] they can be very slow."[29]

With classic American and British horror movies he had admired from his youth—*The Exorcist* (1972), *Carrie* (1976), *The Shining* (1980), and *Don't Look Now* (1980)—together with *Altered States* (1980), *The Blair Witch Project* (1998), and *Vampyr* (1932), which feature family/domestic/psychological horror, possession, or a haunted place, Japanese horror movies of the late 1990s and early 2000s were a likely source of inspiration for the new version of *Antichrist*.[30] This returned to the trajectory of *Medea* and *Dogville* in which a strong woman struggling against a repressive culture epitomized in a male antagonist avenges the crimes against her—with her revenge as unimaginable and apocalyptic as her powers have been suppressed. Derived from the Asian avenging ghost story, Hideo Nakata's *Ring* and Takashi Miike's *Audition* feature suffering and vengeful women with preternatural powers (and, always, long dark hair). *Antichrist*'s cycle of patriarchal condescension and female revenge evokes *Ring*, in which a clairvoyant woman, scorned by male scientists, is avenged by her daughter, who inherits her powers and unleashes them on the world; associated with oceanic chaos, female power takes virally proliferating forms and destroys indiscriminately. But *Antichrist* has yet more in common with *Audition*, which has similarly been interpreted both as a feminist revenge film and as a misogynistic reaction against feminism. Much like *Antichrist*, the film shifts from a family melodrama into what has been dubbed "torture porn" or "Asian extreme" cinema: to avenge the abuse she suffered as a child, a beautiful, melancholy woman seduces men and turns them into maimed, doglike wretches. In *Antichrist*'s last act, von Trier would switch genres, veering wildly from Bergmanesque marital melodrama into uncharted visceral and emotional territory. Von Trier substitutes the equivalent Western mythology in which, as Nigel Andrews puts it, She is "finally driven to visit on the world the witching powers attributed to her sex through history."[31]

On October 3, von Trier and I discussed *Audition*, my students' favorite Japanese horror film at the time, at some length. Fascinated with how Asian cultures produce images "much different from what you are used to," he asked me about the motif of the long black hair, often covering the face in the most horrific scenes, and I had suggested that its roots in the tradition of the avenging female ghost (*onryō*), a submissive victim (with long black hair) in a funeral kimono (white dress), whose vengeance reenacts a cultural cycle.[32] Her hair signifies both the traditional, submissive woman and the sensual animality of her vengeful powers, once revealed.

> LB: [In *Audition*], the woman with the hair is at first a completely passive person and then she takes her revenge, which is disturbing because the guy actually is fairly nice. [The film is] typical in that the woman is a victim and yet she's terrifying and tortures him far beyond what the crime [seems to deserve]. Usually my students bring up this issue: "Did he really deserve that?"
>
> LVT: That may be the same thing about *Dogville*. The punishment is, yeah.
>
> LB: Yeah, it's very like *Dogville*. So, there's a paradox where her victimization produces an even worse victimization, and it just goes on in a vicious, never ending cycle.
>
> LVT: Yeah. But [*Audition*] was very hard to watch.
>
> LB: Why?
>
> LVT: Oh it was just very cruel.
>
> LB: But people often call you cruel.
>
> LVT: Ah. Yeah, yeah, yeah. I would like to be cruel. I'm not cruel enough. Let's see what you say after [you see] this film that I have on my wall here.

LB: Yeah, get some cruelty into it—that would be fun.

LVT: I'll try [laughs]. I'm working on it.[33]

The interview concluded with his summary of the core idea of the film, which had not changed from the description from 2004. The film is

> based on me looking at plants and whatever, living things and how much they suffer. . . . that it's really a nasty idea, life. And especially human life, because . . . [it's] one thing to be an animal and tortured and made to suffer your whole life and then to die in the end, but being a man, it's . . . much worse, because first of all, the man knows that he's going to die, and furthermore . . . that it's morally not right to kill other beings—or anyway there can be some emotional problems—and to know that for every step we take we kill a lot of animals, or plants, or whatever, and for every breath we take we kill. So it's . . . that being a human is really a nasty joke. There's nothing new in that but when you talk about drama it's . . . [pauses] it's very . . . [long sigh]. If it were a film—life—a very well written film, that is . . . now, that would . . . be a horror film of substance.[34]

This existential nihilist understanding of the bionetwork ecology not as green and rationally comprehensible, but as chthonic and chaotic, would be refracted through the next three films, if from very different prisms.

THE NEW SCRIPT

The draft he spoke of in the October 2007 interview, eventually revised and titled "*Antichrist*, second draft 26.1.2008," sixty-four pages in Danish, Schepelern describes as "a totally new script" with "only some elements in common with the first one": the story of a male anxiety patient treated by a female therapist becomes one about a grieving female anxiety patient treated by a male therapist who is also her husband. Completely new is the prologue with a couple enjoying acrobatic sex while their child falls out the window. The elements of anxiety, madness, horror, and therapy remain, but the childhood trauma motive, together with the father, his church, and the religious elements outside of the name of the woodland home are gone.[35] Instead, sexuality and gender (which were, oddly, nonissues in the early versions) are the center of the story. The most striking images and scenes found in the earliest notes—the bridge, the burning feet, the distorted, "screaming" forest, the oak tree raining down acorns, the ticks, the deer with the miscarried fawn, the talking fox, the birds—were all retained, however, to powerful effect.

Several ideas and scenes were reinvented in ingenious ways to fit the new plot. The female therapist plans to turn Jeremy's case into an article; She has attempted to write a thesis on "gynocide." Mary/Brenda becomes affected in ways that eventually belong to Gainsbourg's She: "Mary comes home . . . she doesn't say anything, but is a little mean . . . Raps the baby's fingers as it tries to take a cake and eats it herself. The child cries. We see Mary wearing the cross in reverse. Zoom out and up past trees and birds and nature and all the way out into space."[36] The zoom over the trees would be repurposed for She's visionary experience of "the cry of all the things that are to die." Mary's cruelty to the baby becomes the flashback in which She abuses her child Nic by putting his shoes on the wrong feet. In "Anti-x idea 6," she consults the Bible and discovers that the word "God" has been replaced by "Satan"; a similarly possessed text becomes the primary turning point in the finished film: when He climbs up to the attic where She has stored the work for her thesis and discovers a phantasmagoria of images of and from the witch trials together with her notes, whose handwriting becomes grotesquely distorted.[37]

The characters are now a modern, educated, middle-class couple in their late thirties to early forties with an only child, living in a modern apartment in Seattle, Washington, that looks more like Europe, referred to only by the gendered pronouns "He" and "She." As the film proceeds, the characters, setting, and plot are pared down to the bare essentials, becoming increasingly allegorical. Thus, in scenes in which people would be expected, they are blurred (the funeral procession) or left out (the train interior on the way to the cabin) until the film becomes a literal two-hander. There is no road to their cabin, which has no electricity. They must hike into this wilderness, where they are completely cut off from the real/modern world.

As mentioned, one of the early notes for the first version of the film describes a sort of reverse garden of Eden story: a sadistic Genesis in which Satan is revealed as the creator of the world, which has always been "fallen," an anti-Judeo-Christian story in the broadest sense. "I am disappointed by religion," von Trier told Karin Badt in 2009. "I am not a believer. Every time you think about religion, it becomes more obvious that it is an invention of men. I am quite sure there is something beyond but these books—like the Bible, and religions—like Scientology—don't seem very divine to me."[38] But the new script was concerned less with this "disappointment" with religion than with "politically correct" secular humanism, idealistic "green" movements, and female sexuality. With its universally gendered couple, and excepting its allusion to Adam brought down by Eve's seduction by Satan/Nature, it abandoned the earlier story's Judeo-Christian references and arcane religious symbolism. The result is far more abstract than the first script—or any of his other films, for that matter. The animals mentioned in the notes remain, but, rather than taking on religious connotations, are biotic embodiments of psychological conditions: Grief, Pain, and Despair. Profane rather than sacred trilogies abound: mother, father, and (dead, abused) child, prologue, main feature, epilogue, the Three Beggars (deer, fox, crow), their outlines repeated in a child's puzzle that the couple dislodge as they make love, their titles in the figurine the child knocks over as he lurches toward the open window, and the strange constellations that reveal themselves to the husband near the end of the film. In this way, von Trier takes ancient, iconic Judeo-Christian symbols such as Eden and divests them of their original meanings by multiplying connotations, and thereby undermines and skews them.

In contrast to the more or less unisex therapist and patient Brenda and Jeremy, gender defines the film's two characters allegorically, and, in the most radical change, the couple's genders are reversed. He is in the dominant position as therapist and "professor"; She is the failed student of history, women's studies, or some such humanities agenda, having begun but never finished her PhD thesis, whose title "Gynocide" is taken from a chapter from Andrea Dworkin's radical feminist tome *Woman Hating* (1974). Otherwise, their backgrounds are nonexistent, other than the reference to She's traumatic experience a year ago in Eden alone while writing her thesis with Nic (another name for Satan) in tow. The couple are now a secularized Adam and Eve whose former paradise is revealed to be von Trier's "European jungle." The story becomes a battle of the sexes as ancient as the association of woman with chthonic nature, whose fecundity is threatening—wasteful and murderous—from a rational humanist (male) perspective. The meaning of the title, now with the final "t" replaced by the female symbol, associates woman with the Antichrist in what appears to confirm the wife's reversion to witchcraft. Like the spelling of *Nymphomaniac* with two parentheses to pictorialize an insatiable vagina, however, this was a winky flourish, a flagrantly "inappropriate" provocation. Moreover, the new version of the film would project a materialistic, darkly ecological understanding of natural process, traditionally gendered female, as chthonic, chaotically fecund, and violent.

The first versions of *Antichrist* had returned to the pattern set by the Europe trilogy. These are led by idealistic male protagonists who journey to the heart of darkness—to solve a crime or fight a disease—and lose themselves to the malignity surrounding them, thanks in part to their reliance on rubrics and rational systems. *The Element of Crime*'s cop Fisher tracks the serial killer Harry Gray by following his mentor's profiling system (of putting oneself in the mind of the killer) and takes on the Gray's attributes to the point of completing his "work." Fisher represents "the humanists who've often had central roles in my films," von Trier explains. "And everything keeps going wrong for them! He's working from the assumption that good and evil don't exist. But they're there all right . . . whether they're represented by people or nature."[39] *Epidemic*'s Niels (Vørsel) and Lars (von Trier) research the history of the plague as they write a screenplay about an epidemic in the present. In the script, projected as a polished film-within-the-film, young Dr. Mesmer (von Trier again) attempts to mitigate the epidemic's symptoms by ministering to the dying and ends up spreading it. In a parallel trajectory, the filmmakers use a hypnotized female medium to summon the plague, infecting all assembled before spilling over to the audience. In each case, the "cure" invokes or spreads the disease. In *Europa*, the protagonist travels to Germany in 1945 order to show the defeated country "a little kindness" and is sucked into a maelstrom of postwar corruption and international power politics. Similarly, to conquer his anxiety, in the early drafts of *Antichrist* Jeremy and his therapist undertake cognitive exposure therapy by returning, like each of these ill-fated male protagonists, to the source of trauma. Jeremy becomes possessed, a condition that spreads to the therapist.

In switching genders, however, the new draft continued the more recent and notorious trajectory that von Trier had maintained since *Medea* in 1988, where a strong, idiosyncratic female protagonist, a naïve victim-heroine (the Gold Heart heroines) and/or a canny rape-revenge heroine (*Medea*, *Dogville*) is the center of the film's conflict and source of its emotional charge. Virtually all of these heroines are positioned against oppressive and hypocritical male authority figures. They also tend to be complex and divisive, allowing actresses to triumph while provoking accusations of misogyny against the filmmaker. Like Medea or *Dogville*'s Grace, *Antichrist*'s grief-stricken mother She, pushed to the limits of her sanity by her therapist husband, summons the powers at her disposal and retaliates devastatingly only for him to murder her in a perpetuation of an age-old cycle of misogynistic violence.

EARLY VON TRIER, THE FEMME FATALE, AND FIN DE SIÈCLE ROMANTICISM

"Everything that I'm doing is based on stuff from way back. So no wonder that everything looks the same. It all comes from the same [sources]," von Trier told me in September 2006.[40] This confession, by no means new, was especially apt for *Antichrist*. If his newfound interest in Japanese horror and the onryō was one possible incentive for the gender switch, it was no doubt compelled by the fascination with the feminine, female sexuality, and female power discernable throughout his oeuvre, especially in his early work. As the press book's "confession" suggests, von Trier's depression took him back to a place where he could recover the "dangerous" themes, characters, and images from some of his earliest and most baldly personal works, including two thirty-minute films and two unpublished novels. These feature mentally unstable men who are drawn to dangerous women, sadomasochistic eroticism, and transvestitism.

The films made during this apprenticeship, and that he has officially kept out of circulation (but are unofficially accessible on YouTube), are permeated with sadomasochistic sexuality and influenced by classic pornographic literature—Pauline Réage's (Anne Desclos) novel *L'histoire d'O* (*The Story of O*, 1954), and the Marquis de Sade's *Justine* (1797) as well as films such as Liliana Cavani's *Il portiere di note* (*The Night Porter*, 1974) and Pier Paulo Pasolini's *Salò o le 120 giornate di Sodoma* (*Salò, or the 100 Days of Sodom*, 1975). His independently produced experimental film *Orchidégartneren* (*The Orchid Gardener*, 1978), whose protagonist Victor Marse (played by von Trier) he describes aptly in 2011, shaking his head at the memory: "I am in a Nazi uniform, I am a transvestite, I am killing a pigeon, it's misogynist as hell—it's a caricature of a Strindbergian character running around raping children. Every scene in the film is politically so uncorrect."[41] A sequence in *Menthe la Bienheureuse* (1979), loosely adapted from *The Story of O*, features a woman in chains, with a closeup of a ring in her labia, being whipped. Around the same time, von Trier had planned a film based on Leopold von Sacher-Masoch's famous novel *Venus im Pelz* (*Venus in Furs*, 1870) and wrote a detailed fifty-page script (*Verdande—af et oversanseligt menneskes bekendelser* [Verdande—from the confessions of an oversensuous human being]) that was never produced.[42] At the Danish Film School he ful-filled a *Dokumentarøvelse* (documentary exercise) with a film about a pedophile that Schepelern describes as a kind of *Lolita* satire, and he wrote a script based on Sade's *Philosophy in the Bedroom* (1795) but was forced by his instructor to destroy it and made a short film based on a story by Boccaccio instead.[43]

Von Trier's unpublished writings from *before* he committed himself to film-making are even more revealing, especially one of two novels he wrote along with several other prose pieces when he was nineteen and twenty, *Eliza eller Den lille bog om det dejlige og det tarvelige* (Eliza, or The little book about the delightful and the vulgar, 1976). This included the motif of the witchlike seductress, a female mas-turbation scene in which a baby's cry is heard offscreen, a sequence in which the male narrator believes he has been bewitched, another in which he sees blood and fears castration during intercourse with a seductive woman,[44] and another in which he encounters the seductress's young blond son, whose feet, he discovers to his horror, are deformed from being forced to wear his shoes on the wrong feet.[45]

"I am quite fond of the moment when Charlotte goes out to the woodland and masturbates whilst her husband looks on, unsure of what to do," von Trier has commented. "I think the atmosphere at this moment is very unique—it is a beautiful sequence also but it is also quite strange and even scary. . . . I did not have to say much to Charlotte—she just knew what to do and how to por-tray this character."[46] The masturbation scene echoes a sequence in *The Orchid Gardener*, where a young woman is shown masturbating alone in a room. With no clear link to the plot, the scene was, unlike the rest of the film, shot by von Trier himself, with a former girlfriend in the role.[47] Both masturbation scenes resemble Gustav Klimt's drawings of masturbating women, among the first in Western art to show women's sexual self-sufficiency. But they are equally "an invitation to voyeurism," suggesting "a painter or director who can use his authority to have the actors perform sexual acts."[48]

Von Trier's novels were turned down by several publishers and remain unpub-lished, and for years he kept the two films from his apprenticeship out of sight (allowing them to be shown only to invited audiences). As Schepelern puts it, the young Trier's first projects were "filled with anxiety, perversion and sexual-ity in an un-clarified mixture that was far too extreme and bizarre to find response."[49] *The Orchid Gardener* helped him get into the Danish Film School, but the acceptance committee remembered many years later concluding that either they had discovered a genius or made a huge mistake,[50] and when he showed the film to a university audience, they had only one question: "*Why?*"[51] "When I was younger," he says, "even more than today, I needed to show the dark sides very much."[52] When he achieved professional respect for the technical virtuosity of *The Element of Crime* and *Europa*, and wide international recognition and even popularity with *The Kingdom* and *Breaking the Waves*, it was not because his obsessions had been dispelled, but because he had found ways to integrate them into stories with characters and images that communicated widely. As examined by Peter Schepelern, early script drafts for *Breaking the Waves*, which many still consider his best film, are eye opening. Conceived as early as August 1991 as an adaptation of de Sade's *Justine*, it evolved from an "erotic melodrama" with frankly pornographic elements as the heroine becomes increasingly debauched, to the more commercial (yet far more complex and fundamentally disturbing) "religious melodrama with erotic overtones."[53]

As von Trier admits, "As for the provocative themes, in that respect I haven't changed at all. I still deal with exactly the same things, but in a more controlled way."[54] In this light, *Antichrist* is a fascinating reversal of the process that had become established. The original project, an almost straightforwardly personal story about anxiety and the patient-therapist relationship, had *lacked* any really provocative material other than the mildly blasphemous (or nihilistic) suggestion that Satan had created the world. After his depression, however, and needing an "emergency project," of art as self-therapy, he consciously reverted to the obsessions of his early work for emotions and issues that would match his desperation. As Schepelern puts it, "*Antichrist* is a return, a revival of the complexity and perversity of the early universe, a portrait of the artist as a young man, *retrouvé* and unchallenged, returning to all the unfinished businesses of youth. In this respect von Trier's claim that it is 'the most important film of my career' can be explained."[55] Switching gender, making the therapist male and the patient female, he distanced the raw material while radically sexualizing the material, therefore making it, in the light of von Trier's alleged history of misogyny, *more* personal.

A STRINDBERGIAN INFERNO?

As von Trier admitted in his "Director's Confession," he turned for inspiration to his earliest and most "dangerous" influences, mad geniuses whose psychoses were more than a little tinged by misogyny: in addition to Strindberg, the German author Friedrich Nietzsche, and Norwegian painter Edvard Munch. Strindberg's creative psychosis, like Munch's and Nietzsche's, was famously linked with his turbulent relationships with women. Thus, with more than a little histrionic irony, von Trier reclaimed their collective and largely Nordic insanity for his most blatant psychodrama.[56]

Von Trier has stated that among his films *Antichrist* is "the one that comes closest to a scream,"[57] referring to Munch's painting *Skrik* (*The Scream*, 1893), and that "cette composition est proche de ce que j'ai ressenti en le réalisant. J'y ai puisé toutes mes peurs et mes émotions" [this composition is close to what I felt when I realized it (the film). I drew all my fears and emotions from it]. [58] In one of *Antichrist*'s most chilling moments, She says, "I heard a sound," and the camera pans up and over "the tree tops at the edge of the meadow. . . . across the endless and ever rising forest scenery. . . . 'I heard the cry of all the things that are to die!'" in a direct reference to Munch's image.[59] The 1895 lithograph version has a motto in German: "Ich fühlte das große Geschrei durch die Natur" (I felt the great scream throughout nature). Peter Watkins's 1974 television docudrama biography of Munch "was a revelation" to von Trier. "When I saw it, I had to go and paint—and scrape the paint with the handle of the brush as well. Strindberg's and Munch's madness was the height of artistic romanticism for me then," he later told Björkman.[60] Munch, of course, represents woman as alluringly fatal in paintings such as *Madonna* (1894–1895), in which the virgin mother is a dark femme fatale with a blood-colored halo (and a frame ornamented with wriggling semen and a fetus-like figure in the lower left-hand corner); *Vampire* (1893–1894), where a woman with lush red hair is sensuously draped over her male victim's neck; and *Death of Marat* (1907), where a nude Charlotte Corday stands beside the murdered Marat.

Von Trier's kinship with Nietzsche's version of the mad genius, his confrontational stance, and transvaluation of conventional Judeo-Christian values is obvious throughout his work and his provocations, which propose the "anti-" to whatever is politically correct. With its title taken from Nietzsche's blistering attack on Christianity (1895), written in 1888, shortly before his inferno period, *Antichrist*'s title is possibly "an homage—and a nostalgic reference," as Schepelern suggests,[61] and although von Trier claims to have kept it on his bedside table for years, whether he actually read it is disputed.[62] Regardless, as Bodil Marie Stavning Thomsen suggests, the title's substitution of the female sign for the final "t" is a transvaluation of the crucifix that aligns with Nietzsche's concept of the Antichrist as a Dionysian force with the "potential for resistance," in this case through female chaos.[63] And it is not for nothing that in Jacob Thuesen's *De unge år: Erik Nietzsche saagen del 1/The Early Years: Erik Nietzsche Part 1*, 2007, written by von Trier and based on his experience at the Danish Film School, his alias is one "Erik Nietzsche."

As for his affinity with Strindberg's madness and misogyny, this had gone at least as far back as 1976, when, in what was his first public adoption of the aristocratic German "von," he published a newspaper article about Strindberg's period of creative psychosis (1894–1897). This featured a photo of "writer and artist Lars von Trier" posed outside the estate in Holte (near von Trier's home) where Strindberg wrote *Miss Julie*.[64] A Nietzschean understanding of existence as a struggle between weak and strong and a "will to power" rather than a merciful God informed Strindberg's psychosexualized version of naturalism, which portrayed the relationships between men and women, often spouses, as bitter power struggles, especially in the pre-*Inferno* plays *Fadren* (*The Father*, 1887), *Fröken Julie* (*Miss Julie*, 1888), and *Den starkare* (*The Stronger*, 1889). Von Trier's film is a similarly unrelenting struggle between "male" intellect and "female" nature, a chaos through which creatures procreate and suffer, struggle, kill, and die. In the 1887 autobiographical essays "Hjärnornas kamp" ("The Battle of the Brains") and "Om själamord" ("Soul Murder"), Strindberg compares the "stronger" mind to a kind of waking hypnosis or thought transference capable of coercing a "weaker" or more impressionable mind. In *Antichrist*, He employs cognitive therapy and hypnosis-like visualization exercises in attempts to normalize his increasingly agitated wife, who in turn uses sex to distract and dominate him. As for the wife's witch hysteria, this uncannily resembles the novella *En häxa: Historisk berättelse* (*A Witch: An Historical Narrative*, 1890), one of Strindberg's last pre-*Inferno* works and a case study of sorts: in seventeenth-century Sweden, not long after witch burning has been abolished, a young woman susceptible to others' influences becomes fascinated with the powers and stigmas ascribed to witchcraft, convinces herself that she possesses them, and, in a hallucinatory final scene, executes herself through the sheer force of her imagination. From 1896 to 1897, Strindberg was tormented by visions and anxiety described in the novel-like text *Inferno* (1898), allegedly based on the writer's diaries.[65]

Playing off his and Strindberg's shared proclivity for psychodrama, von Trier presented *Antichrist* as a similar projection of his own personal and mental struggles. The obvious connection is Strindberg's epistolary novel *Han och hon: En själs utvecklingshistoria, 1875–76* (*He and She: The Story of a Soul's Development*,

1875–76, 1919), compiled in 1886 from the passionate correspondence between himself and his future wife Siri von Essen, which, like von Trier's film, universalizes its gendered protagonists. His autobiographical novel *Le Plaidoyer d'un fou* (*A Madman's Defense*, 1895), moreover, presents a marriage from the husband's histrionic and embittered male perspective. Arguably, *Antichrist*'s transmutation from realistic chamber drama into a delirium shared by the couple compares with Strindberg's post-*Inferno* modulation into modernist expressionism, surrealism, and overt psychodrama in *Ett drömspel* (*A Dream Play*, 1901), in which characters "split, double, multiply, evaporate, condense, dissolve and merge" within the consciousness of the dreamer. As Strindberg explains in the play's preface, "A dream is usually painful rather than pleasant, a tone of melancholy and compassion for all living creatures permeates the rambling narrative."[66]

The inchoate surrealism of Munch and Strindberg merges in the film with the equally potent and early influence of Andrei Tarkovsky, to whom *Antichrist* is dedicated, and *Antichrist* has "the same complexity, the same ambiguous layers of meanings and symbols" as Tarkovsky's most personal film *Zerkalo* (*The Mirror*, 1975),[67] which von Trier had Gainsbourg and Dafoe watch before shooting started.[68] *The Mirror* is set in an archetypal woodland cabin, the home the exiled protagonist remembers sharing with his mother. Collapsing distinctions between characters and between past and present to convey the fluidity of identity, spatial experience, and psychological time, *The Mirror* sustains a continuously subjective perspective. With its archetypal "He" and "She," von Trier's psychodrama similarly returns to the repressed and therefore mystical space of Eden. There is also the Tarkovskian theme of nature impinging on the human that permeates the Europe trilogy as He and She descend into insanity and existential despair.

IN TREATMENT: *ANTICHRIST*, MENTAL ILLNESS, AND THERAPY

For von Trier, as for his heroes Munch, Nietzsche, and Strindberg, mental illness, therapy, and its tools had been important motifs since his earliest creative endeavors. The disturbed patient is invariably romanticized and Gothicized, as "good art is not always an expression that the artist is in a particularly happy place. There is always something slightly sick about great art."[69] Similarly, alternative or suspect therapies, especially hypnosis, may be abused but always reveal or bring on the awful truth. The psychologist, therapist, or doctor, on the other hand, is just as invariably derided or sent up—as is one famous Copenhagen psychiatrist, Dr. Daniel Jacobson, a psychologist who treated both Munch and Strindberg. In von Trier's assessment, "Strindberg's novels got much duller and Munch's paintings were far less interesting after their meetings with Professor Jacobsen [sic], so he was a bit of a villain in my eyes. They might have felt better, but their art was damaged by those consultations. . . . No, artists are meant to have it bad, because it makes the results so much better!"[70] Unsurprisingly, his unpublished novel *Bag fornedrelsens porte* (Behind the gates of debasement, 1975), which he describes as autobiographical, includes a scene in which the disturbed young protagonist "has a long sarcastic conversation with a psychiatrist," and in *The Orchid Gardener* (1978), the protagonist, a tormented artist, is in a sanatorium.[71] Throughout the Europe trilogy and *The Kingdom*, grotesquely misguided or demon-possessed doctors, backed by sinister and corrupt medical institutions, are targets of ridicule. Conversely, preternaturally innocent and prophetic mental patients abound: in *The Kingdom*, the brain-damaged child Mona, who spells out the name of the arrogant neurosurgeon, Stig Helmer, who botched her operation, in alphabetic blocks, and an ominous (and always accurate) chorus of two dishwashers with Down syndrome. These would evolve into the "good" women of the Gold Heart trilogy, holy fools like Bess, Karen, and Selma, who are regarded as simple or irrational by their communities. *Antichrist* lines up with its predecessors, with the deluded rationalist pitted against his wife/patient, who becomes perversely attuned to the natural world, to the real.

Yet the film is unique in drawing directly from von Trier's experience with cognitive exposure therapy (or, as he calls it in the early plot synopses, "flooding"), which is portrayed as relentless and torturous for the patient. Administered by the husband, preoccupied with his exercises, experiments, and diagrams, therapy becomes condescendingly pedantic and patriarchal, positioning her as an ignorant student or a deluded child. As her self-appointed therapist he dismisses her psychotherapist's diagnosis (of an "atypical" grief pattern) and treatment ("he gives you too many drugs") along with the guilt and self-loathing she frequently confesses, leading her to internalize and project onto herself the misogyny that was the subject of her feminist thesis. However, it is precisely through her female "insanity"—enabling her communion with chthonic nature—that Gainsbourg's She accesses the "truth" that the unconscious reveals.

In short, "male" reason, especially when confined to cognitive therapy, is limited at best and disastrous at worst; hence, as Sinnerbrink suggests, He suppresses his grief by projecting it into her therapy, until She "literally *forces*" him to experience it, provoking him to act out "the violent misogyny that was the subject of her abandoned thesis."[72] Moreover, the film's misandrous representation of the therapist—to the extent that cognitive therapy and the rational male archetype are presented as interchangeable—is juxtaposed against a misogynist fear of the chthonic feminine. And if many of the first to react proclaimed *Antichrist* misogynistic, equally as many differed, seeing it as a film *about* misogyny, with socialist-feminist historian Joanna Bourke suggesting that "the man's violence is the heartlessness of rationality" that "sneers at the woman's research" and "bullies her into exposing her inner demons."[73] Contending that "a lot of male critics don't get it," Jessica Hopper reads *Antichrist* as a study of male hubris and compares von Trier's vision of a world "in full masochistic flower" to radical cultural feminist Andrea Dworkin's refusal to "look away from the relentless blunt force trauma of patriarchy."[74] However glibly, von Trier has said, "I've always been the female character in all my films. . . . the men tend to just be stupid, to have theories about things and to destroy everything" or the equivalent.[75] Gainsbourg has just as often supported him, asserting in interviews at the time that she felt that she performed as his surrogate. "Lars really showed me what he felt," she says. "And so I felt very close to him. I felt he wasn't just coordinating everything, a spectator, but as if he was with me, feeling [those emotions] too."[76] To the extent that the first version of the story was autobiographical (in being about a male anxiety patient and a female therapist in a relationship apparently familiar to von Trier), the development of the film, as traced in the preceding pages, backs up her interpretation.

From its earliest conceptions, the film's central argument exposes the limitations of anti-Freudian cognitive therapy over Freud's theory of the unconscious, to which von Trier has evidently long felt drawn. Midway through the film, She flippantly pronounces herself cured, whereupon He confesses to having had "some crazy dreams." "Dreams are of no interest to modern psychology. Freud is dead, isn't he?" she quips with deadly irony. "The whole thing about this cognitive therapy is very sarcastic from my point of view," von Trier told the *Independent*: "I have been undergoing [it] for some years, and the therapy he [Dafoe] is doing in the film—in a very bad way—is cognitive therapy. The very modern thing about these people is that Freud is dead and has no significance any more, which I don't know. I know a little about Freud but I would not be able to say if he is dead or not."[77] In fact, von Trier typically uses Freudian concepts to explain himself and his influences,[78] and as Schepelern suggests, he fits all too well Freud's notion of the artist, the literary artist in particular, as a "daydreamer" who expresses his childish regressions and neuroses creatively in forms that entertain the public, thereby validating himself.[79] If anything, in his last four films, von Trier has employed this notion as a metatext.

Hypnotherapy, which Freud used while developing his talking cure, and like other alternative forms of knowing or gnosis, is presented as fascinating, mysterious, and dangerously ambiguous, yet invariably "right" in von Trier's oeuvre. As in *Antichrist*, von Trier's fascination with hypnotherapy and similar techniques permeates the Europe trilogy in direct parallels between hypnosis and cinema, hypnotist and filmmaker. In *The Element of Crime*, Fisher undergoes hypnosis to relieve incapacitating headaches and blackouts, only to recall the events that led him to become a serial killer. In *Epidemic*, filmmakers hire a hypnotist to regress a subject back to a plague-infested Europe, whereupon she becomes a medium for the disease which eventually is cinema itself. *Europa* opens with a hypnotist in voice-over speaking to the protagonist and the viewer simultaneously as he puts "us" into the trance that is "Europa." Echoing *Europa*, which begins with the soft rhythmical clatter of the train over the tracks, *Antichrist* features a train sequence in which husband/therapist employs a guided visualization and trance through which She envisions returning to their woodland cabin. She enters and moves through the forest at night, floating through deep blue foliage accented by mists and concentrated points of sparkling light. In the visualization, She encounters cues for the ensuing episodes: the fairy-tale footbridge, the fox hole, the dead tree, blowing grass. At his insistence, she lies down in the grass and imagines herself blending with the green and with the elements, obliterated in nature, and her fears seem to have been temporarily conquered. The strangeness of her visualizations, however, says otherwise, and they act as a transition into an increasingly surreality through which the husband's rational therapeutic narrative is disrupted and dislocated.

While working on *Antichrist*, von Trier made experimental use of the unconscious, which he accessed through induced dream and trance states, in addition to his usual practice. As for the latter, in a long *Politiken* interview with Nils Thorsen in 2014, he confessed to having used alcohol topped off with a specific drug cocktail (which he refuses to disclose) to boost inspiration for most of his films, especially at the writing stage: the intoxicants erased anxiety and doubt, allowing him to blaze through the labyrinth of decisions any manuscript presents.[80] And more: "It has always been a way to reach the parallel world," he explains. "Creativity is, in a way, the parallel world," adding that "this is somewhat similar to being on a shaman journey, which I have also used, and which is traditionally often carried out on intoxicants. So the rush has always been a way to get to that world. And those experiences are fully valid. I believe in a way that creativity is to seek that world."[81] Asked by Thorsen in 2011, "What was the thought that you based *Antichrist* on?," von Trier answered:

> "I don't know if it was a thought or a feeling and this film is hard to talk about also because it was made in a more intuitive way where I just tried to dream on to some pictures. Mostly from shamanic travels I had made [ten years] earlier."
> He lights up.
> "Now they have started to use the isolation tank!," he exclaims. "They say it is so fantastic. And they have been lying there for hours. And got *pictures!*"[82]

This explanation, however fragmented, suggests a conscious, rational decision and a more than usually concerted effort to "dream" up visionary encounters. Thus, while having "only . . . what some might call 'the bare necessities' in the way of a plot," as von Trier noted in the press book, *Antichrist* is among the most surrealistic, complex, and allegorical of his films, while also perhaps the most calculatedly indecipherable, provoking perfectly balanced opposite interpretations and reactions.[83]

Anti-Wagnerian Romanticism: *Antichrist* and the Bayreuth *Ring* Project

Setting the film in the United States, near Seattle, Washington, von Trier explicitly sought out a primeval German forest location that could pass for old growth forest in northwestern United States.[84] Other than the European "jungle" documentary that provided the film's core concept, together with his own experience of therapy, the most important inspiration for *Antichrist*'s primordial location, setting, style, and sound design, was German Romanticism and Richard Wagner. As he told Per Juul Carlsen in a 2011 interview, "The Germans have always influenced me. . . . I have always flirted with the good Herr Wagner, and in *Antichrist*, we inched toward a kind of German Romantic painting [inspired, especially by Caspar David Friedrich]. Indeed, sturm und drang and everything that followed."[85] The fascination with Wagner has informed many of von Trier's topics and aesthetic choices, most especially the Europe trilogy. *The Element of Crime*, inspired by the helicopter shots in *Apocalypse Now* (1979) through which Americans pilots terrorized the Vietnamese to *The Ride of the Valkyries*, was made with Wagner's *Parsifal* and *Tristan* playing throughout the shoots to motivate the actors, enhancing a trancelike mise-en-scène whose ochre lighting makes the film stock itself look degenerated and diseased.[86] In *Epidemic*'s film within the film, the strains of *Tannhäuser*'s overture accompany the pestilence's fatal dissemination and recur in the framing film's climactic moments.

From this largely "masculine" obsession with the Third Reich, von Trier turned to female melodrama in the Gold Heart trilogy (1996–2000) with the theme of female self-sacrifice, a German Romantic lynchpin. As *New York Times* music critic John Rockwell suggests, in these films he creates the emotional equivalent of music, and the soaring intensity of the actresses' performances represents "a new kind of hyper-emotional artistic experience" comparable to that evoked by music.[87] (As for Dogme 95's collaborative minimalism, marketed as a corrective to the excesses of globalized Hollywood blockbusters, von Trier invented to constrain what one might call his own "Wagnerian" tendencies, including an obsession with the technical and manipulative aspects of filmmaking.) Although nominally a musical, with a four-minute overture and a final aria cut off by the heroine's death, *Dancer in the Dark* aspired to the melodramatic emotional reaches of opera, as von Trier has commented, to the extent that Danish composer Poul Ruders thought that it was meant to be just that, adapting it as the opera *Selma Jezková* (2010).[88] More recently, Missy Mazzoli and Royce Vavrek's "savage, heartbreaking," "powerful," and "spellb[inding]" adaptation *Breaking the Waves* (2016) won the inaugural Best New Opera Award from the Music Critics Association of North America and an International Opera Award nomination for Best World Premiere.[89] It should come as no surprise, then, that von Trier told an interviewer in 1999 that "to film Wagner . . . would be the ultimate goal of my life. . . . I could die happy," or that in 2001, he was commissioned by Wagner's grandson Wolfgang Wagner (1919–2010) to stage *Der Ring des Nibelungen* (1848–1874), four epic musical dramas based on the Norse sagas and Germanic mythological material (in which forests are a significant location, especially in *Die Walküre* and *Siegfried*).[90] In a public acceptance statement, he called the assignment "a dream come true," a call to which "one responds as unquestioningly as a soldier, subordinating himself" to the Bayreuth tradition while believing that "I have an intuitive knowledge of the way the definitive staging should look."[91] But, after working on the project for two years, in close collaboration with conductor Christian Thielemann, he withdrew in 2004, having concluded, according to the announcement on the Bayreuth Festival's website, that despite two years of "excellent progress," the "dimensions and requirements" of the sixteen-hour stage production would "clearly exceed his powers," and he had come to "the dawning truth that a realization was beyond his reach."[92]

"Wagner's ruling vision for the *Ring* settings— . . . the one described in the rubrics of his poem—was that of the wild grandeur and infinite changeability of nature," Patrick Carnegy explains.[93] A fanatical alpine walker, he gave nature and landscape an especially active role in the drama. In so doing, he created "huge problems both for himself and for all subsequent producers of the *Ring*. It is not only the states of mind and actions of the characters which are mirrored in the music and . . . settings. Air, earth, fire and water are no less vital players, both in their own right and as symbolic correlatives of the characters."[94] Thus, instead of a theatre artist, for his scenic design he commissioned Viennese landscape painter Josef Hoffmann (1831–1904), who made extensive preliminary landscape studies in the alps, to bring life to nature on the Bayreuth stage.[95] Wagner's original productions of the *Ring* attempted to convey the sense in which actions and characters, many of whom are variations on or descendants of the Norse gods, are associated with the power and inscrutability of nature and with specific natural forces: Wotan (Odin) with thunder and lightning, the Norns with darkness, Erda (Mother Earth) with the primordial and chthonic, the Rhinemaidens with water, the sleeping Brünnhilde with a protective circle of fire and the sun she greets upon awakening. Action and emotion are reflected in moods of the weather. Moonlight floods into Hunding's hut to articulate the lovers' rapture, while sunlight penetrates the Rhine and reflects its gold to suggest dawning awareness. At least partly because of the challenges this created for directors, Wagner's version of natural supernaturalism has more often than not been succeeded by abstract modernist, psychoanalytic renderings, or industrial or contemporary production designs with historical and sociopolitical commentary. Yet all the evidence suggests that von Trier's goal was to embrace Wagner's original vision, based on a Romantic understanding of nature and the sublime, engineering it through modern media technology inspired by cinema and immersive, world-building computer games. Indeed, as Rockwell notes, the Bayreuth announcement of von Trier's "proclaimed goal to create a new staging concept of a Wagner-opera, in celebration of Wagner's original ideas and settings" could not have been more tantalizing for Wagnerites. Thus, the Munich daily *Süddeutsche Zeitung* called von Trier's withdrawal "the greatest disappointment in the opera history of this decade."[96]

In a "Deed of Conveyance" that he subsequently posted on Zentropa's website, von Trier publicly shared his key ideas for the aborted *Ring* project in the hope that others could use them. These were a fascinating blend of Wagnerian "monumentalism" with a "less is more" aesthetic that, on the surface, recalls the powerful minimalism of Dogme 95. The document devotes most of its attention to the aesthetic practice of "enriched darkness," which employed obscurity, videos, and fluid scenery to guide the audience's vision and revealed its origins in cinema, specifically horror movies' reliance on darkness to create suspense and fear, and video games (he had been playing *Silent Hill*, which also partly inspired *Dogville*'s gameboard-like set.)

> Actually, the concept is filmic. In horror films in particular, the technique of hinting without showing has been tried and tested, and adopted to great effect by electronic games. In both media we are familiar with arriving at a darkened house with the frail beam of a torch our only source of lighting. Not to mention in real life: at night, no matter how delightful and safe our neck of the woods may be, it inevitably becomes populated by demons, evil and mythological forces; and as we all know, they are all the more real and terrifying for not being illuminated.[97]

As the "Deed of Conveyance" together with his notes, diagrams, and research materials suggests, his plans attempted to realize Wagner's intentions through cinematic means: projecting videos of the German forest and rugged alpine inclines, of massive ("monumental") trees with networks of roots, rocks, and streams, to provide a truly immersive experience. This was in stark contrast to the contemporary trend in which directors transplant the plot to another period or universe, adapting it to a sociopolitical or psychoanalytic context. Von Trier adhered to the original 1876 staging, which blended naturalism with mythic romanticism. For example, when recreating the alpine sublimity of act 2 of *Die Walküre*, "the entire act appears as a long tilt/crane ride up a mountain. The mountain is . . . 8 times the height of the Bayreuth stage."[98]

If they proved too ambitious to engineer for a live performance on a theatrical stage, von Trier's ideas and preparations, including precise plans and
diagrams for the production of *Die Walküre* and *Siegfried*, were realized in
various, striking, and significant ways in all four of his postdepression films.
Melancholia, with its Wagnerian score, is merely the most obvious case. As von
Trier told Stig Björkman, a great many of the "metaphysical and monumental
images" and other scenic ideas for *Antichrist*, "have their origin in that project,"[99] and this assertion, also made elsewhere, is supported by a study of his
research notes, photographs, and drawings.[100] This repurposing of the *Ring* was
apt: the Bayreuth production he had hoped to stage through cinematic techniques derived from horror movies and computer games; conversely, in *Antichrist*, he must have envisioned a horror movie infused with Wagnerian monumentalism, mysticism, and a Norse pagan ambience.

The hefty folder with von Trier's research, drawings, and notes for the *Ring*
project at the Danish Film Institute includes a spiral notebook with images
of past Bayreuth productions together with several separate sheets with
photographs of forest landscapes. These are stored with his own sketches and
a collection of location photographs.[101] All together they suggest von Trier's
keen interest in realizing Wagner's romanticism, based, like German Romantic painting, in a sense of interdependence between nature, the gods, and the
human sphere, together with an obsession with forest imagery, individual
tree shapes, large twisting roots, and grottoes. Most of the historical photographs are renderings of Joseph Hoffman's production design for the first
Bayreuth performance. A striking photograph of the original scene design
for Siegfried's second act depicts a grotesque romantic forest setting with
the dragon Fafnir emerging from his lair whose jutting rocks are surrounded
by roots, trees, and shrubs sketched in naturalistic detail. In *Antichrist*, the
key location of the fox's hollow partly concealed by a mass of roots—where
Dafoe drags himself and fights an uncannily undying raven—resembles this
image.

The climactic moment of act 1, scene 3 of *Die Walküre*, where Wotan's twins
Siegmund and Sieglinde, having been separated since childhood, are reunited
and fall ecstatically in love, typically takes place in Hunding's hall, which is
supported by a huge living ash tree whose branches pierce the roof, with its
foliage extending over it. In the tree is a magical sword that can be released and
wielded only by a designated hero. In von Trier's sumptuously romantic ("monumental") version of the scene, nature, manifested through lighting (enhanced

FIGURE 1.1 Renderings of Joseph Hoffman's production design for the first Bayreuth performance of 1876.

Modell av den originale Bayreuth-dekorasjon til 2. akt av «Siegfried».

FIGURE 1.2 The original Bayreuth scene design for Siegfried's second act: the dragon Fafnir emerges from his lair, its jutting rocks surrounded by roots, trees, and shrubs in naturalistic detail.

darkness), videos, and blocking, is the central character. The scene is described in detailed notes for the piano-vocal score (from the Peters edition), with page and bar indications heading each description:

50.2 four spot[light]s starting outside on the branches and roots of the big tree . . . approach infinitely slowly [toward] the sword's space. it is the story of the big tree. . . .

54.11 S. [Siegmund] comes in and embraces her in the light.

56.12 It's as if a wind is blowing through the entire forest . . . in three four quick glimpses (partial video). . . .

58.5 The moon breaks through the clouds and illuminates the creek behind the house. (video) + moonlight

58.12 S. steps out. . . . into the water.

58.17 S. looks up the creek toward the moon and follows it upward. . . . .

59.5 Sl. [Sieglinde] is also coming out now . . . the two have their own light. In the following, Sl. is slowly lured by him from plateau to plateau as the creek forms up towards the moon (video). He is constantly a little ahead. everything with [the] brook is seen through the branches of ash.

74.10 bird flock flies past the moon and away (video)

76.1 S. and Sl. continue to climb upwards. . . .

78.10 S. and Sl. reaching straight up so they become silhouettes against the moon (video), but at the same time S. is looking down again. with sudden energy . . . he slides down the slope to the foot of the tree. light also after him.

81.2 S. has reached the ground under the tree . . . every trace of H[unding]'s house is gone. The ash stands alone in shallow water among a thousand small young ashes. . . .

82.3 they go down to the tree together

83.2 . . . the house is gone. . . .

85.13 Sl. helps S. up the trunk. He pulls her up.

85.14 S. pulls out the sword in the trunk and fucks her against the tree. As he does it the whole tree trembles. . . . we pan away from the two, from the large branch we saw swinging first . . .

86.11 we follow the movements of the great branch upward and higher and higher up to the twigs that also shudder.

86.24 We end on the first twig we saw in the wind at the start of the act. Now directly in front of the moon (video) It vibrates for a long time then it calms down. Light down on everything. End Act.[102]

Von Trier's concept of the scene, clearly influenced by German Romantic painting, heightens the both the mythological and sexual subtexts surrounding the sword, the adulterous and incestuous Wälsung couple in the momentous act of conception, and the tree, an ash recalling Yggdrasil, the World Tree at the center of the cosmos and the cycle of new life and death in Norse paganism. Where in previous versions Siegmund and Sieglinde consummate their passion offstage, von Trier takes their intercourse to the next level, with the shuddering of the tree indicating the momentous events to come (Siegmund's death and their son Siegfried's birth), with a grandiosity worthy of William Butler Yeats's "Leda and the Swan" ("A shudder in the loins engenders there / The broken wall, the burning roof and tower / And Agamemnon dead").[103]

The tree at the center of Hunding's hall may also have suggested *Antichrist*'s set design for the massive oak that stands next to the cabin, its canopy extending over the roof upon which it incessantly rains down acorns. But it was the most iconic of *Antichrist*'s sequences (which furnished the image for Zentropa's publicity poster) that von Trier would make both "monumental" and eerily perverse use of these scenic ideas, many of which resonated with the darker elements in Norse mythology. After the camera moves in gradually to a closeup of She masturbating in the forest, He joins her, and the couple have "demonic" intercourse against a great tree around whose knotted roots the limbs and hands of the dead are entangled. In this mythical space, the boundaries between nature and the human, sex and death, become indeterminate.

This blurring of boundaries is consistent with the mythology surrounding Yggdrasil. Beneath the roots of the ash flows a spring where the Norns live and from which they water it, yet one of its roots leads to Hel, the realm of the dead.[104] One of von Trier's sketches for act 2 of *Siegfried* depicts, against a back-projected video of mountains, a stark, splintered trunk with spiky remnants of branches that would become another of *Antichrist*'s most haunting repeated images. In the first, early in her visualization exercise, She sees herself passing a similar, chillingly stark and splintered dead tree. In the last, as He, a broken man, exits Eden just before the epilogue, a crane shot pulls back to reveal, in an image suggested by Hieronymus Bosch, innumerable corpses surrounding the dead tree, the residue of chthonic sacrifices long past—a possible reference not only to Hel (overseen, in Snorri Sturluson, by Hel, the queen of the underworld)[105] but also to the "hall of the dead," Valhalla.[106] Notably She associates trees, the oak in particular, with nature's wasteful fecundity, exemplified in the acorns that, like the fledgling bird, fall and

FIGURE 1.3 He (Willem Dafoe), framed by the canopy of the oak tree extending over the cabin's roof, is bombarded by acorns and engulfed by aggressive vegetation.

FIGURE 1.4 He (Willem Dafoe) and She (Charlotte Gainsbourg) have "demonic" intercourse among the roots of the great tree intertwined with the limbs and hands of the dead, blurring the lines between the human and nature, sex and death.

"die," an interpretation that corresponds with shamanistic beliefs that unborn souls reside in trees, and that a falling leaf designates a death.[107] In the *Ring*, bridges are signifying props, notably the rainbow bridge built by Wotan to permit the gods a direct route from Midgard to Valhalla near the end of *Das Rheingold*, and that corresponds with Bifrost in Norse mythology. Similarly in *Antichrist* the footbridge crossed in both dream states and in waking life, like the various trees, acts a portal between ordinary and enchanted realms. This is echoed in *Melancholia* in the bridge that that neither the horses nor the golf cart will cross.

FIGURE 1.5 One of von Trier's sketches for act 2 of *Siegfried* depicts, against a back projected video of mountains, the stark, splintered trunk of a dead tree with the spiky remnants of branches.

FIGURE 1.6 As He (Willem Dafoe), exiting Eden, passes the dead tree, long-buried corpses are revealed surrounding its trunk.

Thus, if von Trier never achieved Wagner's vision of Norse mythology on the Bayreuth stage, he realized a dark and visceral variant in *Antichrist*. The film's earthy/unearthly images of trembling fronds, trees, and cavern-like spaces together with effects of visual and aural dislocation evoke, paradoxically, through a heightened form of naturalism, a sense of mythical time and space.[108] Where Wagner's gods and heroes are represented by and command the elements, She invokes the forces of nature by allying with "the sisters" who can "send down hailstorms."

With *Antichrist*, von Trier abandoned the overscripted, Brechtian cinema of the USA duology and returned to the technical virtuosity, oneiric logic, and Tarkovskian ambience of his early monochromatic and color-coded films, with the Wagnerian goal, it seems, of creating an immersive sensory environment and a maximum level of affect. Reaching "into the old toybox," as von Trier put it, he rediscovered slow motion, slowed further with a Phantom HD (high-speed) camera and other visual effects, such as black-and-white and montage, which he employed in the five-minute, twenty-second, forty-two-shot prologue, as the blissfully unaware couple reach orgasm and the child falls silently to his death, evoking grief, the stasis of melancholia, and fatalism.[109] The use of black-and-white infers that the events of the prologue happen on a different, mnemonic or oracular, layer of narration.[110] The use of high speed (ultra–slow motion) suggests that the events we see are beyond ordinary concepts of time and elevates commonplace—or, conversely, pornographic—close-ups to the level of sublime art. An elaborate montage choreographs the movements of the lovers and allegorizes the narrative. Juxtaposing the narrative trajectory of parents and the child, the camera points out details the characters are unaware of, anticipations and omens that viewers understand only in retrospect. The omniscient camera spots, under the boy's playpen, his shoes standing in the wrong position, the left to the right and vice versa (announcing a motif that will be important to the plot); the bottle gulping out water—a symbol of waste but also ejaculation; the child's wooden puzzle that She grazes with one buttock, loosening the pieces to reveal a deer, a fox, and a crow; on the desk three metal figurines labeled "Grief," Pain," and "Despair" (eventually matching three of the chapter titles) and a book with loose note papers, signifying academic studies, rifled by the wind from the open window; the teddy bear tied to a balloon and floating in the air, perhaps luring the boy toward the window; the laundry tumbling in the dryer. The child falls from the third floor of a modern city apartment building on a street lined with parked cars under a light blanket of snow. Apart from the snow, which aestheticizes the shot, nature is absent from the prologue. At the same time, after the penetration shot, as Ger Killeen has observed, virtually every sequence in the montage "emphasizes motion and the physics of motion, the ineluctable operation of gravity": the couple knocking over the bathroom tumbler with the toothbrush, She's foot kicking over the scales, the wooden picture-puzzle, and the bottle that gulps out its liquid, with the laundry in the drier echoing their tumbling from room to room and eventually and fatally, the child's fall. ("We all fall down" is the refrain of the song playing over the end credits of von Trier's plague film *Epidemic*). Adding a symbolic layer to the prologue, the formal elements elevate it beyond the realistic domestic situation. All these ordinary props and movements are swept into the aesthetic discourse by the high-speed cinematography, precisely calculated montage, black-and-white, and the classical music soundtrack and are made hypnotic and symbolic, shifted to a timeless mythic or allegorical level whose events will play out fatefully over the next ninety-eight minutes.[111]

From the pyrotechnics of the prologue, von Trier shifts markedly to the Dogme-style naturalism and deep blues and greens of the contemporary narrative. Here nature is no backdrop to the human drama, which it increasingly and without warning interrupts, but an obscure, uncannily nonhuman ambience, an "enhanced darkness" that surrounds and gradually engulfs the human characters and domestic drama. The first hint is the dimly lit hospital room scene in which the camera ominously tracks in on the rotting stems in a vase of lilies as they slowly dissolve into the murky water. Later, a therapy sequence is interrupted by a series of cutaways to the forest: a stationary shot, with "a hard artificial light in the night," of "young birch trees bent down into arches by wind and weather;" dense undergrowth shot through by a flickering light source; and a shot of the forest passing with increasing rapidity until it blurs completely.[112] Images of Gainsbourg's face contorted into a scream emerge from the blur and fade back into it with increasing rapidity until it "becomes impossible to fix the eye."[113] At crucial points, as when She explains her symptoms, the naturalism of the domestic drama is interrupted by haptic images, blurred and grainy slow-motion close-ups that immerse the spectator in bodily sensations of anxiety: footage of a pulsing throat, sweating skin, and trembling hands. Thus, even before we enter the forest, as Thomsen has suggested, the film is a disorientingly immersive viewing experience, shifting from human to nonhuman points of view: for example, in the visualization sequence where the fox hole is shown from inside (from the fox's—and eventually He's—perspective) as She glides across the sight line, to a crow's-eye view of She passing the tree of death that, as she remarks, "rots so slowly."[114]

Key shot sequences described in the final script are designed to erase the boundaries between the human and the nonhuman. In a transition from the chilling sequence in which She recalls hearing nature's cry, followed by

FIGURE 1.7 In She's (Charlotte Gainsbourg's) visualization of entering Eden, the fox hole is shown from the inside, the fox's perspective, as She glides across its sight line.

the crane shot over the forest canopy, scene 57 describes an elaborate lap dissolve:

> *Stationary shot of her neck in the cabin. She is standing quite still. Slow dissolve from the previous scene. For a long time, we cannot differentiate between the shadows of the forest and the shadows of her hair. It is as if the two images combine. . . . As if the tree tops have made room for her, for the picture of her neck and hair. Now the former scene fades away. After it is gone, the green colour still clings to her and her neck and her hair. She is tinted green as in the first shot of her in the meadow. Now he enters the frame and the green tint disappears.*[115]

This transition is all the more unsettling for the way it echoes the comparatively innocent visualization sequence in which She "just turn[s] green."

Likewise, as the script makes clear, the camera forces He to see things from a nonhuman perspective. In a transition from scene 61 to scene 62, after he crumples up the letter about the child's autopsy, tosses it in the firewood basket, and "pensively" lies down beside her,

> suddenly he seems to spot the camera.
> *The handheld shot is suddenly transformed into a stationary shot that glides into a linear movement up and away from him.*
> He looks inquiringly at the camera.
> SCENE 62, EXT. "EDEN"/ UNDER THE OAK—DAY.

Stationary shot, slow motion.

With a loud crash, suddenly he is on the ground outside "Eden" in extreme slow motion. He is under the oak in front of the cabin. He is looking into the camera. It is as if many of the acorns raining down on him stand still in the air. First we are in a close shot of him.

Cut to stationary full shot slow motion of him against the oak and the cabin.

In the foreground, hundreds of little oak plants grow unnaturally fast out of the ground, only to die in spasmodic movements as they are overshadowed by others. Out of the image grows the cry of a child.[116]

In encounters with the Three Beggars, He interacts with a nature whose viscera is quite literally exposed, threatening the human subject's sense of bodily integrity. In the meadow he spots a beautiful hind, who, sensing his presence, raises her head and "stare[s] at him intensely." Abruptly the camera cuts to a medium lengthwise shot that reveals a still-born fetus "still hanging in its vernix half-way out of the hind's genital opening."[117] In the next encounter, he warily approaches a patch of rustling ferns and pulls them apart, the camera closing in to expose the fox tearing at its own entrails. Abruptly rearing and turning its head, the fox utters the words that became a meme: "Chaos reigns!" In another abrupt cut, as Dafoe stands stock still with grim astonishment, rain (punning on "reigns") pours from the skies, swamping him, in a motif that culminates in the epilogue's final scene. In the third encounter, he takes cover in the fox hole and uncovers a half-buried, "undead" crow that repeatedly comes back to life to alert She to his location. With chapter 4, "The Three Beggars," the anthropomorphic perspective denoted in the previous chapters named for the human emotions "Grief," "Pain," and "Despair" is taken over by the shamanistic animals, as She announces, "When the Three Beggars come, someone must die." When she "sacrifices" her clitoris and her scream echoes throughout the forest, the hind raises her head and gazes into the darkness toward the source. Once more, the crow's muffled caw is heard, revealing the location of the wrench under the porch before magically aligning, together with the hind and the fox, next to She's prone body, before He frees himself to complete once more the cycle in which female nature blooms, bleeds, and dies. The Tarkovskian motif of the encroachment of the nonhuman on the human world, tapped throughout *The Element of Crime*, *Epidemic*, *Medea*, and *The Kingdom*, becomes *Antichrist*'s primary allegory and "special effect."

Since the Dogme 95 Manifesto, von Trier had been known for his opposition to manipulative and immersive film scores. In fact, the Vow of Chastity prohibited nondiegetic sound entirely. *Breaking the Waves* and *Dancer in the Dark* either anticipated or partly drew on Dogme's prohibition. The church's prohibition of music or bells was a running joke in the earlier film, which expressed Bess's (and von Trier's) love of 1980s rock and pop music by limiting it to the chapter breaks, where it played over exquisite picture postcard–style landscape paintings by Per Kirkeby. In *Dancer in the Dark*, von Trier's naturalistic version of a musical cum opera, the song and dance routines filtered through Selma's imagination were set off as such. But beginning with *Dogville* and *Manderlay*, made concurrently with his work on the *Ring*, von Trier began to employ classical baroque music to lend an atmosphere of formality, grandeur, and elevation to the narrative. This began with the use of Vivaldi, Handel, Albinoni, and Pergolesi in *Dogville* and *Manderlay* and led to his use of Wagner in *Melancholia* and Bach and César Franck in *Nymphomaniac*.

In *Antichrist*, the elegiac aria from act 2 of Handel's opera *Rinaldo*, "Lascia ch'io pianga la dura sorte" ("Let me weep over my cruel fate") plays over the prologue and epilogue, to the exclusion of all diegetic sound, to create "a solemn meta-layer of synesthetic effect where music and picture melt together, reciprocally exchanging meaning."[118] Despite the complexity of the choreography, what was perfect about the aria, sound designer Kristian Eidnes Andersen explained, was the emotional simplicity of its melody, its "quality of direct expression." This he "made even more simple" with a click track followed by the musicians and mezzo soprano Tuva Semmingsen,[119] and von Trier asked the performers to "make more noise" to expose the physical presence of the instruments.[120] In Handel's opera, the aria is sung by the knight Rinaldo's beloved, Almirena, who has been abducted by a queen with witchlike powers. The suffering woman seems to parallel or predict the suffering of the woman in the film, although, later, as it plays over the epilogue, this seems skewed or ironic, suggesting, as Ger Killeen has noted, that the words of the aria "serve as a lament by the parents for the tragic death of their son" and its consequences. "Better, perhaps," Killeen adds, "is to see them as a lament for the human condition in general, the inevitable traumatic encounter with the real which is the fate and lot of everyone."[121]

It is *Melancholia* that von Trier has called a quintessentially "romantic" film, in which themes from *Tristan and Isolde* prelude compose the film's sole leitmotif, that Wagner's impact on sound design becomes obvious. According to Thomas Grey, the *Ring*, which introduced Wagner's "'leitmotivic' method of composition" was "an attempt to imitate nature itself as an organic process of growth or evolution. Musical motives are introduced in their simplest form— . . . the notes of a major triad or part of a diatonic major scale—and become more complex with the passage of musical and dramatic time, the unfolding of events or history."[122] In *Antichrist*, any such notion of nature as progressive or harmoniously organic is exposed as false: nature is wastefully fecund, chaotic, dissonant, and violent. Where, for instance, act 2 of *Siegfried* lulls us with "forest murmurs" and a bird whose singing informs the hero about Brünnhilde (via flute and glockenspiel, within the quiet undercurrent of sustained strings), nature in *Antichrist* is represented by alarming ambient sounds, shock chords that arrest the action, earsplitting shrieks, low-pitched drones, and a talking fox with a demonic voice.

For the narrative proper, von Trier worked with Andersen to create something completely novel yet leitmotivic all the same. Especially for a "horror" film, the "biggest challenge was to avoid clichés" while "adding this psychological pressure, this unease" in which "less is more."[123] The result was what Andersen has called a "mix of sound design and a musical score," composed naturalistically of "organic sounds not touched by mankind," obtained exclusively from materials such as "sticks, branches, stone,"[124] or by blowing on blades of grass or running horsehair over thin branches, that Andersen looped and combined. In an abrupt shift from the melodic and intricately choreographed prologue, the handheld footage of the domestic drama is punctuated by the sound of bending and clashing trees, "breathing" ferns, and acorns clattering on the tin roof, as well as the sounds of the human body (which Andersen recorded after swallowing a tiny microphone). The latter accompany what the script designates as the "Anxiety

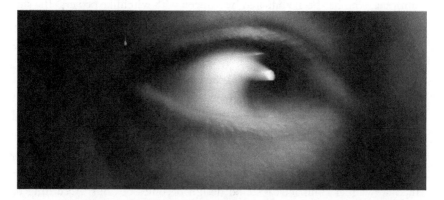

FIGURE 1.8 In a sequence from *Antichrist*'s "Anxiety Montage," extreme handheld close-ups articulate She's visceral experience of a panic attack.

Montage" that functions as a leitmotif: extreme handheld close-ups of ten designated regions of She's body during a panic attack whose literal viscerality—
the experience of embodiment from the inside—paradoxically produces a hallucinatory affect.[125] In this orchestration of a nature that is immanent rather
than other, that manifests from without and within, *Antichrist* invokes the vast,
encompassing cry of "all of the things that are to die."

A NORSE PAGAN ECOLOGY

If, like Wagner, von Trier aimed for an immersive affect that evoked the terror
and ecstasy of the sublime, the point of *Antichrist*'s aural naturalism was the
opposite of Wagner's leitmotivic romanticism. Wagner associated the primal
and natural with a pure golden age, and the end of *Die Götterdamerung* envisioned
"a new, 'utopian Anthropocene,' " according to Grey, "a potential new harmony
of human consciousness with its natural environment," a harmony that belied
many of its Norse pagan sources.[126] Von Trier takes a far grimmer—and, as I
will argue, darkly ecocritical—view signaled in the epilogue, where He is forced
to acknowledge both the failure of his overweening rationalism and his inter-
dependent coexistence with chthonic nature. There the He feeds on berries to
survive, glancing warily back at the shamanic animals who are rendered momentarily benign, when a horde of faceless, indifferent, but otherwise ordinary-
looking women engulf and walk past him. *Antichrist* was after all meant to be a
horror film. But, as we have seen, as the film developed it shifted from a more
conventional religious binarism to a secularized, existentialist, and Norse pagan
perspective. Thus, in a 2009 interview with Gunnar Rehlin, von Trier explained,
"I would rather believe in the old gods, those who were God and Satan at once.
I'm not religious. I've tried, but I don't believe in anything."[127]

   On one level that appealed to American and global audiences, the woodland
cabin is meant to be redolent of colonial New England and witch persecution
in a Puritan vein. Cabin horror films like *Evil Dead* (1981), *The Blair Witch Project*,
and, more recently, *The Witch: A New-England Folktale* (2015) resonate from an
American tradition going back to the Salem witch hysteria, Charles Brockden
Brown, Nathaniel Hawthorne, and Arthur Miller's *The Crucible* (1953), and, consequently, *Antichrist* resonates from that perspective as well. Hence "Eden"
devolves into "Satan's church" to embody the dichotomous extremism with

which the Puritans regarded nature: both as the garden before the Fall, and the threat of savagery and reversion. According to this scenario, nature inspires Gainsbourg's vindictive sexuality, linking her through her thesis to witchcraft, and drives Dafoe toward insanity and murder.

On a deeper and perhaps less conscious level on von Trier's part, the rendering of the (German) forest location and the witch burning theme, as I have argued, corresponds with Norse pagan mythology and a heritage of Nordic cinema in which nature is powerful and often cruel, feared and respected, and with a harsh justice that emphasizes revenge and sacrifice.[128] In *Antichrist*, Nature *is* Satan's church in that the forest, the central image of which is the great tree that rains down acorns or dying hatchlings crawling with feasting ants, is pagan. It—or, rather, they, as there are, as we have seen, several manifestations of the tree archetype in the film—alludes both to the Tree of Life or the Tree of Knowledge in some fallen version of Eden (whose trees are imported from various pagan tree cults) as well as to a Darwinian nature "red in tooth and claw."[129]

Although typical of von Trier in challenging audiences with a taboo issue and embracing the tensions inherent in it, *Antichrist* shocked even the most inured viewers by unearthing a deeply rooted fear of (and evident desire for) the chthonic feminine. Repressed within Judeo-Christian culture, this mixed fear of and reverence (already discussed in the work of Munch and Strindberg), together with the motif of witchcraft and witch burning, has long been a current in Scandinavian cinema. As early as 1958, British film critic Dilys Powell remarked, "Whenever Scandinavian cinema has five minutes to fill, it burns a witch."[130] The witch-burning motif is overwhelmingly obvious in key films of specific forebears von Trier has acknowledged over the years: Benjamin Christensen's *Häxan* (1922); Carl Dreyer's early films, including *Blade af Satans bog* (*Leaves from Satan's Book*, 1921), *La passion de Jeanne d'Arc* (*The Passion of Joan of Arc*, 1928), *Vampyr* (1932), and *Vredens dag* (*Day of Wrath*, 1943); Alf Sjöberg's *Himlaspelet* (*The Heavenly Play*, 1944); Bergman's *Det sjunde inseglet* (*The Seventh Seal*, 1957) and *Jungfrukällan* (*The Virgin Spring*, 1960); and, in a sense, Andrei Tarkovsky's "Swedish" film *Offret* (*The Sacrifice*, 1986)—as well as von Trier's own *Medea*, adapted from a Dreyer script. Even more important, all feature protagonists torn between the now-dominant Christian (or secularized Christian) and deep-seated pagan values to which they in some sense revert, and they frequently empathize with the "devil's" (or Odin's) point of view, which is usually possessed by (or possesses) a woman suspected of being a witch. Reflecting these same tensions, sympathies, and narrative arc, *Antichrist* subtly acknowledges von

Trier's Nordic roots.[131] Perceiving this, and in spite of its English language and American setting, the Nordic Council awarded *Antichrist* its 2009 Film Prize for a work rooted in Nordic culture. The prize recognized it as a "visionary work" out of which rises "a darkness without contours, a chilling loneliness, as well as pain as the primal force of human survival," a work that "questions convenient religious thought and attacks accepted rational and controlling ambitions, pushing the viewers towards the edge of their own deepest fears."[132]

Recent ecocritical perspectives help to contemporize this discussion in ways that lead to the next chapter of this book. As She and her pagan "sisters" recognize, humans and nature do not take separate subject and object positions, but coexist, influencing one another in an interdependence that Timothy Morton has described as a "dark ecology," and that opposes Western environmental perspectives in which binary oppositions between nature and culture perpetuate notions of the nonhuman as benign and passive on the one hand and sublime on the other.[133] Accordingly, and like von Trier's previous rational humanists, Dafoe's He ascribes to a subject-object binary that is revealed overwhelmingly to be false, whether in his series of encounters with the Three Beggars or his vision of a new constellation, of deer, fox, and crow. Along these lines, Kristoffer Noheden explores how, in *The Element of Crime*, *Antichrist*, and *Melancholia* the protagonists' "altered subjectivities" through hypnosis, anxiety, and depression interconnect with "an encroaching non-human world [and thus] undermine the normative 'anthropocentric gaze' and may invite new perceptions and experiences" of the universe. Drawing on Morton, he argues that these three films confront "the limits of reason with gnostic epistemologies" and force audiences to contemplate a "radical coexistence" with the nonhuman, "from microbes and companion animals to rocks and galaxies, all of which have their own forms of agency," to which *Antichrist*'s epilogue is the perfect testimony.[134] Morton finds the world a dense mesh of interconnection, a mesh that "twists and turns, generating riddles and distorting perspectives like a maze filled with so many funhouse mirrors," or, alternately, a black prism.[135] As seen through the mesh, the world is a decaying "Gothic mansion" rather than "a lush green meadow." Nature, accordingly, is neither "green" nor passive or sublime and certainly not "cosy."[136] A journey through the origins and development of *Antichrist* exposes equally the Judeo Christian "Eden" and the ecowarrior's idealization of nature as lies and reveals that the film is above all about the masculine/rational mind's repression, belated recognition, horror, and grief when confronted with the real.

2

MELANCHOLIA

Wagner, Superkitsch, and Dark Ecology

ORIGINS AND DEVELOPMENT

Melancholia originated as a psychological inquiry inspired by conversations between von Trier and his therapist, who (in von Trier's words) theorized that "depressives and melancholics act more calmly in violent situations, while 'ordinary, happy' people are more apt to panic. Melancholics are ready for it. They already know everything is going to hell."[1] Searching for a crisis of magnitude, von Trier came across web pages about interplanetary collisions such as Nibiru, and, possibly after watching a television documentary, he decided on Saturn, a gas giant about nine times the size of the Earth, as a model for the planet.

Von Trier's plans for the film developed further during conversations and correspondence with actress Penélope Cruz, who had written von Trier expressing her desire to work with him on a new film and had brought up her fascination with Jean Genet's play *The Maids* (*Les Bonnes*, 1947), in which two maids, Claire and Solange, based on the infamous Christine and Léa Papin, kill their mistress.[2] (About the sisters, Genet enigmatically remarked that "maybe the characters are me, maybe they're not," much as von Trier would explain his Justine and Claire.)[3] The two ideas merged and developed into a story that contrasted the reactions of the depressive Justine and the "normal" Claire to the threat of a rogue gas planet hurtling toward Earth. "Penélope can ride. So I used that, too," von Trier said.[4] The title, together with the character of Justine, was obviously inspired by von Trier's own depression. Cruz, who was expected to play Justine, dropped out over a scheduling conflict, and after consulting with American filmmaker Paul Thomas Anderson, von Trier offered the role to Kirsten Dunst, who accepted, with Charlotte Gainsbourg as Claire.[5]

A New Approach to Script Development

While writing *Melancholia*, von Trier was forced to make substantial changes in his working methods. For years, his procedure embodied the Romantic stereotype of the solitary, substance-abusing artist. After jotting and dictating numerous short notes, outlines, and summaries, he outlined the plot, visualized as a horizontal line on his office wall drawn with a black marker, gradually filling it in with vertical black and red lines indicating turning points, events, musical cues, and images, then sequestered himself, while drinking alcohol, usually vodka (together with a drug cocktail for which he will not provide the recipe), for a short, intense period of time, completing a first draft within a few days to two or three weeks. But his depression and its toll on his physical health, exacerbated by the alcohol and drugs, put an end to these solitary, if spectacularly productive, binges.[6] Since his depression he had suffered from hand tremors that made it impossible for him to write or type at any length. Eventually he embarked on a healthier procedure for writing scripts through collaborations with Vinca Wiedemann, Jenle Hallund, and a number of assistants. As his producer Louise Vesth described the process, a person sits with a computer that is linked to a television, which shows the text as von Trier "is telling what he wants to put in the script."[7]

Vinca Wiedemann, who had broad experience as a film editor, screenwriter, producer, commissioner, story supervisor (and subsequently became rector of the National Film School of Denmark from 2014 to 2019), worked with von Trier in this capacity on *Melancholia* and *Nymphomaniac*. Although she typed his dictation two hours a day at an appointed time, the process was never as straightforward as it sounds, and it eventually developed into a far more collaborative relationship. Often, as she describes it,

> Lars would be at an earlier stage than [that] of dictating [and] would gradually unfold the story. So the first time the story would just be, "I know that I want to make a story that begins with a wedding and that ends with the collision of two planets." . . . And that [there will be] two sisters . . . and then he would

elaborate from there. So that would be his overall structure and then he would gradually fill in more and more. That's his working method. . . . That's why the drawing [the outline on his office wall] is there, so he can see the overall construction. . . . work with that and then gradually fill in more.

But Wiedemann's role also involved discussing, questioning, and prodding:

> If he was in a bad mood, he would say, "I know nothing about my story." And I would try to interview him. "Well, what about her? What about him? Where do they live? . . ." to [get] his imagination going. Because of course you know much more than you think, it's that it's just not conscious yet. So I would kind of help him track it from the unconscious to the conscious, and then [to] all the decisions he would have to make, and that way he would have to make them because he would have to give me a response.

When asked if she contributed suggestions, she replied that her job was to supply "bad" ones: "So, I would say 'She lives in a big house.' 'No. How stupid.' 'No, of course. She lives in a blah, blah . . .' The suggestion I would make would make him think of what he thought it would be like, or [whether or not] it ma[de] sense." Clearly, Wiedemann had an active role in storing, recovering, and establishing links:

> If he had a clear vision, I wrote it down. If there was not a clear vision, maybe it would pop up, maybe today, maybe tomorrow, maybe in a month. So [on any given day] I will just write down the fragments that he has today and I will try to explore whether there's more to it . . . , and if not, maybe it will come some other day or maybe it will not be there and maybe [he] will think next time this was stupid, take it out, and I will take it out.[8]

Melancholia was essentially a trial run for what would become a more collaborative method. Wiedemann insists that her contributions at that point were facilitative rather than creative or inspirational, but, as Vesth has explained, her designated role became increasingly dialogic and expanded to include research and story supervision, especially while working on *Nymphomaniac*, which meant that she had control over the final script.[9]

At around the same time Wiedemann became attached to the project, von Trier hired writer and director Jenle Hallund in the role of general consultant. He and Hallund had met on the set of *Limboland* (2010), which Hallund codirected with Jeremy Weller and Zentropa produced.[10] There, impressed with her ability to read, interact with, and direct a group of young, disaffected second-generation immigrants, nonprofessional actors featured in explosive situations, he asked her to help him with the relationship between the two sisters and to bring her own experience of extreme situations, including depression, to bear. In a June 2019 interview, Hallund explained that before she met von Trier she was "not a fan" because his heroines "were always suffering and . . . led by somebody else or something else instead of themselves." Hence, she made it her goal to "give [Justine and Claire] a bit of, uh, internal drive. . . . that was definitely [the subject] of many discussions that Lars and I have had." Hallund remembers that working on the characters was "a lot of fun . . . because I have sisters myself . . . and a lot of melancholy and depression running in the family."[11] Whatever the causes, Justine and Claire manage to evade the female martyr syndrome that has afflicted so many of von Trier's previous heroines.[12] Each sister is strong in her own right, and *Melancholia* is unique among von Trier's films in that the film's primary relationship is between two women.

Evidence suggests that the film was written and produced relatively quickly and that the shoot, from July 22 to September 8, 2010, was, contrary to its title, a pleasure. "*Melancholia* was a totally different shoot than all the other shoots I've been on," von Trier's longtime assistant director Anders Refn explained in 2018. "It was a very happy shoot. . . . a wonderful summer, warm, and we were shooting in the castle where the film is set," and the crew and cast worked so efficiently that they finished shooting three days early.[13] In the evenings after work, the film's party scenes spilled over into the communal dinner for the cast and crew: "Two French sound guys were brilliant chefs," and at the end of every working day, "they threw down their microphones and tape recorders . . . and ran into the woods and picked mushrooms, and started cooking and making risotto." Meanwhile, the "guys playing in the band [for the wedding] had big jam sessions. . . . And people were dancing through the night. John Hurt [who played Justine's father] was . . . was dancing all night. And people were so sweet to each other, there was such a good atmosphere."[14]

In contrast, as is well known, *Antichrist*'s shoot had been strained because of von Trier's precarious condition, with Refn and cinematographer Anthony Dod Mantle, who had been cinematographer for *Dogville* and *Manderlay*, ready to take over in von Trier's absence. The fact that he could not wield the camera frustrated him, triggering relapses and conflicts. Afterward, von Trier blamed Mantle primarily for his dissatisfaction, claiming that the cinematographer disregarded or "improved on" von Trier's direction and that the film was as a result too polished, without enough contrast between the prologue and the narrative sections, between the handheld sequences—which he wanted to have an edgier and more ragged feel—and the "monumental" scenes.[15] For *Melancholia*, therefore, he looked elsewhere, hiring Hoyte Van Hoytema, acclaimed for his work on *Let the Right One In* (2008) but who subsequently dropped out, and finally Manuel Alberto Claro, recognized for his dazzling work on Christoffer Boe's *Reconstruction* (2003). Evidently, Claro had a combination of temperament, intelligence, knowledge, and skill that a vulnerable von Trier needed at the time. According to Refn,

> Manuel is opposite to Anthony; he's very fast-working, and he worked multiple practicals, with very little lighting. Of course, we had some big lamps, also, when we did the slow-mo, because it was shot with a Phantom camera. But Manuel is very intelligent in the way of using very little light. And that fit very well with Lars's way of working, because you don't have to wait for hours for the light like you normally do on traditional films.[16]

FROM PRIMAL SCREAM TO THOUGHT EXPERIMENT

Von Trier decided early on to make clear from the beginning that the world would end, depriving the audience of suspense, while privileging the psychological and emotional reactions of the characters to crisis. Or, rather, he substituted anxiety and dread for suspense, creating a narrative of affect rather than action. Like *Antichrist*, *Melancholia* originated as a psychodrama, and Justine's perspective is a projection of his own experience of depression. It was, as von Trier has said, about a "state of mind" rather than the end of the world per se.[17] However, supported by Refn's and others' observations, it reveals von Trier in a very different space from that in which he made the previous film. If he explained *Antichrist* as a primal scream therapy from the depths of his depression, his statements about *Melancholia* suggest that it was truly a post-depression film, looking back on the experience from an analytical perspective, conceived quite objectively, as a case study, or, as Thomas Elsaesser suggests, as a psychological and philosophical "thought experiment," based on the premise originally suggested by his therapist.[18] Thought experiment films, according to Elsaesser, "deal in hypothetical situations, and thus are fictions, often presented in the form of a didactic parable or an imaginary scenario. However thought experiments are also 'What if?' conditionals, and as such they are suppositions. . . . ways of making inferences based on real word evidence, posited in such a way as to allow for deductions that can predict future outcomes."[19] In fact, many of von Trier's films originated as hypothetical situations in which the characters represent some aspect of himself. Explaining how he "thought up" *Dogville*, he described the film as "a very good exercise—to kind of put yourself in a very difficult situation and see how things will turn out."[20] As such, rather than traumatizing and polarizing audiences, *Melancholia* achieved intellectual distance while evoking discussion from a wide range of psychological, philosophical, and aesthetic perspectives.[21] Described in the press notes and elsewhere as "a beautiful film about the end of the world" and permeated with Wagner's music, it achieved a notable aesthetic distance as well: in being "Wagneresque," its melancholy "was perfect, how it should be," as Hallund puts it.[22]

Regardless—or perhaps for that reason—it has proven a seductive, profound, and complex emotional experience for many viewers and critics. As Caroline Bainbridge observes, the film's "invitation into the melancholic state of mind is . . . difficult to resist," colored "as it is by the director's own well documented experiences of mental illness and collapse,"[23] and the film deeply affected viewers with a history of depression whose testimonies have congratulated von Trier and Dunst for "get[ting] it right,"[24] Steven Shaviro and Rupert Read among them.[25] "So many people I meet somehow connect to that film," Claro told me in 2018. For many "young people. . . . in their twenties," *Melancholia* is "the first film that really they connected to. And people who are not film buffs."[26] In a powerful personal testimonial, Trevor Link explains that "by creating an exteriorization of what is inherently, tragically a self-destructively interior process, a film like *Melancholia* allows a depressed person to draw strength from these images: . . . in them, the truth of the world as imagined or feared by the depressed mind is made real, finally, rather than continuing to plague him or her as a terrifyingly palpable, yet elusive, phantasm." He adds further that "von Trier is right, as he implies in *Melancholia*, that there are truths that depressed people have accessed that are valuable. His film is a powerful and hopeful affirmation of this."[27] Bainbridge, who specializes in psychoanalytic approaches, was so devastated by the film that she was incapable of talking or writing about it for several years. In "The Melancholic Gaze" (2019), she attempts to account for her response to the film and theorizes that through projective identification it offers a therapeutic encounter for depressives.[28] Writing several years later at the height of the COVID-19 pandemic, mental health blogger Natalia Antonova finds hope in the film's point that "people with psychological problems may just be useful as the world ends—and the apocalypse, I believe, is not linear, each of us is a little, walking apocalypse, and so the world is therefore always ending."[29] In another pandemic-inspired piece, in the May 2020 *Atlantic*, Mallika Rao notes that in "today's context," Justine might be "the mascot for misunderstood seers, the Cassandra of the screen."[30]

Remarkably, *Melancholia* does not psychologize Justine's condition—in striking contrast to *Antichrist*, in which psychological theories and treatments, however disastrously, frame She's mental and emotional collapse. There is no mention of past trauma, no therapist, no diagnosis. The film refuses clinical objectivity—or, as Shaviro puts it, von Trier "depathologizes" depression entirely.[31] This is despite the devastating accuracy of Kirsten Dunst's portrayal, which was based in von Trier's experience and no doubt enhanced by her own.[32] Although "melancholic depression" is a clinical term, the title eventually refers less to a mental or emotional disorder than the film's mood, tone, weltanschauung, and, arguably, philosophy of existence. Most discussions of melancholia pay respects to Freud's essay on "Mourning and Melancholia," in which depression is a failure to grieve, a persistent attachment to a lost object.[33] Along these lines, and drawing on Julia Kristeva's *Black Sun: Depression and Melancholy* (1992), Elsaesser argues that Justine's mother's refusal of empathy suggests that Justine's is a case of Oedipal melancholy, one that stems from von Trier's experience with his own mother.[34] But if Gaby's maternal failure is bluntly exposed, *Melancholia* is otherwise perversely lacking in a psychological backstory, diagnosis, or treatment. Significantly, as von Trier's collaborators Wiedemann and Hallund have both emphasized, one of their tasks was to help spot and eliminate conventional psychological explanations for characters' behaviors.[35] Ultimately the film's omission of a clear originating event or past trauma should be understood not as an oversight but as an assertion of the validity of Justine's (and von Trier's) experience. Like *Nymphomaniac*'s Joe, who authorizes herself by reclaiming the archaic and misogynist term "nymphomaniac" over the politically correct (but pathological) term "sex addict," Justine claims her melancholia as a worldview and a calling.

Justine's state of mind *is* the film. Her face, her eyes heavy-lidded and blank, fills the opening frame as dying birds fall from the sky. As Claro explains, the overture represents what Lars regarded as "previsions that Justine can see because of who she is. The first ten minutes are her viewpoint."[36] This is followed by part 1, which, in spite of the wedding party's large cast, focuses intensively on Justine's emotions and reactions, so that later, in part 2, when she speaks like a seer, claiming to "know things" ("There are no other places. We are all alone [in the universe].") we believe her. If part 2 opens with Claire in charge as a calming and nurturing figure, it becomes the story of her breakdown, and as she becomes distraught and dysfunctional, unable to console her own son, Justine discovers empathy in his fear and despair, bringing the three together to face the end.

WAGNER, THE *GESAMTKUNSTWERK*, AND CANNES 2011

As von Trier's second film to draw on his abandoned Bayreuth project, *Melancholia* was, unlike *Antichrist*, overtly Wagneresque. "What was it I wanted?" he asked rhetorically in the director's statement included in the production notes: "With a state of mind as my starting point, I desired to dive headlong into the abyss of German Romanticism. Wagner in spades!"[37] In an interview included in the film's DVD extras, he explains that "very early on in the project" he chose the prelude to *Tristan and Isolde* as the film's keynote, stressing that it is not what most would "consider melancholic music," but "romantic music," and that this has "somehow turned the whole thing into a very romantic film."[38] A document labeled "Directors [sic] Intentions," which von Trier signed in Copenhagen, March 2010, asserts that his primary aim was to

> carry on a kind of form from my previous film "Antichrist," in which the strictly narrative level to a greater degree submits itself to the rest of the stylistic means of the film. I see a film which starts in an overture of lyrical, but also ominous and confusing scenes to the score of Wagner's "Tristan and Isolde." These scenes do not yield any meaning per se, but in the course of the film they will create associations and unrest as they fall into place in a greater perspective. From its monumental opening, the film continues in a strictly documentary style. . . .

Eventually, the style of social realism is disrupted in the effects of the invading planet on the Earth . . . as supernatural light phenomena and a general suspension of the physical laws of our planet.[39]

Hence, while taking obvious elements from the disaster and science fiction genres, *Melancholia* was an experimental work of cinematic art in which aesthetics and affect predominate over plot; score and image over narrative; and often, to a degree that is atypical of von Trier, the sonic over the visual. Noting that a total of 29 minutes of this 130-minute film are taken up with cues from Wagner's opera,[40] David Larkin observes that this "choreographic matching of the visual to the musical is not only unusual for von Trier, it is the reverse of the industry norm whereby the composer is usually given a close-to-finished set of images to which to add music."[41]

The film begins with the longest single cue in the film, sustained over 16 frames and of extreme slow motion (shot by the 5000-frames-per-second Phantom Cam) choreographed to bars 1–83 of the prelude to *Tristan und Isolde*, whose images and musical motifs recur, in altered forms, in parts 1 and 2. Tellingly, von Trier often calls his prologue an "overture."[42] As Larkin describes it, "The final ascent to the musical climax (bars 74–83) lends to the accompanying images—the catastrophic planetary approach and collision as seen from a god's-eye perspective—a climactic quality of their own."[43] Moreover, the prologue ends not with the relatively subdued final section of the prelude but with a snippet from the prelude to act 3 of *Tristan*, with added rumble noises as the earth is consumed by the encroaching planet, thus signaling its return to accompany the final credits.[44] In other sequences, Wagner's music is cut and manipulated to fit the narrative and emotional moment. Altogether the Prelude is heard nine times: in the prologue (00:00–08:00); when Justine leaves the party (00:22); when she swaps out the art books (00:43); during the balloon launch (00:47); Justine and Claire riding in the mist (01:04); Justine watching the planet (1:19); Justine at the stream (01:22); Claire, carrying Leo (Cameron Spurr), attempting to flee (01:52); and the ending (02:00).

As Claro has said, "We saw the opening images . . . as intricate paintings: different parts of each image might have slightly different perspectives, for example, which adds a sense of artifice and unreality—as in Renaissance painting. The whole opening sequence is stitched together from many, many shots." Although von Trier's use of paintings was inspired by Tarkovsky's approach to creating images, more generally, "we wanted in this sequence to have the expressive and emotional freedom that painting has."[45] *Melancholia*'s scenic design also incorporated the work on the Bayreuth *Ring* project, continuing and enhancing a style influenced by the German Romantic paintings that inspired Wagner's original set designs. The film allowed von Trier to combine monumental architecture with sublime landscapes and uncanny manifestations of weather. The prologue's eighth frame depicts Claire, Leo, and Justine arranged on the lawn, with the Gothic castle's battlements brooding behind them, bordered by the blue planet on the left and the moon on the right. In frame 7, Justine, like a goddess orchestrating the powers of nature, raises her fingers to the sky, and lightning flashes from her fingertips. In part 2, in a scene designed to look like a German Romantic painting, while offering an exquisite instance of "enriched darkness" as well, Justine reclines naked on the bank of a stream like a Rhinemaiden and offers herself to the planet whose beams highlight the contours of her body.

In the file of von Trier's Wagner materials at the Danish Film Institute is a photograph of the "Awakening Scene" from the 1954 production of *Siegfried*, designed by Wagner's grandson Wieland Wagner, in which Brünnhilde, sleeping under Wotan's spell in a ring of fire, is aroused by the hero's kiss and exults in the light of the sun.[46] Described as "one of Bayreuth's most sublime stage images," it is pared down to three elements, the earth, the lovers, and the sun. The photograph reveals the curved outline of the earth, with the figures of the lovers lying together at the center, as the dawning sun rises over them, dwarfing them, the scene representing the rekindling of life. The photograph has been partly pasted over another, less arresting design, singling it out, suggesting that it had made a memorable impression. However paradoxically, the image is suggested in the powerfully minimalist design for *Melancholia*'s ending, in which the planet is envisioned as a vast yet oddly tranquil light blue orb that rises over the gently sloping earth, the tiny figures of Justine, Claire, and Leo, united as a family, outlined against it as it fills the sky.

In his interview with Claro, Rob White suggests that, in contrast to von Trier's previous films, "the aesthetic of *Melancholia* is something new, digital, closer to videogames or fashion photography," noting that "the Bruegel painting in the opening sequence burns, as if to make way for a new art that might even mock, or anyway reinvent, painting."[47] Yet it should be pointed out that von Trier's films were already typically aesthetic and technical experiments, genre hybrids, and transmedial feats, as in the Europe trilogy's sustained riff on neonoir and art film staged as hypnotic trance, or *Breaking the Waves*'s chapter titles, which overlay picturesque landscape paintings with nearly indiscernibly moving elements accompanied by music. Long before *Melancholia*, *Breaking the Waves* and *Dancer in the Dark* had employed the alternation of two styles, a documentary naturalism and an expressionistic experimentalism that drew inspiration from the noncinematic arts, such as music and painting. This experimentalism momentarily peaked with *Dogville*, which von Trier developed concurrently with the Wagner project and described as a "challenge" to the limitations imposed on the arts. He called it a "fusion film," a fusion of art forms, "between film, theatre, and literature."[48] *Antichrist* signaled von Trier's shift to a transmediality inspired in part by his work on the *Ring* cycle—with the stunning black-and-white prologue choreographed to a Handel aria, painterly slow-motion dream sequences, sound mixes taken from organic materials and processes, and a dazzling range of influences and allusions. *Melancholia*, however, was his first film to aspire blatantly and self-reflexively to the *Gesamtkunstwerk*, Wagner's concept of a "total" work of art drawing multiply from cinema, music, painting, architecture, and drama. This drama's cosmic scope and Wagnerian grandeur moreover enlarges what might have been a merely "personal" film about depression, lending it philosophical and political as well as psychological import and resonance, and *Melancholia* has consequently been recognized as addressing several of the major cultural, existential, and ecological crises of our time. Von Trier's "Wagnerian" ambitions, however unfortunately, together with "the charged aura of evil that hangs over Wagner since the Holocaust," also triggered the scandal that dominated the film's reception and that continues to dominate the conversation surrounding Lars von Trier.[49]

Cannes 2011 opened amid intense speculation about a face-off between *Melancholia* and Terrence Malick's *The Tree of Life* for the Palme d'Or. Both were massively ambitious, experimental, lushly cinematic films by world-class auteurs with cosmic scope and serious philosophical implications. The former expressed a Judeo-Christian search for existential meaning that returned to the origins of the universe, the latter an atheistic philosophical pessimism that envisioned the end of all life. If the Cannes showdown to some extent played out, with *The Tree of Life* winning the Palme D'Or and *Melancholia*'s Kirsten Dunst awarded Best Actress, it was skewed by the notorious *Melancholia* press conference and von Trier's disgrace and exile—amid speculation about whether *Melancholia* would have won the big prize had von Trier kept his mouth shut (like Malick, who, perhaps wisely, refuses to make public appearances). As it turned out, this was no idle speculation. Speaking to the French publication *Liberation* in

May 2020 and calling it a "magnificent" film, Olivier Assayas (who served on the jury alongside jury president Robert De Niro; actors Jude Law, Uma Thurman, and Martina Gusmán; producer Nansun Shi; writer Linn Ullmann; and filmmakers Mahamat-Saleh Haroun and Johnnie To) confirms that before the scandal, all but two of the nine jury members favored *Melancholia*: "At first, there were only . . . Jude Law and I, who thought that Terrence Malick's 'The Tree of Life' could also claim the highest prize. The reason other members joined our cause was because they had lost their favorite."[50]

Despite von Trier's exit, *Melancholia* was esteemed and awarded a number of prizes in multiple categories, including the Best Actress Award at Cannes and the European Film Award for Best Picture and Best Cinematography, as well as various awards from critics circles and top ten lists and, in contrast to the walkouts, scandal, and division in response to *Antichrist*, *Melancholia* was acknowledged to be "among Mr. von Trier's finest."[51] As von Trier himself has noted with no little irony, that it has "the most happy ending I have ever made."[52] Even Jonathan Romney, who is anything but a von Trier fan, described it as "severe and graceful" and remarked that watching it persuaded him to forgive von Trier for making *Antichrist*.[53] In hindsight, Roger Ebert confessed that "if I were choosing a director to make a film about the end of the world, von Trier the gloomy Dane might be my first choice."[54] Some mixed or negative reviews found part 1 a needlessly lengthy rip-off of Thomas Vinterberg's *Festen* (1998). On von Trier's use of Wagner's music, two prominent American music critics took opposing perspectives. The *New Yorker*'s Alex Ross panned the score's excerpting of Wagner's music for "manag[ing] to be at once clumsy, unoriginal and perverse."[55] The *Washington Post*'s Tim Page found "teaming a new film with *Tristan* . . . an audacious decision . . . yet, after all, it works. . . . I loved it."[56] Whatever the case, more than one critic found the experience of watching the film "incredibly uplifting" (Stephanie Zacharek),[57] or claimed to have left the theater "light, rejuvenated and unconscionably happy" (J. Hoberman),[58] or soaring, "in a state of ecstasy" (Lisa Schwarzbaum).[59]

Von Trier himself, who usually judges his success in terms of numbers of walkouts, may have regarded the favorable response as a bad sign. His public statements before the film's release were decidedly ambivalent. His statement for the press book claimed that when his producer presented him with a mockup for a poster and a trailer after the film was made, he felt "ready to reject the film like a wrongly transplanted organ," describing it as "cream on cream. A woman's film!" As for the German Romanticism, "is that not just another way of expressing defeat. . . . to the lowest of cinematic common denominators? Romance is abused in all sorts of endlessly dull ways in mainstream products. . . . I cling to the hope that there may be a bone splinter amid all the cream that may, after all, crack a fragile tooth."[60]

In an interview with Per Juul Carlsen for the May 4, 2011, issue of the Danish Film Institute's journal *FILM*, he put the issue more bluntly. The film

> consists of a lot of over-the-top clichés and an aesthetic that I would distance myself from under any other circumstances. . . . It reminds me of those Luchino Visconti films I always enjoyed that were like whipped cream on top of whipped cream. I went overboard, blasting Richard Wagner. I made the film with a pure heart and I couldn't have done it better, and everyone did a good job. But when I see clips from it, I think, "I'll be damned. That was unpleasant." . . . this film is perilously close to the aesthetic of American mainstream films. The only redeeming factor about it, you might say, is that the world ends.[61]

Von Trier went on to speak of his love/hate relationship with Wagner, Germany, his own complicated heritage and identity, and the "Nazi style," which complicated his ambivalence toward the film. In *In Search of Lost Time*, he explained, Proust concludes that Wagner's *Tristan and Isolde* is the "greatest work of art of all time,"[62]

> so that's what we pour all over this film, pushing it for all it's got. I haven't used so much music in a film since "The Element of Crime" . . . but here we wallow in it. It's kind of fun, actually. For years, there has been this sort of unofficial film dogma not to cut to the music. Don't cut on the beat. It's considered crass and vulgar. But that's just what we do in "Melancholia." When the horns come in and out in Wagner's overture, we cut right on the beat. It's kind of like a music video that way. It's supposed to be vulgar. That was our declared intention. It's one of the most pleasurable things I've done in a long time. I didn't have to force it out, like in "Antichrist," not at all. Cutting on the beat is pleasurable.[63]

The reference to *The Element of Crime*, his first feature, is telling. Von Trier shot the film without recording sound so that he could have the "music of Wagner [selections from *Parsifal* and *Tristan und Isolde*] blasted at full volume from the loudspeakers on the set, in order to infuse cast and crew with the right spirit of things."[64] A practice "used during the silent era," this was "very beneficial to the atmosphere. . . . It's a Wagnerian milieu."[65] Similarly, during the shooting of *Melancholia*, as cinematographer Manuel Claro has mentioned, "the Wagner was played on set a lot (and we listened to it before shooting too), and it worked quite differently for different people, with some being moved and others finding its epic, tragic dimension annoying."[66]

The 2011 *FILM* interview with Carlsen proved fateful. From his enthusiastic discussion of the "vulgar" pleasure he took in cutting on the beat to Wagner, von Trier moved directly to the pleasing shock of learning from his mother on her deathbed that he was half-German, then to his interest in Nietzsche and Thomas Mann, then to his aborted *Ring* project, then to *Antichrist*'s German Romanticism, and eventually, inexorably, to the Nazis, who "certainly cut on the beat":

> They didn't pussyfoot around. I've always had a weakness for the Nazi aesthetic. A Stuka will outlive a British Spitfire in our consciousness by millennia. . . . While a Spitfire has all those rounded forms and was a very beautiful airplane, the Stuka was a revelation. . . . a dive-bomber that swooped down and dropped its bombs with great precision. A special feature . . . was that its bombs were equipped with a little whistle [the "Jericho trumpet" sirens that became the propaganda symbol of German air power] which is staggeringly cynical but also a sign of artistic surplus. Someone was thinking, 'How can we make this bomb even worse than it already is?' The whistles were supposed to erode the enemy's morale.[67]

It was this buoyant, if dangerously frank, interview that led to von Trier's downfall. On the morning of the May 18 press conference that followed the screening, after thirty-some minutes of questions and answers and banter, together with von Trier's lengthy and humorous description of his next project—a "three or four hours long" porn film starring Dunst and Gainsbourg—moderator Henri Behar allowed for two additional questions. Kate Muir of the London *Times* asked if he could "talk a bit about your German roots and the Gothic aspect of this film?," adding that "you mentioned . . . in a Danish film magazine your interest in the Nazi aesthetic and you talked about your German roots at the same time. Can you tell us a bit more about that?" As usual, and echoing some of his remarks in the interview with Carlsen, von Trier's comments were replete with droll self-mockery, with jibes at his Zentropa rival Susanne Bier:

Yes, well, the only thing I can tell is that I thought I was a Jew for a long time and was very happy being a Jew . . . and then I found out that I was really a Nazi. You know, um, because my family was German, Hartmann, which also gave me some pleasure. So . . . what can I say . . . I understand Hitler. But, um, I think he did some wrong things, yes absolutely, but . . . I can see him sitting in his bunker in the end. . . . No, I am just saying that, that, that I think I understand the man. He's not what you would call a good guy, but . . . I understand much about him and I, um, sympathize with him a little bit. Yes, not in a, but come on, . . . I'm not for the Second World War, and I'm not against Jews, . . . even Susanne Bier. That was also a joke. I am of course very much for Jews, no, not too much, because Israel is a pain in the ass, but still . . . how can I get out of this sentence? No, I just want to say about the art of the . . . I'm very much for Speer. . . . Albert Speer I liked. He was also maybe not one of God's best children, but he had some talent that was . . . possible for him to use during . . . [sigh] okay, I'm a Nazi.[68]

Even before von Trier had finished talking, journalists were logging tweets. "Great hilarity at the *Melancholia* press conference," the *Telegraph*'s Florence Waters noted, adding ten minutes later, "Von Trier knows how to turn a press call into a cockpit, and opens himself up further to taboo subjects."[69] But, two hours later, it was the *Hollywood Reporter* that officially broke the news that von Trier had "pulled a Mel Gibson," with the soundbite-worthy headline "Lars von Trier Admits to Being a Nazi, Understanding Hitler."[70] By early afternoon, a media firestorm including the Associated Press, States News Service, Press Association, AFP (Agence France-Presse), and United Press International covered von Trier's remarks while largely ignoring the film itself.[71]

That evening, after festival officials asked von Trier to explain his comments, he apologized for his behavior, saying that, in his desire to entertain, he had allowed himself to be "egged on." In a public apology made through his U.S. distributor, Magnolia Pictures, von Trier wrote, "If I have hurt someone this morning by the words I said at the press conference, I sincerely apologize. I am not anti-Semitic or racially prejudiced in any way, nor am I a Nazi."[72] The following day, after an emergency meeting, the Cannes festival board of directors announced its regret that the press conference had "been used by Lars von Trier to express comments that are unacceptable, intolerable, and contrary to the ideals of humanity and generosity that preside over the very existence of the

Festival" and proclaimed von Trier "a *persona non grata* at the Festival de Cannes, with effect immediately."[73]

It should be observed, however, that as von Trier meandered toward his point he voiced sympathy less for Hitler than for Hitler's architect and rally stage designer, Albert Speer. To another journalist's final question about whether he would attempt a more ambitious film, his deadpan answer was, "Yeah . . . we Nazis have a tendency to . . . do things on a grander scale"— muttering, a "*Final Solution*—with journalists." Those in the audience who realized he was joking pronounced the remarks merely "stupid." But what becomes quite clear, and as Andrew O'Hehir argues, what he was "*trying* to say wasn't stupid at all." In fact, it related "directly" to *Melancholia*'s "artistic method and themes": "With its spectacular photography, sumptuous costumes, setting, and hypnotic use of the orchestral prelude to Wagner's *Tristan und Isolde*, this movie may be the ultimate cinematic expression of the German Romantic aesthetic [that] was an enormous source of inspiration for Adolf Hitler and the Third Reich— the thread that leads from Goethe and Schubert to the worst crimes of the 20th century."[74]

From his student films on, a fascination not just with German Romanticism but with German history and the Third Reich has informed von Trier's thematic and aesthetic choices, in part because of his complicated Jewish German heritage. This began during the German occupation of Denmark in neutral Sweden, where his mother, Inger Høst, a communist leader and feminist, and Ulf Trier, a Jewish socialist, met. Young Lars identified intensely with his Jewishness, which gave him a shared history—"a sense of belonging"—but that he discovered he "didn't have any right to at all" when, on her deathbed in 1989, Inger revealed that Ulf was not his real father and that, desiring a child with "artistic genes," she had conceived Lars with her employer Fritz Michael Hartmann (whose family was of German extraction and included important figures in Danish music, especially the composer J. P. E. Hartmann [1804–1900]). As von Trier has put it, his biological father, who refused to acknowledge his son, was "more of a Nazi," which produced an acute identity crisis.[75] But if his student films are any indication, that crisis had begun at least twenty years prior. The notorious scenes in *The Orchid Gardener* in which von Trier dresses alternately as a woman and a whip-wielding SS officer was inspired partly by Charlotte Rampling's drag performance in Liliana Cavani's *The Night Porter* (1974), about a sadomasochistic erotic relationship between a former SS officer and a concentration camp survivor. (An imperious, much older Rampling plays Justine and Claire's mother in *Melancholia*.) His "graduation film" *Befrielsesbilleder* (*Images of Liberation*, 1982) *deconstructs* the history of the German occupation of Denmark and its aftermath, exposing Danish collaboration and showing suppressed newsreel footage of liberated Danes assaulting Danish informers, Danish Nazis, and women who had slept with German soldiers. In his final moments the protagonist, a German officer betrayed by his Danish mistress and executed in a forest, imagines himself a sacrificial victim who at death ascends to heaven.

As he explained to Stig Björkman, "If you look down towards Europe, the first thing you see is Germany. Seen from Denmark, Germany is Europe,"[76] and historically Nazism was "the great European tragedy."[77] Images of Germany imagined as a map over- or underlying Europe appears throughout von Trier's Europe trilogy films. With their German Expressionist noir aesthetic and thematic obsession with trauma, they project the image of a diseased and disconnected Germany. *The Element of Crime* portrays the Holocaust as an apocalyptic nightmare from which the protagonist cannot awake, and von Trier has a bit part as a Jew. *Epidemic* includes a scene in which Udo Kier as himself tells at length the story of his birth during the bombing of Cologne. The third film, whose shooting was interrupted by von Trier's mother's deathbed confession, is set in Germany in 1945 but is titled *Europa*, conflating Germany, or the scar it has left across the continent, with Europe. It concerns the Allied demilitarization and denazification of postwar Germany, and in depicting Germans, Jews, and Americans in shades of gray, extends the themes of von Trier's "graduation film." Leo, a naïve German American, is hired as a sleeping-car conductor for Zentropa, a railroad company owned by one Max Hartmann. Seduced by Hartmann's daughter Katarina, a Nazi partisan or "Werewolf," Leo is tricked into facilitating an assassination and blowing up a bridge and drowns. Von Trier again plays a Jew, bribed by an American colonel to sign documents exonerating former Nazi collaborators deemed essential to Germany's recovery. In a crucial scene—slouching, bespectacled, nose accentuated—he scowls over the doctored papers, stands, embraces Hartmann (named for von Trier's biological father), and claims, "Max Hartmann is my friend. He hid me in his cellar and gave me food." Repulsed, Hartmann retreats to the bathroom and commits suicide. As Katharina explains, her father saw Germany as his "model railway" and repressed knowledge that his trains conveyed Jews to camps, a fact the film brutally brings forward in a hallucinatory image. Neither Hartmann, neither Max nor von Trier's father, is a simple villain, and von Trier's performance is equally ambiguous and self-reflexive: he spits on Hartmann's doorstep as he exits.

Lost in Translation: *Melancholia*, Wagner, and the Nazi Aesthetic

Once the *Hollywood Reporter* reduced von Trier's rambling, self-reflexive joke into a sound bite, any understanding of this complicated heritage and body of films was lost on most audiences.[78] Whatever the case, as the previous discussion should have made clear, one thing was true: with its sumptuous overture and repeated evocation of the infinitely unresolving "Tristan chord" as its sole leitmotif, *Melancholia* was von Trier's most truly operatic—and specifically Wagnerian—film, soaring and falling with Justine's emotions and prophetic visions. Page described it as the cinematic equivalent of *Tristan und Isolde*, quoting Wagner on its representation of "endless yearning, longing, the bliss and wretchedness of love; power, fame, honor, friendship all blown away like an insubstantial dream."[79] Moreover, with its music overlaying painting and drama, alluding to works of art and cinema over several centuries, the film seemed to aspire to transcend the medium of film, to approach the *Gesamtkunstwerk*, Wagner's ideal synthesis of ideas, visual arts, poetry, and music.

So too did the pageantry and rites Hitler used to arouse national pride, with his cult of Wagner—all engineered by Speer and recognized for its power to move masses of people.[80] After he and Mick Jagger watched Leni Riefenstahl's Nuremberg rally film *Triumph of the Will* (1935) fifteen times, David Bowie, one of von Trier's greatest heroes, said, "Hitler was one of the first great rock stars. . . . He was no politician, he was a great media artist. How he worked his audience. . . . He made an entire country a stage show."[81] And, as Friedrich Kittler has memorably argued, Wagner's "music-drama is the first mass-medium in the modern sense of the word," in replacing opera's symbolic order of representation (libretto, musical score) with data streams that "correlate in the real itself to the materiality they deal with."[82] As for von Trier's Wagner project, after studying von Trier's "Deed of Conveyance" in relation to Wagner's aims, *Opera Quarterly*'s Ryan Minor points out that von Trier argues against lighting the stage "democratically" while stressing the importance of "conceal[ing] the technology" and "manipulating to the extreme," concluding that the document reveals a director completely "dedicated to a Wagnerian aesthetic of over-whelming emotional intensity and willing to pull out all the stops to achieve it."[83] Finally, the practice of von Trier's "enriched darkness" at Bayreuth would have required "(hidden) human labor on an extraordinarily Wagnerian scale . . . armies of stagehands equipped with night-vision goggles, continu-ously moving the sets"—validating Adorno's charge that Wagner "strives unceas-ingly to spirit away its own origins in human labor."[84]

Like Wagner, from the beginning of his career, von Trier has aimed above all for a powerful effect, and correspondences that might be found between *Melancholia*'s Wagnerian Romanticism and the Nazi aesthetic, as his comments to Carlsen especially suggest, are neither fanciful nor accidental. Arguing that Hitler was less interested in politics than in architecture and, ultimately, in creating a culture, Frederic Spotts discusses the Nazi aesthetic in terms of overlapping themes including "monumentalism," sacrifice, and destruction.[85] Hitler's obsession with massively oversized neoclassical architecture is legend-ary, together with the Nuremberg rallies engineered by Albert Speer, whose "cathedral of light"—130 searchlights at forty-foot intervals—shot beams into the sky to 25,000 feet, producing an illusion of columns ascending into infin-ity.[86] Drawing on the aesthetic power of darkness that the Romanic artists and writers venerated, Speer staged Hitler's greatest visual events during the night to create a sublime effect.[87] Indeed, Speer's atmospheric illumination may have partly inspired the "enriched darkness" that von Trier had planned for the Bayreuth *Ring*. In both *Antichrist*'s and *Melancholia*'s DVD commentaries von Trier uses the term "monumental" to refer to images, icons, and effects, among them Tjolöholm Slott, the spectacular castle setting and grounds, and the magical light show of the nighttime balloon launching. And what could be more monumental than Wagner's *Gesamtkuntswerk*, in the sense of the ulti-mate or total special effect?

Transcendence through sacrifice is at the center of the Gold Heart trilogy—in Bess's perverse sexual martyrdom to save her husband's life in *Breaking the Waves*, and in Selma's sacrifice of her life to save her son's eyesight in *Dancer in the Dark*. Similarly, in *Melancholia* the theme is modulated by the concept of the Liebestod, German Romanticism's keynote—especially in Isolde's final aria in *Tristan*, where love's consummation is sublimated in death. In an important distinction, however, Justine is not in love with a person or an ideal other than annihilation itself, as embodied in the approaching planet. Consider the sequence in which Claire watches as Justine (Persephone, Cassandra, Isolde,

FIGURE 2.1 Justine (Kirsten Dunst) bathes in the light of the blue planet, gazing up with infinite longing.

and Brünnhilde in one) gazes up with infinite longing at the death planet looming from the night sky while bathing in its blue light —to provide what von Trier in the DVD commentary called "a picture . . . Adolf would have liked."[88]

Hitler experienced destruction as aesthetic pleasure and death as purification or cleansing (as per the Holocaust). Speer reported seeing him ecstatic while watching a documentary of London in flames after German air raids.[89] Similarly, in Wagner death is not tragedy but purification and redemption; Justine, like the lovers in *Tristan*, yearns for "the boundless realm of endless night," where she will know only "endless, godlike all-forgetting." As Wotan cries in act 2 of *Die Walküre*, "I want only one thing now." "The end! The end!" (Nur eines will ich noch: das Ende! Das Ende!)

In *Melancholia*, the moment when the Tristan chord merges with the roar of the consuming planet aims to be the most exquisite and cosmic instance of destruction in von Trier's work. And there are many. Consider the postapocalyptic landscapes of the Europe trilogy, the plague in *Epidemic* that manifests through the film, the genocidal vengeance with which *Dogville* is exterminated, the slow-motion death of the child that opens *Antichrist*, or von Trier's gleeful deconstructions of official histories. In the prologue, after rhythmically repeated images of falling, sinking, looming, and circling, the two planets perform a dance of magnetic attraction ending in death, at one point "kissing," and it concludes as Melancholia sucks the earth sensually into its bosom.[90] And this is just the beginning. It is no wonder that audiences sat stunned throughout the end credits.

In an otherwise brilliant essay, Steven Shaviro asserts that *Melancholia* is unique among von Trier's films in being "non-ironic, heartfelt, and sincere."[91] Other critics immediately picked up on the self-reflexive irony inherent in its grand gesture or—as von Trier put it—the "bone splinter" in the cream. As O'Hehir says, "He's embracing all of [German Romanticism], the Eros and the Thanatos, the sensuality and the mannered artfulness and the love of destruction," yet "suggest[ing] that the tendency that leads to magnificent art and poetry and the one that leads to totalitarianism and the cheesiest grade of 1990s music videos are all essentially the same."[92] Contrasting the film's tone with the earnest didacticism of *The Tree of Life*, Amy Taubin finds that the film "is built on an ironic deployment of German Romanticism that both acknowledges and resists its allure and power."[93]

While representing von Trier at his most Wagnerian, *Melancholia* is equally informed by the Wagnerian antithesis, a Brechtian dialectic that critiques its own excesses. It deconstructs its pretensions as a *Gesamtkunstwerk* in particular, signaling its postmodern self-awareness with a heavy hand, indicating through obsessive intertextuality and irony that its expansive multimediality is a grandiose performance. The title is a quadruple reference to (1) the director's well-publicized clinical depression, represented in (2) the heroine's depression, (3) a rogue planet absurdly *ten* times the size of Earth, and (4) Albrecht Dürer's 1514 engraving *Melencolia I*, which features a female figure meditating on what appears to be a planet. The film's pretensions are announced in a surreal slow-motion stream of allusions (many within allusions) to the arts: in addition to music, painting (Pieter Bruegel the Elder's *Jagers in de Sneeuw* [*The Hunters in the Snow*, 1565]); literature (John Everett Millais's *Ophelia* [1851–1852], representing a scene from Shakespeare's *Hamlet*, 4.7); and cinema—the Bruegel pays homage to Tarkovsky's *Solaris* (1972), where it is featured, the falling horse to *Andrei Rublev* (1969), the burning house to *Zerkalo* (*Mirror*, 1975) and *Offret* (*The Sacrifice*, 1986). In the narrative proper, in addition to Genet's *The Maids*, the two sisters who switch roles as nurturer and patient echo Ingmar Bergman's *Persona* (1966). The film's second frame, an overhead shot of a pedestaled sundial and lawn flanked by parallel rows of teardrop-shaped yews with eerily doubled shadows line an expanse down to the fjord, evokes the famous garden, topiary, and sculped human figures (which alone cast shadows) of Alain Resnais's *L'Année dernière à Marienbad* (*Last Year at Marienbad*, 1961), the ultimate European art film. The film's writer, Alain Robbe-Grillet, said that he recognized in the film "my own efforts toward a somewhat ritual deliberation, a certain slowness, a sense of the theatrical, even that occasional rigidity of attitude," which, he added, "suggests both a statue and an opera."[94]

Like its castle (and certain Nazis' residences), *Melancholia* is a repository for plundered art—and instead of becoming immersed in a spectacle of destruction, we are distantiated through intellectual awareness and aesthetic contemplation. Then there is the Kubrickesque marriage of "high" and "low" art: the cinema of Tarkovsky, Bergman, and Resnais, with science fiction extravaganzas like Roland Emmerich's *2012* (2009). Defying Emmerich and his like, von Trier ends the world in the prologue, "spoiling" the conclusion in a series of CGI visions of the collision from outer space, a "distant and majestic tableaux [that] seem[s] to recall the icy infinities of Stanley Kubrick's *2001*."[95] He follows with the film's title in the style of a charcoal tombstone rubbing—a tongue-in-cheek gesture comparable to (if less offensive than) his replacement of *Antichrist*'s final "t" with the woman symbol. This is followed by simple black-and-white title cards for the film's two contrasting sections, "Justine" and "Claire," that nevertheless continue on *Dogville*'s Brechtian stylization.

Much of part 1 is black satire that plays off European cinema's most pretentious, decadent, and apocalyptic party sequences—Jean Renoir's *La règle du jeu* (*The Rules of the Game*, 1939), Luis Buñuel's *El ángel exterminador* (*The Exterminating Angel*, 1962), Michelangelo Antonioni's *La Notte* (1961), and Luchino Visconti's *Il Gattopardo* (*The Leopard*, 1963) in particular—that epitomize modernist alienation. Bordering on caricature, Justine's parents are awful in opposite ways. The dialogue, described by some critics as ham-handed, approaches farce, in the imperiously enunciated speeches of Charlotte Rampling's marriage-hating mother; John Hurt's drunken, lecherous, spoon-stealing father; Udo Kier's fussy wedding planner; or Stellan Skarsgård's Jack, Justine's implacable boss. Part 1 is introduced by a real-time, shaky-cam (Dogme-styled) joke about a stretch limousine too unwieldy to make the turns in the estate driveway, the first of many comments about the assumptions of privilege and outsized ambitions driving global capitalism. The preposterous castle setting, together with its surreal nineteen-hole golf course, represents the American empire on a collision course with reality imagined as the end of the world. Monumentalism, destruction, and sacrifice, the signatures of the Nazi style, are thus employed to an end that could not be more different from the Third Reich's imperialistic aims: to comment on the vanity, absurdity, and vacuity of all empires, institutions, and rituals—indeed, of all monuments.

LARS VON TRIER'S *GÖTTERDÄMMERUNG*

Conceptually, as a "beautiful film about the end of the world," *Melancholia* likely owes less to *Tristan* than to *Die Götterdämmerung* (*Twilight of the Gods*) and the Old Norse concept of Ragnarök that underlies it.[96] The prologue to act 1 of the *Ring* cycle's final opera opens as the Norns, the three daughters of the Earth Mother, Erda, who weave the rope of destiny, lament the past and attempt to foretell the future until their vision is cut off. They tell of the gods' and demigods' corruption and despoiling of the world in their lust for acquisition and power, represented in Alberich's originating crime, the theft of the Rhine gold and forging of the Ring, and Wotan's appropriation of a limb from the world tree for his spear, resulting in the death of the ash that was the source of all life. The tree has been hacked into logs that are piled around Valhalla in preparation for the gods' immolation, which follows immediately on Brünnhilde's igniting of and self-immolation in Siegfried's funeral pyre at the end of the opera—or, as Erda predicted in act 4 of *Das Rheingold*, "Alles, was ist, endet" (Everything that is, ends). As Wagner scholar Thomas Grey suggests, Wagner's version of Ragnarök is provoked by crimes against nature, beginning with Alberich's theft of the gold and the forging of the ring, leading to alienation, while suggesting "the depredations of industrialism and the 'cash nexus' deformation of human relations."[97] Like *Die Götterdämmerung*'s prologue, *Melancholia*'s overture projects Justine's melancholy prevision of the end of the world. Meanwhile, there is John (Kiefer Sutherland), who, like Alberich and Wotan, has sacrificed love in a quest for wealth and status and hosts Justine's wedding to display his mansion and golf course, later making much ado of his generator, telescope, and technical prowess. Near the conclusion, Justine insists that we should not grieve for the earth, suggesting that the apocalypse (as in Wagner) is a kind of cleansing.

Evidently with echoes of *Die Götterdämmerung* in mind, Alex Ross finds that von Trier's "aestheticized vision of the end of the world . . . buys into a cheap conception of Wagner as a bombastic nihilist": *Die Götterdämmerung* is not "glorying in their destruction but anticipating the approach of a better world; it marks a change of regime. . . . Wagner gives us hope, however vague."[98] But von Trier's film is not nihilistic in any "cheap" sense, nor does it end bombastically. True, *Melancholia* gives no hope for a better world; according to Justine, life on earth is all there is. Yet, in contrast to the conclusion of *Die Gotterdammerung*, we do *not* see von Trier's Valhalla in flames, and the film's affect is constrained. At first, the concluding shots repeat the overture's distantiation of affect. To the strains of the Tristan chord amid a distant rumbling, we watch the blue planet rise serenely above the horizon, and the image is less terrifying than beautiful. (Thus far, as suggested earlier, this scenic design may have been inspired by a photograph of Brünnhilde's blissful Awakening Scene, or just as possibly, as Richard Grusin has suggested, the final shot of *E.T. the Extra-Terrestrial* [1982].[99] Yet, as composer Kristian Eidnes Andersen has described it, the sound design for the ending was meant to create a powerful internal tension from the "struggle" between the "epic" reverberations of Wagner's music and "the violent realistic sounds": "You're [now] close to the little boy, you're close to the two sisters, and together with this small world, together with some of the best music ever written, . . . struggling with [the actuality that] now we are going to be destroyed." He and von Trier "imagined that it would be physical," but brief, to the extent that "in two seconds everything would disappear" as the screen is abruptly engulfed in flames, followed by several seconds of black screen.[100] So, on the one hand, the black screen signals von Trier's refusal of the pseudo-Wagnerian endings of Hollywood disaster films, whose digitalized spectacles of disaster are witnessed by an elite group of survivors, stand-ins for the audience, and thus offer a cheap form of transcendence. On the other hand, and together with the emotional struggle Andersen describes, the black screen forces the audience to encounter the Real.

The Wagner notwithstanding, the film ends not by achieving the Romantic sublime, in which a vicarious sense of transcendence and power is evoked through a spectacle of terror, chaos, and destruction, and that the Nazi aesthetic perfected, but more like what Shaviro has dubbed the "anti-sublime,"[101] or what Edmund Burke understood as "the beautiful," and that evoked the "social" emotions rather than fear.[102] Along these lines, it is moving and significant that, in von Trier's ending, Justine for the first time turns her back on the planet (to which she has consistently exhibited an almost erotic attachment) in order to bring the remnants of her family together.

Sarah French and Zoë Shacklock refine this idea by bringing Brian Massumi's work on affect to bear on Jean-François Lyotard's discussion of the sublime. They propose the concept of an "affective sublime," one that does not cancel sublime transcendence so much as muddles it, causing a cognitive hiatus together with "an involuntary visceral response characterized by the coexistence of pleasure and pain."[103] This is experienced by the body because it cannot be put into words. *Melancholia*'s prologue, for example, is replete with individual images that radiate meaningful possibilities but that cannot be assimilated into a coherent narrative or conceptual framework. It therefore

> produces a cognitive failure, as a result of the spectator's inability to locate the images in time or space and a sublime feeling that stems from the excess of emotional and aesthetic weight imbued in the images coupled with an inability to comprehend their actual meaning or significance. . . . we see everything and nothing at all. Displaced from the intellect and cognition, the "meaning" of the sequence is instead grounded in the body.[104]

French and Shacklock's words correspond with von Trier's "Directors Intentions," which describe the prologue as consisting of "lyrical, but also ominous and confusing scenes" that "do not yield any meaning per se, but in the course of the film they will create associations and unrest."[105] The prologue offers a concentrated dose, as it were, of the film's affect as a whole: the music, the images, the structural design, together with the restless, handheld shooting style, achieve a peculiar "churning suspension" in which affect predominates over cognitive understanding. We are forever in transition, and time is suspended: "The disaster is on its way, but it has not yet arrived; unless . . . this not-yet, this non-advent, this suspension of time, so that the present does not pass and the future does not arrive, is itself already the disaster."[106] A frequent complaint is that part 1 is too long, but the torpor, repetition, and stasis—the sense of not getting on with a story, of excessive affect over action—expresses Justine's state of mind.[107] Thus, to suggest, as several critics did, that part 1 is an overstated variation on *Festen*'s desperately protracted house party is to admit that von Trier succeeded. Action and conflict in the usual sense are replaced by repetition and contrast as Justine leaves, returns, rises to some occasion, and again falls back. Tonal shifts constantly rend the film. Rather than sustaining a progression, parts 1 and 2 mark series of reversals of perspective (from Justine to Claire and vice versa) through contrasts in content, theme, lighting, color, and sensibility. The sumptuous Wagnerianism of the prologue descends in part 1 into caustic satire alternating with heaving emotionalism, while part 2, beginning at the nadir of

Justine's depression, opens as Bergmanesque melodrama and builds to stomach-churning anxiety and despair.

Essential to this "affective sublime" is the score, which repeats the Tristan chord throughout the film, incessantly building tension toward a resolution that never occurs, producing a sonic equivalent of the repeated slow-motion images of Justine, encumbered in her wedding dress or by tendrils of clinging yarn, or of Claire, carrying Leo, sinking into the ground as they attempt to escape the inevitable. As Shaviro notes, Wagner's prelude "marks what the Lacanians would call the film's death drive: a kind of unsurpassable, idiotic reiteration," and von Trier "quite deliberately empties [it] out."[108] Thinking along similar lines, music scholar David Larkin notes that Proust's description of *Tristan und Isolde*'s leitmotif technique in volume 5 of *La Prisonnière* (*The Captive*) might easily be applied to von Trier's use of the prologue in *Melancholia* and was likely an inspiration for it.[109] Playing through a piano score of *Tristan* before attending a concert where excerpts from the opera will be performed, Proust's narrator is

> struck with how much reality there is in the work of Wagner as I contemplated once more those insistent, fleeting themes which visit an act, recede only to return again and again, and, sometimes distant, dormant, almost detached, are at other moments, while remaining vague, so pressing and so close, so internal, so organic, so visceral, that they seem like the reprise not so much of a musical motif as of an attack of neuralgia.[110]

While composing *Tristan,* Wagner was profoundly influenced by Arthur Schopenhauer's philosophical pessimism and especially his *Aesthetics*, book 3 of *The World as Will and Representation* (1819), in which he theorized that, alone of all the arts, music was exceptional: rather than a mere representation (according to Plato's theory of forms), music was a direct expression of the metaphysical will. Famously, Schopenhauer postulated that life, which embodies the will, is irrational and instinctual, a matter of endless striving, grasping, suffering, and making others suffer, and its end—and goal—is death. As Bryan Magee, in *The Tristan Chord: Wagner and Philosophy* (2000), interprets Schopenhauer's thought, humans are "cruel, greedy, stupid, aggressive, and heartless," the world teems with violence, oppression, and exploitation, and nature is "no better," as "in every instant thousands of screaming animals [are] being torn to pieces alive."[111] Thus, Wagner's *Tristan und Isolde*, specifically the "Tristan chord," aimed to express the essence of human experience as Schopenhauer saw it, as discord and striving, yearning without resolution in an infinitely suspended final chord.[112] Although von Trier's understanding of Wagner's music and ideas, much less of Schopenhauer, is largely intuitive,[113] the Wagner-Schopenhauer connection sheds light on his use of Wagner in the film.[114] As von Trier explained his philosophy of existence, apropos of *Melancholia*, to Chris Heath of *GQ* magazine, we are all animals who fight for the best place on the truck on the way to the slaughterhouse. "There's a lot more to life than that, but that is part of the truth," he said, before interjecting an observation about Proust's veneration of great art and church windows. "That gives me some joy, but I still think life is a terribly bad idea," adding that if God created life ("which I sincerely doubt"), he didn't think it through. "I think you should have a say when you're born—'Is this really something you want to do?'"[115]

Schopenhauer found that the pain of existence could be palliated in three ways. Moving from depression to something like acceptance, Justine discovers all three. One is asceticism, or denial of the will, to which Justine's melancholia eventually leads. Immune to carnal pleasures (even Alexander Skarsgård can't turn her on, and her favorite food tastes like ashes), she becomes serene as the planet approaches.[116] Secondly, according to Schopenhauer's *Aesthetics*, moments of transcendence may be achieved through the contemplation of art, as von Trier, citing Proust, has suggested. Hence the film highlights Justine's aesthetic sensibility—which has been co-opted, a fact that contributes to her depression

FIGURE 2.2 Justine (Kirsten Dunst) manifests compassion, enabling herself, Claire (Charlotte Gainsbourg), and Leo (Cameron Spurr) to come together in the "magic cave" at the end of the world.

until she willfully gets herself fired—in the contemplative moment in which she replaces Malevich's abstractions with the artistic inspirations for the prologue's images. As the end approaches, in an ironic "staging" of the end of the world, Justine and Leo construct the "magic cave" (the odd term suggesting the many enchanted grottoes in Wagner). The frame of a teepee made of stripped branches placed on a gently sloping hill, a reminder of the earth's curvature, her art speaks of the emptiness of all monuments. Third, the work of constructing a haven for the child, work that is both aesthetically and ethically powerful, demonstrates Justine's recovery of morality through compassion or empathy, in which the suffering ego may be transcended through confusion of one's suffering with another's.[117] At last, she becomes able to grieve for someone other than herself. In that fragile human construction, a split second before the screen bursts into flames, asceticism, art, and compassion come together.

LOCATION AND CAPITALIST REALISM: EREMITAGE, TJOLÖHOLM, SUPERKITSCH, AND JUNKSPACE

"While disaster films generally take place in the creepiest locations, sewers and worse, this story is set in a wonderful castle" and consequently conjures up the "sort of mental images [as] in fairytales," von Trier explained to Per Juul Carlsen. "I certainly hope there's some reality underlying it," he added.[118] But why did von Trier choose a "fairytale" setting and this particular location for staging the end of the world?

The script's name for the manor estate, "Eremitage," suggests a strong satirical intention on von Trier's part. From a Danish context, the name was probably suggested by Eremitageslottet or Eremitagen (the Eremitage Hunting Lodge) in Dyrehaven (the Deer Park), an eighteenth-century Baroque mansion that was the king's hunting lodge, located a few miles from von Trier's home. In the context of the film's American setting, "Eremitage," combining "ere," archaic for "before," with "hermitage," referring to a retreat, forms a portmanteau word suggesting nostalgia and a utopian escape. Possible nods are to Samuel Butler's *Erewhon* (1872), about a satirical Victorian antiutopia whose name is "nowhere" spelled backward, together with Andrew Jackson's Hermitage, the seventh president's plantation home near Nashville, Tennessee, and Alexander Sokurov's *Russkiy kovcheg* (*Russian Ark*, 2002), filmed at the monumental Russian State

Hermitage Museum. Like Manderlay, the name of the plantation in von Trier's 2005 *Dogville* sequel, which puns on Manderley, the Gothic mansion in Daphne du Maurier's *Rebecca* and "The Road to Mandelay," Rudyard Kipling's paean to British imperialism, or like "Eden," the name of *Antichrist*'s woodland cabin, the name reeks with irony.

But the name was dropped from the film, and, as it turned out, much of *Melancholia*'s sociopolitical commentary was wielded through more subtle means: through a multivalenced implementation of its iconic Swedish location, Tjolöhoms Slott, south of Göteborg near Fjärås, overlooking Kungsbacka Fjord. The location was hugely inspirational, Claro maintains, in his work as cinematographer, for many of the "monumental" shots, key allusions, and thematic highlights.[119] While most glosses mention only that the exteriors were shot on location, the interiors are featured in many key scenes: the front entrance and great hall in the bean-counting scenes, bathtub scenes, corridor sequences, the bouquet tossing, and Justine and Claire's intimate talks in the "Turkish room" in last part of the film.[120] Like many of the director's settings, von Trier's Tjolöholm is profoundly paradoxical. Shot to enhance its inherent monumentalism, it represents the summit of human aspiration and culture tragically doomed to extinction, on the one hand. On the other, it epitomizes the greed, excess, and empty materialism of late capitalism—or what Justine in part means when she asserts that life on Earth is "evil." We might even venture that this evil has brought on the apocalypse in the form of a rogue planet.

Tjolöholm is one of Sweden's national treasures, but the film's end credits ("FILMED ON LOCATION IN VÄSTERGÖTLAND") neglected to mention its name—perhaps because the setting is intended to be generic. Or perhaps because, like all but two of von Trier's seven films since 2000, *Melancholia* pretends, however winkingly, to be set in America, the frequent target of his satire. Because America "for me always to some degree stood for capitalism," it was the appropriate setting for the ultimate catastrophe.[121]

Whatever the case, *Melancholia* sounds and looks distinctly European or transnational if not exactly Scandinavian, yet (thanks to its iconic location) far more Scandinavian than von Trier's other pseudo-American films. As if to brandish the "fact" of transnationality, *Melancholia* features an international cast with cacophonous and unexplained accents, even within the same family: Gainsbourg's French-British intonation, Charlotte Rampling and Hurt's British accents, Skarsgård's Swedish inflexion, and Hollywood stars' Sutherland's and Dunst's flat American intonations.

FIGURE 2.3 Tjolöholm Slott as the monumental backdrop for Melancholia.

If Tjolöholm is a Swedish national monument, its history and architecture are as transnational, hybridized, and anachronistic as the film itself. One of Sweden's newest castles (actually a mansion built to resemble a castle and listed as a "slott"), it was begun in 1898 on property purchased by James Fredrik Dickson, heir to a founder of the Scottish East India Company, and completed in 1904.[122] Claro describes Dickson as "an immensely wealthy Scottish importer of Siberian wood" who moved to Sweden with his wife/cousin Blanche to cash in on the shipbuilding industry.[123] A breeder of hackneys, he purchased the property to develop Scandinavia's largest privately owned stud farm and commissioned architect Lars Israel Wahlman, an Anglophile and devotee of the Arts and Crafts movement led by William Morris, to build a neo-Tudor castle with interiors in the Morris style. This predominates, "the Elizabethan façade" having "hints of Art Nouveau . . . , and . . . flowing lines and stylised flower and plant themes [that] reoccur throughout the whole castle."[124] Claro is less complementary, describing the castle as an anachronism even before completion: as "a tycoon's dream palace that [Dickson] never got to live in because he died during a drinking binge" shortly after construction commenced.[125] (The website reports discreetly that "he died of blood poisoning . . . contracted by wrapping foil from a bottle of wine around a cut finger to stop the bleeding.")[126] His ambitious, socially committed wife, Blanche, then oversaw the project to completion.[127]

Thanks to Blanche, Tjolöholm reflected not only Morris's Arts and Crafts aesthetic but many of his sociopolitical ideals, derived from art critic and social theorist John Ruskin. In an eccentric blend of feudalism with socialism, Ruskin had proposed a society that returned to a medieval guild model and idealized Gothic architecture for its organicism, digressive construction, and handhewn figures, which reflected (in his view) the antithesis of capitalist industrialization. Morris, and Wahlman in turn, applied these ideals through the abundant use of natural materials and handcrafted designs—especially in the village Blanche commissioned for the estate workers, with its quaint red and timber cottages and assembly hall in Swedish "National Romantic" style, and Gothic church. Claire's anachronistically condescending references to "the village" and "little Father" (the head butler) may be in keeping with Tjolöholm's, and especially Blanche's, originating ideals.

But Tjolöholm was equally a showpiece for late nineteenth-century industry, which provided Dickson's internationally based fortune. So, however paradoxically, this neo-Gothic castle epitomized turn-of-the-century modernization in Sweden and was the antithesis of Morris's anachronistic utopia. The Dicksons flaunted up-to-the minute luxury appliances and specialized in outsized gizmos: a steam-driven power plant that supplied electric lighting, central heating, hot and cold running water, a circular-flow shower, a meter-tall hair dryer that ran on paraffin, wall-to-wall carpeting, a 1.5-ton horse-drawn, petrol-powered vacuum cleaner with massive hoses that were lifted up through the windows, and a telephone—all rare extravagances at the time.[128] Now owned by the city of Kungsbacka, Tjolöholm is a Disney World for the artier class, celebrated for its guided tours and open house traditions—concerts, parties, children's theatre, antique auto show, and festive Christmas market (with local crafts, food, and romantic carriage rides)—and as a tourist attraction and resort where one can stay overnight or for a season, swim, hike, fish, and play golf, or get married, as Tjolöholm is, unsurprisingly, the dream location for many lavish weddings.

From von Trier's jaundiced point of view, in which Kiefer Sutherland's John is James Dixon's double, Tjolöholm suggests the global commodification of culture with an American neoliberal flourish. John has not inherited his wealth, explains Claro; he is the self-made man with no real understanding of the heritage he has bought into.[129] Brandishing his Midas touch, he bullies Justine into enjoying her (his) wedding: "Do you have any idea how much this party cost me?" he asks rhetorically, and answers, "A great deal of money. A huge amount of money. In fact, for most people. . . ." John's pride in his eighteen-hole golf course, technological prowess, fascination with astronomy, and trust in "the real scientists" complements the Dicksonses' devotion to the comforts of machine culture. Yet the film complicates John's character by making his infatuation with science almost boyish. We know, however, that in a von Trier film, science, rationalism, tycoons, and, especially, idealists will fail, and in the film's most didactic moment, when the experts' predictions are shown to be wrong, he skulks off to the stables and commits a coward's suicide, leaving his family to face catastrophe alone.

Like Disney World, Kane's Xanadu, or Horace Walpole's Gothic Revival monument Strawberry Hill, Tjolöholm exemplified power and capital through its amalgamation of past styles within a modern structure. Von Trier's comments about the location suggest that he had this point in mind. Claro mentions that he had first envisioned a "more modern and therefore more cheesy" location before falling in love with Tjolöholm at first sight.[130] Thorsen's biography, based on a series of interviews with von Trier, describes him as elated over the location photographs, pronouncing it "Superkitsch! Absolutely perfect!": "A tremendously rustic box full of different styles and with a huge garden with shape cut trees . . . a bit Scottish and with all sorts of legendary figures all around."[131] Von Trier's use of the term "kitsch" likely means more than "cheap" or "lowbrow" taste. For Hermann Broch, kitsch is parasitic and soulless—it mimics an original with no regard to ethics and is a perversion of art's mission (of pursuing an infinite idea).[132] For Adorno, kitsch is the product of mass marketing and consumer culture, the antithesis of the avant-garde, and exemplified the false consciousness inherent in capitalism.[133] Kitsch, according to Walter Benjamin, offers "instantaneous emotional gratification without intellectual effort—without the requirement of distance, without sublimation."[134] Not incidentally, Hitler revered what the avant-garde critics, many of them Jewish, disparaged as kitsch, deeming it "everything that is health" as opposed to the "degenerate" art he eventually banned,[135] and Saul Friedländer summed up Nazism as a culture of kitsch and death.[136]

"Superkitsch" further suggests a post-postmodern awareness (both ironic and sincere) through which an object is so extravagantly bad that it's "cool." In this kitschy guise, Tjolöholm may be a predecessor of what Dutch architect Rem Koolhaas has called "junkspace" in reference to twentieth- and twenty-first-century architecture as postmodern commodity: designed to satisfy immediate gratification through accommodation, superficial luxury, and nostalgia from a perspective of ironic knowing. Coined from the term "space junk," signifying "the human debris that litters the universe, *junk-space* is the residue mankind leaves on the planet. The built . . . product of *moderniza-tion* . . . what remains after *modernization* has run its course or, more pre-cisely, . . . its fall-out." Expressing and encouraging the drive to consumption, junkspace is perhaps epitomized in the upscale shopping mall, with its disori-enting oversaturation and repetition varied via bricolage and scaled down to a user-friendly level. "A single shopping center now is the work of generations of space planners, repairmen and fixers, like in the middle ages; [similarly] air conditioning sustains our cathedrals."[137] As John's late capitalist moderniza-tion of the *concept* of the castle, *Melancholia*'s Tjölöhom suggests junkspace in several respects—but perhaps most pertinently in von Trier's vision of its future as cosmic debris.

Melancholia's castle stands for high art co-opted as commodity or advertis-ing. Like the prologue, it stands as a microcosm of the film itself. It is an archive of culture, as suggested in the prologue's sumptuous succession in ele-giac slow-motion of allusions to European music, art, and cinema from vari-ous periods. In this tapestry of allusions, the film takes on its darkest irony in view of Justine's profession as an overqualified art historian, newly promoted from copy editor to the art director of an ad agency—with a caveat from her boss, Jack (Stellan Skarsgård), who turns the occasion into a challenge to invent a tag line for her newest ad design, derived from Pieter Bruegel the Elder's famous image of gluttonous satiety *Het Luilekkerland* (*The Land of Cock-aigne*, 1567), one of the paintings Justine subsequently chooses from a book in

FIGURE 2.4 Justine's advertisement, a riff on Pieter Bruegel the Elder's image of gluttonous satiety *The Land of Cockaigne* (1567), features three models in an outré *Vogue*-style photo shoot.

the art library.[138] Bruegel accentuates the grotesque, splaying three human figures in random directions under a round table laden with food and drink; Justine coolly substitutes three models in an outré *Vogue*-style photo shoot.

As Rupert Read observes, the ceaseless talk about Justine's need to be "happy" about her lavish wedding, the film underlines the absurdity inherent in "the idea that one can be 'made' happy by . . . *things*."[139] Thus we understand that the wedding party—and part 1 in general, which was denounced by some critics as hyperbolic—is not "*meant* to be realistic," especially as seen in the behaviors of Jack (whom Read compares to something out of Sade) and his minion, Tim (Brady Corbet), which represents "a Kafkaesque absurdist extreme of no-escape: The profit-motive and a rigorously utilitarian attitude to other people won't leave you alone for even one moment, not even at your wedding. This gives us some insight into our market-mad world, by touching uncomfortably on . . . its contemporary essence."[140] In its use of hyperbole and Wagnerian "bombast" for satirical social and political commentary, part 1 of *Melancholia* has more in common with von Trier's "Amerikan" films *Dogville*, *Manderlay*, and *Dear Wendy*, inspired by Kafka's *Amerika* (1927) and Brecht's plays set in the United States, than one might initially suppose.

Melancholia envisions a world under the spell of "capitalist realism" in the sense that Mark Fisher uses the term: to signify the pervasive cynicism of our current state of mind, "the widespread sense that not only is capitalism the only viable political and economic system, but also that it is now impossible even to imagine a coherent alternative to it." Further, because everything capable of being imagined is recuperated by the system, branded, and turned into profit, the future "harbors only reiteration and re-permutation . . . nothing new can ever happen"; the future is exhausted. Under such conditions, Fisher says— echoing Fredric Jameson and Slavoj Žižek—"it is easier to imagine the end of the world than it is to imagine the end of capitalism."[141] Accordingly, *Melancholia*'s Amerikan castle is a Gothic space haunted by archaic rituals associated with surplus value: the stretch limousine too long for the driveway, the bean counting, cake cutting, and balloon launch, the pancakes Claire serves on the morning of the day the world will end. Supporting this commentary are allusions to modernist aesthetic traditions documenting bourgeois apathy and alienation amid exorbitant wealth, such as the guests in *The Exterminating Angel*, who are unable to leave a lavish dinner party, or the man and woman in *Last Year at Marienbad*, condemned to perform variations on their roles amid empty halls, baroque statues, and geometric gardens.

FIGURE 2.5 Justine (Kirsten Dunst) envisages herself weighted down or impeded in images that suggest the materialization of surplus.

Justine's melancholia stems not from the psychological trauma of loss but from having *too* much, from surplus value, to the extent that the Earth itself has become junkspace.[142] Hence the massive gas planet Melancholia is not Earth's nemesis so much as its mirror image, written in cosmic terms: like it, life on Earth consumes everything in its path and turns it into junk. Hence Justine envisages herself weighted down in images that suggest the materialization of surplus—the billowing wedding dress, the clinging tendrils of gray yarn and the castle edifice that epitomizes "happiness" as an impediment or an obligation she cannot fulfill—and seeks to escape. The paradox of surplus value is articulated most tellingly in what von Trier and Claro called the "Wagner moments," the "more elevated moments where you're watching a planet or a landscape" through Justine's eyes, the visual objective correlatives for the musical cue, the Tristan chord that, in breaking with chromaticism, creates the tension of yearning without fulfilment or resolution, an aching anticatharsis of endless desire.[143] It is appropriate, then, that in its immensity, beauty and mystery, the planet indicates absence or aporia; in the third frame of the prologue, the image suggests a vacuum or black hole into which the earth is sucked.[144] This vacuum, accented with a red dot flare, a fake imperfection that von Trier in the DVD commentary remarks having "put in," reminds us that the planet is a *digitalized* image—an image of nothing—that aptly heralds the end of modernization.[145] Tjolöholm, *Melancholia*'s fairy-tale castle, together with the film's Wagnerian excess, does stand for the tragedy of human aspiration and culture doomed to extinction, but in the much-diminished sense of junkspace about to become space dust (or, more properly, cyber dust).

THE ANTHROPOCENE AND ECOGRIEF

Most, if not all of von Trier's films have nihilistic implications, but *Antichrist* was a turning point in that the film not only projected pessimism, it was an argument for nihilism as the only way to understand existence. It was the product of von Trier's understanding through depression that existence ("Nature") is not only meaningless but full of endless suffering, with those who suffer causing others to suffer, ending in death. *Melancholia* expanded that argument philosophically: the conceptual implications of its cosmic drama have much in common with the current philosophical trend toward materialism, skeptical realism, and transcendental nihilism led by Ray Brassier and Quentin Meillassoux. Brassier's *Nihil Unbound: Enlightenment and Extinction*, as explained in his preface, argues that nihilism (often equated with depression) is not "a disease, requiring diagnosis and the recommendation of an antidote," nor is it "a pathological exacerbation of subjectivism . . . but on the contrary, the unavoidable corollary of the realist conviction that there is a mind-independent reality . . . indifferent to our existence" and oblivious to human values. "Nature," he writes, "is not our or anyone's 'home,' nor a particularly beneficent progenitor."[146] The major premise of transcendental nihilism is based on what scientists, rather than correlationist philosophers, tell us, that planetary extinction is inevitable and imminent, that all life—including the very thought of life—will end. With this premise in mind, Shaviro claims that the planet Melancholia "is not a projection of Justine's personal melancholy. If anything, we should say the reverse: that Justine's personal state of misery is itself a kind of interiorization . . . of the cosmic, deflationary truth of planetary extinction."[147]

When Justine abruptly asserts that "the Earth is evil" and that "no one should grieve for it," she has a closely related if not ancillary idea in mind: that of the Anthropocene—the current geologic epoch (since the Industrial Revolution and perhaps earlier), understood as anthropogenic. This concept is based on widespread evidence that the Earth's ecosystems and biosphere have been and are continuously altered by humans, hence contributing to "evils" such as global warming, environmental change, the acidification of the oceans, and mass extinctions. Extrapolating from *Antichrist*, we can say that what humans perceive as evil is inherent in nature but, as evidenced by the Anthropocene, is made infinitely more evil *by* humans. From this perspective, because *Melancholia* ends in mass extinction on a cosmic scale, Justine's depression can be understood as an embodiment of our collective ecogrief. But rather than raise the issue of anthropogenic ecological disaster directly through representation, action, and dialogue, as most apocalyptic science fiction films do, *Melancholia* approaches the subject through the back door: through production design, characterization, and an emphasis on affect over action.

Paradoxically, when one considers its Wagnerian extravagance, *Melancholia*'s production design works similarly to *Dogville*'s and *Manderlay*'s Brechtian staging, in which the United States is represented by a bare soundstage with painted lines that direct the viewer's attention to ideological commentary. Dominated by Gothic architecture and sculpted gardens girded by an expansive lawn merging with a golf course, *Melancholia*'s set design is at the same time luxurious and rigorously contained. Confining the viewer's attention to a human elite who take landscaping, stables, and perfect weather for granted, it represents nature cultivated and framed by Western culture. As the planet approaches and brings on atmospheric changes and bizarre weather, as Kristoffer Noheden admits, *Melancholia* depicts a natural rather than anthropogenically caused apocalypse. Yet the film asserts "parallels between the Earth–Melancholia relation and human relationships with the non-human world, and alludes obliquely to the scale of ecological destruction current in the Anthropocene."[148]

As von Trier has stated, "When the earth is ready to crumble between our fingers, whatever we do in the way of heroic conquests or petty family squabbles doesn't matter," and as a science fiction disaster film, *Melancholia* is remarkable for prioritizing the feminine, affect, and vulnerability over masculine reason, technophilia, and action.[149] With this in mind, Selmin Kara observes that it, together with other recent films with apocalyptic resonances such as *The Tree of Life* (2011), *Beasts of the Southern Wild* (2012), and *Gravity* (2013), corresponds with a line of thinking that acknowledges our current impasse in ecological crisis and the inevitability of mass extinction and that is variously called "post-masculinist rationality"[150] and an "ethic of vulnerability."[151] Drawing on Wendy Brown's "post-masculinist politics" and Darin Barney's "post-masculinist courage," Joanna Zylinska discusses this as a "minimal" ethics that concedes uncertainty in situations we cannot control as opposed to masculinist bravado that seeks to exert rational and instrumental dominance.[152] Mira Hird's "ethic of vulnerability" goes on to acknowledge the agencies of nature and nonhuman actors that affect us.[153]

From this perspective, Justine's melancholy follows on that of *Antichrist*'s She in being juxtaposed against rational dominance and in her attunement to the dark agencies of the nonhuman. From the beginning of part 1, cosmic and earthbound natural occurrences draw her attention to and separate her from the social community, and she simultaneously expresses and transcends her depression—her lack of interest in "normal" life—through her empathetic relationship to nature. Arriving at her wedding party two hours late, admonished by Claire and John, she gazes up at the sky and asks, "What star is that?," and the camera lingers on the red star Antares "a bit too long" before running to the stable to greet and caress her horse.[154] While her reluctance or inability to fulfill social obligations at first seems childish or frivolous, her preference for the outdoors to interiors and the nonhuman to people and society (the child Leo the one exception) becomes thematically important. Repeatedly in part 1, as an unruly, earthy version of an imprisoned fairy-tale princess, she flees from the castle to the grounds, trashing her gown, a potent symbol of what is weighing her down. (She drags her train into the stables, and on a later excursion, when her billowing skirt becomes entangled in the golf cart's gears, she rips it, frees herself, and strides on.) Squatting on the green to urinate, she looks up at the planet, and finds a moment of transcendence. Interrupting obligatory sex with her new husband, Michael, she strides outdoors followed by Tim, still in pursuit of a tagline, then pivots and shoves him onto a sand trap and rapes him. In part 2, as she recovers from the depths of her depression, she basks in the sunshine on the terrace and uses her fingers to eat jam out of the jar. She is especially in sync with the chaotic states induced by the planet's gravitational pull, signaling the impending natural disaster. More simply, her response exemplifies Morton's "dark ecology" in which nature and human are uncannily and "radically coexistent," as in the prologue when she lifts her hands to the sky while St. Elmo's fire arcs from her fingers.[155] Chaos indeed reigns in *Melancholia*, but to Justine's delight, when "fountains of insects spew from the ground" and dance in the air around her as she stretches out her arms.[156] Showered with snowflakes while picking berries on a sunny day, she smiles with wonder, and while bathing in the planet's blue light, she recovers bliss. In this way, *Melancholia* represents the brighter side, as it were, of *Antichrist*'s "dark ecology," and

FIGURE 2.6 Justine's (Kirsten Dunst's) joyous response to a "dark ecology" in which nature and the human are uncannily and radically coexistent, as insects fly up from the ground and dance in the air around her.

Justine embodies a happier variation on She's gnosis. Like Gainsbourg's She, Justine establishes a relationship with nature that is uncanny, prescient, yet vulnerable, but that in contrast is represented as positive—indeed, as the only valid state of mind at the end of the world. Through the experience of this radical coexistence, she is able to empathize with Leo and Claire in their mutual vulnerability and to discover compassion.

POSTCINEMATIC ATAVISM

If von Trier may not originally or even primarily have conceived the film as a meditation on dark ecology and ecogrief, with our current and escalating fear and horror over climate crisis, mass extinctions, and pandemics, *Melancholia*, now widely available for streaming on Amazon Prime and other venues, has resonated increasingly with anxious and grieving viewers. What is clearer, however, is the film's anticipation of, confrontation with, and grief over its own end as cinema—and especially as European art cinema in the grand, Cannes award–winning style. As Xan Brooks commented at the Cannes Film Festival in 2011, "If *Antichrist* felt like it could have been the first film ever made—raw and crude; a primal howl—this often feels as though it could be the last. It's old and disillusioned, fighting for breath as the noose draws tighter and the planet pulls closer."[157] Similarly, if more positively, and from his perspective as von Trier's cinematographer, Manuel Claro observes that although "what he was doing in

the nineties until *The Boss of It All* has been very much what I call destruction
of cinema" in reaction to cinema's pompousness. Indeed, with the Dogme 95
Manifesto, von Trier became associated with radical minimalism and the revolutionary potential of digital cameras that provided the tools for anybody to
make movies.[158] But, in his postdepression phase, beginning with *Antichrist*, von
Trier has been "very respectful and he's come back to . . . his big love for cinema." Claro adds:

> A lot of the main energy in cinema is reactionary. . . . obsessed with a con-
> cept of beauty that goes back to Wagner, maybe earlier, . . . [a notion of] the
> individual . . . and nature and true beauty. . . . Modern art and music and a
> lot of other forms of expressions, they have moved on. . . . And cinema is a little
> bit stuck, because of the commercial aspect of cinema and also . . . [because]
> most people use cinema for distraction . . . and not for enlighten[ment].[159]

And in its overt—and overtly ambivalent—homage to modernist European classics and to Wagner and the *precinematic*, *Melancholia* acknowledges cinema's
anachronism while anticipating and mourning and celebrating its passing.

What Brooks and Claro suggest, if from opposing perspectives, might be
explained as von Trier's deliberate and self-reflexive employment of "post-
cinematic atavism," a return to past or archaic cinematic traits that have been
jeopardized in a post-cinematic era of increasing digitalization.[160] The prologue,
with its dense layers of allusions to precinematic art forms, including German
Romantic, Pre-Raphaelite, Renaissance, and medieval painting, is especially relevant here. It is also paradoxical, having been created largely through digital
means and for ending in obviously digitalized images of interplanetary collision from a cosmic perspective, into which von Trier winkingly inserted fake
lens flares. As a Wagnerian "music video," the prologue flaunts post-cinema's
ability to incorporate all the arts while representing what is impossible for
humans to witness: their extinction. When representing the end of the world
for the second and final time, however, von Trier proffers, rather than a spectacle, the ultimate in cinematic or digital minimalism: a black screen. For an
apocalyptic science fiction film, there is a conspicuous absence of references to
technology—or even electronics other than a computer (there are no cell phones
or television sets)—and the diagram of the planet's "Dance of Death" (whose title
alludes to a medieval allegorical concept) that Claire prints off is conspicuously
drawn rather than digitalized. Five-year-old Leo's invention of a primitive wire

tool for measuring the planet's distance from the Earth amounts to a self-reflexive joke about the film's lack of technology. Eremitage as embodied in Tjolöholm Schott pretends to be a picturesque throwback to the preindustrial era, and the "magic cave" that turns out to be a reference to an aboriginal America provides a fitting final location. Apropos of Freud's Thanatos, it is as if we have traveled back to the beginning of our time.

The Tree of Life, to which *Melancholia* was so often compared in 2011, is as utterly sincere in its cinematic modernism as it is in its Judeo-Christian eschatology and, consequently, in its atavism. In contrast, *Melancholia* is blackly ironic and self-reflexive in its unflinching confrontation with extinction, by way of a treasure trove of allusions to Western art and culture. The Wagnerian *Gesamtkunstwerk* has special relevance here, as in aspiring to it von Trier indulged in a blatant atavism while deploying its digitalized transmediality as a means to move on. *Especially* as cinema in the grand style mourning the end of cinema, it pushed cinema to its limits, forcing it to become something else—"reinventing," as Claro suggests, fusing science fiction/disaster and art cinema, music video, moving paintings while pushing the limitations of cinema through transmedial innovation. *Nymphomaniac*, the subject of the next chapter, moreover, would be a completely different and far more expansive—and quite possibly democratic—take on the *Gesamtkunstwerk*.

3

NYMPHOMANIAC

Digressionism, Collaboration, Hypotexts, Paratexts

Rather than the capstone of a "depression trilogy," *Nymphomaniac* was a departure from *Melancholia* and *Antichrist* in nearly every respect.[1] Instead of an expressionistic product of his depression, the film was a lengthy, two-volume rumination on many subjects, among them von Trier's long-term struggle with alcoholism, which he confessed in 2014 to having battled recently with relative success. Although the film, especially *Volume II*, was at times "depressing" in the loosest of senses, the subject of *Nymphomaniac*, according to Manuel Claro, was addiction. Adding that *Melancholia* had been "a cinematographer's 'candy store,'" as Claro put it, "you had to be really bad to fuck it up." Von Trier, Claro related, itched to "do something really punk": something bold but "ugly" and low-fi—"the settings, the subject matter, everything"—and, as it turned out, extremely talky, by turns artless and blatantly artificial, hilarious and disturbing.[2] With its narrative frame of two people conversing in a single, sparse, drab room, "it was a very tricky film to do." Visually, it "was just nothing," Claro continued. "It was all words." Nor was it meant to be erotic. "We were looking for realism and the sex wasn't supposed to be 'sexy.'" It was shot "in what you could call 'normal bedroom light.'"[3] The sound design was minimalist yet "iconic," according to Kristian Eidnes Andersen: "The main thing was the construction of this apartment, which becomes less and less and less." What you hear is "quite simple or not effectful. So you felt that you were in this little apartment without being in a set piece."[4] As for genre, where *Antichrist* had been an experiment with horror and *Melancholia* with science fiction, it was for

Andersen "a very good long book," one that von Trier himself compared to an "Amager shelf," a Danish variation on the curio shelf or cabinet "where you can put things from your past." Yet if *Nymphomaniac* referred extensively to "his past works . . . his past ideas and past struggles,"[5] it was conceived and written through a process substantially different from von Trier's previous films and embodied what he pronounced a new form or genre: "Digressionism."[6]

Concluding the May 2011 interview with Nils Thorsen for *Melancholia*'s press kit, von Trier shifted to the topic of his next film and joked,

> I've given Peter Aalbæk a choice between two titles: "Shit in the Bedsore" and "The Nymphomaniac." And he seems to think that a film with the title "The Nymphomaniac" might be easier to market. [laughs] . . . I'm researching on nymphomania. And Marquis de Sade. I've found that 40 per cent of all nymphomaniacs are also cutters, in the sense that they cut themselves. But then again, it's politically incorrect to speak of nymphomania, because the concept in itself is seen to indicate that we cannot relate to female sexuality.
>
> As I understand, many of them cannot obtain satisfaction, so they use sex like cutting because it is something within their control. I suppose they carry around a fear or pain that they conceal beneath that.

Pausing, he adds, "But it's no fun if they're just humping away all the time. . . . Then it'll just be a porn flick."[7] At the Cannes press conference on May 24, just before his infamous Nazi comments, von Trier garnered laughs by claiming that his next film was to be a three- or four-hour porn film with "these two" (Kirsten Dunst and Charlotte Gainsbourg). As it turned out Gainsbourg did star in what became, in the original director's cut, a five-and-a-half-hour film.

It was about time for von Trier to make his "porn" film, also his "monumental film about the female erotic desire," as he put it in an April 12, 2012, statement of intentions.[8] As explored in chapter 2, his juvenilia and film school projects had flirted with the darkly erotic, and Sade had long been an obsession. Since the early drafts of *Breaking the Waves*, von Trier had introduced nudity and explicit sex into his films, and *The Idiots* was widely recognized as early "extreme" cinema for an orgy scene that included a few seconds of real sex performed by porn actors. The first minute of *Antichrist*'s prologue featured an extreme if brief close-up of penetration, an obvious "porn shot" (performed by a body double) intended to throw the audience off balance while warning them to be prepared for anything in what would follow. But *Nymphomaniac* would be von Trier's full-fledged attempt to integrate explicit sex acts into his repertoire and into the cinematic language.

PUBLICITY AND PARATEXTS

The Cannes press conference disaster, having left von Trier *persona non grata* for an indefinite period of time, deprived him of his platform for launching films, rendering him unable to speak of such provocations.[9] In October 2011, unnerved and concerned about legal repercussions after his remarks about Hitler, after being questioned by the Danish police courtesy of charges made by the French police in August, he voluntarily gagged himself, announcing that "due to these serious accusations I have realized that I do not possess the skills to express myself unequivocally and I have therefore decided from this day forth to refrain from all public statements and interviews."[10] Deprived of Lars von Trier's voice, the publicity for *Nymphomaniac* had to stand on its own, and it emphatically did, although von Trier participated in the marketing meetings, with several important contributions. As marketing director Philip Einstein Lipski has said, von Trier's silence was actually "very liberating."[11] Beginning in February 2013, when Zentropa's website released the first still (a nude Gainsbourg framed by two African men), on its first poster. Then came a poster/logo designed by von Trier, featuring two parentheses framing an open space in an abstraction of a vagina, with the complimentary tagline "Forget About Love." Shortly thereafter came a photo shoot staged as an elaborate tableau with each cast member frozen in the act of a single, distinctive "indecent" act. This was followed by picture of von Trier with duct tape covering his mouth, speaking by not speaking, and a press release announcing his invention of a new genre, "Digressionism," listing the chapter titles, explaining the film's official campaign. The campaign would be incremental, beginning with a trailer and a series of monthly "appetizer" clips, one for each chapter. In October, the brilliant "orgasm" posters featuring head shots of each actor en flagrante and (mostly) with mouths agape, based on an idea by The Einstein Couple, Lipski and his wife, Maria Einstein Biilman, and photographed by Casper Sejersen, were released, marketing *Nymphomaniac* as a film in which everyone gets off.[12]

Sejersen's posters evoked the diversity, wit, and lightheartedness of *Volume I* in particular, and the entire campaign whimsically played off the irony of von

FIGURE 3.1 *Nymphomaniac*'s "orgasm" poster campaign, based on an idea by The Einstein Couple and photographed by Casper Sejersen, featured head shots of each actor en flagrante and mostly open-mouthed.

Trier's enforced silence. But it also predicted an unprecedentedly graphic experience and in so doing was party to an elaborate ruse. Zentropa hinted initially that the film would show real sex, and Shia LaBeouf, who would play Jerôme, bolstered this notion by claiming he got the role after sending von Trier a sex video of himself with his girlfriend.[13] Subsequently, however, carefully worded "leaks" revealed that porn stars and prosthetic genitalia were used as body doubles during close-ups. In the final analysis, as Claro argues and further evidence suggests, von Trier's interest was less in the film's sensational subject matter than the form and process through which it was produced.[14] As a file in his "Director's Intentions" folder explains:

> With "Nymphomaniac," I wish to transfer qualities from literature to film that have not been seen before. The story is the underlying structure as always, but digressions and associations are layered liberally on top of this, as in the best literature.
>
> In "Nymphomaniac," it will be done through a frame story in which the film's central female character tells a listener about her erotic life. In reality this means that all the main story's characters, comments, and thoughts can be developed in images. As such, becoming an important style element, often illustrated by the use of archival material. The archival material, as opposed to the film's chapters—which are presented in a style befitting each chapter—will appear in the completely random form in which it was produced (in terms of colour, recording medium, contrast, etc.) and will therefore stand out from the main part of the film and together with it create a kind of collage.
>
> My idea is to make a much freer film compared for example to Melancholia, both dynamically and aesthetically. Thus in a way a naturalistic film with a poetic layer born of the film's main story, with the purpose of adding, elaborating, and enriching images, as well as characters and narrative. I envision an explosive film! A film that by using the tools of the best novels allows a deeper perspective.
>
> A monumental film about the female erotic desire, with claims and counterclaims, conflicting angles, and moral—or perhaps immoral—observations. Through the main story, we make room for the most strident arguments and set up the wildest thesis, because the main story allows room for discussion about everything: the film itself, human beings, life!
>
> Lars von Trier
> April 2012[15]

As early as the May 2011 press kit interview for *Melancholia* conducted by Nils Thorsen, von Trier is as excited about his plans for his next film as the one to be screened immediately at Cannes. He suddenly tells Thorsen that he has started to read books: Thomas Mann's *Buddenbrooks*, Fyodor Dostoyevsky's *The Idiot* and *The Brothers Karamazov*. "Why the hell do films have to be so stupid!" he bursts out in a rhetorical question, followed by another: "Why do all lines have to be about something? A plot. When books have a red thread, they only brush it momentarily! . . . Whereas a film is completely tied to the plot. Even a Tarkovsky film has nowhere near the same depth as a novel. It could be fun to take some of the novel's qualities—even that they talk nineteen to the dozen, which is what I like in Dostoyevsky—and include that."

When Thorsen asks how those qualities might appear in a film, von Trier replies, "Well, this room holds a thousand stories. . . . a lot of material which doesn't issue from an image. For instance, the story of the origin of this chair. How has it been used previously and why is it exactly this chair here and not another chair which perhaps ought to have been here." Thorsen asks, "You mean, a depth in the story which is usually perceived as diversions in a film?" Von Trier answers, "Yes. Why does the bottle look like that? . . . Why do we drink that water? Is it cheaper? Or the bar code on it. How did that originate?"[16]

Digressionism

Some time after shooting *Melancholia*, von Trier gave up alcohol (for the most part), with which he had increasingly self-medicated for anxiety since filming *Breaking the Waves* in Scotland in 1995.[17] In his first public statement since his self-imposed silence after the Cannes debacle, via a long interview with Thorsen for *Politiken* in November 2014, he announced, "Now I am about to make an attempt to keep alive by removing all the various intoxicants, but at the same time I have to try keep the creative line. . . . And I simply don't think that it will be possible. Because no creative initiative of artistic value has ever been made by former drunkards and drug addicts."[18] He persisted nonetheless, and the screenplay for *Nymphomaniac* was the first thing von Trier had written sober: "But it also took me a year and a half," he complained. "Also because I am partially depressive and almost can't pull myself together for anything."[19]

Of the drug cocktail he had used for creative inspiration, he stressed that he did not use it recreationally or in "random situations."[20] It had two functions: it generated ideas and images but also, perhaps more important, obliterated anxiety and simplified choices. When Thorsen asked him if it inspired ideas to which he would not otherwise have had access, he replied, "I'm absolutely sure of that. And it helped me make decisions. . . . Because more options look equally inviting. But as I had set myself up with alcohol . . . I was quite ready to make decisions and just move on. And it's the doubts that take time. When you stop and think: I could go the other way too. For me it was just: right, left, straight. It left all doubts. And that's great."

Asked if he ever made the wrong choice, von Trier replied, "I didn't. It was only the superfluous doubt I came to terms with," adding that "the parallel world costs," but "it's a case of use, not abuse. For I have had a purpose I can vouch for."[21] With digressionism, on the other hand, he had found a model and a procedure that might "forgive" or even make a virtue of indecision and inclusivity.

Von Trier's Book Group: Reading, Arguing, Writing

Melancholia had been a trial run for a collaborative working relationship with Jenle Hallund and Vinca Wiedemann that developed throughout the making of *Nymphomaniac*, now enhanced by an important reading component. With the "parallel world" inaccessible, von Trier turned to a regimen of reading, contemplation, and discussion of long nineteenth- and twentieth-century classic European novels together with brainstorming and writing in sessions enriched with research conducted by them and other assistants. Although he read voraciously when he was young, he explained to Thorsen, he had gone for thirty years without reading a book.[22]

Von Trier had been interested in making "literary" films before. *Dogville* (2003) and *Manderlay* (2005) were inspired as much by David Edgar's theatrical adaptation of Charles Dickens's *Nicholas Nickleby* (1838–1839), directed by John Caird and Trevor Nunn and filmed as a four-part television miniseries in 1982, and Stanley Kubrick's 1975 adaptation of William Makepeace Thackeray's *Barry Lyndon* (1844) as they were by Brecht. Both Victorian novels were long, episodic Bildungsromans. But the immediate inspiration for digressionism was the reading program on which von Trier and Hallund—and eventually von Trier and

Wiedemann, together with suggestions from his longtime mentor Peter Schepelern—had embarked.[23] According to Hallund,

> After *Melancholia*, I read a lot. Lars didn't read at all at that time. And read a lot of the old books, like old Russian books, . . . Tolstoy and Gorky and, Thomas Mann, so [when] I got employed to work with him on what should he do next, we decided that we were going to read together . . . not sit and eat together, but . . . meet once a week and read this much. And we did. So we read [Fyodor Dostoevsky's] *Crime and Punishment*. . . . We read [Tolstoy's] *Anna Karenina* and [Dostoevsky's] *The Idiot*. . . . And, that's where the idea of digressions came [from in] *Nymphomaniac*. . . . this sort of literary [way of filming] that you don't have to stick to a dramaturgical order of events.[24]

To Thorsen, von Trier mentions reading "Dostoevsky and everything. In his novel 'Doctor Faustus,' Thomas Mann wrote that now something will happen violently, but that it is his privilege as a writer to determine how and when to mention it," he explains. "And it won't be now," he adds, with a knowing laugh.[25]

Wiedemann elaborated on their joint reading of Marcel Proust's seven-volume *À la recherche du temps perdu* (*In Search of Lost Time*, 1871–1922), the most obvious model for *Nymphomaniac*'s narrative structure, and in comments that echo (and/or perhaps influenced) von Trier's intention as stated in his "Director's Comments" quoted in full earlier. In contrast to the rigorous plotting "we're used to in filmmaking," she explains, "once you read the whole" of Proust's novel, you realize "it's a depiction of life itself."[26] "It's such a big piece. . . . If you read it quickly, you miss everything, you miss the point. So you just have to get immersed into the reading. And this was what Lars wanted to do with *Nymphomaniac*."[27] Literature, the novel, and Proust especially offered a model for what was for von Trier a totally different *process* for writing scripts: "He [von Trier] realized he couldn't do a quick development [or] . . . a short script. He just had to start out without knowing the end."[28]

Von Trier adapts Proust's concept of involuntary memory as a motif that foregrounds thought processes, conscious and unconscious, as his heroine, Joe (Charlotte Gainsbourg), is prompted by odd props in Seligman's (Stellan Skarsgård) apartment that bring up associations that advance her story. In turn, Seligman's digressions are inspired by incidents and allusions in Joe's narrative, inspiring more memories and associations. Within this framework, the story of

Joe's life emerges in fits and starts. In chapter 1, "The Compleat Angler," Joe's attention is held by a fishing fly absurdly attached to the wall. The episode develops as she relates how as young teenagers she (Stacy Martin) and her friend B (Sophie Kennedy Clark) competed for bag of chocolates to be won by whoever seduces the most men on a train; meanwhile, Seligman digresses on parallel observations about the techniques and delights of fly fishing. It ends as Joe uses oral sex to make an extremely difficult catch, swallows, elaborately licking her lips, followed by a shot of her lustily, triumphantly devouring the bag of chocolates. In the shooting draft,

> *Seligman sits for a while nodding to himself. Then he smirks.*
> SELIGMAN: I can hear that you have literary role models. Only with you it's not the taste of a piece of a madeleine cake moistened with lime blossom tea . . .
> JOE: What???
> SELIGMAN: Yes well, I'm sorry, that was perhaps a culturally blasphemic digression—a story about memory. It describes how two flavours in combination set off a chain of memories. I'm assuming the man in the compartment ejaculated?[29]

It is not for nothing that Joe's neglected child is named Marcel. When the theme is introduced for the second time, in scene 58, it is signaled by the beginning of the first movement of Belgian French composer César Franck's *Violin Sonata in A Major* (in a version for cello and piano), regarded as the model for Proust's fictional composer Vinteuil's sonata, a phrase from which triggers Swan's memory of his love for Odette. The phrase thenceforth illustrates music's power to trigger involuntary memory, which von Trier invokes:[30]

> *Insert 1: Montage of shots of forests, amongst them archival pictures, in different seasons.*
> Music: César Franck's violin sonata in A major (the Vinteuil-sonata).
> SELIGMAN V.O.: You walked in the forest?
> JOE V.O.: Yes, I walked in the forest as a part of my cure against exaggerated lust . . .
> SELIGMAN V.O.: Any particular forest?
> JOE V.O.: The forest of my youth . . . And everything was just as it had been then. I took the same walk again and again . . .

Joe appears on a path in the forest just prior to defoliation. Amongst other things, we see Joe's P.O.V. of her feet as they walk along the path. She passes a water mill.

JOE V.O.: Right turn by the watermill . . . and right again by the ash tree, which has the most beautiful leaves in the forest . . .[31]

The forest of Joe's youth is that of *Antichrist* and Norse mythology, referenced in the ash tree, here reclaimed as the forest of von Trier's youth in its original, Edenic state.

As these examples suggest, and apropos of *In Search of Lost Time*, *Nymphomaniac* is self-reflexive to a degree not seen before in von Trier; it is a web of allusions to moments in his previous films.[32] The name Seligman comes from *The Orchid Gardener*, and Seligman's claim that his name "means the happy one" echoes the title of *Menthe la bienheureuse* (*Menthe—the Happy One*, 1979).[33] A shot of a bird on a branch is identical to the opening shot of *Befrielsesbilleder* (*Images of Liberation*, 1982). Fischer, the name of a lover on Joe's answering machine, may allude to the protagonist of *The Element of Crime*. The train sequence (in which Joe and B compete for willing men) recalls *Europa*, whose most suspenseful sequences take place on a train. Joe's red vinyl minishorts in that chapter replicate Bess's "tart" outfit for luring men in *Breaking the Waves*. The cellar corridors of the hospital sequence echo *Riget* (*The Kingdom*, 1994), and a shot featuring dead leaves, an automatic door, and the sign "OPGANG 2" (Entrance 2) is taken directly from it. Jerôme's request in chapter 6 to hear about Joe's lovers echoes Jan's request that Bess seduce other men and titillate him with her accounts. The Shostakovich waltz heard when Joe and B as young girls play "frogs" in the bathroom von Trier used in the commercial *La Rue de la vie* (1993). Seligman's exclamation of "Hopla" is from "Pirate Jenny's Song" from Brecht's *Threepenny Opera*, a key inspiration for *Dogville*. Perhaps the most melodramatic self-reference is when in chapter 6 Joe leaves her child during the night, and he nearly falls from the balcony to his death, reiterating *Antichrist*'s prologue, complete with "Lascia chio pianga" playing over it. The shot of twelve-year-old Joe lying in a field of grass, which opens the chapter, replicates one of *Antichrist*'s most iconic shots—of She visualizing her absorption into nature and "turn[ing] green." In the restaurant scene in which Joe uses her vagina as a cache for elegant dessert spoons, to the consternation of the waiter (Udo Kier), refers to John Hurt's spoon stealing in *Melancholia*'s wedding dinner scene. In chapter 5, Joe, overwhelmed by her lineup of lovers, makes choices on how to treat them by throwing dice, recalling Automavision, the computerized director of *The Boss of It All* (2006), which dictated camera movement by chance. Jean-Marc Barr and Udo Kier, who had leading roles in several of von Trier's early films and now often function as mascots of a sort, as Schepelern notes, show up in cameos.[34]

If the film came from inside von Trier's head, it takes the form of a dialogue throughout: two people in a minimally furnished room debate issues ranging from the ridiculous (the proper way to eat rugelach or to parallel park) to the pedantic (Zeno's paradox) to what remain some of the most significant and stubborn philosophical, ethical, and political issues of our time. Although ancient oral literary models come to mind, the frame story for *One Thousand and One Nights* (English translation, 1706–1721) or Giovanni Boccaccio's *The Decameron* (1349–1353) for example, this dialogic narrative situation was inspired to a greater or lesser extent during the brainstorming and writing stages in which Hallund and Wiedemann participated. Hallund, with whom von Trier had a close personal and sexual as well as professional relationship that has since been made public, suggested that much of the content of Joe and Seligman's discourse and to some extent its debate structure originated in discussions between von Trier and herself, with von Trier's arguments eventually, for the most part, given to Joe, and Hallund's (who is a passionate—and unconventional—feminist) to Seligman:[35]

> Lars and I've had lots of arguments. . . . That's a creative process. And it's a good kind . . . a lot of *Nymphomaniac*—the dialogue—was written on [the basis of] our conversations, . . . but he gave a lot of my arguments to Stellan and his own to Charlotte. I used to go back and forth, . . . but [the film included] a lot of what we discussed. And we had fierce arguments, really volatile because we're both quite passionate people. That was probably the film that had most of our conversations in it. I mean literally, a lot of them. . . . That's also the way we worked. I did research, but mainly I did conversation. I have a lot of ideas and I just spit them out, and I have opinions, and then we discuss and we argue.[36]

Hallund stresses that the process was open ended, although von Trier clearly had final say, and that the film itself was similarly meant to be open, dynamic, and "life affirming."[37] In contrast to Hallund, Wiedemann began as an amanuensis on *Melancholia*, progressively contributing more and more to the dialogue and the content, eventually becoming *Nymphomaniac*'s story supervisor, which mean that she had control over continuity and the details of the script.[38]

If writing alongside Vinca Wiedemann was introduced as a replacement for von Trier's intoxicated method of entering the "parallel world," the arrangement worked something like Dogme 95, which he invented with Thomas Vinterberg as a set of constrictions designed, among other motives, to force himself to give up authorial and technical control.[39] Wiedemann speculates that von Trier's genius (and limitation) has been his ability (and compulsion) to envision a film as a totality before starting to write.[40] "This of course limits the kind of stories you can make," Wiedemann adds, "because . . . you just have to put it down on paper" rather than allowing it to develop depth and complexity. Von Trier "always fought this problem, that things felt . . . like a construction," because, she believes, "he had to contain it in his brain." Attempting to "bypass this feeling of a construction," he encouraged actors to improvise and played games with himself that forced him "to give control to someone else, but then again, drawing it back."[41] This dialogic writing process was, therefore, one more game, a rather elaborate one, to thwart his compulsion to make overly constructed films.

That compulsion was perhaps most obvious in his first feature, *The Element of Crime*, written as a conundrum whose ending is determined in the premise: a profiler methodically projects himself into the mind of a serial killer and inevitably completes the killer's mission. It peaked with the Brechtian, allegorical USA duology, which arguably turned rigorous construction into a virtue—and, conversely, the script of *Dear Wendy* (2004), which he gave over to director Thomas Vinterberg to bring to life. Subsequently, as products of von Trier's depression whose plots were subordinated to affect, the expressionistic *Antichrist* and *Melancholia* represented breakthroughs. Then, having tapped his depression, as Wiedemann suggests, "came this [desire] to do a movie that was like one of these big novels, when you need to type down without knowing everything and beforehand. . . . he knew that this would potentially add to his art. I believe that after *Melancholia*, he suddenly felt that this way of collaborating on the script would allow him to make a bigger thing [and] because he felt that he could trust me." Or, rather, she adds, "on *Melancholia* we found the way to collaborate and on *Nymphomaniac* we used the method to make this big thing."[42]

While subordinated to the narrative, Socratic dialogue and post-Brechtian dialectic had long been a hallmark of von Trier's films, which usually end by posing questions or offering equally negative alternatives. *The Idiots* and, subsequently, *Dogville* and *Manderlay* were analytical, dialogue-heavy thought experiments based on Danish and American communities and their behaviors, respectively, that featured protracted lectures followed by debates and theatrical voting scenes. As noted in chapter 1, the postdepression films foreground and progressively heighten this dialectic by incorporating the structure of a two-hander: with the perspectives of He and She, Justine and Claire, Joe and Seligman, and Jack and Verge juxtaposed. With *Nymphomaniac*, however, the story is subordinated to the frame narrative and depends on dialogue and involuntary memory to advance, proliferating rhizomatically. As von Trier's producer Louise Vesth explains, "Digressionism . . . meant that the script was not only the drama between these two guys talking in a room, it was also . . . thinking about [and then] leading to something, leading to something, leading to something else, leading to something else."[43]

Gesamt

As such, *Nymphomaniac*'s digressionism turned the notion of the *Gesamtkunstwerk*, with which *Melancholia* had flirted so outrageously, inside out. In place of Wagner's sublime and seamless totality, von Trier now aimed for an assortment, medley, or collage, a *Gesamtkunstwerk* with its seams showing, in which the disparate "contents" of the film assumed prominence over any overarching auteur's vision, and in which the processes of thought are foregrounded. It is as if von Trier takes the audience backstage to expose the "Wagnerian technologies"—to use Gundula Kreutzer's term—that masked the apparatus that made Wagner's productions a seamless transmedial experience.[44] Individual chapters and a multitude of archival materials are given discreet shapes, grains, colors, and aspect ratios, shifting from warm and vibrant in young Joe's earlier years to black-and-white for chapter 4, "Delirium," about the torturous death of her father (Christian Slater), and from a 2.35.1 base aspect ratio to a 1.85.1 format in chapter 3, which features Mrs. H (Uma Thurman), the furious wife of one of Joe's many lovers. "We had very strict rules for each chapter," Claro explained in a *Film Comment* interview, to "separate and define the different stories clearly."[45]

As a long-winded exhibition of authorial self-indulgence, however, *Nymphomaniac* might be deemed egregiously Wagnerian. Consider its release in two

two-hour "volumes" (117 and 124 minutes) in 2013, including eight chapters with elaborate title cards, followed by the five-and-a-half-hour director's cut (148 and 178 minutes), whose DVD cover featured a blow-up of two parentheses in the shape of a vagina framing a full-length shot of a jaunty von Trier in a white suit, T-shirt, and straw hat (likely modeled on Dirk Bogarde in Luchino Visconti's 1971 film *Death in Venice*).[46] From this perspective, Anders Refn sees the film as a magnum opus, as von Trier using "his whole palette of experience . . . to sum up what he has learned from moviemaking, and put it into this film about addiction and sexuality. And art. . . . with . . . organ, flute, and all these figures. Because what Stellan represents is this refined, intellectual, asexual person" that Lars also is.[47]

That the *Gesamtkunstwerk* was on von Trier's mind was indicated when, in mid-August 2012, shortly after completing the script and before shooting started later that month, the Copenhagen Art Festival announced a "challenge" from the "Master" to the people, a crowdsourced art project called *Gesamt*. Where digressionism spun out from a single origin point, *Gesamt* was to be a compilation and synthesis of a multitude of minds and bodies. Aspiring filmmakers, composers, and musicians were to choose from any or all of "six great works of art," create a five-minute film or audio recording taking direct inspiration from it, and submit it to von Trier's partner and collaborator Jenle Hallund. Von Trier was credited with the concept, and Hallund's task, as director-editor, would be to select, edit, and integrate the submissions. The sources of inspiration were limited (provocatively) to James Joyce's novel *Ulysses*; Albert Speer's Zeppelinfeld at Nuremberg, the former Nazi rally marching grounds; Paul Gauguin's painting *Where Do We Come From? What Are We? Where Are We Going?*; Sammy Davis Jr's. music; César Franck's *Sonata in A Major*; and August Strindberg's play *The Father*.

While standing on its own, this initiative, ending in a collage-like synthesis of stories, styles, videos, stills, and musical compositions, also functioned as a paratext simultaneously in relation to *Melancholia*, as von Trier's most Wagnerian film, and *Nymphomaniac*, whose eccentric disparity challenged the notion of a universal, seamless, auteurist work of art. Perhaps equally, it alluded back to *Limboland* (2010), a Robert Best Feature Award–winning film directed by Hallund and Jeremy Weller from the improvisations of eight young, angry, culturally alienated second-generation immigrants playing themselves. However, as the press release announced, *Gesamt* would turn Wagner's elitist concept into an egalitarian one: "By using the idea of Gesamt in a user-generated film project we [von Trier and Hallund] are taking the [*Gesamtkunstwerk*] concept one step further: A universal work of art is not only created by many different art forms but also by a diversity and multitude of people."[48]

Like the methods embodied in *Nymphomaniac*, the "rules" for *Gesamt* were apparently meant to advance an open-ended creative process: "What the result of *Gesamt* will be, no one knows—yet. There is no script, just a cinematic experiment that gradually comes to life by people, thoughts, images and sound that merge into each other and form new meanings and constellations. The final work . . . is [to be] a reflection on our time and the people who live in it: a community masterpiece."[49] "Because it is based on ordinary people's creativity and imagination," Hallund ventured, "it has the potential to reveal the health of a civilization by exposing its soul. Together we can try and create a cacophonous testimony of the human condition's greater purpose than power and profit."[50] As Cecilie Høgsbro Østergaard analyzes the experiment, "Here, then, *Gesamt* does not mean 'total,' but *together, in common*. In fact, crowd sourcing really turns the entire idea of the Gesamtkunstwerk upside down. According to modernist mythmaking about the latter the masses do not create the Gesamtkunstwerk; rather, the masses are created through it. Crowd sourcing is about the opposite: it is about showing the masses as individuals."[51] The result, a four-track film shown simultaneously on four screens and titled *Disaster 501: What Happened to Man?*, combined 142 of the total 501 contributions from 52 countries at the Kunsthal, Charlottenborg, Copenhagen, from October 12 to December 30, 2012.

While respectful of the project's egalitarian intentions, Østergaard's review of *Disaster 501* was also skeptical, with good reason: von Trier's title lent the concept "juicy totalitarian overtones" that contradicted the "cautious democratic expectations about communication, audience involvement, and 'community'" that the Copenhagen Art Festival aimed for.[52] These overtones were fully intended to provoke—together with connotations lent by two of the given sources of inspiration: Strindberg's *The Father* (often read as misogynist) and Albert Speer's "monumental" Nazi rally stage. That Strindberg and Speer were controversial influences on *Melancholia* and *Antichrist* was widely known from von Trier's "Director's Confession" and his infamous "Nazi comments." (Other proposed sources were apparently, simply, on von Trier's mind: for instance, Franck's *Vinteuil Sonata*, which would be featured in *Nymphomaniac*'s idyllic forest scenes.) But *Gesamt* was also typical of von Trier's provocative coinages in reclaiming a word with negative connotations by spinning its meaning in an opposite direction—for example, "Dogme" (dogma) appropriated to designate the liberation of cinema—while retaining the original meaning as well (Dogme as a set of prohibitions)—to create a thought-provoking tension. Considering its paratexual role in relation to his previous and forthcoming films, *Gesamt* might be compared to Bakhtin's concept of carnival as a suspension of auteurism and elitism for a celebration of the creativity of ordinary individuals, the *Gesamtkunstwerk* reclaimed—however temporarily.[53]

In its radical open-endedness, *Gesamt* was similar to several early experimental performance art projects, paratexts, and spin-offs from concepts informing von Trier's films, and that gave up control by turning on chance and improvisation. *Verdensuret (Psykomobile #1: The World Clock)* and *D-Dag (D-Day*, 2001), both of which were born out of the impulse that produced Dogme 95, for example, occupy an intermediary space between cinema, theater, performance art, and game. *Psykomobile*, which he called "a drama 'happening,'" assigned characters to fifty-nine actors in twenty rooms who changed moods (anger, melancholy, joy, lust) as dictated by the arbitrary movements of an ant colony in Mexico (von Trier and Albinus). *D-Dag*, a collaboration consisting of four different seventy-minute films, each made by one of the four Dogme brothers and with the same plot (four people rob a bank and mask the explosion with the noise from the New Year's celebration), was, ultimately, much like *Gesamt*, a onetime crowd-sourced "happening": on January 1, 2000, viewers could edit their own versions from the four films shown live on four different screens, using their remote controls. In relation to *Nymphomaniac*, then, *Gesamt* might be seen as the product of von Trier's recent experimentation with collaborative script development, as a paratextual tribute to his personal and working relationship with Jenle Hallund and Vinca Wiedemann, and ultimately as a radically collaborative variation on digressionism while it was still in the making.

Yet "I'm not sure that I would call this process very collaborative," as producer Louise Vesth cautions:

> He uses people around him for creative purposes. . . . He tells you a scene to get a reaction and however you react, he uses that, or you [might] even come up with an idea. . . . but [generally] he gets people to react [to] the things he already knows he wants to do. . . . it's also true that he wants something to play with, but he doesn't really want them to give him their ideas. He wants them

to reflect on his ideas in order to place them the right way in this picture, to refine them. . . . [and] if I'm telling him what I think he will do the opposite.[54]

Digressionism as Essayism

With Vesth's point in mind, we might say that *Nymphomaniac* is less like the *Gesamt* initiative (or the *Gesamtkunstwerk*, for that matter) than an essay film. As Claro puts it, the conversation between Joe and Seligman, Jenle Hallund notwithstanding, is von Trier's dialogue with himself (2018), together with literature and a host of other genres and texts, making *Nymphomaniac* dialogic in the Bakhtinian sense. Moreover, the essay (or essayistic) form offered von Trier the provocateur, gagged since his vow of silence after 2011, a voice. Digressionism, as Claro submits,

> gives Lars the opportunity to pretty much speak about whatever he wants— you don't have to think about plot, you don't have to think what makes sense within the story. You can just have the characters wander off to whatever they want to discuss. And then he makes it work with [the rest of the film] and I think it has been giving him a sense of freedom. He has found a form with . . . *Nymphomaniac* and *The House That Jack Built* where he feels he can pretty freely incorporate whatever he has on his—uh, okay, he needs to get off his chest. [laughs] I say it a little jokingly because I really hear Lars's voice in both films. And it's both in Jack and it's in Verge and it's in Seligman and also in Charlotte's character. All of the voices are Lars's voice. He's in his head discussing things from one side and then the other side. It's his inner dialogue.[55]

In a review of Chris Marker's *Letter from Siberia* (1957), André Bazin became the first to analyze a film in relation to the essay form. He distanced Marker's practice from cinema proper, describing *Letter*'s "primary material" as a "verbal intelligence" as opposed to the cinematic image. Distinguishing Marker's "horizontal" montage from traditional montage, he claimed that "a given image doesn't refer to the one that preceded it or the one that will follow, but rather it refers laterally . . . to what is said."[56] Hence *Letter* is not cinema—or not-cinema—but, rather, an essay documented by film.[57] "The important word is 'essay,'" Bazin writes, "understood in the same sense that it has in literature—an essay at once historical and political, written by a poet as well."[58] Bazin's description of Marker's use of montage fits *Nymphomaniac*'s structure, which links heterogeneous ideas and materials. It also matches von Trier's "Director's Comments" about aspiring to make a film that "transfer[s] qualities from literature to film"[59] as well Claro's understanding of *Nymphomaniac* as "visually . . . just nothing"—"all words."[60]

Countering the notion that the essay film consists largely of talking heads and words, however, Kenneth B. Lee asserts that much writing on the essay film embraces "the form's ability, through the combination of images, sounds and words, to express the process of subjective thought. In the words of Hans Richter, who coined the term in 1940, the essay film: *'allows the filmmaker to transgress the rules and parameters of the traditional documentary practice, granting the imagination with all its artistic potentiality free reign.'*"[61] In fact, the essay film "explicitly reflects on the materials it presents, to actualise the thinking process itself," as seen in Seligman's segue from Joe's story about oral sex and chocolates to a meditation on Proust and the nature of memory.[62] Employing what Bodil Marie Stavning Thomsen calls the "diagrammatic," von Trier most often realizes the process of thought cinematically through superimposition and horizontal montage, as in Seligman's digression from Joe's tale of losing her virginity (via three vaginal and five anal thrusts, with the numbers superimposed on the moving image of the couple) to his riff on Fibonacci ratios, literalized through interpretive numerical and figurative diagrams imposed on the screen.[63] Likewise, Seligman's analogy between Joe and B's game of scanning a train for horny men and fly fishing is actualized through maps and documentary footage illustrating different segments of Joe's story. This and similar cinematic "figures of thought" pepper and enliven *Volume I* until, in *Volume II*, as Joe complains about the poor quality of Seligman's digressions, their conversation turns into a series of increasingly polarized debates.

Traditionally the essay film was regarded as nonfiction, an offshoot of documentary, or a cross between documentary and experimental film that, characterized by subjectivism and self-reflexivity, is typically "ruminative, digressive and playful."[64] Much recent critical interest, however, is in essayism in narrative fiction cinema, as in Timothy Corrigan's *The Essay Film: From Montaigne after Marker* (2011) and Elizabeth Papazian and Caroline Eades's *The Essay Film: Dialogue/Politics/Utopia* (2016), whose first chapter, "Essayism and Contemporary Film Narrative," by Corrigan, focuses on Malick's *The Tree of Life* (2011) and Lech Majewski's *The Mill and the Cross* (2011).[65] *Nymphomaniac*'s essay, so to speak,

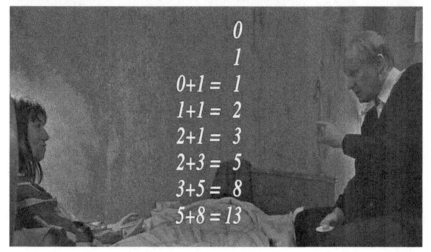

FIGURES 3.2 AND 3.3 *Nymphomaniac* actualizes the process of thought cinematically through superimposition and horizontal montage. Below, Seligman (Stellan Skarsgård) digresses from Joe's (Charlotte Gainsbourg's) tale of losing her virginity to discuss Fibonacci ratios, which are literalized by superimposing the numbers on the screen.

emerges from the dialogue, which proceeds from a tension between narrative and digressive impulses—or, rather, the film's digressionism turns on a conflict and eventual compromise between what Gilles Deleuze and Felix Guattari have deemed an "arborescent" structure, chronological and hierarchical like a gene-alogical tree, and "rhizomatic": horizontal and nonhierarchical and composed of heterogenous links.[66] "Originally, [von Trier's] vision was to do something much more punky and crazy and we tried to do that but it started to feel forced,"

Claro explained. "So it became a balance between an open experience but still wanting to tell a good story."[67]

Viewing *Nymphomaniac* as an essay or essayistic film makes sense of a strain in von Trier's work that flaunts a discursive and metadiscursive edge. *Epidemic*, *The Idiots*, *Dogville*, and *Manderley* are narratives with a satirical-analytical-essayistic style that employ what Søren Birkvad has called "negative didactics"— through embedded lectures, debates, shock tactics, and free-ranging social and political critique along with Godardian self-reflexivity.[68] Borrowing his key term from Bazin, Corrigan has analyzed Abbas Kiarostami's *Close-Up* (1990) together with *The Five Obstructions* (2003), which von Trier made with Jørgen Leth, as "refractive" essays, a type of documentary that "reflexively examines the changing values of modern cinematic images."[69] *Nymphomaniac* features a dialogic process that Papazian and Eades find characteristic of many essay films: in this case, between subject and object, female and male, action and rumination, emotion and reason, fiction (inherent in storytelling) and fact.[70]

Much writing on the essay film espouses "a resistance to the didactic, the pedagogical . . . or the polemical," as Lee points out;[71] it "takes on ideas in a casual, even playful way that eschews professional, scientific rigour, and is often infused with details of everyday life."[72] Understood in this way, we can make sense of the film's obsessive but irreverent portrayal of experts, therapies, cases, and testimonies, which in the diegesis ends in open or mock-pedagogical discreditation, as Joe defies the pathological terminology ("sex addict") and advice of psychologists, social workers, and medical personnel, deeming them enforcers of political correctness who would obliterate her identity.

Von Trier's use of experts and cases while researching and writing followed a similar course. Vesth stresses that the "DNA" of each of his films has been "built from hours and hours and hours of research: books that he has read, paintings that he has seen, music he has listened to, people, experts that he has spoken to, interviews [conducted] by other people and delivered to him."[73] Research on *Nymphomaniac* (which, she notes, is really two films) was especially exhaustive. According to Vinca Wiedemann, there were two kinds of research at the script development phase. The first was based in discussions with sex therapists like her mother, Maria Marcus, sex therapist and author of a book on female masochism (*Den frygtelige sandhed*,1974; *A Taste for Pain*, 1981), and psychologists and medical doctors such as Aalborg University sexology professor Christian Graugaard, who worked with von Trier as an academic adviser, together with input (via interviews and testimonials) from a wide range of women with experiences with hypersexuality.[74] Suzanne Brøgger, author of the autobiographical *Fri os fra kærligheden* (1973; *Deliver Us From Love*, 1976), which may have partly inspired Joe's early philosophy of the zipless fuck, was not available. But von Trier interviewed several other women who had published candid books about their sexual experiences: Suzanne Bjerrehuus (*Livet i mine mænd* [The life in my men, 2002]); Anne Linnet (*Testamentet* [The testament, 2012]); *The Sexual Life of Catherine M.* (2001), an autobiographical memoir by French art critic Catherine Millet; and the therapist Laila Topholm, who has spoken publicly about her former sex addiction, including her shame over leaving her two young boys alone at night.[75] As Schepelern explains, these and many other testimonials provided episodes (including the woman who "hosted" a gang rape in an industrial area and the provocative scene with the two African brothers). Secondly, there was research on the vast range of "other kinds of digressions," from botany to knot tying.[76]

Von Trier's mania for accuracy notwithstanding, more than one of the experts (including Christian Graugaard and Maria Marcus), were piqued when he ignored or departed from the diagnostic models they had given him. Paraphrasing her mother ("This is not what a masochist is. This is not what a nymphomaniac does"), Wiedemann explained that "he didn't really care. He just wanted to get the inspiration and . . . [then] take off from some really marginal, tiny little detail. . . . [like] the chocolate candy in the train sequence. That was what he was most interested in. . . . That's a delightful sequence based on someone's story."[77] And so, rather than a case study based on an exhaustive archive of facts and models, Joe arguably functions as a literary device—or as a nexus for a collection of loosely connected vignettes.

If anything, the consultations with experts seem to have informed von Trier of what he wanted to avoid. After the interview of July 25, 2019, Wiedemann emailed me to explain that although she and Lars talked about "a lot of thematic issues," they "did not do this as an analytic tool for him to decide how the scenes or his characters should be. Then what did he use it for? Maybe rather for him to be sure that he did not take any conventional choices, that it did not become a psychological or political cliché."[78] Unbidden, and like Wiedemann, Hallund brought up von Trier's abhorrence of psychological clichés and refusal of psychological realism. "Lars never thinks about psychology. He thinks about what do I want my character to do," she says. "He's never had to dissect his ideas into cheap psychology" and, however often he consults them, does not make changes based on experts' recommendations.[79] Unsurprisingly, Hallund shares von Trier's disdain, protesting that, because of popularized psychology, American and European cinema has become increasingly based on a "very narrow" idea of human nature and the stories that can be told:

> Everything is tested upon . . . psychologized legitimacy. . . . And I hate it. I see
> so many films and I know exactly what's going to happen. People see films and
> they think that this is life reflected. . . . So that's how we become, because . . .
> cinema and films [are] teaching us how to be human. And if everything has
> been taught through the prism of psychology, we just partition off so many
> elements and components to the human. . . . so the world becomes smaller . . .
> and more stupid.[80]

And so, rather than a case study of sex addiction, then, *Nymphomaniac* open-endedly explores or "essays" the subject of female sexuality. According to Hallund, the film

> brings it [sex] back to what it is. It's the source of life and it's a source of feel-
> ing it. . . . and he's tried to strip away every single taboo around it. . . . I
> think it's one of his most life affirming films. And I know that people think
> that *Volume II* is very tough with the violence. But my argument with this has
> always been that she chose it, nobody was buying, she was in control and she
> wanted to feel something. She didn't want to be hurt. She doesn't want to be
> abused. . . . she orchestrated that. She was the master. And that's very impor-
> tant because it was all about her will to feel something despite what was going
> on around her.[81]

She stresses that the film "was an exploration of addiction too, because . . . it's so much part of Lars's personality, this idea of 'I'm an addict.'" Yet she thinks that "he managed to . . . not define it as an addiction. [The film] alluded to the fact that it could be or that we label it like that. But isn't it really just an existential celebration of life through your body? And isn't it society that stigmatizes, ever to let Joe chastise herself, because society couldn't accept and she couldn't function in a society where she lived her free sexuality?"[82]

By the end of the film, however, what precisely von Trier is saying about Joe's sexuality—much less female sexuality, hyper- or otherwise—is still radically open to interpretation, as Joe repeatedly dodges or diverges from norms and labels. Is *Nymphomaniac* about the female self-empowerment through sexual freedom (as Hallund and much of *Volume I* might suggest)? Or is it, as Claro suggests, an exemplum about the horrors of addiction (as much of *Volume II* seems to be)? Is the film itself intended to be erotic, or is it, as Claro maintains, a joke on the porn consumers who no doubt often stumble on to it? Notably, as Papazian and Eades observe, "fragmentation, indeterminacy, and failure are as intrinsic to the essay film as the notion of an attempt."[83]

This indeterminacy is whimsically complicated by the revelation (per the picaresque tradition that was one of von Trier's several models) that Joe is an unreliable narrator and Jerôme a wildly, conveniently inconsistent character, a transparent plot device whose various guises are almost impossible to sum up. In chapter 5, Seligman notes that "there are some completely unrealistic coincidences in the story about Jerôme. First, by chance, you are hired to be his assistant and now you're taking a walk in a forest that just happens to be littered with photographs of him. And if that's not enough, he is actually present and like a God pulls you up to him through the clouds!" Joe replies, "So what? That's the way this story goes and I'm the one telling it and I know what happened. Do you want to hear it or not?"[84]

CINEMATIC HYPOTEXTS: THE 1970S AND SCANDINAVIAN BLUE

In a metacinematic moment at a sex addiction therapy group meeting, the heroine introduces herself: "My name is Joe . . . And I'm a nymphomaniac." She is promptly corrected by the therapist ("We say 'sex addict'"). Yet she stands by her identification with an archaic, misogynistic stereotype of insatiable female sexuality. In such fashion the film pronounces itself a "throwback to the Seventies . . . a period associated with a strain of sex cinema that sold itself on the idea of scandalous, excessive female desire," as Jonathan Romney puts it, naming the usual American suspects *Deep Throat* (1972) and *The Devil in Miss Jones* (1973).[85] These "adult" films ushered pornographic movies into Western culture and were followed by an international wave of landmark art films replete with nudity and explicit sex: Bernardo Bertolucci's *Ultimo tango a Parigi* (*Last Tango in Paris*, 1972), Nicholas Roeg's *Don't Look Now* (1973), Liliana Cavani's *The Night Porter* (1974), Pier Paulo Pasolini's *Salò* (1975), and Nagisa Oshima's *Ai no korida* (*In the Realm of the Senses*, 1976). All of these films came out in

Denmark between 1974 and 1976 and were seen by von Trier, who was eighteen to twenty years old at the time.[86]

Anticipating *Deep Throat* by more than two decades, however, a wave of Scandinavian erotic ("blue") films was already a widely recognized export by the early 1970s. By concocting and exploiting a myth of Scandinavian and, especially, female sexual emancipation, Swedish and Danish cinema lent the European art film its own brand of the outré and risqué. Many of these focused specifically, as *Nymphomaniac* would, on the coming of age of a rebellious, sexually driven "nymph." The sensual "summer film," Arne Mattsson's *Hon dansade en sommar* (*One Summer of Happiness*, 1951) was a precursor to Ingmar Bergman's international breakthrough *Sommaren med Monika* (*Summer with Monika*, 1953), whose blend of neorealism, melodrama, and nudity turned Harriet Andersson into Sweden's first postwar erotic star.[87] But the Scandinavian erotic art cinema peaked in the mid-to-late 1960s with two far more explicit films, Mac Ahlberg's *Jeg—en kvinde* (*I, a Woman*, Denmark, 1965) and Vilgot Sjöman's *Jag är nyfiken— en film in gult* and *Jag är nyfiken en film in blåt* (*I am Curious [Yellow]* and *I Am Curious [Blue]*, Sweden, 1967/1968), the latter of which Jack Stevenson pronounced a "watershed event in American popular culture" that helped "set in motion the country's wider sex revolution."[88] Internationally popular Swedish sex education/sexploitation film hybrids followed, including Torgny Wickman's *Ur kärlekens språk* (*Language of Love*) tetralogy (1969–1972) and *Anita—ur en tonårsflickas dagbok* (*Anita: Swedish Nymphet*, 1973), featuring a young Stellan Skarsgård. Moreover, after the 1969 law abolishing censorship of pornography in Denmark, Danish softcore porn became a popular export, perhaps most notably the *Sengekant* (Bedside) series (1970–1976) of eight films directed by John Hilbard that blended pornography with the folk comedy genre.

This transnational trend was precisely the sort that von Trier ought to have appreciated, if primarily in hindsight (as it peaked when he was less than eighteen years old). Scandinavian erotic cinema embodied Danish concepts of *frisind* ("liberalism, libertarianism, broad-mindedness") and *frigjorthed* ("emancipation . . . in relation to conventional norms" of "sexuality and politics"), values that flourished in the 1960s and 1970s[89] and that a precocious Lars Trier, born in 1956 to cultural radical, nudist, feminist parents, cut his teeth on—and flaunts yet simultaneously challenges in his films.[90] Evoking these values and the era (in which the film is partially set) while recapitulating von Trier's own history of provocation, *Nymphomaniac* has brought attention to—and in a sense caps—this

Scandinavian blue heritage and its most successful international exports.[91] These (Swedish and Danish) films cover three sometimes overlapping subgenres: the female coming-of-age narrative, the topical sociopolitical sex film, and the sex education film. In character types, narrative trajectories, and structural and stylistic eccentricities, *Nymphomaniac* has striking and revealing commonalities with this tradition, an awareness of which illuminates the film's conflicted relation to genre, to Scandinavian cultural radicalism, and to feminism.

Von Trier's intense, complex female protagonists, like Joe of *Volume I*, follow on the tradition of Dreyer and Bergman. Whether directly or indirectly, Joe also embodies the popular feminism infusing early Swedish and Danish erotic art films that privileged female desire. Born from erotic summer films of the 1950s, whose settings and themes became motifs in later sexploitation, Scandinavian blue initially followed the naturalism of Mauritz Stiller and Victor Sjöström in placing their heroines in natural settings and associating awakening sexuality with an all-too-brief, idyllic Nordic summer. In *Summer with Monika*, the open sunlit spaces of the Stockholm archipelagos in which Andersson's instinctively pagan Monika is juxtaposed against the oppression of the city as a grim and claustrophobic urban neorealism. Although framed by Harry's (Lars Ekborg) coming of age, the film was unprecedented for the raw sensuality of Andersson's performance and a dramatic shift to Monika's point of view. In an iconic shot near the end of the film to which Truffaut, in *Les quatre cents coups* (*The 400 Blows*, 1959) and von Trier, in *Breaking the Waves*, would pay homage, Monika, having left husband and child for the evening, lights her cigarette from the burning end of another proffered by an unseen man, turns her face to the camera, and stares in defiance at the audience, taking possession of the film. In today's popular imagination the film is less about Harry than about Monika's sexual empowerment and rejection of her designated role as wife and mother, and Harry's story is all but shucked off in the reedited American sexploitation version, Kroger Babb's *Monika: The Story of a Bad Girl* (1955).

As in *Monika*, a sexually inexperienced male protagonist (Skarsgård) provides half of *Nymphomaniac*'s frame story and many of its talking points. But it is Joe who narrates the story of her erotic life, building from her first moments of masturbatory pleasure and underscoring her rejection of domesticity and motherhood. Yet if Joe's affinity with nature, highlighted in her forest walks, resembles Monica's, her sexual empowerment aligns more obviously with *I Am Woman*'s Liv (Essy Persson), based on the 1961 autobiography of a self-diagnosed Danish nymphomaniac, Agnethe Thomsen (as Siv Holm). A young woman from an evangelical family, some of Liv's earliest sexual experiences (like Joe's) are associated with religious ecstasy and her father's virtuoso violin. Soon Liv's demands become threatening to her consorts, as when she mounts her prudish fiancé or strips naked in an open field, her frank desire repelling him. The film ends as a brutal partner's sexualized violence merely stimulates her appetite, and her laughter of self-recognition peals in exultation.

The iconic image of Persson's Liv, head thrown back, lips parted, might have been a prototype for *Nymphomaniac*'s celebrated "O-face" campaign. Like Liv, young Joe revels in her power, seducing a succession of men, and becomes a dispassionate homewrecker shunned by other women. Desensitized by her excess, she similarly seeks out extreme stimulation from a sadistic K (Jamie Bell). Throughout, Joe insists on the persistence of desire and the unfeasibility of monogamy and love, as illustrated in the narrative's overarching and beleaguered relationship with Jerôme. "In love" with Jerôme, and after having his child, she loses the ability to achieve orgasm and lives in a torment of frustration. Unable to satisfy her, Jerôme suggests that she find other men, but her lust persists along with his (and her) jealousy. Hence Joe concludes that love equals "lust plus jealousy," or desire distorted by possessiveness, and early in *Volume II* she leaves Jerôme and their toddler; later, when she finds herself pregnant again, she performs her own coat-hanger abortion. Like Monika and Liv, she is unable to reconcile her *frigjorthed* with the patriarchal family, a theme that corresponds with much of the pro-sex feminism of the 1960s and 1970s. One example is the work of Danish avant-garde feminist and frequent *Suck* magazine contributor Suzanne Brøgger, whose essays in *Deliver Us from Love* attacked monogamy and the patriarchal family.[92] (Von Trier also likely draws on the socialist feminism of his mother.) Thus Schepelern finds that, viewed optimistically, the film can be "seen as a feminist defense of freedom and equality"—specifically, the belief that women have the right, usually reserved for men, to sex without emotional attachment.[93] This view is supported when, forced to undergo sex-addiction therapy or lose her job, Joe responds much like both Monika and Liv; she owns her desire and lifestyle and walks out on "society" altogether.

Nordic Soul-Searching and Negative Didactics

At the outset, Joe warns Seligman that she is a "terrible" human being and that her story will therefore be "long. . . . and moral," indicating that *Nymphomaniac* descends from, yet plays against, a postreligious inheritance of guilt from "cultural father figures" including Søren Kierkegaard, Strindberg, Henrik Ibsen, Dreyer, and Bergman, or the "Nordic soul searching" typified in the Swedish director's angst-filled cinema.[94] In Vilgot Sjöman's *I Am Curious (Yellow)* and *(Blue)*, this tradition was continued and tweaked for the new waves of the 1960s. Blending a lightly humorous tone with the "post-religious equivalent" of angst, it exemplified a "negative didactics" that employed "meta-conscious aesthetics and political reflexivity" to interrogate capitalist society.[95] Described by Stevenson as a "bold" Godardian experiment whose like "Scandinavian cinema would not see until von Trier and the Dogme 95 movement," and as a nearly four-hour, two-volume sexual and ideological odyssey, it anticipated the satirical-analytical-didactic style and experimentalism of *The Idiots* and *Dogville* and, especially, the two-volume *Nymphomaniac*.[96] Shot on location in available light, with the crew often visible (as in *The Idiots*), it rebelled against genre and dramaturgy, blending documentary and fiction and claiming to be plotless and improvised, with a metanarrative about the fraught relationship between director, star Lena Nyman, and her on-and-off love interest Börje. As in *Monika* and *I Am Woman*, the premise concerns its "curious" female protagonist's sexual coming of age; this, however, is inseparable from her equally intense ideological quest, as she interviews, polls, and badgers Stockholm citizens and international celebrities (Olof Palme, Yevgeny Yevtushenko, Martin Luther King Jr.) about class, gender equity, and civil rights, Franco's Spain, and Swedish socialism. Amid these investigations, she explores sexuality to achieve "libidinal rationality," Herbert Marcuse's term for a level of personal development in which sexual mores are understood in relation to the political economy.[97]

By way of a similarly genre-defying digressionism, *Nymphomaniac* brought the Nordic soul-searching tradition into the twenty-first century. Von Trier foregrounds the film's "negative didactics" in an omnivorous range of topics and styles, and its digression-prone frame bleeds into the narrative proper, often engulfing it, with episodes "spontaneously" inspired by articles in Seligman's apartment and embellished with his (and the increasingly competitive Joe's) analysis and analogies, together with other Brechtian/Godardian alienation effects. *Nymphomaniac* and *I Am Curious* are similarly transgressive mixes of pointedly gendered dialogue, explicit sex, identity politics, and social critique. In *I Am Curious*, sex is politicized in discourse over birth control, abortion, and women's rights as well as in the forthright, uneroticized nudity of its heroine Lena Nyman's "flawed" (short, plump, untoned) body. Similarly, Seligman and

Joe speak out on topics for which von Trier has been censured and censored: racist language, anti-Semitism versus anti-Zionism, and misogyny, and Joe's abortion, featured in a graphic sequence followed by a protracted ethical discussion. Joe's slender, androgynous body, like her name, makes its own political statement as the site of the narrative "I," rather than simply the object of the gaze. In the lightly humorous first chapter, "nymphomania" leads to a parody of collective action as Joe and best friend B rebel against "love-fixated society," vow never to have sex twice with the same man, and lead a sex-positive organization for exploring desire. In a sequence reminiscent of von Trier's earlier 1960s "throwback," *The Idiots*, they protest in the streets, vandalize shop windows, and create "happenings," signaling that the adult Joe's personal choices will have social and political implications.

As one of the Scandinavian film industry's top-grossing exports, *I Am Curious* demonstrated that "educational" content in a docudrama format and with social and political relevance was often strategic in mainstreaming Scandinavia's erotic films. Focusing on reception, Kevin Heffernan explores the film's commitment to bore audiences, which paradoxically made the sex acceptable and even hip for the "respectable" American middle class.[98] However, like most of these early Scandinavian erotic art films—only more so—its genre and purpose were in contention. Was it a drama, a romantic comedy, or a dirty movie? Was it a film about current social and political trends and issues? Was it meant to be entertaining, sexually stimulating, instructive, or provocative—or (most likely) all of the above? *Nymphomaniac*'s hybridity bored, confused, polarized, and provoked audiences in similar ways.

Sexploitation or Sex Ed?

Like that of *I Am Curious*, the international success of Torgny Wickman's hardcore documentary *Language of Love* tetralogy had as much to do with its educational and moral pretentions as with its sexually explicit scenes. On the one hand, Sweden's 1955 mandate requiring sex education in schools, together with the popularization of sexology in the work of Kinsey and Masters and Johnson, lent these films legitimacy.[99] The ostensible purpose of *Language of Love* was didactic: to teach healthy sexual practices as well as sexual equality and tolerance. To this end, however, they included sequences of actors performing masturbation, fellatio, heterosexual, and gay, lesbian, and disabled intercourse often enhanced by split screens, diagrams, and animation to show multiple regions of the body simultaneously. Most of the footage, however, was devoted to discourse among middle-aged, tea-drinking experts (including popular Danish sexologists Inge and Sten Hegeler, and Maj-Briht Bergström-Walan) in a casual setting and featured appearances by gynecologist Sture Culhed in a white physician's coat. Excerpts from the films were eventually made into a series of shorts used in Swedish and Danish schools.[100] Internationally, however, *Language of Love* came to epitomize "Swedish sin" after being parodied and mistakenly identified as the "porno" that Robert DeNiro took Cybill Shepherd to in Martin Scorsese's *Taxi Driver* (1976).[101] Nevertheless, the contention over genre—whether such films were sex education or pornography—enhanced their international success.[102]

Although hard to imagine as public school material, *Nymphomaniac* is equally (if differently, and often ironically) "educational," with its middle-aged, tea-drinking couple discoursing tediously about the technicalities and ethics of Joe's sexual history, and with Seligman's (and often Joe's) abstruse commentary de-eroticizing Joe's "porn." Chapters are announced with pedantic title cards—for instance, "Chapter 6: The Eastern and Western Church (The Silent Duck)"—and the "lesson" is spelled out or recapped with superimposed captions, numbers, diagrams, maps, and scrapbook-like inserts. Like *Language*'s graphic comparisons of positions and techniques, Joe's jubilant analogy between having sex with different men and Bach's polyphony (chapter 5) is made via a three-way split-screen. In chapter 2, young Joe, in pigtails and a schoolgirl's uniform in an old-fashioned classroom, using a pointer, map, and her own anatomy to teach herself a series of "lessons," is depicted in a Victorian-styled erotic fantasy montage in Seligman's mind. The film's most shocking sequence, however, may be its most "educational": *Volume II*'s abortion sequence, which, in an abrupt tonal shift, achieves the step-by-step clarity of a YouTube "How To" video.

Wickman's documentaries marketed themselves not only as scientific but as "infused with a sense of didactic mission."[103] While supported similarly by testimonials, scientific materials, and experts, as we have seen, *Nymphomaniac* pointedly diverges from such norms and diagnoses, especially when Joe decisively rejects sex addiction therapy. And if therapy is pointedly built into the confessional narrative situation in a parody of psychoanalysis, with Seligman and his apartment furnishing a couch, the talking cure, and a Rorschach-like association process, this turns blackly satirical in the final scene exposing Seligman's hypocrisy. While recalling *Antichrist*'s therapeutic situation (which facilitates the wife's descent into madness), *Nymphomaniac*'s therapeutic framework also bears uncanny resemblances to *Anita: Swedish Nymphet*, Wickman's fictional case study/romance/softcore hybrid starring voluptuous Christina Lindberg and a young Stellan Skarsgård as Erik, a psychology student whose interest in Anita is an ambiguous blend of intellectual excitement and erotic attraction. Like Joe, Anita is found battered and bruised by Erik, who ministers to her wounds as he listens to her story. Intermittently advised by the kibitzing Professor Lundberg, he turns this "rare and damaged nymphomaniac" into his thesis topic and eventually "cures" her by evoking her first orgasm.

Such parallels caused Darragh O'Donoghue to assume that von Trier "modell[ed]" *Nymphomaniac* on this "niche artifact of Scandi-softcore"[104] (although von Trier has denied having heard of it).[105] If Seligman's vaunted sixtyish virginity is not an ironic reference to the Swedish superstar's early career in Scandinavian erotic cinema, it should be.[106] Yet it is the differences between these two films that are most revealing. If Anita submits to Erik's "scientific" expertise and to sanctified monogamy (the film ends at a church as the organist plays Mendelssohn's *Wedding March*), Joe is increasingly combative and reproves Seligman for responding with the "clichés of our times." Especially near the film's conclusion, Seligman proffers the message that was as "politically correct" (liberal humanist, feminist) in 1960s and 1970s Scandinavia as it is today, defending Joe as a "human being" and a "woman demanding her right" against Joe's protests. Further, where *Anita*'s psychoanalytic frame story is in earnest, *Nymphomaniac* caricatures Freud in Seligman's physical impotence and overly fertile (and often clueless) erudition. Freud attempted to lead his patient to self-understanding through infuriatingly oblique and (for example, in Dora's case) uncomprehending interpretations of the symbols in the patient's dreams, and Seligman's attempts to make sense of Joe's erotic life veer off into abstraction—while playing off the "autistic" side of von Trier himself. Where Erik's therapy "cures" Anita, Seligman betrays Joe's trust in a conclusion whose contrast with *Anita* could not be more stark, thanks to Seligman's role as von Trier's (typically) weak male. Where Anita achieves sexual satisfaction and is integrated into patriarchal monogamy, sexual fulfillment persistently eludes Joe, who ends up a social outcast.

Scandinavian art films with graphic sex confounded audience expectations shaped by genre, and *Nymphomaniac* plays off the same kind of confusion with knowing wickedness. With its plethora of effects that replicate the apparatus of an "educational" film, *Nymphomaniac* deconstructs its own "porn," rendering it first into light comedy but, finally, in *Volume II*, lending it a darkly unstable, "feel-bad" irony. Likewise, through its confessional/"therapeutic" narrative concluding in noncommunication and disaster, as well as Joe's negative experience with group therapy and abortion counseling, it eviscerates therapy culture. Finally, in parodying the discourses of sex education and therapy culture, *Nymphomaniac* mocks the idea that sexuality can be understood from a rational and "healthy" perspective. The parallels highlight von Trier's frustration of audience expectations, whether for a positive therapeutic outcome, for sexual arousal, or for a conclusion with a "meaning."

The fallout from the Scandinavian blue era included a global flood of pornographic films and a more conservative cultural climate. As the appetite for sex films spread overseas, Scandinavian exports began to imitate the American exploitation that their earlier erotic films had in part made possible, and the erotic art film became passé—or hardcore sequences were clandestinely inserted into their narrative settings.[107] And as the erotic art film yielded to overt sexploitation, the humiliation of the sexualized woman in a noirish or Sadean setting became a fixture, as in *Dværgen* (*The Sinful Dwarf*, 1973), and a number of films about "decadent" Copenhagen. This trend provoked a late 1970s and 1980s shift in which second-wave feminist ideology (especially in the United States and the UK) became dominated by an anti-porn crusade. Sadly, the Nordic "nymph," once associated with bucolic sex, became an exploitation cliché. So if the pessimistic and graphically violent turn taken by the end of *Volume II* was predictable from von Trier's earlier films, it also followed an-all-too-common trajectory in which, as in as in Bo Arne Virbenus's *Thriller: en grym film* (*Thriller: A Cruel Picture* / a.k.a. *They Call Her One-Eye*, 1973), the hypersexualized woman is punished or retaliates on a massive scale. Becoming addicted to pain as she once was to pleasure, alienating Jerôme and neglecting her child, Joe joins the criminal underworld as an extortionist who uses sexualized torture and blackmail. Repeated overstimulation results in a loss of sensation, her genitals a massive sore, crippling her passion for life.

Like early Scandinavian sexploitation, and as usual for von Trier, *Nymphomaniac* embodies a fundamental contradiction: between Joe's defiant assertions that her sexuality is natural, healthy, empowering, and essential to her identity, as demonstrated in *Volume I*, and her insistence that it is an affliction or addiction, her abjection deserved, as suggested by the end of *Volume II*. This contradiction (or trajectory) is exacerbated by the fact that Seligman, the postfeminist man, caricatured as an asexual yet would-be rapist, provides the mouthpiece for the film's "feminist" messages (as will be explored further). Or with how, despite the nods to feminism (often articulated by Seligman and shot down by Joe) *Nymphomaniac* "sideline[s] any kind of female community."[108] From Monika to Liv, Lena, and Anita, the sexually adventurous woman is a loner abhorred by "good girls," wives, and mothers. Despite the emphasis on female friendship and solidarity in *Volume I*, Joe becomes an anathema to the married woman Mrs. H (Uma Thurman) and makes short work of a female support group, and her mentorship of her young female ward P ends in betrayal.

Difficult to classify, whether as art or exploitation, feminism or misogyny, fiction or documentary, sex-ed or pornography, didacticism or sensationalism, these hybrid Scandinavian sexploitation films brought sexuality and politics together in cinematic discourse, breaking ground as they roused censors and brewed scandals. In the early twenty-first century, *Nymphomaniac* is similarly if more radically divided in intention, genre, tonality, and meaning. Whatever the case, the film has restaged the controversies surrounding sex and female agency that these Nordic films once inspired, to provoke and to generate debate in today's porn-saturated yet reactionary climate.

NYMPHOMANIAC'S SADEAN DISCOURSE

If its title identifies *Nymphomaniac* as a throwback to the 1960s and 1970s, the term itself dates much further back, however, to eighteenth-century medicine, so that the film reminded critic J. Hoberman of an obscure doctor's tome, *Nymphomania, or A Dissertation Concerning the Furor Uterinus* (D. T. de Bienville, 1775) the first scientific study of female hypersexuality.[109] A more direct eighteenth-century link, however, is with the Marquis de Sade, with whose works von Trier has had a long-term engagement, and that he mentioned revisiting while planning the film in 2011.[110] Although the publicity played off of the film's hardcore content, and the hype followed suit, the true site of its vaunted obscenity, as in Sade, is both its discourse (beginning with the archly scandalous title spelled with a gaping set of parentheses in place of the "o"), and its premise as the narrative of a female libertine.[111]

As Joe narrates the picaresque story of her life—or her genitals, as she has little use for love, family, or career in any conventional meaning—Skarsgård's

Seligman comments at length, drawing on a massively eclectic knowledge base that includes everything *but* sex, as *Nymphomaniac* dissects and theorizes Joe's "pornographic" narrative through Seligman's abstruse digressions and baroque visual illustrations. Von Trier's most flamboyantly allusive film, it references or reflects a surfeit of musical, literary, religious, and historical texts: Bach, Handel, Mozart, Rammstein, Isaac Walton (*The Compleat Angler*, 1653), Proust, Mann, Dostoevsky, Poe, *One Thousand and One Nights*, Brecht, and *The Story of O*—one likely source for the parenthesis in the title—along with most of von Trier's own previous works. But, as *Film Comment*'s Nick James, suggests, it is Sade whom von Trier "channels" as he had done at least since *The Orchid Gardener* in 1978, his application film for the Danish Film School.[112] In that *Nymphomaniac* is an archive of references to von Trier's previous films, reading it through a Sadean lens can illuminate some of the central controversies raised by his work. One is whether, in a twenty-first-century context, its "Sadean" strategies are provocative and, if so, how.

In 1978, von Trier's interest in Sade was filtered through cinematic obsessions such as *The Night Porter* and *Salò*, as shown in *The Orchid Gardener* in a series of tableaux in which he stars, posing alternately as a naked Christ figure; as a woman who wrenches the head off a bird, smearing her/his cheek with blood; and as a Nazi officer who dips a whip in honey and then salt. An episode from his Danish film school career is more explicit, however: "I wrote a script for *Philosophie dans la boudoir.* . . . A grand drama in three acts, splendidly vulgar. . . . But Gert Fredholm, who taught direction, told me to destroy the script. It wasn't enough that I couldn't make the film. Any evidence that a script made for a film like that had been written at film school had to be destroyed!"[113] This experience becomes a funny and pivotal sequence in *De unge år: Erik Nietzsche sagaen del 1* (*The Early Years: Erik Nietzsche, Part I*, 2007), von Trier's somewhat fictionalized autobiographical script, directed by Jacob Thuesen, which he narrated in voiceover. The title character protests, to no avail, that "Sade was a revolutionary in his day," and this brutal suppression changes the sensitive young Nietzsche into a cynical, opportunistic—and successful—filmmaker. Von Trier evidently turned this act of censorship into a challenge: to make "Sadean" films, much as Sade had been challenged by his incarcerations in the Bastille to write *Les 120 journées de Sodome ou l'école du libertinage* (*120 Days of Sodom*, 1785) and *Justine* (1791). Hence was born one of von Trier's basic strategies, of converting provocation into art—that is, turning prohibitions or taboos into prerequisites, rules, or even controlling principles for his films and initiatives. The unwritten rules for a Hollywood film became the prohibitions of the Dogme 95 "Vow of Chastity," and his USA: Land of Opportunity trilogy was inspired by critics who attacked him for setting *Dancer in the Dark* in the United States without ever having visited it.[114]

He went on to adapt elements from Sade's novels in several of the most important films of his maturity. The first draft of *Breaking the Waves*, a female melodrama turned into an excruciating "spectacle of suffering," a form of provocation that has become his trademark, was first written as an erotic drama adapted from Sade's *Justine*.[115] He modeled Bess and Grace of *Dogville*, who are subjected to different kinds of sexual slavery, on Sade's Justine, whose name is given to the clinically depressed heroine of *Melancholia*. *Dogville* and *Manderlay*, von Trier's most obviously political films, concur with Michel Foucault's understanding of the sadomasochism inherent in power relations and conclude in sadistic applications of that point designed to make audiences squirm.[116] *Melancholia*'s Justine, whose depression places her beyond sexuality or the affairs of the world, may be an ironic homage. But, thus far, von Trier's Sadean allusions and affinities had functioned primarily on the level of theme, characterization, structure, and affect, including some or all of the following: the featuring of an innocent and/or promiscuous heroine, a novelistic mode, overbearing allegory, and deliberately monotonous repetition with variation and building through increasingly intense modes and levels of torture and suffering, not least the audience's.

Nymphomaniac arguably culminated von Trier's obsession with Sade to that point. On the most obvious level it poses as a pornographic film that plays off the oppositional perspectives embodied in the intersecting, Janus-faced *Justine* and *Juliette*, originally published as *Histoire de Juliette ou les Prospérités du vice* (*Juliette, or Vice Amply Rewarded*, 1797–1981). Together the two novels demonstrate Sade's lesson that vice will invariably triumph over virtue. Two orphaned sisters come of age in pre-Revolutionary France and take opposite paths. Sade opposed the Enlightenment philosophies of Jean-Jacques Rousseau and Thomas Hobbes, which attempted to reconcile nature, reason, and virtue as basis of ordered society, understanding nature to be unreasonable, violent, and destructive, and a life of hedonism and crime to constitute the only reasonable existential response. Thus, Sade deems Justine's virtue perverse and "well-chastised"—so that, in von Trier's words, she is "exploited, raped, or whipped by everyone she meets," with "everyone" grouped into representatives of the church, the aristocracy, the sciences, and the law.[117] Justine's devotion to "virtue" leads inevitably to her degradation until she is split down the middle by a bolt of lightning to the amusement of the omniscient narrator, who concludes with this "politically correct" moral: "May you be convinced . . . that true happiness is to be found nowhere but in Virtue's womb," capped with a winking reference to "compensation by Heaven's most dazzling rewards."[118] A mocking inversion of Samuel Richardson's novel *Pamela; or, Virtue Rewarded* (1740), the revised 1791 edition was *Justine, ou de Malheurs de la Vertu* (*Or, Good Conduct Well Chastised*). Or, as Guillaume Apollinaire wrote over a century ago, as quoted in the prefatory note to the 1949 Pauvert edition of *Juliette*, Justine is "woman as she has been hitherto: enslaved, miserable and less than human."[119]

In contrast, *Nymphomaniac*'s Joe is a sexual outlaw from the beginning. Having "discovered" her "cunt at the age of two," she lives in pursuit of untrammeled desire—and so is more like *Juliette*, Justine's opposite. If Justine is killed off by a derisive narrator, Juliette's education in pleasurable depravity enables her to thrive, to acquire wealth, luxury, and power. This begins with a coterie of lascivious lesbian nuns and is followed by a succession of libertine nobles who exhaust perverse variations on sexual congress and engage in incest, torture, murder, and cannibalism. *Nymphomaniac*'s Joe embodies aspects of both of Sade's heroines. The frame story introduces her as a type of Justine, as abject, betrayed both by her lesbian lover P and her former lover Jerôme, who have left her beaten and urinated on in an alley, setting us up to expect that, like most von Trier heroines, she will be punished. But Joe is no martyr; obeying her nature, rejecting conventional mores, she lives out her desires and can be seen as a somewhat humanized twenty-first-century pro-sex postfeminist version of Juliette. Desensitized by her excesses, Joe seeks out "dangerous men" and increasingly more extreme sources of stimulation, including sadomasochism. Eventually forced to accept therapy or lose her job, she responds by owning her "cunt and [her] filthy dirty lust." In her final career move, Joe assumes a more performative and proactive sadomasochism: employed by L (a suavely sinister Willem Dafoe), she works as an extortionist who sniffs out men's secret sex "crimes" (masochism or pedophilia, for example) and, backed by a couple of heavies, finesses the most appropriate sexual tortures. Like Juliette, she finds satisfaction in sadism and crime while training her much younger lesbian lover in the business. Thus, like Sade and his imitators, whose porn scenes are repeated in increasingly violent and deviant permutations, von Trier works through repetition, complication, and intensification. Yet perhaps we should think of *Nymphomaniac* as "the book . . . Sade never got to write," in that Joe is *neither* Justine nor Juliette, but "a hybrid: a woman driven by deep and not entirely comprehended desires . . . in conflict with equally incomprehensible social norms," as Lowry Pressly asserts in *Los Angeles Review of Books*.[120]

Still, *Nymphomaniac* is arguably concerned less with what Schepelern calls the "summing up of the woman" central to von Trier's greatest films since *Medea*, than about its own discourse of excess, its desire or compulsion to "say everything."[121] Now that von Trier "has made an unmistakably Sadean film," Pressly continues, it's "funny and . . . telling" that the reviews highlight the sex, when "as in . . . Sade, the site of the film's eroticism is in its discourse, in the telling of the story."[122] Orgy scenes alternate with lengthy philosophical treatises—with Juliette and her entourage of rogues joining other libertines for a session of "frigging" followed by treatises on theology, morality, aesthetics, naturalism, and metaphysics. "You have killed me with voluptuousness. Let's sit down and discuss," says the heroine after one such orgy in an example noted by Barthes, the "discussion" modulating into another orgy that ups the ante in kinky violence.[123] Often "anticipating Freud, but also inverting him, describing it in the same terms as the orator's art, Sade makes sperm the substitute for speech" and vice versa.[124] In *Nymphomaniac*, Joe's narrative/libidinal drive, demonstrated through von Trier's variations on hardcore porn, is pointedly matched by the florid vigor of his Enlightenment-style rhetoric (or digressionism) of her interlocutor. This is peppered with topics on which von Trier has been censured in the name of political correctness—such as Joe's use and staunch defense of sexist and racist words (including "cunt," "nymphomaniac," and "Negro")—and Seligman's distinction between anti-Semitism and anti-Zionism (which provide a defense of von Trier's remarks about Israel being "a pain in the ass" during the Cannes 2011 press conference). More often, however, Seligman's discourse, much like Sade's savage parody of classical reasoning used to support Enlightenment ideals, is the butt of the joke, as Seligman is another in the long line of overweeningly rational and verbose male characters ridiculed in von Trier's films.[125] Representing Logos, they are often philosophers (*Dogville*'s Tom Edison), psychotherapists (*Antichrist*'s He), or pompous amateur scientists (*Melancholia*'s John). As a pedantic version of the intellectual omnivore, Seligman resembles all three. As Joe tells of her sexual escapades, competing for narrative dominance, Seligman comments, analyzes, and catechizes, usually on abstract topics such as Fibonacci numbers or church history, with Joe increasingly responding in turn on practical mechanics: of parallel parking, eight-cylinder engine spark plug caps, James Bond's Walther PPK automatic, and the like. A Gargantuan hybrid, an intermediary cross between cinema, novel, compendium, and essay, all in all the film most closely resembles the Menippean satire, anatomy, or novel of ideas, an essayistic, often dialogic, and implicitly satirical genre favored by Sade's greatest (and lengthiest) hits.

What distinguishes *Nymphomaniac* from von Trier's previous Sadean films is the elaborateness of its cinematic adaptation of a Sadean discourse, two types of which correspond with the film's two volumes. The first, which prevails in *Volume I*, is "saying everything" (through repetition and variation, as theorized by Roland Barthes and Marcel Hénaff).[126] The second, featured in the unmediated, corporeal sadomasochism of *Volume II*, is that of "showing everything," or "speaking the unspeakable," as Peter Michelson puts it.[127] Both are types of anatomy, the first figurative, the second literal.

Volume I: "Saying Everything"

For Barthes (writing in *Sade/Fourier/Loyola*), Sade reduces the erotic scenario entirely to discourse, and for Hénaff's Sade, "there is no sexual pleasure that is not spoken. . . . the libertine body . . . must speak incessantly of its own doings."[128] Sade's goal was encyclopedic, or "the saturation of the Catalog"; moreover, pleasure (via vice or crime) "exists only in proportion to the quantity of language invested in it."[129] Quality is not without importance, however. Barthes notes that one of Sade's most common rhetorical tropes is therefore "metonymic violence": juxtaposing "heterogeneous fragments belonging to spheres of language . . . ordinarily kept separate by moral-social taboo."[130] "To bring together incest, adultery, sodomy, and sacrilege," for instance, a man "buggers his married daughter with a host [as in wafer]." Another sentence juxtaposes "the church, 'fine style,' and pornography," and so on.[131] Von Trier relishes this sort of figure, which resembles an elaborate form of swearing. In chapter 3, the medieval Catholic *Confiteor, mea maxima culpa,* is hilariously reiterated as *mea vulva, mea maxima vulva,* the self-loving pro-sex credo of Joe's adolescent clique, only to reemerge, as Lynne Huffer notes, "as the secular humanist" confession of twelve-step recovery: "My name is Joe, and I'm a nymphomaniac." In a blasphemous tableau related at the beginning of *Volume II*, one that inverts the transfiguration of Christ, Joe relates her memory of her first orgasm at the age of ten as a spiritual epiphany. This is rendered as a levitation scene, one that alludes to *Antichrist* by way of a mystical sex scene between the protagonist and a "witch" in Andrey Tarkovsky's *Offret* (*The Sacrifice*, 1986), and is capped by a vision of two women, clothed in light and hovering over the ground, whom Seligman identifies as the "notorious" nymphomaniac Valeria Messalina, the third wife of the Roman Emperor Claudius and the whore of Babylon.

While von Trier delights in such impious inversions, more notable and pervasive is the film's visual representation of the body in ways that dissect, moralize, politicize, and de-eroticize Joe's porn. Beauvoir observes that, rather than evoking or explaining erotic affect, Sade's minutely detailed representations of debauchery "systematically exhaust the anatomical possibilities of the human body."[132] Von Trier sustains a similar alienation effect through similar means. Indeed, if *Nymphomaniac*'s form was intended to be free and open-ended, the sex was just the opposite: exhaustive in scope and elaborately constructed to conform to games, rules, and conditions, this rigor intensified by the on-set constrictions on filming the graphic sex scenes with body doubles.[133] In a comprehensive analysis of Sade's poetics, philosopher and anthropologist Marcel Hénaff details Sade's replacement of the (idealized and figurative pre-Enlightenment) "lyrical body" with the "libertine body": the body demystified, mechanically reduced to its materiality by Enlightenment rationalism and turned into a "pleasure robot."[134] Expressing—and travestying—the biological reductionism of the "medical gaze," the libertine body is the body anatomized, turned over to "the scalpel of classifying reason," much as explored by Foucault in *The Birth of the Clinic* (1973): "Dis-affected from any expressive relationship . . . the Sadean body ultimately models itself on flayed matter, the *échorcé*, of the medical dissecting lab. [It] is by definition a body exhibited, divided up, and inventoried, which is why it is so lightly handed over to the torturer."[135] One probable influence was the early French materialist Julien Offray de La Mettrie's *L' Homme Machine* (*Man a Machine*, 1748), which Sade read with enthusiasm.[136] In *Nymphomaniac*, what often comes across merely as abstraction and alienation is savagely political as well as psychosomatic.

Although Hénaff organizes Sade's poetics into five rhetorical elements, I focus on the first two, representation, or "the demystified body" and the "will to say everything," which often overlap in the examples to follow.[137] In *Nymphomaniac*, as in Sade, the libertine body is anatomized, de-eroticized, and politicized through a plethora of visual and rhetorical devices involving nondiegetic, often noncinematic text, as mentioned previously: spelling out the lesson in overlaid captions, diagrams, and maps, shifts of aspect ratio or from color to black-and-white, scrapbook-like inserts, and so forth. One of these is arithmetical reduction or the quantification of the body, a practice at which Sade's Juliette is especially adept. (In the current era she would be texting or tweeting mid-orgy to report on her friends' latest round of ejaculations and orifices.) At the Monastery of the White Friar, Clairwil is "fucked another fifteen times in the mouth, ten in the cunt, and thirty-nine in the ass; and I forty-six in the ass, eight in the mouth, and ten in the cunt. All told, another two hundred fuckings each."[138]

Likewise, in *Nymphomaniac*, the body is quantified and dissected through enumerations of thrusts, strategies and appendages (the silent duck), sex toys (whips), lovers, and catalogues (of body parts). In chapter 2, Joe tells at length of being "relieved of [her] virginity" by Jerôme, who completes the task in eight laconic thrusts: three vaginal and five from behind (Sade's favored orifice), in a rigorously organized sequence with numbers superimposed on the screen. (Seligman portentously interjects that three plus five is a Fibonacci sequence, which becomes a recursive motif.) This episode exemplifies Jerôme's and Seligman's (stereotypically male) abstraction. But Joe's sexual prowess cum addiction is exponentially matched by her increasing quantification and dissection of sex—for example, in her technique of masturbating on the train to fetishized images of singular parts of various men's anatomies that remind her of Jerôme's features, represented on the screen as a silhouette with a jigsaw puzzle or paper-doll-like dissection of his body, and in her techno-prowess (demonstrated in parallel parking, with eight-cylinder engines, and guns).

Joe's obsession with adding and upping the ante lends irony to the paradox in which, as Schepelern suggests, satiety eludes her, comparing it to Metz's "imaginary object" of desire.[139] In an ironic commentary on Joe's "Fill all my holes" refrain, at a posh restaurant Jerôme promises her a fiver if she can insert a dessert spoon "up into her cunt." She inserts seven or eight, which clang one by one to the floor as she exits. Eventually, as Hénaff explains, "because the [libertine] body is divided up, mechanized, and quantified, amorous relationships can mean nothing but combinations, which can be attained only through the construction of a system of variations meant to establish the greatest number of articulations among available bodies."[140] In *Volume I*, the result is a variation on what Jan Simons calls von Trier's "game cinema," approached as a collection of data (characters and locations) and algorithms (roles or actions) that together define a field of possibilities (a matrix or state space) and graphically illustrated in the way that *Dogville* and *Manderlay* are laid out on a sound stage like board games.[141] By adapting a trope from the eighteenth-century epistolary novel in which Joe's friends, business associates, and sex partners alike are designated by alphabetical letters, von Trier suggests the extent to which Joe's lovers become cyphers and combinations thereof. From the beginning, young Joe approaches sex successively as a sport, a game, and (apropos of Dogme 95) a secret society with vows and rules. In her first real sexual escapade, she and best friend B compete to see who can have sex with the most men on a train (in a sport Seligman compares to fly fishing), with numbers highlighted on an imaginary scoreboard. Where B racks up points quickly, Joe lags behind but ultimately wins by five points by betting on S, a "difficult" man who insists that he is saving his sperm for his ovulating wife and requires a complicated set of moves. Next, Joe's adolescent "flock" of girlfriends form a secret society and take a vow of promiscuity (inverting Dogme's vow of chastity), swearing never to have sex with the same man twice, and confess both their conquests and violations of this rule. Then, as a young adult with several appointments a day, she makes decisions and creates variations by rolling dice, assigning each number a reply ranging from "almost passionate" (1) to "no answer" (6).

Searching for a musical equivalent for Sade's writing, scholar Philippe Sollers seizes on Bach's contrapuntalism, and it is no accident that chapter 5, *Volume I*'s final sequence, embraces an analogy between Joe's sexual experience (which she limits for the sake of illustration to three men) and Bach's baroque organ music. This is dissected through a three-way split screen to convey the contrapuntal

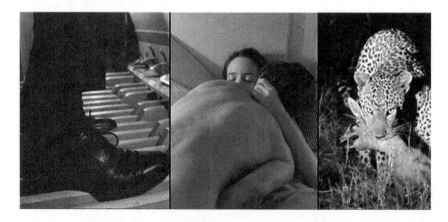

FIGURE 3.4 *Volume I* ends in a virtuoso three-way split-screen sequence that embraces an analogy between Joe's multisensory polysexual experience and the contrapuntal polyphony of Bach's "Ich ruf zu dir, Herr Jesu Christ" from *The Little Organ Book.*

polyphony of "Ich ruf zu dir, Herr Jesu Christ" from *Orgelbüchlein* (*The Little Organ Book*, 1708–1726).[142] Articulating the multisensory and polyphonic nature of Joe's cumulative sexual experience, this is the film's most expressive sequence. Yet its technical virtuosity only serves to demonstrate how far we've come from a pre-Enlightenment "lyrical" body.

Von Trier is clearly indulging his own, well-publicized obsession with numbers, rules, and games. Applied to sexual bodies, however, the effect is distinctly Sadean even as he adapts it to his own purposes. Overall it produces a *Verfremdungseffekt* that speaks of Joe's detachment, which Schepelern explores and that might, in another context, be analyzed in the light of what Hénaff calls, apropos of Sade's texts, "apathetic desire,"[143] or alienation from others and herself, while provoking the equivalent—analysis and intellectual/esthetic appreciation as opposed to arousal—in the spectator.[144] Like reading Sade, watching the director's cut of *Nymphomaniac* is, and supposed to be, repetitive, tedious, and painful, a matter of suffering on the audience's part. As Nicola Evans suggests, in von Trier's films "the passage of time itself" is a masochistic experience.[145] Hence in today's reactionary yet sex-saturated climate, *Volume I* is provocative paradoxically for the Sadean abstraction of its dissection of Joe's porn.

The question remains: Beyond all these effects and in-jokes, what is von Trier's purpose or message? And how do we square von Trier's Sadean discourse with Hallund's understanding of the film as "life-affirming," or with the positive and collaborative filmmaking experience described by Hallund, Wiedemann, Pearce, and Claro? In Sade, such rhetorical strategies are equally sadomasochistic on a personal level and, arguably, satirical on a sociopolitical one. For example, Horkheimer and Adorno interpret Juliette's calculating and ruthless behavior as representing Sade's critique of the "bourgeois subject freed from all tutelage,"[146] the embodiment of an Enlightenment philosophy in which reason, detached from experience and suffering, becomes identical with domination.[147] In *Nymphomaniac*, however, it is Seligman's detachment that entertains and exasperates by turns until the end, when his hypocrisy is directly exposed. As for Joe's Juliette-like blend of apathy and hedonism and how we're supposed to feel about it, this is a more complex problem.

Which brings us to the issue that comes up in any discussion of Sade and von Trier: the woman in the text, misogyny, feminism, and—perhaps ultimately—the way the woman is used in the film as a provocation and for effect. This is especially crucial when *Volume II* shifts from the rhetorical or figurative anatomy of *Volume I* to anatomy in the literal, unmediated, corporal sense, to overt sadomasochism staged as (woman's) melodrama and calculated to make audiences suffer.

Yet, as Hénaff asserts of Sade, "only women [being associated with nature] are accorded the privileged function of the narrative *I . . . historienne*, or storyteller,"[148] with their libertine interlocutors [aligned with male culture] supplying the analysis.[149] This is important if, as Barthes has said, "the master is he who speaks; the object is he or she who remains silent . . . separate by a mutilation more absolute than any erotic torture."[150] Juliette represents the paradox of the female libertine narrator, whose body/text transgresses gender identity. According to Apollinaire, quoted in the prefatory note to the 1949 Pauvert edition, Sade wanted woman to be "free as a man," calling Juliette "the woman whose advent [Sade] anticipated, a figure of whom minds have as yet no conception, who is arising out of mankind . . . who shall renew the world."[151] From Apollinaire's perspective, "Fill all my holes," Joe's nymphomaniacal refrain, would be an assertion of insatiable, polymorphous desire, and a refusal of monogamy, the procreative imperative, and the social order—or Hallund's Joe, whose "free sexuality" is "an existential celebration of life."[152]

In many respects Joe *is* Sade's revolutionary, a sexual outlaw who has "no use for society, [as] society has no use for me," calling her therapy group leader "society's morality police, whose duty is to erase my obscenity from the surface of the earth." This speech, which follows Joe's abrupt exit from therapy, is followed by an equally abrupt cut to a shot of Joe setting a car on fire—to the Talking Heads' "Burning Down the House." At least two prominent feminists have defended Sade in ways that illuminate this moment and Joe's choices in general. Simone de Beauvoir's "Must We Burn Sade" (1951–1952) defended Sade for his critique of bourgeois institutions, ideology, clichés, and false comforts.[153] Humorously, but similarly, Joe and B protest against bourgeois "love" as "lust with jealousy added" and institutionalized in patriarchal heterosexual monogamy, and by the end of *Volume II*, Joe's love for Jerôme ends in her domestic entrapment, frigidity, betrayal, and battery. A major theme is her rebellion against the maternal role, resulting in her abandonment of her child, her subsequent abortion, and her "foster" daughter P's corruption and betrayal.[154] The film can be appreciated further by way of Angela Carter's *The Sadeian Woman and the Ideology of Pornography* (1978), which approached Sade as a political satirist and paradigm for a "moral pornographer," whose texts might be read as a "critique of current relations between the sexes." Aiming for "the total demystification of the flesh and the subsequent revelation, through the infinite modulations of the sexual act, of the real relations of man and his kind," such a pornographer might "penetrate to the [obscene] heart of the contempt for women that distorts our culture."[155] Neither Sade nor von Trier, however, is ever that straightforward.

That said, *Nymphomaniac* arguably culminates von Trier's long-term interest in female-audience-oriented eroticism. In the late 1990s, von Trier's Zentropa Entertainments became the first mainstream company to produce (quite successful) hardcore pornography through its subsidiary Puzzy Power, whose manifesto called for pornography produced and directed for women by women. While authored by a man (with significant input from women), *Nymphomaniac*'s male gaze is deflated by Seligman's asexuality and qualified by the slender androgyny of Gainsbourg and Martin. Female sexuality is portrayed overall as "polyphonic"—surveying the variations that female pleasure and pain can take—hence subverting the phallic "Law." That quest, however, is unsuccessful, as the sadomasochistic melodrama of *Volume II* makes clear.

Volume II: Showing Everything / Speaking the Unspeakable

In nearly all of von Trier's films since the Europe trilogy, male power is a pretense asserted in order to be deflated. In *Nymphomaniac* this theme is literalized in a succession of jokes about male genital vulnerability, as in Joe's oral rape of the aforementioned would-be father to the hangdog clinginess of Mr. H, and the sexual exhaustion of Jerôme. In an episode—based on a testimonial—featuring Joe with two African brothers with impressive "dueling" erections, von Trier delights in violating the taboo against showing erect penises (outside of porn) while joking about penis size fetishization (especially in porn). While the elephant in this room is over-the-top racist stereotyping implicit in Joe's (and von Trier's) exoticization of Black male sexuality, the primary joke is that the men are less interested in Joe's body than in competing with each other through that body as they argue in dialect over who gets which of her orifices. In the opposite way, Joe's "morphological study" of flaccid penises displayed in a brisk series of stills (which Romney calls the "penile equivalent to mug shots") reverses the compositional rhetoric of porn.[156] Overall, as Joe acquires exotic specimens to "fill all [her] holes," the film flaunts male frontal nudity as much as, if not more than, female nudity, playing off the vulnerability of the male genitals, whether erect or soft, confronting the heterosexist male gaze with its literalization in abject flesh. It is no accident that the last dick we see is Seligman's "very floppy" one (as described by Skarsgård, quoting von Trier).[157]

Von Trier's hardcore close-ups are sensational, but, as Rosalind Galt has noted, the purpose of the sensation is "the overturning of conventional ideologies of image composition," destabilizing patriarchal visuality. When Joe's father dies, his corpse in the background is framed by Joe's legs in a necrophilic female-subjective money shot: the eye is drawn to the drop of liquid running down her right thigh, provoking simultaneous "repulsion, arousal, and empathy" while "privileging . . . female sexual pleasure over patriarchal scripts."[158] When in close-up, female genitals, like the aforementioned penises, are rendered clinically (that is, unmediated and corporal) in images that thwart a conventional erotic or sadomasochistic response—for example, in the sequences in which Joe is whipped by Jamie Bell's dominator K. (By contrast, consider Dakota Johnson's rosy bottom in Fifty Shades of Grey.) In shots of the fifty-year-old Joe's genitals after years of abuse, the pornographic affect of arousal is sabotaged by a literalization of woman as bleeding wound—as it is to a more traumatizing effect in Antichrist's rendering of She's autocliteradectomy.

Von Trier's disturbing porn close-ups compel us either to look away or to watch analytically and, often, politically. A case in point is the film's protracted BDSM subplot (chapter 6) presided over by K, who names Joe "Fido" and deploys an assortment of knots, whips, and lashes, as well as the "silent duck" (fisting) to provoke orgasm, and, as Richard Brophy comments, von Trier films the "sadomasochistic relationship" with a real "verve, an excitement . . . missing from the rest of the movie."[159] Together, Seligman and Joe strain to explain her attraction to sexualized violence and pain. Seligman asks what K's "business" is, and Joe explains it as "a system of violence" not unlike that of many Western institutions, with Seligman commenting that "the Passion of Christ" is "full of systematic violence. Via Dolorosa. . . . The thirty-nine lashes." It should be noted that in making cruelty "a new kind of pleasure principle," Sade subverted the mystifications inherent in the mind-body dualism of the Enlightenment.[160] Perhaps we are to see, by way of Sade, Antonin Artaud, Georges Bataille, and Michel Foucault, how violence informs the power relations represented in our institutions, expressing our true passion, our real savagery, and how we disavow sadomasochism at our peril.

Further, as Galt suggests, in the BDSM scenario of Volume II, von Trier is staging his own relationship with the spectator in a consensual role-playing game. K, the dominant, stands for the filmmaker as he constructs suspense, desire and sensation. The rules are two: "I don't fuck you" and "We have no safe word"—in a provocation of a "politically correct" audience response: if she enters his apartment, she must submit to whatever he chooses to do to her. We enter into a similar (masochistic and "politically incorrect") pact when we submit to a von Trier film, with its "complex affect layering [and destablilizing] bodily, emotional, and political responses" that promises something sensational or exhilarating, but whose requisite is pain.[161]

Three examples of sadomasochistic affect staged as melodrama in *Volume II* adapt but depart from Sade in ways that set off von Trier's provocation strategy as distinctive. One is the director's cut's reputedly "unwatchable" ten-minute self-administered coat-hanger abortion, which provoked several walkouts at Venice,[162] allegedly caused three men to faint at the gala Copenhagen premiere, and leaves Seligman, for the first time, speechless.[163] This sequence cross-cuts between external and internal shots that are mediated by Joe's heaving screams: from Joe's hands and tools and "bleeding wound" to MRIs of the fetus as she extracts it, until an overhead shot reveals a tiny bloody fetus between her legs. In *Juliette* and *120 Days of Sodom* the Sadean libertine viewed the stillborn fetus merely as excrement; this sequence forces us to look at the issue, directly and at length, from opposing perspectives that Joe refuses to acknowledge consciously. A close-up of the coat hanger, a symbol employed by pro-choice groups to recall the brutal specter of illegal abortion in the pre–*Roe v. Wade* era, compels viewers to experience Joe's pain and to take a liberal perspective. The black-and-white MRI video image, on the other hand, is shocking outside of its clinical context (Joe is lying on her own kitchen floor) and packs a self-reflexive triple message: it reminds us of the institutional/medical gaze that determines whose, and in what contexts, flesh may be privileged, probed, or anatomized at the same time that it exposes the effects of the procedure on the fetus, all the while reminding us that we are watching.[164] Taken all together, the sequence conveys a pro-choice message yet suggests right-wing pro-life displays forced on bystanders, traumatizing the spectator by hitting as many trigger points as possible.

The extremes of *Volume II* may be explained further in terms of Artaud's Theatre of Cruelty, designed to erase the line between pain and pleasure, transforming these oppositions into "an undifferentiated intensity that defies classification" but that was intended to be healing.[165] Artaud employed the word *cruelty* "in the sense of an appetite for life" that was both creative and destructive but emphasized destruction to counter the mollifications of

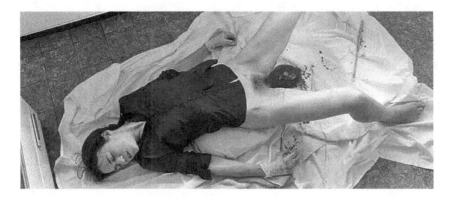

FIGURE 3.5 The ten-minute self-administered coat-hanger abortion sequence in *Volume II* of *Nymphomaniac: The Director's Cut* conveys a pro-choice message while having the effect of right-wing pro-life displays designed to traumatize spectators, thus hitting multiple trigger points.

civilization.[166] In Elena Del Rio's interpretation, the abortion scene is cruel with a rigor and precision that inverts the site Joe's desire and pleasure (the act of fucking via penetration and release via extraction) into self-inflicted pain and mutilation.[167] As Artaudian cruelty, the scene confronts the audience with an extremity that forces us beyond language and the self and results in the disorganization of the bourgeois body. Additionally, in the scene in which Joe tortures the pedophile, she and the viewer watch his experience of simultaneous, therefore intolerable, desire and humiliation as his body and emotions betray his identity. To the extent that we identify both with him and with Joe's cruelty, we experience a disruption of the binary systems of right and wrong, politically correct and incorrect.

The film's last few moments are unwatchable in another sense, and they bewilder, disturb, or enrage even the most favorably disposed audiences.[168] Seligman, who until now has been Joe's ideal interlocutor and first real friend, makes an attempt—as cringe-worthy as it is atrocious—to rape her in her sleep. Suddenly awake, she says, "No," reaches for her gun, and the film abruptly cuts to a black screen as he protests, "But you've had sex with hundreds of men," followed with a sharp sound edit by a shot fired in the dark and Joe's departing footsteps. If this WTF "feel-bad" ending begs to be interpreted as "feminist," it does so with a non sequitur that exploits a cynical cliché from the rape-revenge tradition adored by Quentin Tarantino: that men will be men and women will retaliate with deadly force. Viewed as Artaudian cruelty inflicted on the audience, however, it makes perfect sense.

As these last two examples also suggest, *Nymphomaniac*'s Sadean discourse exposes the constructed nature of the image, with von Trier reminding us that (like Sade's heroines' accounts) Joe's "confession" is his elaborate fiction, ruse, or manipulation. Overall, the film's overbearing rhetoric ridicules the idea that sexuality can be added up or rationally understood. As Christine Evans argues, *Nymphomaniac*'s digressionism obliges us to attempt to interpret the film, yet refuses to reveal any essential psychological or moral truth. Instead it devolves into contradictions, non sequiturs, and a "structure of tautology" that defeats any single reading.[169] Or, as Robert Sinnerbrink put the issue in 2016, von Trier perverts, provokes, and satirizes philosophy in the classical sense, with "anti-philosophy."[170] No sooner does *Volume I* get us rooting for Joe's quest for the "zip-less fuck" than *Volume II* reverts to the fin de siècle, as Schepelern suggests, "to Nietzsche, Wagner, Freud, Munch, and Strindberg" (and, much further back, to Sade): to sex as irrational, "inescapable torment, obsession, and depravity," a sadomasochistic, misogynistic view that Graugaard, von Trier's chief sexologist consultant, discredited to no avail.[171]

Seligman's discursive dominance (which wears a Good Samaritan mask) suggests Sade's demystification of the classical reasoning and philosophical arguments with which his obscenely rich and powerful libertines supported their crimes.[172] While entertaining and harmlessly obtuse throughout *Volume I*, Seligman insists on rationalizing everything Joe narrates, especially in *Volume II*, which includes her criminal career that embraces torture. In the film's final hour or so, digressionism yields to an almost formal debate structure (as in *Dogville*'s conclusion), and he becomes the mouthpiece for what sounds like the film's feminist message. For every time Joe expresses her regrets, insisting she's a "terrible" person who's gotten her just deserts, Seligman defends her, asserting that "you were a woman demanding her right," condemning the double standard: if Joe had been a man, her exploits would have been unworthy of comment. Joe counters with "All this sounds frightfully like the clichés of our times," and "You've probably misunderstood the whole thing."

Lynne Huffer explains these seemingly reactionary rebuttals on Joe's part thusly: "the film's image of the multiply orgasmic, self-pleasing woman has become a neoliberal cliché, a sex-positive coin whose sex-negative flip side is a feminist obsession with worldwide . . . sex trafficking, rape· and . . . media" that turn women's bodies into spectacles that serve men—a dichotomy that harkens back to the juxtaposition of Justine and Juliette. Von Trier confronts us with such dichotomies to force us beyond them, compelling us to unlearn our "spectatorial habits lest we simply repeat . . . Seligman's moralizing intellectual projections."[173] *Nymphomaniac*'s infuriating black screen of an ending works like the cheeky dovetailing parentheses ("()") that von Trier substitutes for the "o" in the film's title: it confuses, enrages, and provokes the kind of disturbance that fosters thinking and debate.[174]

PARATEXTS: JOE'S HERBARIUM

Sadean and Artaudian cruelty notwithstanding, and as his personal assistant Emilie Spliid Pearce suggests, the film was "very personal" for von Trier in ways one might not have expected:

> Especially when you have [shared] everyday life with him and [know] the things
> that he likes to talk about. And especially his relationship to nature is how I
> very much remember. His love of trees. I came into it as an apprentice, a young
> person who hadn't made film and just want[ed] to learn from this guy. And he
> would love to explain to us about trees and stuff in the way that the dad explains
> to the daughter. I can just see a lot of Lars in there. And Joe's mother I think
> is very much based on his relationship to his own mother. Seligman and Joe
> are both him in a way.[175]

Nymphomaniac is for that reason her favorite von Trier film. Together with an understanding of its contexts, inspirations, and the collaborative processes through which it came together, the film reveals new facets of Lars von Trier: that he is (sometimes) a reader, often a storyteller ("like a small boy entertaining family. . . . [who] wants to make people laugh"),[176] frequently "a warm and funny guy," at times a collaborator—and a pedantic lover of trees.[177]

Indeed, where the ecologies of *Antichrist* and *Melancholia* are "dark" or worse, von Trier's relationship to nature blossoms in *Nymphomaniac* into a high Romantic leitmotif associated with trees, nature, youthful innocence, and aspiration that becomes Joe's affirmative keynote. Early on, with a flaming sky as a backdrop, and obviously speaking for the artist, she proclaims, "I've always demanded more from the sunset; more spectacular colors when the sun hit the horizon. That's perhaps my only sin." As her story progresses, she comes to identify her original and "true" self with the trees loved by her physician father. A sentimental and nostalgic sequence in chapter 1, tonally different from anything else in the film, introduces a motif in which Joe recalls walking in the forest of her childhood, noting that "my dad loved telling me about the trees and their leaves and considered it part of a good education." In adulthood, walks in the park return her momentarily to this state of innocence, and turning the pages of her herbarium, a collection of leaves representing her father's teachings, restores her pagan soul.[178] In a flashback to her childhood, Joe's father claims each person has a "soul tree" whose winter outlines reveal one's true nature. Toward the end of the film Joe finds her own soul tree: solitary, bent, with a bifurcated trunk (indicating a breakage) and clinging to a rock, it might have provided the centerpiece of a Caspar David Friedrich landscape. It is this motif that supports Hallund's understanding of the film as "life-affirming," with Joe's assertion of her identity and "free sexuality" in the face of societal regulations.[179]

The tree motif is strategically self-referential, signaling back to von Trier's previous films in which trees, leaves, and nature figure significantly—notably, in the conclusion to *Images of Liberation*, a German soldier is ambushed and dies in the Danish woods. As he uses calls to "talk" to the birds as he did in

FIGURE 3.6 Joe (Charlotte Gainsbourg) discovers her soul tree: solitary, bent, bifurcated and clinging to a rock.

childhood, the forest setting restores his innocence, and at death he ascends to the heavens above the treetops. In a similarly transfigurative representation, Joe experiences a "blasphemous" (orgasmic) levitation while lying in a field of grass. *Nymphomaniac* thus categorically reverses *Antichrist*'s chthonic vision of "Nature [as] Satan's church" as well as that film's take on the Norse mythology lurking in its subtexts.[180] This reversal has its center in Joe's father's discussion of the ash, the "most beautiful" in the forest, and the Norse World Tree (Yggdrasil) from which Odin hanged himself for nine days and nights in order to receive insights and learn the secrets of the runes inscribed on its trunk. Joe's father is evidently the von Trier who believes in nothing but prefers the "old gods."

The forest, often represented by a local park, is juxtaposed against the postindustrial urban settings that limit Joe's horizon and regiment her mind and body. The film opens with a full minute of black screen, followed by sequences near and in Seligman's drab apartment off an alley so dark that he greets a small square of sunlight with delight. Joe's seductions invariably take place in alienated urban environments—in damp and crumbling alleys, airless train compartments, or the sterile light of offices, clinics, and utilitarian rooms. These settings, together with Seligman's dissections and equations, suggest that Joe's sexual addiction and consequent desensitization, as well as Seligman's autistic asexuality, are in part an environmental disease, a product of Western modernization, abstraction and alienation. Postindustrial urban existence has diverted Joe's natural, healthy sexuality into a "mechanical" compulsion that becomes self-destructive and destructive to others. This is what happens to sexuality and identity in a capitalistic sociopolitical structure described by Foucault's *Discipline and Punish* (1975) as fueled by the regulated body. Joe does not sell her body, as Hallund notes (2019), but by chapter 7 she is employed as an extortionist's enforcer, and inevitably her "expertise" is corrupted by the systems in place.

Yet other readings suggest a consolatory side. *Belongs to Joe: Book of Comfort for a Nymphomaniac* (2013), photographed by Casper Sejersen, with text by art historian Cecilie Høgsbro, is a "photographic essay" based on von Trier's shooting script, made concurrently with the shoot and published upon the film's release, takes as its keynote the motif of trees as solace.[181] While drawing liberally from the script, it singles out Joe's herbarium, recreating it as a twenty-four-page insert resembling a lined grade-school notebook. On the cover is penciled in rounded schoolgirl print "my trees," providing a microcosm of the book as a whole. When read in retrospect, this paratexual "book of comfort," in natural yet dreamy, lightly faded shades from nudes to browns and greens, softens and reclaims key sequences and images. The penis montage becomes a meditation on variety and difference. A full nude shot of Skarsgård reveals a deceptive virility. In a pensive and ambiguous variation on Michelangelo's *Pietá*, Stacy Martin lies with her head in Charlotte Gainsbourg's lap.

Belongs to Joe points to the irreducible singularity of *Nymphomaniac*'s heroine, her transcendence of normative categories of "good" and "bad." Elena del Rio makes a similar point by way of Deleuze on Spinozan monism, noting that each body is composed of aggregates in an unlimited diversity that leaves no room for the imposition of moral judgements that assume the existence of a "common" human nature."[182] This perspective is represented most poignantly in Joe's father's tree "readings," which the adult Joe remembers from her childhood. Referring to the naked trunks in winter as "twisted souls, regular souls, crazy souls," he says, "all depending on the kind of lives human beings lead"—what others might call deformities or perversions—he explains as distinguishing features that emerge from the individual's struggle for survival. His depictions of the ash, the lime, and the oak illustrate the immanent value of difference and the idea that the normative notion of "bad" is a social invention. Accordingly, the ash tree's black buds are not an aberration but a mark of singularity. By analogy, Joe's perversion is a mark of her identity, and her empathy with P (who has a misshapen ear) and the pedophile (Jean-Marc Barr) follows this logic. From this perspective, Joe's attempt at sex-addiction therapy means "self-erasure," visualized in Joe's maniacal removal of anything that might stimulate her sexually (virtually everything) from her apartment.[183] And so, at what turns out to be her final therapy group meeting, she is confronted with a mirror image of her former and truer self, the twelve-year-old child from her "transfiguration" scene, and reclaims her identity, asserting triumphantly, "I am a nymphomaniac."

Among other things, this defiant Joe seems to reflect von Trier's decidedly mixed reaction to Alcoholics Anonymous, whose "slave philosophy," as he has called it, requires that one must "flagellantly" submit and morally be made over—when "I like me very much the way I am."[184] And, in his next film, *The House That Jack Built* (2018), we meet an equally if differently defiant—and Dionysian—character in another personal, digressive, essayistic, sadistic (if not quite so Sadean) film, as an exploration of the cruelty inherent in Western art and culture.

On a decidedly edgier note, *Nymphomaniac* is the hypotext for the music video *Gourmet* (2020), in which Danish rapper and director Nikoline (Nikoline Vicic Rasmussen) offers an homage to Joe's description, by way of Bach's polyphony, of the delights of sex with multiple partners. Photographed by Manuel Claro, *Gourmet* is an orgy of fluid sexualities and naked bodies including Sara Helling as a nymph, Tinus De Shunard as the Hindu god Ardhanarishvara, director Mathias Broe as Adonis, actress Sara Hjort Ditlevsen as a (heavily pregnant) Aphrodite, Nikoline as the Valkyrie of Norse mythology, and Lars von Trier as himself in a two-second cameo. This paean to female and pansexuality (with a close-up of fingers penetrating a vagina and a woman taking a man from behind) Nikoline, who has a degree in physics, explains thusly, "For millennia, society has tried to reduce and tame female sexuality to be something passively receptive with whore/madonna complexes and systemic shame. To me, the woman is active and volcanic—from smoldering pheromone ecstasy to explosive and untamed savagery. Our sexuality must, can and is everything."[185] "I have not come here to please you!" she sings and struts. Echoing Joe, paying homage while claiming simultaneously to transcend him, she proclaims herself "the new Trier."[186]

4

THE HOUSE THAT JACK BUILT

Murder as Art/Art as Murder

T he House That Jack Built originated in von Trier's desire to make a film with a male protagonist. In June 2018 he told me, "As I've made quite a lot of films about good women," now he wanted to make a film about a man—specifically "a really bad man."[1] Cowriter Jenle Hallund, who shares credit with von Trier for the film's concept, claims she had often "pushed for" him to make a film with a male protagonist because (as she put it in June 2019, sounding like some of von Trier's harshest critics) "I thought, 'I've seen his fucking suffering women, let's see something else.' . . . I really wanted to see what he would do with a male, . . . you know, 'Who are you if you see yourself, if you portray yourself and everything through a man, what would you come up with then?' It was also how, *how* [would] you, because Lars didn't like working with male actors so much as female actors."[2] Evidently, he took up Hallund's challenge.[3] As he explained to Matt Dillon, he made the film as a kind of self-portrait or, perhaps, self-parody: "Most of the male characters in my films have been fucking idiots, but this guy is like me. [Of all the characters I've ever written], Jack is the one closest to myself. Except I don't kill people."[4]

Nor was Jack his first film with a male lead. Discounting He in *Antichrist*, *The House That Jack Built* was at least von Trier's fifth film with a male protagonist but, as discussed in the previous chapter, those in the Europe trilogy films and *The Boss of It All* are feckless and easily manipulated idealists. And although *The House That Jack Built* is at times a pitch-black comedy, primarily at Jack's expense—in the second and fifth incidents, he sporadically resembles the bumbling leads in von Trier's Europe trilogy—he is unique within von Trier's oeuvre in being actively, productively, and self-reflexively evil. As Hallund explains, both *Nymphomaniac* and *Jack* are "different from a lot of his other films" in that their protagonists and narratives are driven not by external forces beyond their control but by "some kind of individual will," however different—an obsession or addiction, in Joe's case to sex and to murder in Jack's.[5] Jack "wills" evil, as Hallund suggests; he manipulates, performs, epitomizes, and celebrates it.

As von Trier explained to Schepelern, "I was mad about Patricia Highsmith, whose main character [Tom Ripley] is a psychopath in many of her books."[6] Of her five novels about Tom Ripley, Highsmith wrote that she was "showing the unequivocal triumph of evil over good, and rejoicing in it. I shall make my readers rejoice in it, too."[7] In one crucial respect, however, von Trier wanted to go beyond Highsmith: "I read that a psychopath rarely knows he is a psychopath, because he'll always blame somebody else"—as Ripley blames playboy Dickie Greenleaf for being undeserving of his wealth in *The Talented Mr. Ripley* (1955).[8] "But I imagined that this psychopath knew he was a psychopath, which [awareness] he would then exploit."[9] Practicing in front of a mirror, Ripley impersonates Greenleaf to steal his identity and fortune; in a similar mirror sequence Jack practices his performance of humanity by impersonating an assortment of expressions and emotions from photographs and iconic drawings. Citing Bob Dylan's music video for *Subterranean Homesick Blues* (1965), Jack looks straight at the camera while tossing a series of cue cards labeled with characteristics like narcissism, intelligence, irrationality, mood swings, verbal superiority, and manipulation, simultaneously flaunting, celebrating, and deconstructing his psychopathy.

The House that Jack Built is more than a portrait of a psychopath, Hallund argues: it is a radically "psychopathic" film engineered to make audiences uncomfortable. The film is "completely void of direction and morality and condemnation and . . . [having] that kind of irony that is bordering sarcasm that is bordering evil, which permeates the full film because . . . [of] [Jack's] psychopathic distance to everything."[10] Von Trier's understanding of psychopathy, Hallund suggests, comes in part from his experience of being himself:

> Lars is very ironic. . . . And there's that kind of emotional distance to certain things wrapped in irony. And that can be a small sign of psychopathy. . . . Lars

lives with a lot of irony about himself and life . . . and at the same time as he's very personal. So there's a dichotomy about Lars. . . . You can so much feel Lars in this film, I think, . . . the way that he's unflappable about certain things, [where] other people would have to be very emotional, morally outraged—Lars is distanced. And I think that he just played with that part of himself [in the film].[11]

Although von Trier and Hallund are jointly credited with developing the film's concept, he clarified to Schepelern that "we didn't develop it together. She suggested I do a movie about hell and I liked the idea,"[12] explaining to David Jenkins that "it's a long time since we've really visited hell in films. Particularly the journey to hell."[13] The idea of a a film about a serial killer was his own, he said, adding that "The combination of those two ideas worked like an atomic bomb."[14] Two or three years earlier, Hallund had been

very much interested in [William] Blake . . . and then Dante and the *Divine Comedy*. And I saw some Botticelli in London with some of his beautiful paintings of Dante's hell. Then I saw a documentary about these six or seven holes. . . . physical holes . . . that people believe are on this earth, to hell. There was a cave in Portugal, a volcano [Hekla] in Iceland), and an iceberg [cave]. . . . so I gave him this idea three years before. And then Louise [Vesth] called and said, can we use this idea? By then Lars had added on his own idea of the serial killer. . . . and then . . . obviously I'm based in philosophy. I like history of art. So I was interested in Blake at the time, and Blake's heaven and hell. And I was talking to Lars a lot about that. And then we used it in the film.[15]

Like *Antichrist*, *Melancholia*, and *Nymphomaniac*, the film was meant to be an explosive combination of a "low" genre (the horror/serial killer film) with the art film, of schlock references layered with allusions to high culture. The epilogue, announced with the grandiose title "Katabasis," was a blend of philosophical, literary, and mythological concepts and images of hell: beliefs about physical portals to the infernal realm, Blake's *The Marriage of Heaven and Hell* (1790–1793), Dante's *Divine Comedy* (originally *Comedia*, 1320), and Roman mythology (the Elysian Fields), together with Hermann Broch's modernist tome *Der Tod des Vergil* (*The Death of Virgil*, 1945) which von Trier read in translation from the German after a suggestion by Peter Schepelern.

According to producer Louise Vesth, von Trier researched serial killers extensively during the writing process,[16] but Hallund and he have confirmed otherwise: "I think maybe some of it is cultural heritage, if you like, but he did not do extensive research," adding that "he just sort of put two and two together."[17] As early as April 22, 2015, von Trier had decided on the genre and his approach to it, as he told Peter Schepelern:

> [The] serial killer is almost a genre in itself . . . it is at least very, very simple dramaturgy [in] that you know that with a serial killer, everything is dangerous around him, but then I will make it from his point of view . . . interesting I think. And then you will say afterwards: why do you pay tribute to the serial killer? I do not, I make a film seen from the serial killer's point of view. . . . I do like an actor always does, he will defend his character.[18]

For his part, Matt Dillon claims initially to have channeled Ted Bundy, although "once Jack took shape, he became a unique character. That said, Jack is void of any sense of self at his core," Matt Dillon explains, "which is why he morphs into so many different people—he takes on different personalities."[19]

In sum, *The House That Jack Built* is more like a genre film than any of von Trier's other works (with the possible exception of the office comedy *The Boss of It All*), but rather than working from any template, he developed it as a psychopathic character study in first person. Typically, Hallund explains, he takes "an idea of a genre and then he finds the character he wants to make a film about, and then he's absolutely loyal and true to this character and not to the genre."[20] He further resisted the dramaturgical impulse by dividing the narrative into five "incidents" that are further fragmented by the digressive dialogue between Jack and Verge (Bruno Ganz): "So he wrote one and then another incident and another incident. And so it was sort of separate in the way we wrote it, rather than the other way, like an arc where the drama took off."[21] As for the look of the film, at the shooting and postproduction stages von Trier did not provide Claro, his cinematographer, with specific films for reference. "Rather, he gave me photos of accidents or crimes such as those taken by Mexican photographer Enrique Metidines, Mary Ellen Mark's 'white trash' portraits, or views by William Eggleston," Claro explained in 2018. Von Trier wanted an "organic" image that would be "a bit dirty," so they "did a lot of work during colour grading, especially in order to add grain."[22]

PUBLICITY, PARATEXTS,
AND THE 2018 CANNES PREMIERE

Originally, von Trier planned for *The House That Jack Built* to be a television series, but in February 2016, he confirmed that it would be a feature film budgeted at 8.7 Euros ($9.8 million), and by May 2016 had completed a script.[23] TrustNordisk quickly presold it in six different regions, and von Trier began casting for an August shoot near Trollhättan, Sweden, where partner Film i Väst is located, and in Copenhagen.[24] Set in the 1970s and 1980s (before DNA evidence was used in murder cases) in Washington State, with Mount St. Helens often in the background, it is narrated from Jack's perspective over a period of twelve years. On November 2, 2016, von Trier announced that Matt Dillon and Bruno Ganz would play the film's leading roles,[25] followed later by announcements that Riley Keough, Sofie Gråbøl,[26] and Uma Thurman would be joining the cast.[27]

On March 7, in the first publicity photo, von Trier posed as a troll-like version of the scythe-bearing, death-knelling reaper in an iconic frame from Carl Dreyer's *Vampyr*. Three days later he enigmatically announced that the film "celebrates the idea that life is evil and soulless, which is sadly proven by the recent rise of the *Homo trumpus*—the rat king."[28] In May 2017, IFC Films acquired distribution rights to the film and on October 26 issued the "first official look," a photo still of Matt Dillon peering out from a semitransparent curtain, a heavy plastic "membrane" that shields the inside of the walk-in freezer where he stores his victims' bodies—a chilling if obvious homage to *Psycho*.[29] Then, in April, 2018, after nearly a year of postproduction, gearing up for the Cannes Film Festival, IFC Films issued a series of publicity photos: of Dillon with Thurman, Dillon with Keough, the bloodied, plastic wrapped corpse of Lady 2 (Siobhan Fallon Hogan) being dragged into Jack's lair, and Dillon on a construction site against a backdrop of Mount St. Helens.[30]

Marking von Trier's return to the Cannes Film Festival seven years after the *Melancholia* press conference debacle, *The House That Jack Built* was screened out of competition on May 14, sidelining it from the controversy it might have unleashed if a jury had considered it for a top prize, while suggesting that the film would be controversial even for Lars von Trier, thus increasing anticipation. "His film is out of competition because it is such a singular object, a subject so controversial, that this was the best place," Cannes's artistic director, Thierry Frémaux, explained. "And whether we like it or not, we are dealing with a great film and a great filmmaker." He added that "it is time to acknowledge that he was a victim, certainly of his bad jokes, but also of a punishment that was disproportionate and that had lasted long enough."[31]

The Cannes premiere fulfilled expectations for what had up to that point been a rather placid festival. At around the one-hour mark, Twitter exploded with howls and expletives—"Vile!" "Vomitive!" "Disgusting!" "Should not have been made," "Actors culpable!"—and reported that at least one hundred people had walked out. The Grand Théâtre Lumière, which was packed, houses 2,309 people, making the exodus less than 5 percent of the total, however, and a ten-minute standing ovation followed the screening.[32] And when it was screened for journalists the morning following the premiere, very few walked out. The last straw was a sequence featuring Jack as a boy (Emil Tholstrup) snipping off a duckling's leg and watching it flounder in the water. However, PETA (People for the Ethical Treatment of Animals) promptly issued a statement defending von Trier and company for their clever illusionism involving a fake silicon leg and praised them for their realism in showing how serial killers often begin their careers by torturing animals.[33]

On September 26, a controversial set of seven character posters was created by The Einstein Couple, for the CPH PIX film festival in Denmark that marked the film's general release, and featured the director, protagonists, and primary victims in uniquely contorted poses secured with wire.[34] Playing off the grotesquely taxidermized bodies that make up Jack's house of corpses, the posters resonated with the suffering associated with von Trier's most iconic films together with the director's alleged "torture" of actors such as Björk—or, for that matter, Paul Bettany—playing to the controversy surrounding von Trier's return to Cannes.

Then, shortly before the American release of the R-rated version on December 14, in a surprise move, IFC announced a special one-night-only screening of the unrated director's cut on November 28, 2018, provoking the MPAA to "censure" the company, threatening to disallow the "R" rating and creating a minor scandal. Exploiting the controversies already surrounding the film, the marketing copy referred to the director's cut as "the same version that was shown at this year's Cannes Film Festival and prompted both a ten-minute standing ovation and more than a few disturbed walkouts."[35] The strategy worked: many of the screenings were sold out, and the majority of the reviews from them were positive.

FIGURE 4.1 Lars von Trier in one of the seven character posters for *The House That Jack Built* created by The Einstein Couple for the CPH PIX film festival featuring the director, protagonists, and primary victims in contorted poses secured with wire.

DECONSTRUCTING THE SERIAL KILLER

Of the films von Trier made during and after his depression, all of which include self-reflective elements and allusions, *The House That Jack Built* is most clearly a retrospective—and an ironic, tragicomic one at that. For inspiration he again returned to his previous projects and earliest influences, especial the film noir ambience, misogynistic stereotypes, Holocaust obsession, and tropes of the Europe trilogy. Interviewing him shortly after Trier won the Sonning Prize in April 2018, Peter Schepelern brought up a project von Trier had mentioned in a May 1984 interview for the French magazine *Positif* at Cannes, where *The Element of Crime* was premiering: "A World War II movie loosely based on *The Divine Comedy*" (eventually titled *Mesmer-Organisationen* [*The Mesmer Organization*]) as von Trier described it.[36] "Perhaps the World War II is toned down," Schepelern mused, but in *The House That Jack Built,* whether by design or unintentionally, "you have made your *Divine Comedy*."[37]

But *The Element of Crime* itself, and the international wave of Nordic noir of which it was a precursor, is more relevant. When I pointed out to von Trier that his "very first feature was a serial killer film" of sorts, adding that "it's kind of like coming full circle, a summing up, perhaps?" he replied, "You could say that, maybe. Yeah." Pushing the point further, I suggested that *The Element of Crime* was "set in a kind of hell?" "It was set in kind of a lot of water," he deadpanned.[38] And so is *Jack.* The film opens with a black screen against which the faint off-screen voices of Jack and Verge are accompanied by ambient sloshing sounds: "We hear two people speaking with an eerie and strange reverb. Faint sound of something that sounds like someone walking in water."[39] The final descent, the "Katabasis," reveals that Verge has been leading Jack through a cramped watery cavern, a portal to hell. *The Element of Crime* is a similar journey in which Fisher slogs through water toward an abyss, a journey that is similarly framed as a dialogue between the protagonist and a largely unseen guide/interlocutor. It opens as Fisher, a cop under hypnosis for his crushing headaches and amnesia, is guided by his psychoanalyst in voice-over as he "returns" to a postapocalyptic Europe to retrace his steps tailing one Harry Grey, whose serial victims were young girls selling lottery tickets. Like Fisher's analyst/interlocuter, Verge plays the role of priest-confessor, alter ego, or conscience, listening, commenting, prompting, often scoffing, but refraining from final judgement or overt advice.

The obvious link, however, is *The House That Jack Built*'s title and logo—in which the words of the title, in all caps, are collapsed into the shape of a house—and for which the *National Review*'s Armond White accused von Trier of "taint[ing] a foundational nursery rhyme—debasing its formerly innocent traditions."[40] But von Trier had already, unforgettably, tainted it in *The Element of Crime*: in a cage-like cell in a whorehouse in Halbestadt, Kim, the former lover of the serial killer suspect Grey, reads it to her child by Grey as Fisher listens. The nursery rhyme's appeal has always lain in its absurd seriality, recounting a chain of coincidental events that lead inevitably back to Jack: "This is the cow with the crumpled horn that tossed the dog that worried the cat that killed the rat that ate the malt that lay in the house that Jack built." In *The Element of Crime*, this seriality, in resonance with the seriality of the Lotto murders, becomes chilling. Similarly framed, the film's story has already happened, further determining the noir plot in which the antihero is enmeshed in corruption, and lines dividing the good man and the criminal are blurred. Fisher goes "by the book," a tome written by his mentor Osborne, who eventually confesses to Grey's murders. Following Osborne's corrupted logic, Fisher doggedly maps Grey's movements, endeavoring to see, feel, and think like him—until he essentially becomes Harry Grey, who may or may not have existed, unless Fisher *is* Grey. Finally, in attempting to save the final victim, Fisher suffocates her, completing Grey's mission.

Von Trier once described his first feature as a "bastard child of a mating of German with American film"[41]—a blend of German Expressionism with American apocalyptic sci-fi, police procedural, and film noir—but in 1984, *The Element of Crime* was also one of the earliest movies about a serial killer, as the genre did not achieve mass popularity until several years later, in the late 1980s and early 1990s.[42] Moreover, *Element* was one of the first of the contemporary trend in the serial killer genre in which the profiler's method (crime scene investigation, understanding the psychology of the killer) leads to his becoming a serial killer himself. *Element* was also a precursor of the now international genre of Nordic noir, which *The House That Jack Built* arguably parodies broadly through its blue-gray color scheme shot with splashes of red, weather, location, social and political commentary, and the casting of Sofie Gråbol, star of *Forbrydelsen* (*The Killing*, 2007–2012) as the single mother of two young boys who becomes Jack's victim representing the family.[43]

As for the serial killer genre, by 2018, considering the lengthy runs of television series like *Criminal Minds*, *CSI*, and *NCIS* and "a media landscape inundated with a kind of unthinking ghoulish fascination," it had been done to death.[44] Von Trier joked that he chose the project because the women he has been with have been "crazy about serial killers." ("That might have something to do with me," he added.)[45] Evidently an exception to this "rule," Hallund quipped that she thought the film would be "huge" because "men love serial killers. They love killing women. It happens in every single film."[46] Whatever the case, von Trier promised that *The House That Jack Built* would be his "most brutal film ever."[47] As in his other postdepression films, he delights in topping off and deconstructing a hackneyed genre, and in transgressing the boundaries of taste through a discordant blend of a low genre with the art film.

The Harris Template

Ending with Jack's descent into the pit of hell with "Hit the Road, Jack" over the credits, *The House That Jack Built* draws on, celebrates, and mocks the cult of the serial killer. His name resonates with the mythology surrounding the grotesquely artful crimes of Jack the Ripper, who butchered some five prostitutes, exposed their reproductive organs and intestines, ritualistically arranged the bodies and parts, and sent trophies to Scotland Yard, leading to a popular mythology of the serial killer as a gentleman surgeon, or perhaps a painter. (At his most manipulative, misogynistic, and sadistic, Jack slices off Simple/Jacqueline's breasts, placing one on the police car windshield as a signature and message, fashioning the other into a wallet.) For someone who did not extensively research the cult of the serial killer, *The House That Jack Built* registers a keen awareness of the genre tropes, whether in using them for his own purposes or in violating them.

The contemporary serial killer genre was established by Thomas Harris's four novels based on the work of John Douglas, who invented the method of criminal psychological profiling. Harris featured psychologist and cannibalistic serial killer Hannibal Lecter: *Red Dragon* (1981), *The Silence of the Lambs* (1988), *Hannibal* (1999), and *Hannibal Rising* (2006),[48] and their film adaptations, beginning with *Manhunter* (1984).[49] Harris incorporated Douglas's experience, including a nervous breakdown from the strain and demoralization inherent in his method of understanding serial killers, into the personal history of Will Graham, his first protagonist. Despite the unlikelihood of a direct influence, the parallels with von Trier's *The Element of Crime* are uncanny: the intensity of his empathy with Harry Grey has caused PTSD symptoms, including headaches and memory lapses, and leads to a loss of his identity to that of the serial killer.

Thanks to Harris's formula, current serial killer fiction, according to Philip Simpson, interweaves four elements: "The neo-Gothic, the detective procedural, the "psycho" profile, and the mytho-apocalyptic."[50] Put more simply, Harris brilliantly mated the procedural quest for the psychopath with the Gothic novel—per Mary Shelley's *Frankenstein* (1818), Robert Louis Stevenson's *Dr. Jekyll and Mr. Hyde* (1886), Oscar Wilde's *The Picture of Dorian Gray* (1890), and Bram

Stoker's *Dracula* (1897)—whose center of fascination is a "monster" who is also the protagonist's double or shadow. Harris's *Red Dragon* defied the rules of the detective procedural by introducing Francis Dolarhyde in the ninth chapter, forcing readers to share his point of view, back story (of physical deformity and child abuse), hopes, and dreams: thus our interest shifts from the law enforcement protagonist to the psychopath, and from the investigative process to the relationship between the profiler and the killer, which becomes increasingly intimate and dangerous. As in von Trier's *Element of Crime*, Harris's profilers, and with them the audience, operate at the limits of the rational and the social; we lose part of our identity in the crime scene, becoming one with the criminal mind in process of understanding it. Epitomizing this border crossing is Hannibal Lecter, a psychopath who knows he is a psychopath but who is equally a "mind hunter"; a once-respected forensic psychoanalyst, he acts as an informant, consultant, or go-between for FBI agents Will Graham and Clarice Starling. Through Lecter, who inspires fascination, awe, and a perverse empathy, Harris radically destabilized relations and distinctions between protagonist and antagonist, and in the last two Lecter novels and their film adaptations, *Hannibal* (2001) and the prequel *Hannibal Rising* (2007), as well as in the television series *Hannibal* (2013–2015), Lecter essentially becomes the protagonist, the procedural element ancillary. Even so, our identification with a law enforcement protagonist, which functions as a mechanism for disavowing or containing our "uncomfortably and exhilaratingly complex relationship with Hannibal Lecter" is quite possibly the key to the popularity of the serial killer genre as a whole.[51]

In a dramatic departure from the Harris template, von Trier "goes straight to the source," as Hallund puts it.[52] Excising the law enforcement protagonist, he places Jack and his "confession" front and center, coercing spectators to share his murderous gaze and his arguments—hence shocking and disturbing the first Cannes audiences. As for the police, they are omnipresent but mostly nameless, unaware and ineffectual at best and lazy and uninterested at worst, with their ineptitude providing political commentary and comic relief.[53] Omitting the standard mechanism for disavowal, the film confronts viewers with their spectatorship and implicates them in Jack's sadism. "He mutilates Riley Keough, he mutilates children . . . and we are all sitting there in formal dress, expected to watch it?" one traumatized Cannes walkout exclaimed.[54] For all these same reasons, the film delighted hardcore horror and extreme cinema fans.

All the same, von Trier had something like that "uncomfortably and exhilaratingly complex relationship" between the audience and Lecter in mind.[55] When

I asked him if he had seen any of the Lecter films or the television series *Hannibal* starring (fellow Dane) Mads Mikkelsen, he replied, "I have seen Hannibal the cannibal, the film with [Anthony Hopkins]. And there you also feel a certain kind of sympathy for this guy. Even though he's presented as a bad guy in any . . . sense."[56] Earlier, speaking of Jack, he had said, "I was pretty sure that you would think it's horrific what he's doing, but you still would follow him. That means that if the police comes then you're on his side."[57] For example, the sequence at the end of the film, where Jack tries to escape his fate by climbing to a fragment of a bridge leading up from hell, was inspired by Hitchcock: "The film where the bad guy . . . was hanging from the State of Liberty by his fingernails. . . . right? And then Cary Grant came up and tried to save him but he fell, and Hitchcock said . . . 'And that was a mistake from my side. Of course, it should have been the other way around, because nobody cares if a killer falls.'"[58] Challenging Hitchcock's argument, von Trier made the killer not only the protagonist, like Tom Ripley or Hannibal Lecter, but also the narrator, stressing that "you have much more sympathy for Jack than you would have if you weren't carried along. . . . If somebody [merely] said [in third person], 'This killer has done this and this and this,' you would despise him, right? But here we get some thoughts that are human and we learn much more about Jack than just the murders."[59] As he explained to Peter Schepelern, he wanted "to perforate the very concept of evil by letting him be intelligible to us in so many other aspects, so that we are fooled into accepting the killings."[60] This, ideally, leads to a second reaction with an important intellectual and ethical dimension, as he explained further to me: "I like it if people leave the cinema in one mood and then ten minutes after, they say, 'what have we seen? And how have we reacted? That's . . . also to say that —. . . .' You said [that "Incident 3" exposes how] we're predators, . . . yeah, I think that . . . the layer of civilization is much thinner than [we] think."[61] *Dogville* provides the most clear-cut example of this strategy: the film elicits empathy with Grace as her suffering and degradation builds, building in turn our frustration and rage at her oppressors, so that when at her command her father's gangsters shoot all the residents and burn down the town, we experience a cathartic release. The audience's genocidal vengeance is exposed and mocked, however, by David Bowie's deliriously irreverent "Young Americans" over a montage of sacred Depression-era Farm Security Administration photographs during the end credits, producing conflicted emotions, rethinking, questioning, and ethical analysis. Perhaps concerned that *The House That Jack Built*'s audiences might not get to that point, scene 165 in von Trier's "shooting draft" proposes an "end text" discussion sequence in which "the male actor who portrayed Jack, or other of the film's actors, is interviewed in a private setting about his relationship with the film, while the credits roll on one side of the screen. The actor is asked, among other things, why he chose to take on the role, and about his work with the character, plus more general questions like: What do you think the world may get out of this film?"[62]

Later in my interview with him, von Trier brings up "*In Cold Blood . . .* you remember that? That you felt terrible when they were gonna hang."[63] Truman Capote's book and the 1967 film adaptation, which became pivotal in debates about the death penalty, portrayed one of the killers, Perry Smith, as a victim of racism, poverty, child abuse at the hands of parents and orphanages, and chronic pain. Given that serial killers are often victims of child abuse, a staple of serial killer fiction is the traumatic background story. Jack, however, is given no such excuses, and what little information that is provided about his past refers back to Lars Trier's relatively privileged upbringing. We find, thanks to fragments floating through his recollections that Jack is a product of the educated middle class who, like Trier as a child, developed an early interest in architecture and engineering fostered by his mother.[64] Moreover, three vivid (and eerily linked) childhood memories are more enigmatic than explanatory: of young Jack running through a field of reeds in a game of hide-and-seek, then observing a group of men scything a field of grain, followed by the scene in which he mutilates a duckling. While linking snippets from his own childhood with young Jack's predilection for cruelty, von Trier otherwise excludes the clichéd but affective Freudian psychology that Harris used to humanize Dolarhyde, Gumb, and Lecter. Moreover, what we do know about Jack's aspirations and theories about the "art" of destruction hardly makes us feel "terrible" when Jack plunges into the abyss.

So, what, if anything, makes at least some spectators want to "follow" Jack? There is Dillon's manically brilliant performance, together with the fact that *The House That Jack Built* is one of von Trier's funniest and most entertaining films, a horror comedy of sorts, with an assortment of satirical jibes. And if Jack (an unreliable narrator at best) describes his selection of examples as "random," the sequencing of the murders is engineered precisely: to divert, disarm, build amusement, involvement, and even sympathy. The first incident, featuring Uma Thurman's Lady 1, is a variation on the "deserving victim" that Harris offers up early in each of his novels (the irritating journalist in *Red Dragon* or "Multiple Miggs," who assaults the young FBI trainee Clarice Starling in *The Silence of the*

Lambs before Lecter talks him into swallowing his tongue.) After flagging Jack's van down for help, she points out that he looks like a serial killer, muses on how he might kill her and dispose of her body, and finally takes it all back, calling him a wimp, provoking his incel rage. "Incident 2," in which Jack clumsily and lengthily strangles the widow Claire Miller, begins as a comedy of errors as he fumbles through three different, equally eccentric, identities and explanations to gain entry. This Jack is another person; bumbling and uncertain, vulnerable and even compassionate, when, in the midst of strangling his victim, she sputters back into life, he apologizes, sobbing over his failure to make a proper kill, and offers her tea and a bite of a doughnut, which she, absurdly, accepts. Then, overcome by obsessive-compulsive urges and anxiety attacks, he becomes an antic, almost Chaplinesque figure of fun; imagining blood stains under every chair leg and picture frame, he repeatedly returns to the scene of the crime and insists on helping the police search for the missing widow. Unable to lift her body into his van without attracting their attention, he ties it to his bumper and roars off, leaving a grisly streak of blood down the highway. In the nick of time, a "great rain," which Jack interprets as ordained by fate, pours down, washing away the trail. Like Highsmith's young Ripley, however, Jack is a quick study, and by "Incident 3" he has become chillingly, fascinatingly proficient, a ruthless human predator in an elaborately ritualized sequence staged along the lines of "The Most Dangerous Game." Jack has also become suddenly articulate, explaining the ritual of deer hunting as a time-sanctioned, "ethical" heritage. As he gains proficiency and confidence, he takes risks—seeking out and "confessing" to the police in "Incident 4," and attempting to shoot five men simultaneously with one full metal jacket bullet in "Incident 5"—inspiring curiosity as to how his game will play out. All in all, each of the incidents is so vivid and different that we want to see what he will do next.

American Psychos

From another perspective, and as Nigel Andrews puts it in a line quoted on the front cover of the DVD, *The House that Jack Built* is "*Funny Games* meets *American Psycho*"—suggesting that it is a blend of the former's metacinematic cruelty and the latter's pitch-black satire.[65] In both films, the police are missing or easily deceived, and the killers control the narrative. Rather than sympathetic, they are chillingly symptomatic, reflecting the psychopathic soullessness of Western culture and American culture in particular.

Bret Easton Ellis's novel *American Psycho* (1991), which opens with the most quoted line from Dante's *Inferno*, "Abandon all hope, all ye who enter here," from canto 3, is a savage caricature of the culture of acquisition and consumption of the late 1980s narrated by yuppie antihero, misogynist, and serial killer Patrick Bateman.[66] A rambling confessional account with innumerable scenes of graphic, often sexually explicit torture, dismemberment, degradation, and cannibalism, now a cult classic regarded by many as a work of transgressive art, even before publication (after insiders leaked passages to the press) it caused a level of public outrage unlike anything in thirty years.[67]

Where Ellis's novel made its mark through savage caricature, graphic excess, and sheer volume, the 2000 film adaptation, written by unconventional feminists Mary Harron and Guinevere Turner and directed by Harron, pared down Ellis's massive novel to an incisive 101-minute film that made Bateman's often misogynistic violence reflect directly on him. *The House That Jack Built* stands somewhere between Ellis's deeply psychopathic novel and Harron's often wildly funny film, which is clearly a satire: on yuppie "dress-for-success" materialism during the Wall Street boom of the 1980s but ultimately on what Harron, in a deeply ironic understatement, called "men behaving badly."[68] Hallund, who has seen the film, said of Ellis's novel, "I haven't read it. I wouldn't put myself through that." Yet, like Ellis's novel and von Trier's films in general, *The House That Jack Built* "doesn't take a clear moral stance, because it is what it is," Hallund claims. "It's a film about a serial killer and he's faithful . . . to the portrayal of the psychopath."[69]

Moreover, it exposes Jack's narcissism, pedantry, misogyny, and delusions of grandeur and in the end damns him to hell. Like Harron's film, *The House That Jack Built* is a masterfully sustained first-person performance of dramatic irony and black comedy with social and political implications. Christian Bale's Bateman alternates between evaluative descriptions of his friends' designer clothes, condescending speeches about social responsibility and politics, pedantic reviews of mediocre Whitney Houston and Phil Collins albums, and graphic accounts of his murders. Deftly managing a tricky tonal tightrope, Dillon makes Jack ludicrously unaware of the gap between his pretentions and his accomplishments while interspersing his "incidents" with pompous lectures on Gothic architecture, the nature of sublime art, photography, "ethical" hunting, and dessert wine cultivation. Bateman is impervious to the law because he is a cypher, indistinguishable from all the other suits in his class—near the end, he confesses to his lawyer, who mistakes him for another client—and because no one cares, especially about the class of "losers" who become murder statistics. In "Incident 4," after confessing that he is a serial killer of sixty people to the police, who ignore him, and infuriated that no one is noticing him, Jack joins Simple in screaming for help in a pointed "lesson" that "in this hell of a city, in this hell of a country, in this hell of a world . . . no one wants to help. You can scream from now until Christmas Eve and the only answer you'll get is the deafening silence you hear right now!"[70]

Like *American Psycho*, *The House That Jack Built* is set in 1980s America, acknowledging that the genre, like the overwhelming majority of serial killers, is white, male, and American. In simply choosing to make a serial killer film, von Trier extends the critique sustained throughout his six other "Amerikan" films. Specifically, the serial killer antihero represents a breed of Western white male privilege and toxic masculinity that, reacting against feminism in the 1980s, has continued through the #MeToo era. As Andrews comments, Jack "enjoys cruelty perhaps in the name of some totalitarian payday, by men against newly ascendant women."[71] But *The House That Jack Built* has broader concerns than misogyny. Bateman's dual occupation, corporate investment banking and serial killing, plays on an analogy between "mergers and acquisitions" and "murders and executions"; Jack's dual occupation—art/architecture and serial killing—turns on a similarly facile analogy to offer an indictment of the fascist tendencies in modern Western culture.

For his book's primary epigraph, Ellis uses the introduction to *Notes from Underground* (1964), Fyodor Dostoevsky's lecture/confession whose narcissistic, "spiteful," existentialist antihero and unreliable narrator expounds on and exemplifies the evils of modernity:

> The author of these *Notes* and the *Notes* themselves are fictitious, of course. Nevertheless, such persons as the composer of these *Notes*, not only exist in our society, but must exist, considering the general circumstances under which our society was formed. I wanted to bring before the public . . . one of the characters of the recent past. He represents a generation that is still living out his days among us. . . . this personage describes himself and his views, and, as it were, writes to clarify the reasons he appeared and was bound to appear in our midst. The subsequent fragment will consist of the actual "notes," concerning certain events in his life.[72]

Like the Underground Man and Patrick Bateman, Jack is a man of a generation "still living out his days among us": his character, together with the frag-
mentary nature of his confession cum argument, typifies our time. Jack's
motivation may be explained in part in terms of Mark Seltzer's claim that the
"gothicization" of serial killing in American true crime literature, fiction, and
film, together with celebrity culture and a fascination with psychological
trauma and physical wounds, has resulted in a concept of the serial killer as a
charismatic "type of person" and, for some craving fame and a calling, a role
model.[73] Assuming the American liberal capitalist myth in which anyone can
succeed, and, correspondingly, that anyone who does not is a failure, Jack, like
Bateman, turns to serial killing for self-expression, rejuvenation, and a form of
success that he has not been able to achieve through other means. As his skill
and confidence increase, the refrain from David Bowie's "Fame" blasts from the
sound track.

In a running joke in *American Psycho*, Bateman frequently claims to spot Donald Trump, his womanizing billionaire role model and the personification of
the hedonistic extravagance of the 1980s, in upscale restaurants and clubs.
Granted, Jack's modus operandi stems from a different source, but von Trier
makes explicit Trump connections apropos of 2018: in the third chapter, in which
Jack pulls out red baseball caps for his adopted "family" to wear, his deployment of gun culture in an allusion to mass murder, together with von Trier's
publicity statement of February 2017 that referred to "the recent rise of the *Homo
trumpus*."[74] Jack's narcissism, inability to experience empathy, glib "performance"
of human emotions and reactions he does not feel, and grandiose theories and
claims correspond with Trump's personality disorders, as noted by his critics.[75]

Bateman's narcissism, epitomized in his obsession with designer clothes and
maintaining a "hardbody" physique, has its other side in his contempt for the
soft-bodied "bimbos" and prostitutes who, together with homeless vagrants,
comprise the majority of his victims. Prompted by Verge, Jack speaks for von
Trier in explaining his preference for "simple" women as the raw material for
his "art"—moreover in language that von Trier himself has used. "Why are they
all so stupid?" Verge asks:

> JACK: (off) "Who's stupid?"
> VERGE: (off) "all the people you kill—the women you kill strike me as
>   seriously unintelligent"
> JACK: (off) "I kill men too."

VERGE: (off) "But you only talk about the stupid women, unless you think all women are stupid. . . .

JACK: (off) No, but women are easier, not physically, but easier to work with. Easier to cooperate with.

VERGE: (off) To kill, you mean.[76]

Hallund maintains that she and von Trier made Jack's female victims stupid "because Jack couldn't have conceived of them differently, because they served his purpose. So they are . . . not full characters. They are representative of Jack's memory."[77] Likewise, the graphic and extreme nature of Jack's violence against women was key to the film's discussion of masculinity. The film is "about this idea that a lot of the identity of manhood is based upon the destruction of women, [that] it's . . . how you express your real masculinity":

> Jack is a man who can only see himself through his obligation of [sic] women. His only worth is through his obligation of women. Lars chose it like that. . . . which I think is necessary because it's true. A lot of people, a lot of artists, a lot of psychopaths, this is how they feel and this is their psychology. And it's so sad and ridiculous and pathetic, but we buy into it. And that's why I think it's an important film, as it . . . is a portrait of these kinds of men and how they perceive women, how terrified they are of them, how they have to denigrate them in order to feel of any worth.[78]

For many viewers, however, the cruelty of the film, like sheer excess of Ellis's novel, seemed not only to represent misogynistic contempt and rage but to *express* it. "Lars uses that and he abuses that and maybe makes fun with it," she adds. *The House That Jack Built* is unique in portraying Jack's misogyny without psychological rationalizations, without "redemption or reclamation," she argues. Indeed, the film "almost celebrated it because Jack celebrated Jack." Thus "it had that kind of Trieresque irony" Lars is known for, irony "verging on a celebratory kind of attitude"—not unlike that of Highsmith's Ripley or Harris's Lecter.[79] This is consistent with her statement that *The House That Jack Built* is not merely a portrait of a psychopath but a radically psychopathic film engineered to make audiences deeply uncomfortable—at the root of which is von Trier's own conflicted relationship with women: "I think there's . . . a bit of Lars's inferiority toward women expressed in this film and his feeling of a kind of rage against women."[80] Yet "when he [Jack] says things like, 'Why is it always the man's fault' and he sits there with a knife [about to cut Simple's breasts off]? I mean, how can anybody think that that's not a joke . . . showing how pathetic men are?" she asks. "But it was very uncomfortable . . . I hated it." She concludes, "I think it's an important film. But I don't like the film." Elsewhere, she clarifies that it is "an interesting film or well made, but I don't think it's a good film." To call it good "diminishes" it, and "I don't think one should like [it]."[81]

Like Ellis and Harron, von Trier exploits the fascination with serial killers to expose Western culture's toxic masculinity and neofascist nostalgia. *American Psycho*'s Bateman is ultimately pathetic—cowriter Turner calls him a "dork"— and the film, like the book, ends by suggesting that the scenes of torture and murder may have been fantasies, delusions of grandeur in an era in which serial killers have become regarded as celebrities.[82] Jack's celebrity signature, "Mr. Sophistication," similarly points out the gap between reality and his self-regard, as Hallund suggests in her comment that the film is "a portrait of the ridiculous man," adding that "it's also a portrait of a ridiculous artist who justifies his evil by claiming it as art."[83]

Funny Games / Cinema of Cruelty

Austrian filmmaker Michael Haneke shares von Trier's position near the top of the list of European auteurs associated with extreme cinema and similarly accused of sadism, nihilism, and assaults on their audiences. Haneke's earliest and most notorious features *Benny's Video* (1992) and *Funny Games* (1997) addressed and deconstructed an American culture of media violence through a combination of Brechtian distantiation and Artaudian theatre of cruelty. Beginning with *Epidemic*, von Trier has become associated with a similar combination, perhaps most notably in the U.S.-targeted *Dogville* and *Manderlay*. As Angelos Koutsourakis explains, drawing on Stephen Barber,[84] Artaudian theatre of cruelty is not what the term might seem to suggest, the "simulation of horrific and revolting images which aim at producing fixed affective responses," but "an act against social conformism with a view to articulating what Michael Haneke calls *unbequeme Wahrheiten* (uncomfortable truths) . . . that point to broader social crises."[85] Framing their Artaudian "cinema of cruelty" with Brechtian (and modernist) strategies such as the direct address to the audience or documentary footage in fiction film, von Trier and Haneke assure that their assaults on the audience make a point.

Funny Games not only denies viewers the mechanisms for disavowal typically offered by the genre but breaks the fourth wall, directly implicating the audience, taking us to task for our complicity with and enjoyment of screen violence.[86] Two chillingly polite young men, Peter (Frank Giering) and Paul (Arno Frisch), dressed in immaculate tennis polo shirts, shorts, and white gloves, enter and hold an upper-middle-class family under siege at their lake house, torturing and murdering them before moving to the next house, where they repeat the routine. Paul, the more intelligent of the two, "directs" the action, addresses the camera with knowing looks, winks, quips, and rhetorical questions, blurring the border between fiction and the viewer's reality. Asking the victims to bet on their chances of survival, he looks at the camera and asks us to bet also. When Anne (Susanne Lothar) unexpectedly grabs Peter's gun and shoots him, Paul rewinds the video, reassuming control of the narrative. Meanwhile, Peter whines about violations of conventional formulas for sustaining suspense. On one level, they offer a caricature of the puckishly ironic Hitchcockian director using his actors as pawns while playing to and against the complacent audience's expectations.

Like Haneke's films, *The House That Jack Built* synthesizes Brecht and Artaud: offering prolonged and graphic murder scenes with metacinematic or performative elements that alternate with semiformal "lectures" accompanied by Godardian bombardments of text, documentary footage, and archival materials. When Jack murders, the camera pointedly represents his gaze, forcing the spectator, for example, in "Incident 2," to spot his prey, the widow Clare Miller (Siobhan Fallon Hogan), hauling her groceries down a dark road. The first incident unceremoniously deconstructs the serial killer profile. A sullen, disengaged, apparently aimless loner, Jack picks up Lady 1 (stranded with a flat tire and broken jack), who wheedles him into driving her to a repair shop and back. Playing "smart," she provokes him to kill her, whereupon he discovers his calling. Outlining the profile down to the murder weapon, she takes apart the serial killer as a category, modus operandi, and lifestyle, reminding spectators of how an icon has devolved into a cliché. Nervous about riding with a stranger, she notes that "you might as well be a serial killer. Yes, I'm sorry, but you do sort of look like one," adding, "Perhaps it's the van. It's like the kind you'd expect to be kidnapped in or one used for transporting corpses."[87] After her presumption and Jack's patience have reached the tipping point, she proffers the final insult, that he doesn't "have the disposition for that sort of thing," being "too much of a wimp to murder anyone," and he turns her discourse on her by bludgeoning her with the jack, pun fully intended.

By "Incident 3," which takes a page from *Dogville*'s Brecht, Jack presents the murder of the family as a kind of performance art, allegorizing and hence distancing it through an elaborate, blackly ironic discourse on "ethical hunting" introduced by a lecture on the history and art of trophy display. Jack stages the murders as a sport in which he rigorously follows the rules, down to displaying the mother framed by her dead sons, the three in turn framed underneath a border of dead crows. Spectators are cruelly forced to take Jack's perspective as the director of this film within the film, shooting from a tall hunting tower, with his rifle scope taking the position of the camera following the spoor of the bleeding woman (Sofie Gråbøl) as she attempts to crawl away. Perhaps the most painful moments are also the most grotesque, provoking horror, grief, and laughter simultaneously: parodying the "awkward family dinner" scene, Jack, as a rigid father figure, compels the mother to proceed with the family picnic they had planned and to feed the (dead) youngest child, "Grumpy" (Rocco Day)—so named because he did not want to go hunting—a piece of pie. Paradoxically, as in Haneke, such alienation effects implicate the viewer and intensify the impact, and prompted exits at Cannes.

Haneke is the master of the sadistic long, static take, which he uses in *Funny Games* to depict not the violence, but the aftermath of silent suffering. In von Trier's film, much of the grotesque picnic scene after the shooting of the two boys is protracted and hushed as the audience is forced to experience the mother's shock, horror, and emerging grief in an approximation of real time. Like Haneke's most notorious (and many of von Trier's earlier) films, *The House That Jack Built* attracts spectators expecting violence as entertainment and turns it on them, forcing them to experience both the labor and the trauma inherent in the act of killing. Meanwhile, political points are made along the way: about the rise of the "*Homo trumpus*," the hypocrisy of gun culture American style in the name of conservative family values, and about humanity's predatory nature.

Speaking about his role in Václav Marhoul's *Nabarvené ptáče* (*The Painted Bird*, 2020), Stellan Skarsgård mentions a review of *The House That Jack Built* that "complained that the violence wasn't pleasant enough to watch, and it's to me an odd idea that violence always should be pleasant, when in reality it never is." In words that Haneke might have uttered, he continues:

> There's much less violence in this film than there is in any popcorn film, but the violence is truthful. . . . You see people die to the left and the right in all

those action films, and then you see a film about the act of killing, where there's one murder, and it goes on forever and is really brutal and gives you an idea of what it's like to murder someone and to be murdered. . . . you can show [violence] as entertainment and you can mow down 400 star troopers without considering their widows and children, but you also should be allowed to show violence in all its horror.[88]

Paul and Peter are particularly chilling because they are perfect blanks, motiveless and mindless beyond entertaining themselves with "funny games." When Georg (Ulrich Mühe) asks them the inevitable question "Why?," Paul submits a story about Peter's abusive childhood, and Peter begins to sob before both break out in uproarious laughter, taking down the cliché. Similarly, Jack's psychological motivation, other than his ambition and failure to become an artist/architect/auteur, is deftly omitted, as discussed previously, and in keeping with his intention to force viewers to think beyond pop-psychological cliché and to look elsewhere for the point. But where Haneke refuses to suggest causes or solutions other than in the violent media culture that has produced Paul and Peter (who also call themselves Tom and Jerry and Beavis and Butthead), von Trier implicitly indicts the misogyny intrinsic to a type of masculine identity suggestive of male rage in the era of #MeToo, while damning a Western culture of violence and destruction epitomized in fascist aesthetics and ethics, and also, perhaps most compellingly, himself.[89]

THE HOUSE THAT JACK BUILT AS AN ESSAY FILM

Like several critics, Peter Schepelern, von Trier's mentor from the late 1970s at the University of Copenhagen, noted the film's—or is it Jack's?—pretentious, didactic tone created by the "essays scattered through the movie like lectures." This he found ironic in that Lars as a student typically disparaged or skipped lectures, to which von Trier replied, "The lectures are another medium—almost of a book." Thus, pairing the film with *Nymphomaniac* in terms of its transmedial experimentalism, he proceeded to echo T. S. Eliot, seemingly without tongue in cheek, noting that "all culture stands on that of the past. That is why reading books makes you wise."[90]

Wise or not, and *Nymphomaniac* notwithstanding, *The House That Jack Built* is von Trier's most essayistic film. That said, the message inherent in the film is less obvious than Schepelern's comments suggest. As suggested earlier, one of the film's devices, in part following on Highsmith, is seduction: it lures viewers into following Jack's narrative and the logic, however perverted, of his argument. And if the narrative situation, a dialogue between Jack and Verge, resembles *Nymphomaniac*'s digressionism, it does so only superficially. In his 2016 "Director's Statement," von Trier explained that he was dissatisfied with tone and characterization in the earlier film's off-screen dialogue, and that the problem was that the digressions were "written in advance and therefore perhaps not worked into the film in an optimal manner." As for *The House That Jack Built*, he intended to "continue develop[ing] the script and the digressions alongside the shootings" in "close cooperation with the actors."[91] Further, where Seligman often dominates *Nymphomaniac*'s discourse, Verge, eventually revealed as a variation on Virgil, Dante's guide to *The Inferno*, escorting Jack to hell, is less important for his counterarguments, which are short, often scoffing, comments rather than sustained positions. Verge is important rather for his symbolic role as the film's "moral compass" and eventually for the resonances that Bruno Ganz brings to the film.[92] Unseen until the last twenty minutes, the ambience of his disembodied voice, soft, slightly muffled, and distinctively accented, makes him less a character than Jack's alter ego or conscience in an internal dialectic. Hence the film is less a narrative *or* a dialogue than a cumulative argument: interspersed between the film's five incidents and presented directly to an unseen audience through documentary-style stock footage, paintings, drawings, diagrams, and a series of clips from nine of von Trier's own films. Recognizing this, Lawrence Garcia called the film an "astonishing, primarily dialectical work disguised as a narrative: von Trier's digressions, conversations, and provocations are here crafted into perhaps the most forceful, generative and challenging vision the director has produced to date: a summative opus, a "dark light" (the photographic negative) that draws equally from his own cinema and the annals of history."[93]

The House That Jack Built is equally von Trier's most self-referential and confessional film. Marking his return to Cannes seven years after he was pronounced *persona non grata* in 2011, it was, on at least one level, a medium for addressing issues and views he had broached before being muzzled, especially the outraged response to his admission of having felt "sympathy" for Hitler, adding that "I can see him in his bunker in the end."[94] As few of his listeners then realized, he was alluding to (or, at the very least, flashing back on) scenes from Oliver Hirsch-biegel's *Der Untergang* (*Downfall*, 2004), starring Bruno Ganz as a stooped, pal-sied, defeated, yet mesmerizing Führer during the last days of the Reich, which he had recently watched. Ganz's Hitler is three-dimensional and utterly believ-able as never before: he breaks out in frenzied rants and fights delusional bat-tles but is fatherly and gentle to children and demonstrably loves Blondi, his dog.[95] To critics who complained that the film "humanized" Hitler and his hench-men, *Newsweek*'s David Ansen replied, "Yes, and it should: to pretend these villains were less than human is to let ourselves off the hook, to take the easy and dangerous exit of demonology."[96] And so, after his remarks about "sympa-thy" with Hitler were so radically misunderstood, and perhaps with something like Ansen's point in mind, von Trier engineered *The House That Jack Built* to elicit empathy with a serial killer who adulates the iconography and aesthetic of the Third Reich. Then, in a stroke of Trieresque genius, he cast Ganz as Vir-gil, the righteous interlocutor of Jack's imitation of Hitler, the failed artist.[97] Von Trier's point in *The House That Jack Built*, implied in 2011, boils down to a truism: as we must know the past in order to avoid repeating it, we must seek to "understand" Hitler and recognize the Hitler in ourselves. Otherwise we may unwittingly become him—or, in an only slightly less horrific scenario, elect him—as von Trier suggests in his aforementioned allusion to "the rise of the *Homo trumpus*." In June 2018, while discussing the necessity of getting viewers to "follow" Jack, von Trier suddenly blurted, "I think of how the people were teaming up [behind] Hitler, and then there came . . . rumors that it was a dirty, dirty war, and still, because he had this charisma, they stayed with him, . . . not to the very end, but far."[98]

VON TRIER'S MODEST PROPOSAL: SATIRE AND ANTI-PHILOSOPHY

Jack's discourse is a Mephistophelean variation on the digressive strategy behind *Nymphomaniac*'s Seligman. Introduced as a likeable but often clueless pedant, as the film goes on, and especially in *Volume II*, Seligman expresses politically cor-rect (and therefore simplistic or hypocritical) views, leading viewers into a trap sprung in the film's conclusion. Although Jack is obviously unreliable from the outset, his digressions are similarly designed; employing familiar examples and visuals, they lead viewers to try to understand Jack's train of thought, luring us into sympathy with the devil. Von Trier hopes that perhaps then we will see the evil in our own rationalizations—indeed, inherent in the very process of reasoning. Thus *The House That Jack Built* is a potent example of what Robert Sinnerbrink deems von Trier's "anti-philosophy."[99] This employs satire, game-playing, and provocation in ways that undermine Enlightenment rationalism and philosophy through a deconstructive critique derived from Romanticism. "Anti-philosophy" is however, perhaps ultimately, film-philosophy in the sense of generating cinematic thought.

Nymphomaniac resembled anatomy or Menippean satire—a fanciful and disorganized blend of fiction and essay with lightly satirical commentary on a wide variety of topics. *The House That Jack Built* is, relatively speaking, a sustained exercise in dramatic irony more akin to Juvenalian satire: bitter, pessimistic, contemptuously indignant, direct, and brutal, and brilliantly epitomized in the Anglo-Irish author Jonathan Swift's "A Modest Proposal for Preventing the Children of Poor People from Being a Burthen to Their Parents or Country, and for Making Them Beneficial to the Publick" (1729). Swift's target was England's economic and political exploitation of Ireland, and his narrator's argument, in the form of an economic treatise, proposed butchering the infants of the Irish poor and selling them as a culinary delicacy to wealthy English landlords to ameliorate poverty in Ireland. Playing off the incongruity of solving an economic and humanitarian problem with human trafficking, cannibalism, and infanticide, Swift's moral point emerged from the proposal's complete amorality and lack of empathy.

Jack's argument begins with a pedantic lecture on the function of flying buttresses in Gothic cathedrals, followed by his "readings" of William Blake's "The Tyger," "The Lamb," and *The Marriage of Heaven and Hell*. Claiming that Blake's predator, the tiger, offers an ecological balance to prey animals represented by the lamb, he argues that, in the same way, the artist's creative energy is a necessary counterpoint to reason and order. With Jack as his devil's advocate, von Trier marshals familiar tools of satire—Nietzschean inversion (of light and dark, lamb and tiger, good and evil), parody (of art criticism), incongruity, exaggeration, and irony, to support Jack's argument that murder should be understood as Dionysian creativity. Thus if Swift played off the incongruity of solving a humanitarian and political crisis with an economical solution (via sanctioned human trafficking and infanticide), von Trier plays off the incongruity of Jack's defense of murder, an ethical issue, with an aesthetic argument, enlisting Gothic architecture, Romantic art, and poetry. The narrative situation puts a contemporary gothic villain in dialogue with the classical era Roman poet Virgil. Then it abruptly switches from a grainy, documentary-style naturalism and the serial killer genre to a baroque descent into hell drawn from a range of classical literature and art. An even darker irony resonates from casting Ganz, in an homage to his performance as Hitler, as Virgil (representing reason and wisdom), the guide and protector of fellow poet Dante in *The Divine Comedy*, thus putting Jack in the role of Dante Alighieri himself—down to his costume, a red robe Dante typically wears in depictions of *The Inferno*.

In the major premise—and central joke—Jack is a hyperbolic portrait of von Trier himself, representing the psychopath within, his shadow or negative self. Citing von Trier, Hallund has verified that Jack's aspiration stems from von Trier's own "childhood fascination with being an architect,"[100] inspired by his admiration of an architect in his family on his mother's side, together with her nurturing of his creativity.[101] As a child, von Trier, like Jack, also took up photography and became fascinated with the "dark light" of the negative, or light and life materialized, which Jack equates with death.[102] In obvious self-parody, Jack argues that each of his murders is a work of art, in that art uses up, deconstructs, and reconstructs its raw materials, supporting his point with references to von Trier's own films. "There is definitely an element of selv-portrait [sic] there," von Trier admitted in his "Director's Statement" of 2016: "My films have brought a lot of pain to a lot of people. As the little stone in the shoe—Jack is a major stone."[103] Jack the failed artist is the von Trier who is often seen as an autocratic, nihilistic artist who tortured female actors—who, in Björk's words, used suffering women to give his films a "soul." Drawing directly on von Trier's comments in interviews about *Melancholia* as well as the 2011 Cannes press conference, Jack maintains that the most sublime images, the true "masterpieces," are based in destruction and fear—citing the Holocaust (which haunts von Trier's Europe trilogy) while admiring the Stuka, whose screeching "Jericho" whistle was designed to terrorize the enemy, as von Trier did in 2011.[104]

A major cinematic leitmotif spins off a clip from a seven-minute, 8 mm film von Trier made when he was fourteen, *Hvofor flygte fra det du ved du ikke kan flygte fra? Fordi du er en kujon* (*Why Try to Escape from That Which You Know You Can't Escape From? Because You Are a Coward!*, 1970). After encountering a child, seemingly a friend about the same age, who has been hit by a truck, the young protagonist's instinct is to flee. He runs across meadows and streams, haunted by the specter of the child, now appearing with a grotesquely bandaged head. In an expressionistic sequence, he struggles through a field, engulfed in a haptic blur of green, blue, and golden reeds and is forced to confront his adversary and double: the fact of death as inescapable, as well as his conscience, in that his friend haunts him with his resistance to empathy and failure to take responsible action. In four different instances in *The House That Jack Built*, von Trier repeats the segment of the boy running through the reeds. In the second of these, mentioned briefly earlier, the clip is followed by the film's most controversial scene as young Jack in closeup turns and glances at the camera, then, fascinated, gazes at a group of men harvesting grain, moving rhythmically together and accompanied by the sound of their scythes cutting through the stalks, then turns to look at a yellow duckling swimming in a pond. Impassively scooping it up in a fishing net, he slices off one of its legs with tin snips and watches it swim in distraught circles. Von Trier thus makes an explicit connection between his own early film about his fear of and obsession with death, the allure of "the breath of the scythe," repeated poignantly in Jack's brief vision of the Elysian fields, and a formative moment in Jack's development as a killer. In perhaps the most telling of these allusions, the scene with the reeds blends with a surreal underwater shot, supplying a transition from the world of the narrative and Jack's descent to hell.

When I asked him why he quoted his own films, including juvenilia, in such a context, he joked that the choice was economical: "If I said I want[ed] a cut from *Psycho*, I probably couldn't get it," then admitted that "when I got the idea

FIGURE 4.2 Young Jack (Emil Tholstrup) glances at the camera before becoming entranced with a group of reapers in *The House That Jack Built*.

I thought it was kind of cheeky," before adding, "I was afraid that it would be my last film." Finally, he confessed, "Yes, yes, but I like to see it [Jack's serial killing] as a metaphor for art"—one that comments on his own art specifically.[105] When I asked how so, he replied that art is

> hard. You hurt yourself in the hard work, right? And, uh, you hurt your family because you're not there. I was very sure at a certain point that I was the dream father, you know, and after that, all my children have been screaming at me . . . "Why didn't you do this and why didn't you do that and why were you not here?" And that's the story you always hear about directors, that they don't have time for their family.

He added, "When you do a film, you feel like a dictator. And of course, to take it to the level where Jack is, in the end, is very extreme. . . . But you have, to a certain degree, to be a little evil to make a film, because you have to get your will through." He continued, "Yeah, but you know I'm cynical, . . . and you have to be to a certain degree, to direct."[106] This is the filmmaker notorious for manipulating characters, actors, and audiences while distancing himself from the emotional violence he puts them through, to the extent that Skarsgård in 2003 jokingly described him as "a hyper-intelligent child who is slightly disturbed, playing with dolls in a dollhouse, cutting their heads off with nail-clippers."[107] Therefore, when Jack arranges his victims' bodies before photographing them, taxidermizes Grumpy to make him smile, or contorts his entire "corpus" into a house, he literalizes the director's role.

Jack's equivalent of von Trier's appropriation of the German "von" for his auteur's signature becomes "Mr. Sophistication" (as per the Jack the Ripper, Son of Sam, or the Zodiac Killer), signifying the identification with the auteur that allows Lars Trier to detach himself personally from the brutal process of making von Trier's art. "So Mr. Sophistication is the theoretician? Is he also the one who cuts people's breasts off?" Verge asks. "No," Jack replies, "but he gives me good ideas. And he gives me the opportunity to use the third person singular. Such differences grammar affords us. . . . I cut people's breasts off. He cuts people's breasts off. And most surprisingly, [in a wink at the audience] you cut people's breasts off."[108] Ultimately Jack becomes a metacinematic self-caricature, Trier's performance of von Trier at its most disreputable, a summation of the qualities for which he is most berated by critics and commentators: his narcissism, his obsessive-compulsive disorder, his pedantry and didacticism, his manipulation of audiences, and his allegedly Hitchcockian manipulation of women, his characterization of women as naïve "Gold Hearts," whom Jack regards as the most malleable "material" for his art. In "Incident 4," Reilly Keough, cast as "Simple," a drug-addled bimbo with a heart of gold (whose real name, Jacqueline, positions her as his female alter ego), asks in desperation, "Can we just talk about something normal? What you do or things like that."

> JACK: Something you can relate to directly, you mean.
> SIMPLE: (unsure) Yes, I think so.
> JACK: So information about what I do in very simple words, Simple?
> SIMPLE: Yes, thank you.
> JACK: I kill.
> SIMPLE: (a bit surprised) Okay?
> JACK: I've killed sixty people. I'm a serial killer, Simple.[109]

Here Jack quotes directly from von Trier's three-minute short film "Occupations" (2007), a contribution to Cannes's sixtieth-anniversary tribute to the cinema, in which he performed a blackly humorous, murderous version of himself. An obnoxious critic sitting beside him during a screening persists in talking in his ear, bragging about his business acumen and wealth, before condescending to ask, "And what do *you* do?" "I kill," von Trier replies, pulling out a mallet and bludgeoning the man to death. The blood-spattered audience looks on politely before returning their attention to the screen.

MURDER AS ART

Jack's premise that murder can be regarded as sublime art has had a respectable heritage as well as a considerable cachet of late. Joel Black traces the notion to the Gothic revival and to Romanticism as a logical extension of the transgression inherent in the sublime before demonstrating its exponential rise in popularity in the modern era. "Violent acts compel an aesthetic response in the beholder of awe, admiration, or bafflement," he writes in *The Aesthetics of Murder: A Study in Romantic Literature and Contemporary Culture*. "If an action evokes an aesthetic response, then it is logical to assume that this action—even if it is murder—must have been the work of an artist."[110] Although Friedrich Schiller flirted with the idea in his "Reflections on the Use of the Vulgar and the Lowly in Works of Art" (1802), it was Thomas De Quincey's 1827 essay "On Murder Considered as One of the Fine Arts" that stated unequivocally that "murder . . . may be laid hold of by its moral handle . . . *that* . . . is its weak side; *or it may also be treated aesthetically, as the Germans call it*—that is, in relation to good taste."[111] Since then, as Steven Jay Schneider has noted, authors and poets as diverse as André Gide, Oscar Wilde, Jack Abbott, Alain Robbe-Grillet, Yukio Mishima, Marcel Schwob, and Gregor von Rezzori have followed in presenting murder from an aesthetic perspective. And when the antagonists and antiheroes of contemporary films including *Theatre of Blood*, *The Texas Chainsaw Massacre*, *The Silence of the Lambs*, and *Se7en* "turn murder into an artistic product, an artistic performance or some bizarre combination of the two, consumers . . . are once again encouraged, occasionally forced, to acknowledge a side of themselves they normally keep hidden, even from themselves—a side that enjoys, appreciates and admires the display of creative killings."[112] Its Romantic period origins notwithstanding, the concept

> stems from revolutions in the cultural discourses and meanings of "art" corresponding with the rise and popularisation of modern and avant-garde artistic practice. Largely as a result of these practices, "art" itself became more open to and associated with notions of "shock," transgression and offensiveness, with the violation of standing cultural and conceptual categories . . . and with incongruity—just think of Duchamp's "ready-mades," e.g., the urinal in the art gallery—rather than with traditional notions of aesthetic technique, form and beauty.[113]

The rise of the serial killer, defined as having committed three or more murders in succession, is a modern Western mass media phenomenon dating to the late nineteenth and twentieth centuries. The celebrity culture surrounding serial killers, moreover, has blurred the lines between true crime and mythology or fiction, thus intensifying this association. In a 1997 *Film Comment* piece titled "Kill and Kill Again," Richard Dyer lists among the social and cultural causes of the serial killer (including the "anonymity of mass societies," and the "loss of community and a single lifelong family") the "sexual objectification of women in media," a "cult of celebrity," and a cultural infatuation with seriality itself, suggesting that serial killers are the product of a mediated culture in which aesthetic detachment predominates over empathy and ethics.[114] Promising order within disorder and the pleasure of discovering patterns, the narrative of serial killing has an intrinsic mathematical and aesthetic appeal.

It is perhaps unsurprising that the contemporary serial killer genre has increasingly, and often with high seriousness, taken on the notion of murder as art—and vice versa. For Harris's serial killers, each murder is part of a ritual that ends in aesthetic metamorphosis and self-transcendence. *Red Dragon*'s Francis Dolarhyde reconstructs himself into the Red Dragon from Blake's watercolor *The Great Red Dragon Clothed in the Sun* (1803–1805), by tattooing and "building" his body in its likeness and making "home movies" of his transfiguration staged before audiences of dead families.[115] The aforementioned Lecter, a decadent flaneur from the tradition of Baudelaire, whose gourmand-style cannibalism is the mark of his exquisite taste, layers his kinesthetically spectacular murders with allusions to mythology, classic literature, painting, and sculpture—as in *The Silence of the Lambs*, where he seizes on the metaphor of metamorphosis and flight, or in *Hannibal*, where he hangs his adversary in a configuration based on a painting of the five-hundred-year-old murder of the latter's ancestor. Yet it was Bryan Fuller's television series *Hannibal* (2013–2015) that truly literalized the murder-as-art conceit through "an operatic narrative drive,"[116] condensing exposition into allusion, metaphor, and emotionally sustained spectacle against the backdrop of Lecter's (Mads Mikkelsen's) cannibalistic food art.[117]

Von Trier's approach to the metaphor is equally allusive, pretentious, and convoluted, if far less evocative or convincing—and for an important reason. Better at talking about murder as art than exemplifying it, Jack lectures on the cathedral architecture that inspired the Gothic Revival and paraphrases William Blake and, by association, the Romantic philosophical and aesthetic tradition that celebrated the sublime and Dionysian. Believing violence to be inherent in the human creativity, he aligns himself with the Romantic hero as a transgressive artist whose creative energy is inseparable from his revolt against the limitations of life and death. Beginning with his defense of his "art" via William Blake's "The Tyger" and "The Lamb," his key arguments presume the Romantic and Gothic writers' view of John Milton's Satan as more compelling than God and a hell full of energy and interest, whereas heaven, lacking action or conflict, remains abstract and static—leading to the film's culmination in a descent into sublimely roiling lava. In this context, repeated video clips of piano virtuoso Glenn Gould interpreting Bach's *Partita #2 in C Minor, BWV*

826 (1726) project a diabolical figure of frenzied, demonic art. The Bach partita, rendered with what Kristian Eidnes Andersen describes as an over-the-top
flourish, is repeated further in a leitmotif taken up by different instruments
throughout the film, perhaps most spectacularly in the fully orchestrated,
extreme slow-motion tableau based on Eugène Delacroix's painting *The Barque
of Dante* (1822) of Charon's boat delivering Dante to hell.[118] All of this corresponds with what von Trier said to Stig Björkman more than twenty years ago,
in reference to *The Kingdom*: "More than anything, there are more images in evil.
Evil is based far more on the visual, whereas good has no good images at all."[119]

Granted, the five incidents suggest the development of Jack's artistic consciousness and ambition: from found art to ornate tableaus that conclude spectacular performances. If his bludgeoning of Lady 1 with a car jack may be little
more than a bad pun, her deconstructed face takes on the geometry of a cubist
painting, a study in red (as what might be a Picasso is flashed on the screen), "a
deconstruction of a woman," which is "metaphorical murder, if you like, or . . .
a reconstruction," as Hallund describes it.[120] Or, as Bodil Marie Stavning Thomsen observes, this moment, in which Uma Thurman, a cinematic icon of beauty,
"is decomposed into the primary icon of red only to quickly dissolve into an
iconic modern artwork, where personal traits have disappeared, might be seen
as von Trier's first comment on the drive towards iconicity"—iconicity in Jack's
view being intrinsically murderous.[121] As for Jack, in this act he discovers how
he might turn premeditated acts of violence into artistic decisions. "Incident 3"
blends performance art (in which, posing as a father figure, he turns the

FIGURE 4.3 Embedded video clips of piano virtuoso Glenn Gould interpreting Bach's *Partita
#2 in C Minor, BWV 826* (1726) project a diabolical figure of frenzied, demonic art.

FIGURE 4.4 "Incident 3" blends performance art with Jack's most elaborate tableau: a trophy display of the dead family framed by fifty dead crows.

pretense of a family picnic into a hunting exercise) with his most elaborate tableau: a trophy display of the dead family framed below fifty dead crows. Subsequently, Jack gains confidence and a sense of his role: he begins arranging the bodies into compositions, taking photographs, singling out the negatives, signing them as "Mr. Sophistication," and sending them to the local newspapers.

Indeed, like Lecter, Jack is convinced that his "work" is part of a grand aesthetic tradition. But if the murders in Harris's novels and their film and television adaptations genuinely aspire toward, and achieve, a pop variation on the sublime, Jack's kill scenes fall abysmally short—as Verge, representing the critic, often points out. "Oh, aren't you the dangerous man! Smacked her with the jack, did you?" he sneers after Jack relates the first incident. "Tell me something new or shut up!" Von Trier makes Jack a Lecter manqué, a caricature of the character of the serial killer as artist, and ultimately, as Hallund suggests, "the ridiculous man" as the ridiculous artist, and the first, second, and fifth incidents employ humor bordering on slapstick at his expense.[122] While "Incident 3" is Jack's most accomplished work of performance art, resulting in an elaborate trophy display, "Incident 4," in which he turns one of Simple's excised breasts into a message to the police and the other into a grotesque, if patently silly, wallet, is par for the course. Ultimately Jack does not create art; he *theorizes* about murder as art and the art of deconstruction as a rationalization of his failure to create, touting an aesthetic of destruction and "ruin value" derived from Albert Speer, who modeled his buildings on the Greek and Roman precedent of "using both weaker and stronger materials so that they in a thousand years would appear as aesthetically perfect ruins," citing icons associated with monomaniacal and totalitarian dictatorships—"Hitler, swastikas, bombed out cities, crematoria, Stalin, prison camps, the Emperor of Japan, kamikaze pilots, Mao, photos of the dead following the long march, Pol Pot, etc."[123] Jack is aligned with the Nazi aesthetic just before the final incident, which he stages as an homage to the Germans, who, short on ammunition to facilitate their pogroms, "experimented with killing several people with just one bullet."

Perhaps most important, *The House That Jack Built* damningly repositions the discussion of the sublime and the Nazi aesthetic that *Melancholia* embodied, and that he explained, however elliptically, during the Cannes 2011 press conference. Simultaneously celebrating and mocking his attraction to the sublime aesthetic, the film exposes its moral failure as a psychopathic lack of empathy. At the center of the film is the figure of Hitler the failed artist and architect of the Third Reich whose fascination with architecture, painting, sculpture, and music Frederic Spotts explores in *Hitler and the Power of Aesthetics* (2004). Hitler "used the arts to disguise the heinous crimes that were the means to fulfilling his ends, and his vision of the Aryan superstate was to be expressed as much in art as in politics: culture was not only the end to which power should aspire, but the means of achieving it," Spotts concludes.[124] As Hitler drew on Nietzschean and Wagnerian ideas, mythology, and music to support his ideology, Jack uses argument by authority—alluding to philosophy, literature, and art—to defend murder, drawing on some of the most compelling concepts and images not only from Blake, Burke, Kant, and Goya, but also Nietzsche, Albert Speer, and von Trier's own life and work.[125]

Hitler famously failed the entrance exam for the Academy of Fine Arts Vienna, twice. Although his attempts at human figures and expressions were crude, his best drawings and paintings, of buildings and monuments, demonstrated his interest in architecture while suggesting a failure of empathy in his eventual predilection for massing people into geometrical and architectural designs—into colossal icons.[126] And although Speer is frequently credited with the Reich's architecture, as Spots argues, Hitler was the "primus motor of the country's state architecture" and often drew the original designs—for example, for the massive Arch of Triumph for Berlin that he dreamed of creating.[127] Jack's aesthetic ambition is expressed in his serial attempts at architecture, to construct the perfect house on a piece of lakeside property, a failure that he hopes to transcend through *de*construction, both in the serial demolition of his own mediocre constructions and in serial murder, through which he reduces human beings to his signature iconography. Repeated shots of Jack pondering models for his "dream house" are juxtaposed with archival photos of Hitler and Speer looking over models of the "future" Berlin and Munich. Other photographs feature the Nazi Party rally grounds and the Volkshalle or the "Monster Dome," which aspired toward monumental grandeur and embodied the Führer's vision of the Reich as an unparalleled "treasury of art and culture," but was never completed. Jack's obsession with the iconography of the Third Reich aligns the two failed artists/mass murderers whose aesthetic is ultimately a bombastic form of

FIGURE 4.5 Jack's (Matt Dillon's) aesthetic ambition is expressed in his serial attempts to construct his dream house on a piece of lakeside property.

FIGURE 4.6 Jack's only completed construction is the grotesquely monumental sculpture that represents his total "body of work," a house of corpses contorted, wired, and frozen into place.

kitsch, while directly alluding to von Trier's fascination with Speer. Ultimately Jack's only completed construction is the mountain of frozen bodies he molds into grotesquely monumental sculpture that represents his total "body of work," an oeuvre literalized, with a damning finality, as a house of corpses contorted, intertwined, wired, and frozen into place, resembling a parody of Holocaust photographs of mountains of bodies exhumed from mass graves, or of Anselm Kiefer's reflections on the mythology of the Third Reich that fuse Holocaust art and literature, painting and sculpture.[128] As unworkable as a shelter as it is aesthetically incongruous—the antisublime if there ever was one—it is pronounced "usable," by a droll Verge, as a portal to hell.

Appropriately, Jack's house was designed at von Trier's behest by Danish architect Bjarke Ingels, whose "iconic" buildings are spaces where art and architecture intersect, and exhibited in the Copenhagen art museum Charlottenborg from September 21, 2018 (five days before the film's Copenhagen premiere), through January 13, 2019, along with other iconic constructions by the Bjarke Ingels Group (BIG). In this way it was detached from its cinematic context and reduced to a "pure" icon for the concept of murder as art—and art as murder.

Art as Murder: "Katabasis"

The conclusion of von Trier's "Director's Statement" of intentions could not be plainer: "With the character Verge as the moral compass of the story, the film will send our main character to the deepest darkness. My intention is that The House That Jack Built will be my most moral film to date. It is the story of a psychopathic serial killer, who is going to Hell for all his actions. I can hardly imagine a more suitable punishment."[129] Further, in a deft transition to the formal "Katabasis," von Trier alludes to final frame of *The Element of Crime*, seeming to confirm that Jack—and, to the extent that the film is a retrospective, von Trier—is simply getting his just deserts. Profiler cum serial killer Fisher stares down into a sewer hole into the depthless eyes of a loris, a small, nocturnal primate, recalling Nietzsche's famous line: "If you gaze for long into an abyss, the abyss gazes also into you."[130] Jack enters a manhole-sized portal in the floor of his house of corpses before descending through an underground cavern to hell proper. Then, in a moment of déjà vu, the first

lines of the film are uncannily repeated, indicating that Jack, much like
Fisher, has been in hell all along:

> JACK: (off) May I ask you something?
>
> VERGE: (off) I can't promise I'll answer.
>
> JACK: (off) Right, that's exactly what I meant. Are you allowed to speak
> along the way? I was thinking there might be rules?
>
> VERGE: (off, in a bad mood, ironic) Let me put it this way: Very few make
> it all the way without uttering a word. People are overcome with a
> "strange and sudden" need to confess on these trips. And not all of it can
> be said to be of great rhetorical quality, but do carry on merrily, just
> don't believe you're going to tell me something I haven't heard before.[131]

Supporting this view is Verge's presence as the film's moral compass, which
hints at Jack's infernal destiny from the beginning and arguably stands in for
the police, offering spectators an excuse for their fascination, a mechanism for
disavowing or containing our identification with a psychopath. But things are
not that simple. As Hallund suggests, by bringing Jack into "this mythological
context" that includes Virgil, the poet of *The Aeneid*, and Dante's *Divine Comedy*,
the film celebrates, even "immortalize[s]" him. Jack acquires a deep red velvet
robe that alludes to Dante's mantle in the most famous paintings of *The Inferno*.
Although red is a dominant and typically damning color in the film—what with
Jack's red van, red jack, and the recurrent motif of blood—through Dante's red
robe, Jack is "elevated to a status that he doesn't deserve," Hallund claims, adding that "it was a brilliant kind of tool."[132]

The multivalenced resonances of Ganz's Verge—especially when he materi-
alizes in "an old-fashioned suit"—add ambiguity to an experience of hell that is
already rich in incongruity.[133] Throughout the film, Ganz's German accent,
intermittent use of German words (like *schweiss*) and references (to Goethe's oak
at Buchenwald) remind viewers of Ganz's association with German culture and
his most iconic roles, most recently as Hitler in *Downfall* but also as the angel
Damiel in Wim Wenders's *Der Himmel über Berlin* (*Wings of Desire*, 1987) and its
sequel *In weiter Ferne, so nah!* (*Faraway. So Close!*, 1993).[134] When he reminds Jack
that "as I see it, it's you who called me," adding, "I've been with you for a while,
you just haven't noticed me!" Verge takes on resonances of Mephistopheles
through Ganz's marathon stage performance as Goethe's Faust in Peter Stein's
monumental 2000 production, together with the hooded figure of Death in *The*

Seventh Seal, who informs the knight that "I have been walking by your side for a long time."[135]

In the epilogue, von Trier and Hallund's blend of blatantly contradictory sources—among them Dante's *Inferno*, Blake's *The Marriage of Heaven and Hell*, Greek and Roman mythology, and Hermann Broch's *The Death of Virgil*—destabilizes what is often seen as the Dantesque finality of Jack's damnation. As von Trier reminded me in 2018, *Inferno* was a sadistic poem: "Actually the reason Dante wrote this was that he had so many enemies and then he . . . put them different places in hell as a revenge," with their punishments allegorizing the sin.[136] From this perspective, Dante's *Inferno* would have epitomized Jack's aesthetic of torture, terrorization, irony, and iconicity, making it not merely his fitting destination but his paradise. Dante, however, is contradicted by several other, diametrically opposed sources—typical, according to Hallund, of how von Trier "flips things and puts the opposites together," among them "the Roman and Greek mythology . . . [where] the afterlife has the Elysian Fields. So is it a punishment? It's not a punishment. Which religion do you believe in, which mythology are you adhering to? And the mill in hell, that was brilliant . . . when Blake goes into hell, and he sits by the bank of the river . . . of what is supposed to be hell, he's at the top and he sees the mill."[137]

The window to the Elysian Fields evokes a Greek and Roman concept in which paradise is located within the underworld that also includes Tartarus. Jack experiences this as a flashback to the pastoral image from his childhood of the golden fields and the village men laboring in unison to evoke "the breath of the scythe." But the gold-drenched sequence celebrates death's harvest and is laden with pain and suffering. According to the script, the villagers are "all very old and look as if they have been working with scythes all their lives. Their fingers . . . are severely crooked, fitting perfectly to the grip on the scythes. A smiling old man is missing a couple of teeth."[138] Earlier, while narrating his first, ecstatic encounter with the image, Jack waxes poetic: "It was if the meadow lived at its fullest in my consciousness when I listened to its breath," allowing any irony to be supplied by the viewer.[139] And that epiphany directly precedes, and by suggestion inspires, his first act of cruelty, as he cuts off the leg of the duckling. It is no coincidence, of course, that the film's first publicity photo, designed after a frame from Dreyer's *Vampyr*, featured von Trier the auteur posed as the grim reaper with his scythe, tolling the death knell.

The mill image von Trier took from Hallund's discussion of Blake's *The Marriage of Heaven and Hell* (composed between 1790 and 1793, and widely regarded

FIGURE 4.7 Jack (Matt Dillon) envisions the Elysian Fields through a flashback to the pastoral image from his childhood of village men working in unison to evoke "the breath of the scythe."

as a satirical subversion of the binaries of Emanuel Swedenborg's *Heaven and Hell*, 1758), the passage in which Swedenborg and Blake's narrator debate the nature of hell. Swedenborg's angel presents the conventional vision of hell as a fiery pit, whereupon Blake's narrator proposes a "Memorable Fancy" in which the abyss is entered through a mill, a church, and an open Bible, representing social institutions Blake condemned. The mill Blake used to symbolize the oppression and destruction (of nature and human relationships) of the early Industrial Revolution, famously in "the dark Satanic mills" renounced in his poem "And Did Those Feet in Ancient Time" (1808).[140] Although von Trier was probably less interested in Blake's concept of the mill than in the resonance of the image, the poem inspired the scene in which Verge and Jack come upon a forest and two watermills: one is rigid, frozen, and the other groans and creaks as it rushes with water, suggesting (whether deliberately or not) Blake's key theme in which "contraries," or dialectical oppositions, make up the human soul.[141]

Blake's mill also inspired a significant aspect of the underworld's sound design. This is uncanny from the beginning—in the "eerie and strange reverb" of Verge and Jack's disembodied voices together with the ambient dripping and sloshing sounds that accompany the film's opening lines and repeat throughout the film, their footsteps inaudible as they descend—becoming increasingly ominous with the "buzzing" of the suffering damned, heard as they descend further.[142] The effect peaks with the creaking, groaning, whooshing of the mills, supplemented by the "breath" of the scythe, which together take on an increasingly haptic, rhythmical drone. (In the stage directions von Trier suggests that "we hear the buzzing sound rather loudly now; as if it comes from the watermill."[143] For the end scene, Andersen first experimented with more representational effects suggestive of Dante—for instance, human voices, where the sounds of "screaming and protest" were "flying around and . . . horrifyingly loud"—but when that became too much, he turned to evoking screeches from stretched balloons while "abus[ing] a cello," eventually refining and blending a host of "very ugly" sounds to suggest "a chaos of screaming."[144] Yet, in contrast to Dante's rigidly hierarchical arrangement, the circles to which Verge vaguely refers, von Trier's hell thrums with Dionysian energy of Blake's hell, whose "marriage" with heaven reflects the contrary nature of god. Like *Antichrist*'s forest, *Jack*'s hell is haunted with ambiguity. It provides few answers while raising questions: about good versus evil, about reality versus "Memorable Fancies," about whether Jack receives his punishment in some literal sense or whether the last twenty minutes is a projection of his dying mind.

Arguably, except for the single tear of regret provoked by the childhood memory of the reapers and a montage of flashbacks to his suffering victims, Jack's journey to hell is as wondrous as it is cautionary, and we are bound by narrative point of view to experience not only fear and angst but curiosity, fascination, awe, and even, however paradoxically, hope. When, early in their descent, Jack asks about the buzzing sound, and Verge replies, "I don't think you want to know where it's coming from," Jack exclaims, like a Dantesque (or perhaps Faustian) tourist, "I want to know everything!" In this desire, he represents us all. At the shooting script stage, von Trier described the descent as a kind of Kubrickesque "trip," one incorporating images from Jack's experiences, as follows: "The montage is thought also to include some of the iconic images from the film itself, likely electronically distorted, for example the flight through the reeds in acidic, possibly purple, colors. Scenes inspired by 2001: A Space Odyssey."[145] In another surreal, possibly Kubrickesque touch, just before the Delacroix tableau, "Jack and Verge are walking along a small path directly beneath the gigantic waterfall of blood. In the foreground, on the left hand side, stands a porcelain sink from the Victorian era. Super-slow-motion."[146]

Von Trier's "Director's Statement" further envisioned "the epilogue following Jack and Verge's physical descent into hell . . . as poetically grand" and "inspired by the last hundred pages of Hermann Broch's novel: 'The Death of Virgil,' in which the moment of death is drawn out to a state of being, and partly inspired by Dante's 'The Divine Comedy.' . . . The epilogue will blend abstract images of the mind with realism."[147] But where Broch's Virgil's identity gradually dissolves into a kind of universal consciousness, the film's final frames return to a more Highsmithian narrative drive followed by a Hitchcockian cliffhanger: to the sense of adventure, to the love of the game, to Jack's (and von Trier's) inability to resist taking just one more chance.

Broch's novel did, however, lend intellectual heft to Jack's theory of destruction and demolition as art and leads to one of the most self-referential moments in the film, prompting von Trier-as-Jack to think about his own body of work. (According to Hallund, von Trier not only read the novel but brought in a consultant to explain aspects of it to him.)[148] Begun while Broch was imprisoned in Austria by the Germans in 1938, *The Death of Virgil* merged the historical novel with the prose poem to become one of the great Modernist introspective works about the cultural role of art. Drawing on the legend that Virgil planned to burn his manuscript of *The Aeneid*, which had been commissioned by the Emperor Augustus, Broch's Virgil meditates on how art that is used by autocrats to advance an agenda is ultimately corrupted, reasoning that burning his poem could be seen as a kind of redemption of otherwise debased art. Interpreted by scholars as an anti-Nazi statement, in that the Nazis drew on classical and Wagnerian Norse mythology for much of their symbolism and ideology, Broch's meditations were no doubt appreciated by the von Trier who has waged wars against "the clichés of our time" and considered *Melancholia* a Wagnerian "popcorn movie," or who prized walkouts and boos over standing ovations.[149] In von Trier's film, Jack raises the issue with Verge:

> JACK: (off) When you were writing, didn't you yourself plan the destruction of your most popular literary work?
> VERGE: The Aeneid was a commissioned work and was venerated and glorified to the point where it was no longer art.
> JACK: (off) But who says destruction or demolition couldn't be as well—art that is?
> **Scene 123, Stock footage**
> Montage of pictures from classical ruins crosscut with Speer's gigantic constructions.[150]

In the end, Virgil does not burn *The Aeneid*, and Jack's argument for an art of demolition is exposed as an inversion of Broch's Virgil's reasoning, one celebrating a patently facile, fascist aesthetic of ruin value, destruction, sacrifice, and purification—an argument that along with Jack, finds its place in hell.

Yet, as suggested previously as well as in von Trier's stage directions, the descent to hell is less Jack's punishment than an ironic celebration of—and damning monument to—his and von Trier's shared aesthetic. Announced with the title card "EPILOGUE: KATABASIS," marked by a theatrical shift from graphic realism and documentary-style dialectic to dark expressionism and slow-motion tableaus, it is a grandiose realization of the sublime aesthetic and iconic drive that Jack has theorized throughout the film—and, perhaps most important, that von Trier had explored, and increasingly theorized about, since his depression. As the shooting script explains, "The tableaus are conceived from the idea of "the enhanced darkness," or tenebrism, in which most of a painting will be dark allowing a smaller area to be strongly illuminated, giving it a sense of monumentality and focus that through the viewer's fantasy spreads into the darkness and fills out the painting."[151] "Enhanced darkness," the term for the aesthetic principle for Bayreuth project and that von Trier equates with tenebrism, the artistic method often associated with the Italian Renaissance painter Michelangelo Merisi Caravaggio, is most starkly iconic in two of the most dramatic segments of the descent, both in extreme slow motion and reminiscent of Hieronymous Bosch's painings. In the first, Verge and Jack, in two transparent glass orbs on the bottom of the ocean, descend into an abyss; in the second, they inch down strongly illuminated ladders in total darkness. As they reach more familiar markers of hell—the watermills, the slow-motion rendition of Delacroix's *The Barque of Dante*[152] and the streaming lava pit that constitutes the abyss—the aesthetic modulates from tenebrism proper to chiaroscuro, or contrasted light and shadow originating from an irregular source. Von Trier's stage directions for the final scene, for example, explain that "All the light emanates from [the streaming lava] down there,"[153] suggesting Milton's concept of hell as "no light, but rather darkness visible."[154]

The final image of the film, like the images with which Jack sinisterly tops off each of his murders, is a negative image of hell that stands as its capstone. It signifies not simply the notion that Jack has proclaimed throughout, that murder can be art, but, far more chillingly, that art, and the technology used to produce it, is murder. Inspired by the young Lars Trier's experimentation with photography, this discussion presumes the intrinsic uncanniness of the photographic image, which abstracts from life to produce a haunting "undead" icon. Jack's primary fascination is with the negative's ability to make light materialize, revealing its "real inner demonic quality," or the Real that the narrative impetus and the visual drive overlook. As Thomsen interprets it, the negative confines the narrative optic drive to "a haptic, impenetrable—and unqualified—surface, which leaves no room for laughter, irony or humor."[155] After explaining his attraction to the "dark light" of the negative in quasi-scientific language, Jack elucidates his drive to kill (and von Trier's manic-depressive compulsion to create) through an elaborate black-and-white 3D animation of a man walking under streetlamps followed by his shadow, suggestive of the Jungian concept of the shadow, the unconscious, creative, and primitive aspect of the self, "the invisible saurian tail that man still drags behind him."[156] When Jack has just killed, he explains, he is like the man standing directly under the streetlight, whose shadow is at its densest: contained and satiated. And when he starts to walk, the shadow in front of him lengthens and "becomes stronger, like [his] pleasure,"

> but at the same time pain is on its way represented by the shadow behind me from the next lamppost, and at the midpoint between the lampposts the pain is so great it outweighs my pleasure. And with every step forward pleasure crumbles and pain grows behind me. Finally, the pain is so unbearably intense that I have to act, so when I reach zenith directly underneath the next lamppost I have killed again.[157]

Through this metaphor, von Trier may also describe the depression and anxiety that compel him to make films that are projections and transmutations of his pain, and that inflict pain—and Artaudian cruelty—on others.

As von Trier's most pessimistic and also most completely contextualized discussion of the sublime aesthetic of his most recent films—an aesthetic derived in part from his unfinished Wagner project—*The House That Jack Built* links von Trier's concept and practice of "enhanced darkness" and Jack's exploration of the "dark light" of the photographic negative with the drive toward iconicity and a fascist aesthetic of destruction. If the film is controversial for Jack's victimization of women, what is truly provocative is its taking on of Western art and culture with reference to that aesthetic, damning it all, together with Jack and von Trier himself, to hell. The film's cruelty has Artaudian purpose, however. Or, as Jung suggests, we do not become enlightened by imagining ideal concepts but by making the shadow visible. As von Trier appears to understand, one who confronts his shadow "knows that whatever is wrong in the world is in himself, and if he only learns to deal with his own shadow he has done something real for the world. He has succeeded in shouldering at least an infinitesimal part of the gigantic, unsolved social problems of our day."[158]

ENGINEERING HELL: *THE HOUSE THAT JACK BUILT*
AND THE ANTHROPOCENE

In *En Blomst* (*A Flower*, 1971), a a seven-and-a-half-minute film Trier made when he was fifteen, a boy of about the same age (Ole Benzon) finds a seed in a gutter, plants it on a hilltop surrounded by forest, and lovingly nurses it until, when it opens into a flower, he smiles for the first time. As the narrative is interrupted by shots of encroaching cranes and bulldozers and eventually dive bombers flying over the forest, the boy becomes anxious. The film ends as he lies bloodied next to the crushed flower. Juxtaposing images of life and death, nature and machines (representing industry and war), the film expresses the anxiety of a young Trier, whose fears of nuclear catastrophe made him feel "responsible for the whole world."[159] *A Flower* also anticipated von Trier's four postdepression films in their concern with the Anthropocene and the fragility of the ecosystem explored in the previous chapters.

In von Trier's films from 2009 to 2018, architecture is a visual metaphor of the Anthropocene. In contrast to the political concerns of the USA duology and *The Boss of It All*, represented through the town, plantation, and corporation, respectively, the postdepression films have taken a personal and self-reflective turn informed by the more domestic metaphor of the house, whether set against an intricately cultivated landscape (*Melancholia*) or a forest (*Antichrist*, *The House That Jack Built*). Where *Antichrist* explores a masculine projection of "female" nature as chaos refracted through the heroine's internalized misogyny, in *Nymphomaniac*, the heroine finds relief from her all-consuming compulsion, fostered by a soul-numbing urban environment, in her communion with trees. *Melancholia* (2011) and *The House That Jack Built* (2018) are on at least one level overt meditations on the Anthropocene represented through architectural affronts to the natural setting.

The consumerist excess represented by the castle that looms over *Melancholia*'s part 1 comes to stand for what Justine means when she says that "life on Earth is evil. No one will miss it." Jack's architectural efforts make a similar point with brutal irony, ending as he attempts to construct an emblem of his oeuvre in homage to the Nazi aesthetic, a house of contorted bodies wired into an collective whole. But where *Melancholia*'s Tjolöholm is monumentally pretentious, Jack's house is monumentally grotesque, a literalization of his concept of serial killing as art and genocide as architecture. While Blake's concept of Dionysian "energy" supports his main arguments, it is telling that Jack's references to "the great architect, God" are represented on the screen by images of Urizen, Blake's symbol of conventional reason and law, or the imagination in chains, often shown with the tools of the architect in his hands.

Set in the deep forests of Washington State, *The House That Jack Built* offers a culminating statement on human-caused climate change by juxtaposing art-as-destruction against nature-as-life. Like *Melancholia*'s Tjolöholm, Jack's "art-ful" murders and banal architectural efforts are erected against (and blight) an otherwise pristine natural backdrop that includes Mount St. Helens. Jack's serial killing embodies the violence against nature inherent in human creativity and epitomized in Western culture. Moreover (and perhaps correcting misinterpretations of *Antichrist*), evil is unequivocally human and gendered male through a (deliberately) stereotypical opposition of masculine art as violence with female nature as art's material. These settings, together with Jack's cubist iconizations of women, taxidermy art, and the "dark light" of the photographic negative, lead us to contemplate the Anthropocene in terms of the deconstruction and tortured reconstitution of life into dead matter.

In the epilogue, Jack descends into a hell of his—and human civilization's—own making and in which the film has been taking place all along. Like *Melancholia*'s slow-motion prelude, the series of tableaus that constitute the final descent is a composite of citations from classical and modernist literature, art, and music curated by "Verge"/Virgil and personalized from Jack's (and von Trier's) experience. Yet hell's sinister Blakean mills, its "engine," so to speak, are (incongruously, perhaps pointedly) located in a small evergreen forest. And if Jack maintains that the greatest icons depict or invoke destruction—as in the Nuremburg rally grounds, the swastika, or the Stuka, with its Jericho trumpet or whistle of doom—suggesting that the drive toward iconicity is inimical to life, von Trier has Verge respond, in his final illustration before the descent, with a poignant illustration to the contrary. This is an image of the ancient oak tree under whose boughs Goethe legendarily wrote and that remained standing at Buchenwald to survive the war as a reminder of the persistence of nature, life, and love: "Goethe! Here you can talk about masterpieces and the value of icons. The personification of humanism, dignity, culture and GOODNESS, was, by the irony of fate, suddenly present in the middle of one of the all time greatest crimes against humanity."[160] Verge's speech is followed by what stands as Jack's final lecture, summing up his Weltanschauung in words that directly echo *The Marriage of Heaven and Hell*: "Some people claim that the atrocities we commit in our fiction are those inner desires, which we cannot commit, in our controlled civilization. So they are expressed instead through our art. I don't agree. I believe heaven and hell are one and the same. The soul belongs to heaven and the body to hell. The soul is reason and the body all the dangerous things, . . . art and the icons."[161]

Perhaps we should take Jack, for once, at his word. While flagellating von Trier for his nihilism and his love of Artaudian cruelty, *The House That Jack Built* is neither, ultimately, a validation or condemnation of Dionysian art but a ferociously Swiftian "modest proposal" for a necessary dialectic of contraries—of persona and shadow, reason and energy, empathy and cruelty, nature and art: a photographic negative, as it were, an inverted argument for the "marriage" of heaven and hell.

CODA

Von Trier's next project, *Riget III* (*The Kingdom III*), the third season of his hit series of 1994 and 1997, to be shot in 2021 and released in 2022, is based on a treatment/summary that von Trier and cowriter Niels Vørsel prepared around the year 2000.[1] So perhaps he is returning to trilogies after all. But in a free-flowing interview with Christian Lund for the Louisiana Museum of Modern Art Channel in November 2020, von Trier returns repeatedly to the techniques, themes, and inspirations of the duologies of the past decade: transmediality, collaboration, gender politics, genre bending, provocation and deliberate bad taste, performative auteurism, Germany, and atheism as a kind of proactive nihilism.[2]

Early in the interview, he brings up the importance of literature as inspiration, calling it the "basic medium of my life." "What I love about literature," he asserts, "is that one man decides. . . . Even though I am a leftist in the world of art. Perhaps one day a way will be developed to create collective works of art," he adds, in what seems to be a nod toward his recent experiments with the collaborative and the dialogic for *Nymphomaniac* and *The House That Jack Built*, including *Gesamt* and his work with writing partner Niels Vørsel on *The Kingdom Exodus*. But "at the moment," he adds, "I see only that the more unique . . . Kubrick, for instance—who else could compose such a collection of cards?" His next examples, however, suggest his experiments with digressionism (generated in part by collaborative writing), adding that Proust wrote for "pages" about the names of French towns.[3] In *Twin Peaks*, David Lynch "made it a point that it doesn't come together at the end," so that, as in the concept of dramaturgy von Trier has maintained since Dogme 95, "there are small parts in the story—with the same dramaturgy as the whole." Then he moves to the controversial representation of gender that reaches its apex in the postdepression films: "I just thought we should make films about the struggle of the sexes. A world war between men and women. In the beginning, I wasn't thinking about gender politics, and then I made *Breaking the Waves*." Somehow inevitably gender leads to genre. "All I can say is that I've been guided by taking a genre and twisting it—and letting it contradict itself—that is my small thought factory. I wouldn't say that I've changed anything, but I've tried to create a genre that is a blend of naturalism and surrealism, you might say." Earlier, he has reminded us that "a genre is an obstruction too."

Yet ultimately, perhaps, the issue is provocation:

> First of all, I'm convinced that provocations are very important—particularly in a democracy. PC or political correctness is the most dangerous thing imaginable—because no one questions anything. Then everything stops. I've tried through provocations—and various techniques—I've tried to help. Both politically . . . though many probably won't believe it. I've done my best, I'd say, and I've been very dissatisfied with it. But some of the films I think are very efficient.

"I don't know how this last film will fit in," he adds meditatively. "*The House That Jack Built* I haven't come to terms with yet. It was done too much because of indolence." Then his thoughts gravitate toward the issue of taste: in *The Kingdom III*, "there are all kinds of bad taste and splatter . . . That's important to me. . . . Popular taste is bad. Let's think about those bells again [referring to the patently fake church bells, taken from stock footage, that crowned the ending of *Breaking the Waves*]. But actually if you've accepted the film and the religion in the film," bad taste works! The same goes for performance of the self, he suggests, suddenly returning to David Bowie in familiar language: "He is as important as what he does. . . . He was a great part of his [own] work—because he so thoroughly staged himself. Awesome." Surprisingly, von Trier does not bring up his depression and the Cannes 2011 scandal, the keynotes of this decade, directly. "We played games when we were kids. I was the German, of course," he says. Finally, his thoughts go tenderly and meditatively to Bruno Ganz: "I just noticed that I've got Bruno Ganz's phone number. When he was admitted to the hospital, I wrote to him, 'What is life like?' He wrote back, 'I'm in it. That's all I know.' One day later he was dead."

"Listen: I don't believe in God. It's all a fabrication," he interjects, returning to his point about the bells in *Breaking the Waves*. If, beyond their distinctive horrors and virtuosities, the films of his past decade have done us a service, that service lies in how devastatingly they have pierced through the fabrications, especially those structures that support our most dangerous complacencies, to expose the black screen—or the photographic negative—of the Real.

Beyond depression, taking Trieresque provocation to a new level, these films alternate between immersion and confrontation with some of the most regressive, counterintuitive, and taboo ideas and images imaginable, coercing us to think the unthinkable and watch the unwatchable. They epitomize a von Trier who has always considered a theater walkout the indisputable sign that a film is good. Yet the shock is matched by savage wit, intellectual rigor, and a distantiated aesthetic that generates ethical and political discourse. However different from his previous work, these films are perhaps the support for a maxim he used to explain his graduation film *Images of Liberation* in 1982: what is important—indeed, "the definition of true art"—is "that you use an impeccable technique to tell people a story they don't want to be told."[4]

APPENDIX

ANTICHRIST.
Action sketch.
Translated by Peter Schepelern

A young man is plagued by deep phobic anxiety for nature, in all its forms of presentation. He disallows the grasslands of the paved city, and can only shudder at the city's parks at a distance. After some unsuccessful attempts at treatment, the therapist, a woman in the middle thirties, decides to use "flooding," which is a violent exposure of the patient to the anxiety-inducing. It is a matter of finding the maximum stimuli. This proves to be the place where the patient had his first anxiety attack—namely, in a hut named "Eden" in the romantic mountains outside the city. Patient and therapist go to the hut. Along the way, it becomes more and more difficult for the patient to face the impending confrontation. The therapist prepares him patiently again and again by talking him through a visualization of his encounter with nature up there.

It is a shocking wreck that arrives with the therapist for "Eden" in full summer sun. The place looks like anything but something to be afraid of. A wonderful place surrounded by great oaks in a majestic mountain landscape. Behind the small mountain lake, deer graze in full peacefulness. The patient escapes from the grass under his feet into the hut. Where the two are prepared to stay overnight. . . .

In the time of the hut in the signs of fear, the therapist penetrates closer and closer to the plunge of the patient's anxiety, while the site's spooky nature goes up for her. It's like there's something very wrong with nature up here. The oak trees lose their acorns at night in excessively large and noisy amounts over the cabin roof. One night the therapist has been lying by hand too close to the open window she wakes up with a hundred ticks firmly sucked to hand. Slowly it is as if the patient's anxiety spreads into her.

It is the evil in nature that plays out the maximum here. The principle of nature: killing and death and putrefaction are then played out openly and unrealistically magnified. And finally, one day it is that the therapist can also hear it. . . . what the patient in the long nights complained about: the cry of the forest! The screed from the plants that yearn and argue and die. The therapist fears for his psychic health, a night where she medically has stunned and fixed the patient in the midst of an anxiety attack she could not otherwise stop. She is thus the only waking up in the house now the nature outside seems to approach so horrifying. After having secured the shutters, she returns to the sleeping bags to discover that the stunned patient is gone. . . . . and suddenly she gets to see him out there where he is looking at her . . . In one now as part of nature itself. With a seated wolf on either side of him. . . . .[1]

The original Danish:

ANTICHRIST.
Handlingsskitse.

En ung mand er plaget af dyb fobisk angst for naturen, i alle dens fremtrædelsesformer. Han viger uden om græstotterne i den gennemasfalterede by, og kan kun rystende skæve ind i byens parker på stor afstand. Efter en del forgæves forsøg på behandling, beslutter Terapeuten, en kvinde i midt trediverne, sig for at benytte "flooding," som er en voldsom eksponering af patienten for det angstfremkaldende. Det er et spørgsmål om at finde den maksimale stimuli. Denne viser sig at være stedet hvor patienten havde sit første angstanfald, nemlig i en hytte ved navn "Eden" i de romantiske bjerge uden for byen. Patient og Terapeut tager af sted mod hytten. Undervejs bliver det vanskeligere og vanskeligere for patienten at se den forestående konfrontation i øjnene. Terapeuten forbereder ham tålmodigt igen og igen ved at tale ham igennem en visualisering af hans møde med naturen deroppe.

Det er et rystende vrag der ankommer sammen med terapeuten til "Eden" i fuld sommersol. Stedet ligner alt andet end noget at være bange for. Et vidunderligt sted omkrandset af store ege i et majestætisk bjerglandskab. Bag den lille bjergsø græsser hjorte i fuld fredsommelighed. Patienten flygter fra græsset under hans fødder ind i hytten. Hvor de to gør sig rede til at overnatte. . . .

I tiden i hytten i angstens tegn trænger terapeuten tættere og tættere på udspringet af patientens angst, samtidig med stedets uhyggelige natur går op for hende. Det er som om der er noget helt galt med naturen heroppe. Eget-ræerne taber om natten deres agern i alt for store og larmende mængder over hyttens tag. En nat terapeuten har ligget med hånden for tæt på det åbne vin-due vågner hun op med 100 tæger fastsuget til hånden. Langsomt er det som om patientens angst breder sig ind i hende.

Det er ondskaben i naturen der udspiller sig maksimalt her. Naturens prin-cip: Drab og død og forrådnelse, udspilles så ganske åbenlyst og urealistisk forstørret. Og endelig en dag er det at terapeuten også kan høre det. . . . det som patienten i de lange nætter klagede over: skovens skrig! Skriget fra plant-erne der længes og strides og dør. Trapeuten frygter for sin psykiske helse, en aften hvor hun medicinsk har bedøvet og fikseret patienten midt i et angstanfald hun ellers ikke kunne stoppe. Hun er således den eneste vågne i huset nu naturen udenfor synes at nærme sig så gruopvækkende. Efter at have sikret skodderne vender hun tilbage til soveposerne for at opdage at den bedøvede patient er væk. . . . . . . og pludselig får hun øje på ham derude hvor han står kiggende ind på hende . . . i et nu som en del af naturen selv. Med en siddende ulv på hver side af ham. . . .[2]

NOTES

PREFACE

1. Perhaps the most important development in recent French literary studies, genetic criticism is less interested in the "final" text than with reconstructing and analyzing the writing process, by focusing on the "avant-texte," a collection of a writer's notes, sketches, drafts, manuscripts, correspondence, and the like. See Jed Deppman, Daniel Ferrer, and Michael Groden, ed., *Genetic Criticism: Texts and Avant-textes* (Philadelphia: University of Pennsylvania Press, 2004).
2. Paul Ricoeur, *Freud and Philosophy*, trans. Denis Savage (New Haven, CT: Yale University Press, 1970), 5; Eve Kosofsky Sedgwick, *Touching Feeling: Affect, Pedagogy, Performativity* (Durham, NC: Duke University Press, 2003), 36. See also Elizabeth S. Anker and Rita Felski, "Introduction," in *Critique and Postcritique*, ed. Elizabeth S. Anker and Rita Felski (Durham, NC: Duke University Press, 2017), 1–28.
3. Ann Laura Stoler, *Along the Archival Grain: Epistemic Anxieties and Colonial Common Sense* (Princeton, NJ: Princeton University Press, 2010), 50.
4. Granted, approaching *Antichrist*, *Melancholia*, and *Nymphomaniac* as a "depression trilogy" may evoke useful insights. For example, Bodil Marie Stavning Thomsen's *Lars von Trier's Renewal of Film, 1984–2014: Signal, Pixel, Diagram* (Arhus: Arhus University Press, 2018) concludes with a chapter on three "affective figures of depression, melancholia, and mania" (235–340) to demonstrate how this phase in von Trier's career employs affect in radical and distinctive ways.
5. Lars von Trier, interview by the author, Copenhagen, June 28, 2018.
6. Manuel Alberto Claro, interview by the author, Copenhagen, June 28, 2018.
7. Vinca Wiedemann, interview by the author, Skype, July 25, 2019.
8. Wiedemann, interview, 2019.

INTRODUCTION

1. *ArtyFarty*, season 1, episode 4, "Er Von Trier Okay?," aired August 9, 2020, DR2, 2020, https://www.dr.dk/drtv/se/artyfarty_-er-von-trier-okay_201018. Translated from the Danish by Peter Schepelern.
2. Lars von Trier, "Director's Statement," production notes, press kit, *Melancholia* official website, Magnolia Pictures 2011, http://www.magpictures.com/presskit.aspx?id=bbcb733d-8d0e-495a-b a6d-be9a79453d1c (accessed July 15, 2021).

3. Peter Schepelern, "The Making of an Auteur: Notes on the Auteur Theory and Lars von Trier," in *Visual Authorship: Creativity and Intentionality in Media*, ed. Torben Grodal, Bente Larsen, and Iben Thorving Laursen (Copenhagen: University of Copenhagen, Museum Tusculanum, 2005), 111. The German "von," which indicates noble descent, constitutes a defiance of the "Law of Jante" against standing out or flaunting the norm in Nordic cultures.

4. See Linda Badley, *Lars von Trier* (Urbana: University of Illinois Press, 2011), 15–16.

5. Ole Koster, interview with Lars von Trier, Cannes, May 23, 2003, TV2, on *Dogville*, directed by Lars von Trier, disc 2 (Bagsvaerd, DK: Nordisk, 2003), DVD.

6. Scott Roxborough, "Lars von Trier Speared over *Antichrist*," *Hollywood Reporter*, May 18, 2009, https://www.hollywoodreporter.com/news/lars-von-trier-speared-antichrist-84190.

7. Thomas Elsaesser, "The Global Author: Control, Creative Constraints, and Performative Self-Contradiction," in *The Global Auteur: The Politics of Authorship in Twenty-First-Century Cinema*, ed. Sung-Hoon Jeong and Jermi Szaniawski (London: Bloomsbury, 2016), 37.

8. "Lars von Trier Nazi Comments at Cannes 2011," YouTube, 4:26, May 18, 2011, https://www.youtube.com/watch?v=CHKojTI-pNM.

9. Jenle Hallund, interview by the author, Copenhagen, June 12, 2019.

10. Lars von Trier, "*The House That Jack Built* Director's Statement," July 1, 2016. Courtesy of Zentropa Productions.

11. Von Trier, interview by the author, Copenhagen, June 28, 2018.

12. Roger Ebert, "Cannes #10, 'And, at Last, the Winners Are . . . ,'" *Chicago Sun-Times*, May 24, 2009, http://blogs.suntimes.com/ebert/.

13. Roger Ebert, "Cannes #6, A Devil's Advocate for *Antichrist*," *Chicago Sun-Times*, May 19, 2009, http://blogs.suntimes.com/ebert/.

14. Trust Film Sales, "Lars von Trier Shoots *Antichrist* in Eden," *Trust Film Sales*, August 18, 2008, http://www.trust-film.dk/.

15. Stephanie Zacharek, "Best Movies 2011: Why I Loved *Melancholia*, and Why *Tree of Life* Left Me Cold," Slate, January 2, 2012, https://slate.com/culture/2012/01/best-movies-2011-why-i-loved-melancholia-and-why-tree-of-life-left-me-cold.html.

16. Robert Sinnerbrink, *New Philosophies of Film: Thinking Images* (New York: Continuum, 2011); Robert Sinnerbrink, "Provocation and Perversity: Lars von Trier's Cinematic Anti-Philosophy," in *The Global Auteur: The Politics of Authorship in Twenty-First-Century Cinema*, ed. Sung-Hoon Jeong and Jermi Szaniawski (London: Bloomsbury, 2016), 95–114.

17. Lars von Trier, "Director's Confession," *Antichrist* official website, May 18, 2009, http://www.antichristthemovie.com.

18. See Badley, *Lars von Trier*, 14–15, 140; Angelos Koutsourakis, *Politics as Form in Lars von Trier: A Post-Brechtian Reading* (London: Bloomsbury, 2013); and Angelos Koutsourakis, "The Dialectics of Cruelty: Rethinking Artaudian Cinema," *Cinema Journal* 55, no. 3 (Spring 2016): 65–89.

19. Roger Ebert, "Cannes #5, 'For Even Now Already It Is in the World,'" *Chicago Sun-Times*, May 17, 2009, http://blogs.suntimes.com/ebert/.

20. Caroline Bainbridge, "On the Experience of a Melancholic Gaze," *British Journal of Psychotherapy* 35, no. 1 (2019): 143–44.

21. Von Trier, "Director's Confession."

22. Xan Brooks, "Lars von Trier on Filmmaking and Fear: 'Sometimes, alcohol is the only thing that will help,'" *Guardian*, December 3, 2018, https://www.theguardian.com/film/2018/dec/03/lars-von-trier-on-filmmaking-and-fear-sometimes-alcohol-is-the-only-thing-that-will-help.

23. See Tanya Horeck and Tina Kendall, eds., *The New Extremism in Cinema: From France to Europe* (Edinburgh: Edinburgh University Press, 2011); Nikolaj Lübecker, *The Feel-Bad Film* (Edinburgh: Edinburgh University Press, 2015); Mattias Frey, *Extreme Cinema: The Transgressive Rhetoric of Today's Art Film Culture* (New Brunswick, NJ: Rutgers University Press, 2016); Aaron Michael Kerner and Jonathan L. Knapp, *Extreme Cinema: Affective Strategies in Transnational Media* (Edinburgh: Edinburgh University Press, 2016); and Simon Hobbs, *Cultivating Extreme Cinema: Text, Paratext, and Home Video Culture* (Edinburgh: Edinburgh University Press, 2020).

24. Elsaesser, "Global Author," 21–42; Thomas Elsaesser, *European Cinema and Continental Philosophy: Film as Thought Experiment* (London: Bloomsbury, 2019), 57–83.

25. Thomas Elsaesser, "Black Suns and a Bright Planet: *Melancholia* as Thought Experiment," in *Politics, Theory, and Film: Critical Encounters with Lars von Trier*, ed. Bonnie Honig and Lori J. Marso (Oxford: Oxford University Press, 2016), 305–35; Elsaesser, *European Cinema and Continental Philosophy*, 225–51.

26. Lisa Coulthard and Chelsea Birks, "Desublimating Monstrous Desire: The Horror of Gender in New Extremist Cinema," *Journal of Gender Studies* 25, no. 4 (2016): 463–64.

27. Sinnerbrink, *New Philosophies of Film*, 157–76.

28. Sinnerbrink, "Provocation and Perversity," 95–114.

29. Ray Brassier, *Nihil Unbound: Enlightenment and Extinction* (New York: Palgrave Macmillan, 2007), xi.

30. Nina Siegal, "Lars von Trier Wants to Turn All His Films into Diamonds," *New York Times*, February 11, 2019, https://www.nytimes.com/2019/02/11/arts/design/lars-von-trier-diamond-melancholia.html.

31. Siegal, "Lars von Trier."

32. Petur Valsson, "Elevating the Ugly: Lars von Trier's Anti-Aesthetic," paper presented at the Society for the Advancement of Scandinavian Studies, New Orleans, April 28, 2016.

33. Manuel Alberto Claro, interview by the author, Copenhagen, June 13, 2019.

34. Richard Grusin, "Post-Cinematic Atavism," in *Post-Cinema: Theorizing Twenty-First-Century Film*, edited by Shane Denson and Julia Leyda, 2016, https://reframe.sussex.ac.uk/post-cinema/5-3-grusin/ (accessed July 5, 2021).

35. Tom Shone, "*Nymphomaniac, The Wolf of Wall Street*, and Cinema's Bad Sex Renaissance," *Guardian*, March 19, 2014, https://www.theguardian.com/film/2014/mar/19/nymphomaniac-wolf-wall-street-cinemas-bad-sex-renaissance.

1. NATURE AS SATAN'S CHURCH

1. Lars von Trier, "Director's Confession," *Antichrist* official website, May 18, 2009, http://www.antichristthemovie.com.

2. Nils Thorsen, *Geniet—Lars von Triers liv, film og fobier* (Copenhagen: Politiken, 2011), 364. Translated by Peter Schepelern.

3. Knud Romer, "A Hearse Heading Home" (interview with Lars von Trier), FILM #66, Danish Film Institute, May 2009, https://www.dfi.dk/files/docs/2018-02/FILM66%5B1%5D%20%281%29.pdf (accessed July 7, 2021).

4. Von Trier was in the hospital for one day only. He checked in, gave up his pills, and was told that he would need to wait a week to see a psychiatrist. He was assigned to group therapy (which *Nymphomaniac* would ridicule for its political correctness) in the meantime. So he checked out the next day and started seeing a cognitive psychologist. Thorsen, *Geniet*, 364.

5. *The Kingdom* was adapted in that same year, 2004, by horror maestro Stephen King, as *Stephen King's Kingdom Hospital*.

6. Quoted in Dorthe Ravn, "Von Trier vil lave Satan-film," *Berlingske Tidende*, October 20, 2004, https://www.berlingske.dk/kultur/von-trier-vil-lave-satan-film. Translated by Peter Schepelern. In the original Danish:

   > Som jeg forstår filmen, spinder Lars en ende over den store løgn, at det var Gud, der skabte verden. I virkeligheden er det Satan selv. "Handlingen i *Antikrist* udspiller sig omkring en angstterapeut, der får en biolog i terapi, der er blevet bange for naturen. Den er ond, mener han og søger hos terapeuten hjælp til at komme af med sine vrangforestillinger—men har han i virkeligheden ret? Det er spørgsmålet i filmen, der endnu kun eksisterer i den danske instruktørs hoved.

7. Thorsen, *Geniet*, 364; Peter Schepelern, "*Antichrist* I–V," 2015, unpublished manuscript, chapter 2, "Production," 14–15, Lars von Trier Collection (LvTC), Danish Film Institute (DFI).

8. Ib Bondebjerg, "Lars von Trier," interview in *The Danish Directors*, ed. Mette Hjort and Ib Bondebjerg (London: Intellect, 2001), 215.

9. Thorsen, *Geniet*, 364.

10. Lars von Trier, "Ny version: Anti-x idea 6," n.d., "*Antichrist* materialer," LvTC, DFI. In the original Danish:

    > Hun udvikler ondskaben og viljen til at leve. Og slår Nicklas ihjel. Mary tar hjem. Smider notater ud. Mary kommer hjem . . . hun lever en tid godt men træt. En dag hører hun barnegråd. Men det er ikke den lille inde i kravlegården . . . det er græsset ude på betonen. Hun løber ind og flår biblen frem . . . men alle de steder der stod Gud før står nu Satan . . . Zoom ud og op forbi træer og fugle og natur og helt ud i rummet. Slut zoom væk fra den blå planet der skriger. "Og på den syvende dag så Satan at alt var godt . . ." Ellipses in original.

11. Lars von Trier, "Løse ideer projekt efterår 2006" [Loose ideas project autumn 2006], n.d., "*Antichrist* materialer," LvTC, DFI. In the original Danish:

    > Menneskekroppe med fastmonterede bolte igennem lemmer
    > Hullet i jorden
    > Skovens skrig.
    > Ræv der sønderbider sig selv. Den taler ved tankeoverføring.
    > vis gyser, så er skoven de kommer til hvor det onde manifesterer sig en slags omvendt
    >   edens have.
    > Husk en generel distortion . . . billeder strukket ud eller lignende, uden at det er
    >   direkte sebart.

12. Lars von Trier, "*Antichrist* diktatofon noter 10.1.10.2006" [Antichrist dictation notes 10.1.10.2006], 2006, "*Antichrist* materialer," LvTC, DFI. In the original Danish: "Vinden som et gigantisk åndedrag som går gennem skoven."

13. Lars von Trier, "*Antichrist* diktatofon noter 21 og 25.09.2006" [*Antichrist* dictation notes 21 and 25.09.2006], September 21 and 25, 2006, "*Antichrist* materialer," LvTC, DFI. In the original Danish: "Husk billede af nøgent lig under trærødder som ligesom er fængslet af trærødderne der fletter sig ind mellem hinanden."

14. Lars von Trier, "Anti-x ide 2"[Anti-x idea 2] and "Anti-x ide 6" [Anti-x idea 6], n.d., "*Antichrist* materialer," LvTC, DFI. In the original Danish: "Der findes et sted hvor naturen manifesterer sin ondskab. Hvor man kan høre græsset skrige. Dette er mentalt usundt fordi det giver indsigten: at livets ide er ond! At satan skabte verden som en sadistisk ide. Denne indsigt at godhed ikke findes og at den gode Gud ikke er nærværende er forbudt fordi den vil nedbryde verden . . . syndefaldet var da dette gik op for Adam og Eva . . . at de skulle dø. . . ." Ellipses in original.

15. Lars von Trier, "Antichrist kort handlingsreferat" [*Antichrist* brief action report], n.d., "*Antichrist* materialer," LvTC, DFI. In the original Danish:

> Jeremy lever med sin far der er præst og sin lillesøster i stor lykke i deres idylliske hus Eden midt i bjerge og skov. En vinternat dør hans lillesøster af en akut sygdom eller ulykke fordi de ikke kan komme til lægen pga. snestorm. Jeremy ændres og ser nu den før så romantiske natur som ond. Hans angst vokser og til sidst flygter han fra lyden han nu kan høre af skoven der skriger.

> Mange år efter opsøger han en angstterapeut [Brenda], der tager ham med tilbage til "Eden" for at helbrede ham ved en så kaldt "flooding." Han skal eksponeres maksimalt for sin angst for natur ved at konfronteres med det "farligste" sted, nemlig der hvor angsten opstod. Langsomt får hun mere og mere klaret hans symptomer, indtil en nat han er væk og hun får øje på ham udenfor . . . han er begyndt at dyrke satan. Han har inddelt husets grund i de dele hans fars kirke havde nede i byen.

16. Lars von Trier, "Note 16.08.06," August 16, 2006, "*Antichrist* materialer," LvTC, DFI.

17. Von Trier, "Anti-x Ide 2." In the original Danish: "Mary bange . . . finder sammen med Nicklas i dyrisk samleje." Also, in Anders Thomas Jensen's version the man watches the female therapist undress and stands looking at her when she sleeps, but there is no sexual contact." See Schepelern, "*Antichrist* I–V," chapter 2, "Production," 18.

18. Schepelern, 17–18.

19. Schepelern, 16–17.

20. Peter Schepelern, "Hvisken og råb" (interview with Lars von Trier), *Ekko Filmmagasinet* May 17, 2009, https://www.ekkofilm.dk/artikler/hvisken-og-rab/. In the original Danish:

> Det han gjorde, var meget vigtigt for filmen. Det startede med nogle ideer, jeg havde. Så fik jeg depressionen og kunne kun mumle nogle ord til Anders Thomas. . . . Og så skrev han hele historien igennem. Han lavede et manuskript, så vi kunne gå videre med filmen. Og så læste jeg manuskriptet og smed det hele væk. Han læste også mit manuskript og syntes, det var noget rod. Han har måske haft mere indflydelse, end jeg er villig til at indrømme. Men jeg skrev altså det hele om.

21. Thorsen, *Geniet*, 363. Translated by Peter Schepelern. According to Schepelern, "Antichrist I–V," chapter 2, "Production," 18, the second script was followed by a third version ("*Antichrist*, 3. draft," March 16, 2008), now with more details and technical specifications. "*Antichrist* Final Script" (in English, 72 pp.) is dated July 2008.

22. The *Audition* handout, which included background notes and study questions on the film, Japanese culture, and the *onryō*, I rediscovered in 2019, at the head of the alphabetized list of materials in the large folder labeled "*Antichrist* materialer."

23. Von Trier, "Brief om research til *Antichrist*" (Brief about research on *Antichrist*), n.d., "*Antichrist* materialer," LvTC, DFI. In the original Danish:

> Vi skal bruge tekster der beskriver kvinden som værende ond og farlig af natur. Alt materiale som underbygger denne tese. Research som til en artikel eller en retssag. Det kan være skønlitteratur men helst udtrykt i digte, sange, faglitteratur, religiøse tekster og manifester og gerne af både ældre og nyere dato og fra alle egne af verden.

24. Schepelern, "*Antichrist* I–V," chapter 2, "Production," 18–19.

25. Nicholas Page, "Her Dark Materials: *Antichrist's* "Mysogyny [sic] Consultant" Interviewed," The Big Picture, August 6, 2009, http://www.thebigpicturemagazine.com/.

26. Heidi Laura, "Research—om kvinders ondskab—med oversatte citater" [Research on women's evil with translated quotes], August 2007, "*Antichrist* materialer," LvTC, DFI.

27. Linda Badley, *Lars von Trier* (Urbana: University of Illinois Press, 2011), 201.

28. Badley, *Lars von Trier*, 199.

29. Badley, 199–200. Von Trier also mentioned watching Tarkovsky's *Mirror* with "horror music," which turned it into a horror film (200).

30. David Bordwell, "Cinema in the World's Happiest Place," Observations on Film Art: David Bordwell's Website on Cinema, July 2, 2009, http://www.davidbordwell.net/blog/2009/07/02/cinema-in-the-worlds-happiest-place/; Schepelern, "Hvisken og råb."

31. Nigel Andrews, "Beauty and the Unspeakable," *Financial Times*, July 22, 2009, https://amp.ft.com/content/c5d21ac4-76dc-11de-b23c-00144feabdc0.

32. Schepelern, "Hvisken og råb."

33. Badley, *Lars von Trier*, 173–74.

34. Badley, 176.

35. Schepelern, "*Antichrist* I–V," chapter 2, "Production," 18. By the final script, the only trace left of the patient's childhood is that She was in Eden as a child (Lars von Trier, "*Antichrist* Final Script," July 2008, unpublished screenplay, 40, 43, courtesy of Zentropa Productions), but this was removed in the eventual film.

36. Von Trier, "Anti-x ide 2." In the original Danish: "Mary kommer hjem . . . hun siger ikke noget, men er lidt ond . . . slår sin baby over fingrene da den vil ta en kage. Mary spiser den selv. Barnet græder. Vi ser at Mary har korset omvendt på. Zoom ud og op forbi træer og fugle og natur og helt ud i rummet."

37. Von Trier, "Anti-x ide 6." Von Trier has said that when he became most afflicted by depression, his handwriting degenerated similarly.

38. Karin Badt, "Most Hated Director at Cannes: Lars von Trier as Antichrist or Shaman?," Huffington Post, May 29, 2009, http://www.huffingtonpost.com/.

39. Stig Björkman, ed., *Trier on von Trier*, trans. Neil Smith (London: Faber & Faber, 2003), 81.

40. Badley, *Lars von Trier*, 161.

41. Chris Heath, "Lars Attacks!," *GQ*, October 2011, https://www.gq.com/story/lars-von-trier-gq-interview-october-2011 (accessed July 7, 2021).

42. Roman Polanski successfully adapted the book in 2013.

43. Peter Schepelern, *Lars von Triers film: Tvang og befrielse* (Copenhagen: Rosinante, [2000] 2018), 74.

44. Lars von Trier, *Eliza eller Den lille bog om det dejlige og det tarvelige* (Eliza, or The little book about the delightful and the vulgar), 1976, unpublished manuscript, 67. "Trier Eliza-roman renskhrift," LvTC, DFI.

45. Von Trier, *Eliza*, 74.

46. Calum Waddell, "Lars von Trier: Satanic Scandals," Total Sci Fi Online, 2009, http://totalscifionline.com/interviews/3756-lars-von-trier-satanic-scandals (accessed July 7, 2021).

47. Peter Schepelern, *Lars von Triers elementer* (Copenhagen: Rosinante, 1997), 28.

48. Schepelern, "*Antichrist* I–V," chapter 3, "Sexuality," 17.

49. Schepelern, 21.

50. Schepelern, 20.

51. Bondebjerg, "Lars von Trier," 215; Heath,"Lars Attacks!"

52. Heath.

53. Peter Schepelern, *Lars von Triers film: Tvang og befrielse* (Copenhagen: Rosinante, 2000), 207–10, quoted in Jack Stevenson, *Lars von Trier* (London: BFI, 2002), 90–93.

54. Bondebjerg, "Lars von Trier," 212–13.

55. Schepelern, "*Antichrist* I–V," chapter 3, "Sexuality," 21.

56. In an interview with Kristian Ditlev Jensen ("Nordic nonsense," Nordisk Film & TV Fond, n.d., www.nordiskfilmogtvfond.com/managed . . . /lars_eng_version.doc.), an expansive Trier postulates, "If I were to make the [Nordic] 'triangle' it would be with Strindberg in Sweden and Munch in Norway and Dreyer in Denmark." In the same interview, Trier mentions Ibsen but prioritizes Strindberg as his "role model" in theater. Siri Erika Gullestad ("Crippled Feet: Sadism in Lars von Trier's *Antichrist*," *Scandinavian Psychoanalytic Review* 34, no. 2 [2011]: 81), however, notes a striking connection between *Lille Eyolf* (Little Eyolf, 1894), a play by Strindberg's Norwegian nemesis Henrik Ibsen, and *Antichrist*'s inciting event. In Ibsen, a couple's disabled son is revealed to have fallen from a table as an infant as they (at the wife's prompting) were having sex. As in Trier's film, the woman's erotic passion arguably causes the accident and "the child represents an obstacle to [her] exclusive relationship with her husband." Schepelern ("*Antichrist* I–V," chapter 3, "Sexuality," 27), however, claims that von Trier did not know this play.

57. Romer, "Hearse Heading Home."

58. Jean-Luc Wachthausen, "Lars von Trier: '*Antichrist* est ma thérapie,'" *Figaro*, May 18, 2009, http://www.lefigaro.fr/.

59. Von Trier, "*Antichrist* Final Script," 44–45.

60. Björkman, *Trier on von Trier*, 28.

61. Schepelern, "*Antichrist* I–V," chapter 3, "Sexuality," 23.

62. Romer, "Hearse Heading Home"; Wachthausen, "Lars von Trier." Liliana Cavani's Nietzsche film, *Beyond Good and Evil* (1977), which was as much about sex as about Nietzschean philosophy, made a deep impression on him, however. Schepelern, "*Antichrist* I–V," chapter 3, "Sexuality," 23.

63. Bodil Marie Stavning Thomsen, *Lars von Trier's Renewal of Film, 1984–2014: Signal, Pixel, Diagram* (Arhus: Arhus University Press, 2018), 262–63.

64. Björkman, *Trier on von Trier*, 2. Now named Geelsgaard, the estate has been converted into the Børneungecenter for Rehabilitering, Kongevejen 256, 2830 Virum.

65. Olof Lagercrantz's biography *August Strindberg* (Stockholm: Wahlstrøm & Widstrand, 1979) argues that *Inferno* was a literary adaptation that is only loosely connected to the diaries. "August Strindberg writes about August Strindberg but those two are not the same person (440). Or, as Schepelern notes, "Strindberg the person was tormented by his mental troubles but at the same time he was able to regard it as useful material for Strindberg the writer," adding that "this reading of Strindberg's crisis can be compared to von Trier's. He was psychologically disabled, but at the same time . . . [able to] use his personal crisis in a creative way as artistic material. The whole idea came out of depression, nightmare, visions, traumas and therapeutic experiences" ("*Antichrist* I–V," chapter 2, "Production," 12).

66. August Strindberg, *A Dream Play*, in *Miss Julie and Other Plays*, ed. and trans. Michael Robinson (Oxford: Oxford University Press, 1998), 176.

67. Schepelern, "*Antichrist* I–V," chapter 3, "Sexuality," 21.

68. Michael Bo, "De overlevede Antikrist—og von Trier," *Politiken*, May, 23, 2009, http://politiken.dk/.

69. Von Trier, quoted in Ditlev Jensen, "Nordic Nonsense."

70. Björkman, *Trier on von Trier*, 28.

71. Schepelern, "*Antichrist* I–V," chapter 2, "Production," 10.

72. Robert Sinnerbrink, *New Philosophies of Film: Thinking Images* (New York: Continuum, 2011), 172.

73. Xan Brooks, "Mangy Foxes and Fake Firs: The Reel Chaos of the Cannes Film Festival," *Guardian*, May 18, 2009, https://www.theguardian.com/film/2009/may/18/cannes-film-festival-antichrist-lars-von-trier.

74. Jessica Hopper, "In Which Nature Is Lars von Trier's Satanic Church," This Recording, October 27, 2009, http://thisrecording.com/.

75. Kaleem Aftab, "Lars von Trier—'It's Good that People Boo,'" *Independent*, May 29, 2009, https://www.independent.co.uk/arts-entertainment/films/features/lars-von-trier-it-s-good-people-boo-1692406.html.

76. Brooks, "Mangy Foxes and Fake Firs."

77. Evan Fanning, "*Antichrist* Was Lars's 'Fun' Way of Treating Depression," *Independent*, July 26, 2009, https://www.independent.ie/entertainment/movies/antichrist-was-lars-fun-way-of-treating-depression-26553823.html.

78. See Badley, *Lars von Trier*, 6–10.

79. Peter Schepelern, "After the Fall: Sex and Evil in Lars von Trier's *Antichrist*," in *Bridges Across Cultures*, Perugia, Italy, 2013, published in collaboration with *Voces del Caribe*, 2013: 11–12, https://img1.wsimg.com/blobby/go/17d75147-ba5c-4e83-bc9f-efc947767190/BAC2013.pdf (accessed August 9, 2021).

80. "'That's how I wrote the script for *Dogville* in 12 days. It was 278 pages," he told Nils Thorsen. "Von Trier tørlagt, nøgen og på røven," *Politiken*, November 29, 2014, https://politiken.dk/magasinet/interview/art5555223/Von-Trier-tørlagt-nøgen-og-på-røven.

81. Thorsen, "Von Trier tørlagt."

82. Thorsen, *Geniet*, 364. Translated by Peter Schepelern. Also, notably, in the main room of the cabin two small drums of the kind used for shamanistic journeys are occasionally glimpsed.

83. Von Trier, "Director's Confession."

84. Among the research materials are links and articles on virgin forests in America. Von Trier, "*Antichrist* materialer," n.d., LvTC, DFI.

85. Per Juul Carlsen, "The Only Redeeming Factor Is the World Ending," FILM #72, Danish Film Institute, May 4, 2011, HYPERLINK "https://www.dfi.dk/en/english/only-redeeming-factor-world-ending" https://www.dfi.dk/en/english/only-redeeming-factor-world-ending (accessed August 9, 2021).

86. Björkman, *Trier on von Trier*, 69.

87. John Rockwell, "Von Trier and Wagner, a Bond Sealed in Emotion," *New York Times*, April 8, 2001, https://www.nytimes.com/2001/04/08/movies/film-von-trier-and-wagner-a-bond-sealed-in-emotion.html.

88. Badley, *Lars von Trier*, 101–2.

89. See *Broadway World*'s summation of the major news outlets' reviews: BWW News Desk, "Opera Philadelphia Triumphs with *Breaking the Waves*," *Broadway World*, September 28, 2016,

https://wwwbroadwayworld.com/philadelphia/article/Opera-Philadelphia-Triumphs-With
-BREAKING-THE-WAVES-20160928.

90. John Rockwell, "Maybe Lars von Trier's Vision Was Just What Wagner Needed," *New York Times*, June 11, 2004, https://www.nytimes.com/2004/06/11/movies/reverberations-maybe-lars-von-trier -s-vision-was-just-what-wagner-needed.html.

91. Lars von Trier, acceptance statement, October 18, 2001, T VII 80, LvTC, DFI.

92. Rockwell, "Lars von Trier's Vision." Later, in 2011, he concluded that "they didn't have the money for it . . . because I was far too ambitious." Carlsen, "Only Redeeming Factor."

93. Patrick Carnegy, *Wagner and the Art of the Theatre* (New Haven, CT: Yale University Press, 2006), 78.

94. Carnegy, *Wagner and the Art of the Theatre*, 77–78.

95. Carnegy, 77–80.

96. Rockwell, "Lars von Trier's Vision." Rockwell added, "Never mind that Wagner himself was deeply dissatisfied with the original 1876 *Ring*'s staging at Bayreuth, which he oversaw. What Mr. von Trier had in mind might have been another bold step away from the increasingly cliché-ridden attempts to update Wagner by imposing some new dramaturgical conceit on his works."

97. Lars von Trier, " 'Deed of Conveyance': Lars Von Trier on the *Nibelungen Ring*—the Enriched Darkness," Mostly Opera, October 4, 2007, https://mostlyopera.blogspot.com/2007/10/lars-von-trier -on-nibelungen-ring.html.

98. Lars von Trier, "Scenesynopsis, Act II," n.d., T V 55, LvTCC, DFI. In the original Danish: "Hele aktetfremstår som en lang tilt/krantur op ad et bjerg. Bjerget er veli paktisk højde 8 gange Bayreuth-scenens højde."

99. Stig Björkman, "Making the Waves" (interview with Lars von Trier), *Sight and Sound* 19, no. 8 (2009): 16–18.

100. As he told Schepelern, ("Hvisken og råb"), "Yes, I should say that the film to some degree has been colored by the fact that I had a brief encounter of two-three years with Wagner Festspiele. Some of the pictures actually come from ideas I had in connection to the Wagner project, among others the hands that come out from tree roots." In the original Danish: "Ja, jeg vil sige, at filmen i nogen grad er blevet farvet af den kendsgerning, at jeg havde et kort møde på to-tre år med Wagner Festspiele. Nogle af billederne kommer faktisk fra ideer, jeg havde i forbindelse med Wagner-projektet, blandt andet hænderne, der kommer ud af trærødder."

101. Lars von Trier, "Turnbook, Notes, Drawings, and Research from the Opera Project *Nibelungens Ring*," n.d., T VII 55, LvTCC, DFI.

102. Lars von Trier, "Lars von Trier noter til Die Walküre," 2003, T VII 55, LvTCC, DFI. In the original Danish:

"50,2 fire spots der starter ude af grene og rødder af det store træ . . . de nærmer sig alle uendelig langsomt sværdets plads. det er historien om det store træ. vedbend . . . rødder der er vokset gennem noget etc.
54,8 de fire spots er samlet i punktet hvor Sl nu står foran sværdet og dækker det.
54,11 S kommer ind og omfavner hende i lyset.
56,12 det er som om et vindpust stryger gennem hele skoven . . . i tre fire hurtige glimt (delvis video)
57,1 de fortificerede fløjdøre inde i fadeburet blæses op af vinden.
57,5 S, kigger op mod dørene. . . . han trækker hende med op mod dem . . . vi får endnu engang ikke set det sværd.
58,5 de to står i dørene og kigger ud.

58,5 månen bryder igennem skyerne og belyser bækken bag huset. (video) + månelys

58,12 S. træder ud. Det er her bækken er opdæmmet. Han træder ud i vandet.

58,17 S. kigger op ad bækken mod månen og følger den opad. (vi ser ikke månen)

59,5 Sl træder osse ud nu . . . de to har hvert sit lys. I det følgende lokkes Sl. langsomt af ham fra plateau til plateau som bækken danner op mod månen (video). Han hele tiden lidt foran. alt med bæk ses gennem askens grene.

61,4 S. vinker hende hele tiden op til sig. . . .

64,6 Nu kravler hun virkeligt opad! du bist der lenz!

66,5 de to mødes oppe under en busk

68,9 de omfavnes så busken vakler. lys tilt op til fugle der sov i buskens top. De flyver op. (video)

68,13 lys igen på de to.

70,9 glimt af fugleflok flakkende forvildet rundt i skov (video)

74,10 fugleflokken flyver forbi månen og væk (video)

76,1 S og Sl kravler videre opad

78,10 S og Sl. når lige op så de bliver silhuetter mod månen (video), men i det samme søger S. ned igen. med pludselig energi . . . han rutcher ned ad skrænt til træets fod. lys osse efter ham.

81,2 S. har nået jorden under træet . . . hvert spor af H's hus er væk. Asken står alene i lavt vand blandt tusinde små unge aske. S. hopper op og griber efter sværdet uden for billedet (uden for lyset) men får ikke fat. Sl (hviner af fryd og) kommer ned osse.

81,3 idet Sl kravler ned tones månen ud. (video)

81,11 S kommer op og hjælper hende ned

82,3 de går sammen ned til træ

83,2 måske ser vi det først nu: huset er væk . . . asken står ensomt blandt tynde unge træer i vandet

85,13 Sl. hjælper S. op ad stammen. Han trækker hende med op.

85,14 S. trækker sværdet i stammen ud, og boller Sl op ad træet. Idet han gør det skælver hele træet. . . . vi paner væk fra de to, af den store gren vi så gynge først . . .

86,11 vi følger den store grens bevægelser opad og højere og højere op til kvistene der osse dirrer.

86,24 Vi ender på den første kvist vi så i vinden i aktets start. Nu direkte foran månen (video) Den dirrer længe så falder den til ro. Lys ned på alt. Slut akt.

103. William Butler Yeats, "Leda and the Swan," in *The Collected Poems of W. B. Yeats* (Hertfordshire: Wordsworth Editions, 1994), 182.

104. H. R. Ellis Davidson, *Gods and Myths of Northern Europe* (London: Penguin, 1990), 195, 26.

105. Hilda Roderick Ellis, *The Road to Hel: A Study of the Conception of the Dead in Old Norse Literature* (Westport, CT: Greenwood, 1968), 84.

106. Bosch's *The Garden of Earthly Delights* (1503–1515) and *The Last Judgement* (1482) triptychs are among the reproductions in the research folder for *Antichrist*.

107. Davidson, *Gods and Myths of Northern Europe*, 195.

108. Sinnerbrink, *New Philosophies of Film*, 164.

109. Romer, "Hearse Heading Home."

110. *Nocturne* (1980), *Befrielsesbilleder* (*Images of Liberation*, 1982), the Europe trilogy films, and *Medea* all feature slow motion sequences. Specifically, the prologue's slow motion sequence of the bottle spilling its contents recalls similar shots in film school projects *Nocturne* and *Images of Liberation*, which ended in a "monumental" crane shot in which the protagonist, a Nazi soldier, ascends to heaven above the treetops.

111. I thank Peter Schepelern's fine analysis in "*Antichrist* I–V," chapter 3, "Sexuality," 3–4, for a number of these details.

112. Von Trier, "*Antichrist* Final Script," 25.

113. Torsten Bøgh Thomsen, "Foggy Signs: Dark Ecological Queerings in Lars von Trier's *Antichrist*," *Journal of Scandinavian Cinema* 8, no. 2 (2018), 129.

114. Thomsen, "Foggy Signs," 129.

115. Von Trier, "*Antichrist* Final Script," 42.

116. Von Trier, 47.

117. Von Trier, 34.

118. Schepelern, "*Antichrist* I–V," chapter 3, "Sexuality," 2.

119. Kristian Eidnes Andersen, interview by the author, FaceTime, February 1, 2021.

120. "Music and Sound Design," *The Making of Antichrist/Antichrist* (New York: Criterion Collection, 2010), DVD.

121. Ger Killen, "Grace Without Gravity: Lars von Trier's Prologue to *Antichrist*," Headlandia: Words from the Edge of the World, February 6, 2014, http://headlandia.blogspot.com/2014/02/gravity -without-grace-prologue-to-lars.html. Composed for the London stage in 1711 (with libretto in Italian) and loosely based on Torquato Tasso's epic poem *La Gerusalemme Liberata* (Jerusalem Delivered), Handel's opera is about the first crusade.

122. Thomas Grey, "The Idea of Nature in Wagner's *Ring*," in *The Cambridge Companion to Wagner's Ring of the Nibelung*, ed. N. Vazsonyi and M. Berry (London: Cambridge University Press, 2020), 221.

123. "Music and Sound Design."

124. Andersen, interview, 2021.

125. See von Trier, "*Antichrist* Final Script," 14.

126. Grey, "Idea of Nature," 38.

127. Gunnar Rehlin, "Filmen är mitt inferno," Fokus, May 15, 2009, https://www.fokus.se/2009/05 /filmen-ar-mitt-inferno/. In the original Danish: "Jag vill mer tro på de gamla gudarna, de som var Gud och Satan."

128. Linda Badley, "*Antichrist*, Misogyny, and Witch Burning: The Nordic Cultural Contexts," *Journal of Scandinavian Cinema* 3, no. 1 (March 1, 2013): 15–33.

129. Badley, "*Antichrist*, Misogyny, and Witch Burning," 25–26.

130. Dilys Powell, review of *The Seventh Seal*, *Sunday Times*, March 9, 1958.

131. As Rebecca A. Umland and Samuel J. Umland maintain, this trend reflects a deep conflict between Christian and pagan values in the region. With Scandinavia the last of the European regions to convert to the new religion, tension between rival ethical systems—the pagan revenge imperative and Christian forgiveness—remained well into the late medieval period. Residual fears (and desires) that the repressed pagan code might return and "challenge its usurper" is therefore a subtext in early Scandinavian cinema—with the witch film until fairly recently constituting what there was of a Scandinavian "horror" film genre. Indeed, the act of *burning* a witch (as in *Antichrist*), is a "confabulation of (pagan) superstitions and Christian belief" into a single image. Umland and Umland, "Burn, Witch, Burn: A First Look at the Scandinavian Horror Film," in

Horror International, ed. Steven Jay Schneider and Tony Williams (Detroit, MI: Wayne State University Press, 2005), 311, 291.

132. Nordic Council Film Prize Jury, "About the Film Prize," Nordic Co-operation, "Prize Winner 2009," n.d., HYPERLINK "https://www.norden.org/en/nominee/prize-winner-2009-0" https://www.norden.org/en/nominee/prize-winner-2009-0 (accessed August 9, 2021).

133. Timothy Morton, *The Ecological Thought* (Cambridge, MA: Harvard University Press), 2010; Timothy Morton, *Dark Ecology: For a Logic of Future Coexistence* (New York: Columbia University Press, 2016).

134. Kristoffer Noheden, "Hypnotic Ecologies: Environmental Melancholia in Lars von Trier's Films," *Journal of Scandinavian Cinema* 8, no. 2 (2018): 135–148.

135. Morton, *Ecological Thought*, 33–38.

136. Noheden, "Hypnotic Ecologies," 136–37.

2. MELANCHOLIA

1. Per Juul Carlsen, "The Only Redeeming Factor Is the World Ending," *FILM* #72, Danish Film Institute, May 4, 2011, https://www.dfi.dk/en/english/only-redeeming-factor-world-ending.

2. The Papin sisters, who were thought to be lovers, committed a double, mother-daughter murder on February 2, 1933.

3. Catherine Love, "*The Maids* Review: Jean Genet's Would-be Murderers Set Pulses Racing," *Guardian*, November 23, 2018, https://www.theguardian.com/stage/2018/nov/23/the-maids-review-home-manchester.

4. Nils Thorsen, "Longing for the End of All" (interview with Lars von Trier), production notes, press kit, *Melancholia* official website, Magnolia Films, 2011, http://www.magpictures.com/presskit.aspx?id=bbcb733d-8d0e-495a-ba6d-be9a79453d1czzzzzz (accessed July 8, 2021).

5. Thorsen, "Longing"; Howard Feinstein, "Lars von Trier: 'I will never do a press conference again,'" IndieWire, May 20, 2011, https://www.indiewire.com/2011/05/lars-von-trier-i-will-never-do-a-press-conference-again-54069/.

6. Niels Thorsen, "Von Trier tørlagt, nøgen og på røven," *Politiken*, November 29, 2014, https://politiken.dk/magasinet/interview/art5555223/Von-Trier-tørlagt-nøgen-og-på-røven.

7. Louise Vesth, interview by the author, Skype, September 12, 2019.

8. Vinca Wiedemann, Vinca, interview by the author, Skype, July 25, 2019.

9. Vesth, interview, 2019.

10. Jenle Hallund, interview by the author, Copenhagen, June 12, 2019.

11. Hallund, interview, 2019.

12. For example, Genet's play and Penélope Cruz certainly had some influence on the strength of von Trier's female characters and the intensity of their bond.

13. Anders Refn, interview by the author, Copenhagen, June 29, 2018.

14. Refn, interview, 2018.

15. As Refn explained, the shooting was

      very well planned, and Peter Hjorth had made a remarkable storyboard, with all these things written down exactly as they should be done. But then, Anthony always wanted to do it better than Lars wanted it, and Lars got very upset. . . . he felt very patronized by Anthony's "You're sick, and I know exactly what you want, I know better what you want, even better than your own ideas."

These conflicts built to a crisis over a crane shot in the forest that had to be redone. Later in Sweden, where the film was graded, a job shared between director and cinematographer, Refn represented von Trier (Refn, interview, 2018).

Regardless, Mantle's work on the film, which he said was the most challenging of his career (see Morten Piil, "Kindred Spirits," interview with Anthony Dod Mantle, *FILM #66*, Danish Film Institute, June 2, 2009, http://www.dfi.dk/), deservedly won several important awards, including the European Film Award for Cinematography and the Academy Award for Cinematography.

16. Refn, interview, 2018.
17. Lars von Trier, "Director's Statement," *Melancholia*, official website, Magnolia Pictures, 2011, http://www.magpictures.com/presskit.aspx?id=bbcb733d-8d0e-495a-ba6d-be9a79453d1c (accessed July 8, 2021).
18. Thomas Elsaesser, *European Cinema and Continental Philosophy: Film as Thought Experiment* (London: Bloomsbury, 2019), 228–234.
19. Elsaesser, *European Cinema and Continental Philosophy*, 59.
20. Quoted in Linda Badley, *Lars von Trier* (Urbana: University of Illinois Press, 2011), 165.
21. In fact, the "coldness" of the film divided certain critics like Peter Bradshaw ("*Melancholia*—Review," *Guardian*, September 29, 2011, https://www.theguardian.com/film/2011/sep/29/melancholia-film-review); and Philip French ("*Melancholia*—Review," *Observer*, October 2, 2011, https://www.theguardian.com/film/2011/oct/02/melancholia-lars-von-trier-review).
22. Hallund, interview, 2019.
23. Caroline Bainbridge, "On the Experience of a Melancholic Gaze," *British Journal of Psychotherapy* 35, no. 1 (2019): 142–55.
24. Steven Shaviro, "*Melancholia*: Or, The Romantic Anti-Sublime," *Sequence One: Planet Melancholia* 1, no. 1 (2012): 19, https://reframe.sussex.ac.uk/sequence/files/2012/12/MELANCHOLIA-or-The-Romantic-Anti-Sublime-SEQUENCE-1.1-2012-Steven-Shaviro.pdf (accessed July 8, 2021).
25. Rupert Read, "An Allegory of a 'Therapeutic' Reading of a Film: Of *Melancholia*," *Sequence One: Planet Melancholia* 1, no. 2 (2014): https://reframe.sussex.ac.uk/sequence1/1-2-an-allegory-of-a-therapeutic-reading/ (accessed July 8, 2021).
26. Manuel Alberto Claro, interview by the author, Copenhagen, June 28, 2018.
27. Trevor Link, "Depression, Melancholia, and Me: Lars von Trier's Politics of Displeasure," Occupied Territories, November 21, 2011, https://occupiedterritories.tumblr.com/post/13114178124/depression-melancholia-and-me-lars-von-triers.
28. See also Caroline Bainbridge, "'Cinematic Screaming' or 'All About My Mother': Lars von Trier's Cinematic Extremism as Therapeutic Encounter," in *Media and the Inner World: Psychocultural Perspectives on Emotion, Media, and Popular Culture*, ed. Caroline Bainbridge and Candida Yates (Basingstoke: Palgrave Macmillan, 2014), 53–68.
29. Natalia Antonova, "The Touch of Your Hand Behind a Closed Door," Global Comment, April 1, 2020, http://globalcomment.com/the-touch-of-your-hand-behind-a-closed-door/.
30. Mallika Rao, "The *Melancholia* Postulate," *Atlantic*, May 9, 2020, https://www.theatlantic.com/culture/archive/2020/05/watching-melancholia-during-pandemic/611383/.
31. Steven Shaviro, "*Melancholia*," 20.
32. In the September 2011 issue of British *ELLE*, Dunst recalled her 2008 stint at the Cirque Lodge rehabilitation facility, sharing how her experience influenced her performance as Justine: "I brought my own slant [to the role] but I am very much portraying Lars's experience of depression. We met before I did the movie and talked about how the light goes out of your eyes. People

don't talk about depression, so for me it was really amazing that this was going to be portrayed." "Kirsten Dunst Talks Rehab, Depression To British *ELLE*," Huffington Post, August 2, 2011, https://www.huffpost.com/entry/kirsten-dunst-talks-rehab_n_915931.

33. Sigmund Freud, "Mourning and Melancholia" (1917), in *The Standard Edition of the Complete Psychological Works of Sigmund Freud*, vol. 14, ed. James Strachey (London: Hogarth, 1957), 239–60.

34. Thomas Elsaesser, "Black Suns and a Bright Planet: *Melancholia* as Thought Experiment," in *Politics, Theory, and Film: Critical Encounters with Lars von Trier*, ed. Bonnie Honig and Lori J. Marso (Oxford: Oxford University Press, 2016), 317–23; and Elsaesser, *European Cinema and Continental Philosophy*, 240–46.

35. Wiedemann, interview, 2019; Hallund, interview, 2019. Further, in his director's commentary on the Artificial Eye DVD, von Trier explained that he aims for "psychological discontinuity" by shooting a scene several times, each time giving the actors different contexts to bring to it, making choices only at the editing stage. Lars von Trier and Peter Schepelern, audio commentary, *Melancholia* (London: Artificial Eye, 2011), Blu-ray.

36. Manuel Alberto Claro, interview by the author, Skype, November 22, 2013.

37. Von Trier, "Director's Statement."

38. "Interview with Lars von Trier," 2011, "Extras/The Making of *Melancholia*/The Visual Style," *Melancholia*, dir. Lars von Trier (London: Curzon Artificial Eye, 2012), DVD.

39. Lars von Trier, "Directors [sic] Intentions," unpublished document, Copenhagen, March 2010, Courtesy of Zentropa Productions.

40. David Larkin, "'Indulging in Romance with Wagner': *Tristan* in Lars von Trier's *Melancholia*," *Music and the Moving Image* 9, no. 1 (Spring 2016): 43.

41. Larkin, "Indulging in Romance with Wagner," 50.

42. Von Trier, "Directors Intentions"; "Interview with Lars von Trier."

43. Larkin, "Indulging in Romance with Wagner," 51.

44. Larkin, 51.

45. Quoted in Rob White, "Interview with Manuel Alberto Claro," *Film Quarterly* 65, no. 4 (Summer 2012): https://filmquarterly.org/2012/07/11/interview-with-manuel-alberto-claro/ (accessed July 8, 2021).

46. Lars von Trier, "Turnbook, notes, drawings, and research from the opera project 'Nibelungens Ring,'" n.d., T VII 55, LvTC, DFI. Wieland Wagner's stage direction revitalized Bayreuth after World War II by using a minimalistic style that proved to be very influential. Peter Schepelern, "Linda Badley: Melancholia," attachment to email message to the author, June 10, 2020. After he died in 1966, his brother Wolfgang took over as leader of the festival. It was Wolfgang who invited von Trier to direct in 2001.

47. Rob White, "Interview with Manuel Alberto Claro," 2012.

48. Stig Björkman, *Trier on von Trier*, trans. Neil Smith (London: Faber & Faber, 2003), 241.

49. John Rockwell, "Von Trier and Wagner, a Bond Sealed in Emotion," *New York Times*, April 8, 2001, https://www.nytimes.com/2001/04/08/movies/film-von-trier-and-wagner-a-bond-sealed-in-emotion.html.

50. Zack Sharf, "Cannes 2011 Jury Preferred *Melancholia* Over *Tree of Life*, but Wouldn't Award von Trier," IndieWire, May 29, 2020, https://www.indiewire.com/2020/05/cannes-jury-melancholia-palme-dor-tree-of-life-1202234293/.

51. Manohla Dargis, "This Is How the End Begins," *New York Times*, December 30, 2011, http://www.nytimes.com/2012/01/01/movies/awardsseason/manohla-dargis-looks-at-the-overture-to-melancholia.html.

52. Von Trier, "Interview with Lars von Trier."

53. Jonathan Romney, "*Melancholia*, Lars von Trier, 130 Mins," *Independent*, October 22, 2011, https://www.independent.co.uk/arts-entertainment/films/reviews/melancholia-lars-von-trier-130-mins-15-2364172.html.

54. Roger Ebert, "I See It Coming, I Will Face It, I Will Not Turn away," November 9, 2011, https://www.rogerebert.com/reviews/melancholia-2011.

55. Alex Ross, "Melancholia, Bile," The Rest Is Noise, November 19, 2011, https://www.therestisnoise.com/2011/11/melancholia-bile.html.

56. Tim Page, "Filmmaker's Audacious Teaming of His *Melancholia* with Wagner's Music," *Washington Post*, December 23, 2011, https://www.washingtonpost.com/lifestyle/style/filmmakers-audacious-teaming-of-his-melancholia-with-wagners-music/2011/12/15/gIQAWRpgDP_story.html.

57. Stephanie Zacharek, "Best Movies 2011: Why I Loved *Melancholia*, and Why *Tree of Life* Left Me Cold," Slate, January 2, 2012, https://slate.com/culture/2012/01/best-movies-2011-why-i-loved-melancholia-and-why-tree-of-life-left-me-cold.html.

58. J. Hoberman, "Cannes 2011: Lars von Trier's *Melancholia*. Wow," VoiceFilm, May 18, 2011, http://www.voicefilm.com/2011/05/cannes_2011_lars_von_triers_melancholia_wow.php.

59. Lisa Schwarzbaum, "Cannes Film Festival: Lars von Trier's Stunning *Melancholia*—the End of the World and a Challenge to *The Tree of Life*," *Entertainment Weekly*, May 18, 2011, https://ew.com/article/2011/05/18/cannes-film-festival-lars-von-trier-melancholia-terrence-malick/.

60. Von Trier, "Director's Statement." Here he alludes to the famous line from *Epidemic*, his second feature, which anticipated his "deconstructive" Dogme phase: "A film should be a pebble in the shoe."

61. Carlsen, "Only Redeeming Factor."

62. While Proust had immense admiration for Wagner and *Tristan*, there is no exact statement resembling this in any of the seven volumes of his novel. Larkin, however, suggests that von Trier may be alluding to a six-page passage in volume 5, *La Prisonnière* (*The Captive*), "in which the narrator plays through *Tristan* on the piano prior to attending a concert where excerpts from the opera will be performed" ("Indulging in Romance," 42). Larkin also suggests that von Trier may have conflated this passage with a longer one in the same volume in which the narrator refers to later works including *Tristan*, *Rheingold*, and *Meistersinger* as misunderstood masterpieces (55n30).

63. Carlsen, "Only Redeeming Factor."

64. Von Trier, quoted in Thomas Alling, "Sightseeing with the Holy Ghost," in *Lars von Trier: Interviews*, ed. Jan Lumholdt (Jackson: University Press of Mississippi, 2003), 26–27.

65. Von Trier, quoted in Jan Kornum Larsen, "A Conversation between Jan Kornum Larson and Lars von Trier," in *Lars von Trier: Interviews*, ed. Jan Lumholdt (Jackson: University Press of Mississippi, 2003), 42. However paradoxically, the finished film had no score, although the closing credits were accompanied by an original song, "The Last Tourist in Europe" (Der Letzte Tourist in Europa). The "Wagnerian" influence, however, penetrated everything else, the production design—a landscape two-thirds underwater—acting, and movements of the characters that, enhanced by slow motion, trudge over mountains of rubble and slog through sewers or rooms standing in sludge, all with the understanding that the protagonist is a traumatized patient under hypnosis.

66. White, "Interview with Manuel Alberto Claro." Elsewhere, in an interview about his extensive use of Wagner's *Tannhäuser* in *Epidemic*, his apocalyptic horror film of 1987, he used the words "Wagnerian" and "domineering" as synonyms, explaining his choice: "Because it's very

bombastic music. To me it perfectly corresponds to film music." Michel Ciment and Phillipe Rouyer, "A Conversation with Lars von Trier," in *Lars von Trier: Interviews*, ed. Jan Lumholdt (Jackson: University of Mississippi Press, 2003), 62.

67. Carlsen, "Only Redeeming Factor."

68. See Lars von Trier, ' "I Understand Hitler," ' YouTube, 4:26, May 18, 2011, https://www.youtube .com/watch?v=QpUqpLh0iRw.

69. Waters, quoted in Kirsten L. Boatwright, "Constraining Lars von Trier: Issues of Censorship, Creativity, and Provocation," PhD diss., Middle Tennessee State University, 2011, 136.

70. Scott Roxborough, "Lars von Trier Admits to Being a Nazi, Understanding Hitler (Cannes 2011)," *Hollywood Reporter*, May 18, 2011, https://www.hollywoodreporter.com/news/lars-von-trier-admits -being-189747.

71. Boatwright, "Constraining Lars von Trier," 136–37.

72. Melena Ryzik, "Lars von Trier Kicks Up a Cannes Controversy," *New York Times*, May 18, 2011, https://artsbeat.blogs.nytimes.com/2011/05/18/lars-von-trier-kicks-ups-a-cannes-controversy/.

73. Scott Roxborough and Stuart Kemp. "Lars von Trier Named Persona Non Grata in Cannes After Hitler Remarks," *Hollywood Reporter*, May 19, 2011, https://www.hollywoodreporter.com/news /lars-von-trier-named-persona-190227. Interestingly, the noted Danish playwright Jakob Weis devoted the third play in his trilogy about the Danish national character *Kunst, humor og angst* (*Art, Humor, and Anxiety*) to von Trier, titled *Von Trier—Persona non grata* and published as an e-book (Copenhagen: SAGA Edgmont, 2020, https://www.amazon.co.uk/Von-Trier-persona-grata -Danish-ebook/dp/B08M9RZ947). In homage to von Trier, Weis made a vow of self-censorship for three years in which he refused to discuss the play. Kim Kastrup, "Trier-dramatiker giver sig selv mundkurv på i tre år," *Ekstra Bladet*, April 14, 2015, https://ekstrabladet.dk/underholdning /kultur/trier-dramatiker-giver-sig-selv-mundkurv-paa-i-tre-aar/5521978.

74. Andrew O'Hehir, "Pick of the Week: Lars von Trier's Spectacular *Melancholia*," Salon, November 10, 2011, http://www.salon.com/2011/11/11/pick_of_the_week_lars_von_triers_spectacular_ melancholia/.

75. Badley, *Lars von Trier*, 39–40.

76. Björkman, *Trier on von Trier*, 70.

77. Michael Tapper, "A Romance in Decomposition," in *Lars von Trier: Interviews*, ed. Jan Lumhold (Jackson: University of Mississippi Press, 2003), 73.

78. From the village of Mougins, fifteen minutes from Cannes, von Trier continued to meet with journalists, attempting to contextualize and explain his remarks. Recounting his complicated ancestry to Andrew O'Hehir, he stressed that his comments on Speer referred to the architect's aesthetics rather than ideology. He clarified his statement about "understanding" Hitler: "If I said to you that I understood Hitler, you would say, 'What the fuck do you mean?' And I could say, well, in the sense that watching Bruno Ganz playing him in *Downfall* [Oliver Hirschbiegel, 2004] and all that, I understand that he is a human being and it's very important for us to recognize that." He also explained his comments in part as the result of his Danish humor and the common Danish usage of the term "Nazi" to mean, disparagingly, "German." Andrew O'Hehir, "Lars von Trier: 'I Don't Want to be an Adult,' " Salon, May 21, 2011, https://www.salon.com/2011 /05/21/lars_von_trier_interview/. It should also be noted that English is von Trier's second language, and that he rarely travels. In 2014, his wife, Bente, quipped to Nils Thorsen that his problem was "a mild form of Tourette's syndrome," an inability to filter his words.

79. Page, "Filmmaker's Audacious Teaming."

80. Frederic Spotts, *Hitler and the Power of Aesthetics* (New York: Overlook, 2004), 57.

81. Spotts, *Hitler and the Power of Aesthetics*, 56.

82. Friedrich Kittler, "World-Breath: On Wagner's Media Technology," in *Opera Through Other Eyes*, ed. David J. Levin (Stanford, CA: Stanford University Press. 1994), 215.

83. Ryan Minor, "Introduction to Lars von Trier's *Deed of Conveyance*," *Opera Quarterly* 23, nos. 2–3 (Spring–Summer 2007): 339.

84. Minor, "Introduction," 339. See Gundula Kreutzer's *Curtain, Gong, Steam: Wagnerian Technologies of Nineteenth-Century Opera* (Oakland: University of California Press, 2018). "Wagnerian technologies" were designed specifically to mask the apparatus of Wagner's multimedial productions.

85. Spotts, *Hitler and the Power of Aesthetics*, 71–72, 98–100, 105–6,114–17, 321–29.

86. Spotts, 57.

87. Spotts, 33.

88. Von Trier and Schepelern, audio commentary, *Melancholia*.

89. Saul Friedländer, *Reflections of Nazism: An Essay on Kitsch and Death*, trans. Thomas Weyr (New York: Harper & Row, 1982), 70.

90. Von Trier, quoted in Trier and Schepelern, audio commentary, *Melancholia*.

91. Shaviro, "*Melancholia*," 32.

92. O'Hehir, "Pick of the Week," 2011.

93. Amy Taubin, "All Movies Great and Small," *Film Comment*, July–August, 2011, https://www.filmcomment.com/article/cannes-2011-report-1/ (accessed July 8, 2021).

94. Dargis, "How the End Begins."

95. Shaviro, "*Melancholia*," 12.

96. Wagner's title is a German translation of *Ragnarök*, which in Norse mythology refers to a prophesied war among the gods and other beings that ends in the world's destruction and renewal.

97. Kate Soper, *What Is Nature? Culture, Politics and the Non-human* (Oxford: Blackwell, 1995), 29, quoted in Thomas Grey, "Wagner's *Ring* as Eco-Parable," in *Music Theater as Global Culture: Wagner's Legacy Today*, ed. Anno Mungen, Nicholas Vazsonyi, Julie Hubbert, Ivana Rentsch, and Arne Stolberg (Würzburg: Königshausen & Neumann, 2017), 197. See also Christopher Abram, *Evergreen Ash: Ecology and Catastrophe in Old Norse Myth and Literature* (Charlottesville: University of Virginia Press, 2019), whose final chapter is "Reading Ragnarök at the End of the World."

98. Ross, "Melancholia, Bile."

99. Richard Grusin, "Post-Cinematic Atavism," Post-Cinema: Theorizing 21st-Century Film, 2016, https://reframe.sussex.ac.uk/post-cinema/5-3-grusin/ (accessed July 8, 2021).

100. Kristian Eidnes Andersen, interview by the author, Zoom, February 1, 2021.

101. Shaviro, "*Melancholia*," 43.

102. Edmond Burke, *A Philosophical Enquiry Into the Origin of Our Ideas of the Sublime and Beautiful* [1757] (London: Cambridge University Press, 2014).

103. Sarah French and Zoë Shacklock, "The Affective Sublime in Lars von Trier's *Melancholia* and Terrence Malick's *The Tree of Life*," *New Review of Film and Television Studies* 12, no. 4 (2014): 341.

104. French and Shacklock, "Affective Sublime," 340.

105. Von Trier, "Directors Intentions." See also Torben Grodal, "Frozen Style and Strong Emotions of Panic and Separation: Trier's Prologues to *Antichrist* and *Melancholia*," *Journal of Scandinavian Cinema* 2, no. 1 (2012): 47–53, a cognitivist analysis of affect of the prologue in particular and *Melancholia* in general through blocking the normal process of cognition.

106. Shaviro, "*Melancholia*," 12.

107. As Andersen (interview, 2021) explained, Lars intended the first part to be "a little boring and a little too long. And, also the humor . . . becomes a little too long in the start, then you really feel it when you go into the dark" stretches of part 2.

108. Shaviro, "*Melancholia*," 13–14.

109. Larkin, "Indulging in Romance," 42–43.

110. Marcel Proust, *In Search of Lost Time*, vol. 5, *The Captive*, trans. C. K. Scott Moncrieff and Terence Gilmartin, rev. trans. D. J. Enright (New York: Modern Library, 2003), 205–6.

111. Brian Magee, *The Tristan Chord: Wagner and Philosophy* (New York: Henry Holt, 2000), 165.

112. Magee, *Tristan Chord*, 208–9.

113. As Hallund (interview, 2019) explained, von Trier is

> very logical, but he's not very intellectual. . . . If you say something about Nietzsche he wouldn't actually understand what you were talking about. Or, he would understand it, but he wouldn't know that that's what he [Lars] did. Because in the process of making, . . . he doesn't sit down with specific concepts and think "I'm going to reference this and that and that." I mean in a kind of existential intellectual academic sense, he's just like, "Oh, I'm really interested in, um, Albert Speer. I'm really interested in architecture. . . . I love fly fishing." So he [has] . . . a myriad of ideas and passions and needs and phobias, which are particular to him. And he then researches a little bit, you know, not the whole bit, a little bit, and takes things that you can use without thinking of the bigger context. And that's good because if he overintellectualized it would be unbearable. . . . So I think also that it frees him.

114. See Bodil Marie Stavning Thomsen, *Lars von Trier's Renewal of Film, 1984–2014: Signal, Pixel, Diagram* (Arhus: Arhus University Press, 2018), 262–73, who examines the intertextual relations among Schopenhauer's *The World as Will and Idea*, which profoundly influenced both Nietzsche's *The Birth of Tragedy* (1872), Wagner's *Tristan and Isolde*, and *Melancholia*.

115. Chris Heath, "Lars Attacks!," *GQ*, October 2011, https://www.gq.com/story/lars-von-trier-gq-interview-october-2011 (accessed July 8, 2021).

116. Arthur Schopenhauer, *Ethics, Book IV: The World as Will and Representation*, vol. 1 (1818), trans. Judith Norman, Alistair Welchman, and Christopher Janaway (Cambridge: Cambridge University Press, 2014).

117. Schopenhauer, *Ethics*.

118. Carlsen, "Only Redeeming Factor."

119. For example, Claro explains that *Last Year in Marienbad* "became a reference because of the location we chose, especially the rows of trees. Once Lars saw the location, the connection was easily made and we realized we could pay this homage." Quoted in White, "Interview with Manuel Alberto Claro."

120. Manuel Alberto Claro, interview by the author, Skype, November 22, 2013. Other interiors, Claro adds, the golf course, stable, and riding scenes, the balloon launching, Justine's "Rhinemaiden" scene, and the final outdoor sequences were shot at Film i Väst at Trollhättan.

121. Von Trier, quoted in Badley, *Lars von Trier*, 168. According to Claro (interview by the author, telephone, October 5, 2013), the setting was in Pennsylvania, as confirmed by the automobile license plates. See also Linda Badley, "The Transnational Politics of Lars von Trier's and Thomas Vinterberg's 'Amerika,'" *Nordic Film Cultures and Cinemas of Elsewhere*, ed. Arne Lunde and Anna Stenport (Edinburgh: Edinburgh University Press, 2019), 244–60, for an extended analysis of von Trier's films set in, and critical of, America.

122. Elisabeth Olesen, *Adventure Guide to Sweden* (Edison, NJ: Hunter, 2005), 190.

123. Claro, interview, November 22, 2013.

124. Tjolöholms Slott, 2020, http://www.Tjolöholm.se/ (accessed July 8, 2021).

125. Claro, interview, November 22, 2013.

126. Tjolöholms Slott.

127. Anne Sumner, *Tjolöholm: A Woman's Achievement*, trans. Alan Crozier (Fjärås: Tjolöholm Foundation, 2001).

128. Tjolöholms Slott.

129. Claro, interview, October 5, 2013.

130. White, "Interview with Manuel Alberto Claro."

131. Thorsen, *Geniet*, 386–87. Translated by Anders Marklund.

132. Hermann Broch, "Notes on the Problem of Kitsch" (1950), in *Kitsch: The World of Bad Taste*, ed. Gillo Dorfles (New York: Universe, 1969), 62.

133. Theodor Adorno, *The Culture Industry* (New York: Routledge, [1972] 2001).

134. Winifried Menninghaus, "On the Vital Significance of 'Kitsch': Walter Benjamin's Politics of 'Bad Taste,'" in *Walter Benjamin and the Architecture of Modernity*, ed. Andrew Benjamin (New York: Charles Rice, 2009), 41.

135. Spotts, *Hitler and the Power of Aesthetics*, 32.

136. Friedländer, *Reflections of Nazism*. According to Matei Calinescu, *Five Phases of Modernity: Modernism, Avant-Garde, Decadence, Kitsch, Postmodernism* (Durham, NC: Duke University Press, 1987), 234, "kitsch" first became common usage among Munich art dealers to designate "cheap artistic stuff" in the 1860s and 1870s.

137. Rem Koolhaas, "Junkspace," 2001, http://www.cavvia.net/junkspace/ (accessed July 8, 2021).

138. Claro, interview, October 5, 2013.

139. Read, "Allegory of a 'Therapeutic' Reading."

140. Read.

141. Mark Fisher, *Capitalist Realism: Is There No Alternative?* (Winchester: Zero, 2009), 2–3.

142. Abbas Ackbar, "Junk Space, *Dogville*, and Poor Theory" (lecture), December 6, 2013, Film Theory and Visual Culture Seminar, Vanderbilt University.

143. White, "Interview with Manuel Alberto Claro."

144. Ackbar, "Junk Space, *Dogville*, and Poor Theory."

145. Von Trier and Schepelern, audio commentary, *Melancholia*, 2011.

146. Ray Brassier, *Nihil Unbound: Enlightenment and Extinction* (New York: Palgrave Macmillan, 2007), x–xi.

147. Shaviro, "*Melancholia*," 25.

148. Kristoffer Noheden, "Hypnotic Ecologies: Environmental Melancholia in Lars von Trier's Films," *Journal of Scandinavian Cinema* 8, no. 2 (2018): 138. See also Pat Brereton, *Environmental Ethics and Film* (London: Routledge, 2016), 18; and Ursula K. Heise, *Sense of Place and Sense of Planet: The Environmental Imagination of the Global* (Oxford: Oxford University Press, 2008).

149. Carlsen, "Only Redeeming Factor."

150. Joanna Zylinska, *Minimal Ethics for the Anthropocene* (London: Open Humanities, 2014), 15.

151. Myra Hird, "Waste, Landfills, and an Environmental Ethic of Vulnerability," in *Ethics and the Environment* 18, no. 1 (2013): 105–24.

152. Zylinska, *Minimal Ethics*, 15.

153. Hird, "Waste, Landfills."

154. Lars von Trier, "Melancholia, 2nd and Final Draft," March 4, 2010, rev. by VW [Vinca Wiede-
      mann] July 5, 2010, unpublished screenplay, courtesy of Zentropa Productions.

155. Timothy Morton, *Dark Ecology: For a Logic of Future Coexistence* (New York: Columbia University
      Press, 2018).

156. Von Trier, "Melancholia, 2nd and Final Draft."

157. Xan Brooks, "Cannes 2011 Diary: The End of the Festival Is Nigh," *Guardian*, May 18, 2011, https://
      www.theguardian.com/film/2011/may/18/cannes-film-festival-2011-diary-melancholia.

158. Although the Vow of Chastity required Dogme films to be shot on Academy 35, the first Dogme
      films were shot with digital cameras and screened at 33mm.

159. Manuel Alberto Claro, interview by the author, Copenhagen, June 13, 2019.

160. Grusin, "Post-Cinematic Atavism."

3. NYMPHOMANIAC

1. Unless otherwise indicated, references are to *Nymphomaniac: Extended Director's Cut* (2014).

2. Manuel Alberto Claro, interview by the author, Copenhagen, June 28, 2018.

3. Manuel Claro, quoted in John Silberg, "*Nymphomaniac*: How Cinematographer Manuel Alberto
    Claro Brought Lars von Trier's Vision to Life," Creative Planet Network, March 26, 2014, https://
    www.creativeplanetnetwork.com/news/nymphomaniac-how-cinematographer-manuel
    -alberto-claro-brought-lars-von-triers-vision-life-338397.

4. Kristian Eidnes Andersen, interview by the author, Zoom, February 2, 2021.

5. Andersen, interview, 2021.

6. Kevin Jagernauth, "Lars Von Trier Gets Gagged, Reveals Chapter Titles for *Nymphomaniac*, and
    Introduces New Film Genre," The Playlist, May 31, 2013, https://theplaylist.net/lars-von-trier-gets
    -gagged-reveals-chapter-titles-for-nymphomaniac-introduces-new-film-genre-20130531/.

7. Niels Thorsen, "Longing for the End of All," interview with Lars von Trier, production notes,
    press kit, *Nymphomaniac* official website, Magnolia Films, 2011, http://www.magpictures.com
    /presskit.aspx?id=bbcb733d-8d0e-495a-ba6d-be9a79453d1c.

8. Lars von Trier, "*Nymphomaniac*—Director's Comments," unpublished document, Copenhagen,
    April 2012, courtesy of Zentropa Productions.

9. Von Trier originally conceived *Nymphomaniac* as a single film but, because of its length—five
    hours and twenty-six minutes—split it into two films, *Volume I* and *Volume II*. For the film's origi-
    nal release, in Copenhagen on December 25, 2013, a four-hour version was edited with von
    Trier's permission but without his participation. The uncut *Volume I* was screened at the 64th Ber-
    lin International Film Festival in February 2014, and the uncut versions of *Volumes I* and *II* at
    the 71st Venice International Film Festival in September 2014. On September 10, 2014, the com-
    plete director's cut premiered in Copenhagen, with von Trier present, at a red carpet gala
    screening with a half-hour intermission. According to editor Molly Malene Stensgaard at the
    Venice Film Festival, they worked with what became the director's cut for eight months, then
    "used a month to do the shorter version." Essentially, "we just did one film—a film that we really
    liked. A long film with a break, basically." Quoted in Peter Knegt, "Stensgard & von Trier," inter-
    view, Venice Film Festival, *FILM: Danish Films Digital Issue*, August 25, 2014, http://www.dfi-film
    .dk/nymphomaniac-long.

10. Scott Roxborough, "Lars von Trier Imposes Voluntary Gag Order on Himself After Police Ques-
     tioning," *Hollywood Reporter*, October 5, 2011, https://www.hollywoodreporter.com/news/lars
     -von-trier-police-questioning-244514. The French authorities, who have laws against hate speech,

were investigating whether von Trier's statements constituted a violation of a French law proscribing the justification of war crimes.

11. Boyd van Hoeij, "Selling Lars von Trier's *Nymphomaniac*: How to Create a Sexy, Controversial Hit," IndieWire, December 12, 2013, https://www.indiewire.com/2013/12/selling-lars-von-triers -nymphomaniac-how-to-create-a-sexy-controversial-hit-241390/.

12. Van Hoeij, "Selling Lars von Trier's *Nymphomaniac*." According to Lipski, the idea that "anyone who has ever had sex could be interested in this movie" was thus communicated to the audience. See also Jagernauth, "Lars Von Trier Gets Gagged"; and Beth Hanna, "Everyone's Orgasming in New Character Posters for Lars von Trier's *Nymphomaniac*," IndieWire, October 10, 2013, https:// www.indiewire.com/2013/10/everyones-orgasming-in-new-character-posters-for-lars-von -triers-nymphomaniac-195647/. The orgasm portraits were so successful that, in advance of Denmark's annual Bodil Awards, the Danish National Association of Film Critics re-created them (Joe Berkowitz, "Danish Film Critics Do Their Best *Nymphomaniac* Face in Spoof Posters," Fast Company December 18, 2013, https://www.fastcompany.com/3023568/danish-film-critics-do -their-best-nymphomaniac-face-in-spoof-posters), followed by other European journalists' associations (Esther Zuckerman, "Please Don't Let Personalized *Nymphomaniac* Posters Happen," Yahoo News, February 4, 2014, https://tinyurl.com/ysyj2356).

13. Ben Child, "Shia La Beouf Sent Sex Tapes to Win Part in Lars von Trier's *Nymphomaniac*," *Guardian*, August 31, 2012, https://www.theguardian.com/film/2012/aug/31/shia-labeouf-sex-tape-von -trier-nymphomaniac.

14. Claro, interview, 2018.

15. Von Trier, "*Nymphomaniac*—Director's Comments."

16. Thorsen, "Longing for the End."

17. On the ferry to Dover to shoot *Breaking the Waves*, von Trier suffered an anxiety attack and consumed half a bottle of vodka and three sedative benzodiazepines. "Alcohol is the best drug in the world. And I've always used it as self-medication against all the stupid anxieties that keep popping. It seems completely precise, but in length unfortunately negative. And if it's anxiolytic one day, it's anxiety-creating the next," he told Thorsen. (In the original Danish: "Alkohol er jo verdens bedste drug. Og jeg har altid brugt det som selvmedicinering mod alle de dumme angster, som bliver ved med at poppe op. Det virker fuldstændigt præcist, men i længden desværre negativt. Og hvis angstdæmpende den ene dag, er det angstskabende den næste dag.") Von Trier reports having attended ninety AA meetings, at which he is marginalized for not submitting to God. Nils Thorsen, "Von Trier tørlagt, nøgen og på røven," *Politiken*, November 29, 2014, https:// politiken.dk/magasinet/interview/art5555223/Von-Trier-tørlagt-nøgen-og-på-røven).

18. Thorsen, "Von Trier tørlagt." In the original Danish: "Nu står jeg og skal gøre et forsøg på at holde mig i live ved at fjerne de forskellige rusmidler, men samtidig skal jeg prøve at holde den kreative linje, som jeg har lagt. Og det tror jeg simpelt hen ikke kan lade sig gøre. For ingen kreativ udfoldelse af kunstnerisk værdi er nogensinde blevet udført af forhenværende drankere og narkomaner."

19. Thorsen. In the original Danish: "Men det tog mig også halvandet år. Også fordi jeg delvis er depressiv og næsten ikke kan tage mig sammen til noget. Det blev til ganske små pip. Så hvad tids- og livsforbrug angår, har det været et smart regime, jeg har kørt før."

20. Thorsen. In the original Danish: "Har jeg netop ikke brugt i alle mulige tilfældige situationer."

21. Thorsen. In the original Danish:

> Det er jeg fuldstændig sikker på. Og det hjalp mig til at træffe beslutninger. . . . Fordi flere muligheder ser lige indbydende ud. Men som jeg havde sat mig op med alkohol,

og hvad der ellers fulgte, var jeg helt klar til at træffe beslutninger og bare gå videre. Og det er jo tvivlen, der tager tid. Når man stopper op og tænker: Jeg kunne jo også gå den anden vej. For mig var det bare: højre, venstre, ligeud. Det lod al tvivl tilbage. Og det er jo fantastisk. . . . Det er klart, at parallelverdenen koster, men jeg havde sindssygt meget glæde af det. . . . Der er tale om brug, ikke misbrug. For jeg har haft et formål, jeg kan stå inde for.

22. Thorsen.

23. In "Lars von Trier's Reading of World Literature" (email attachment to the author, August 11, 2020), Peter Schepelern explains that, around 2010, von Trier asked "for advice about what literary classics to read," specifically "great, difficult classical literature," and that he and von Trier had several phone conversations in the following years about the subject. Von Trier said that he had read "sufficiently" Dostoevsky, Tolstoy, and Dickens and mentioned having read some Thomas Mann—*Buddenbrooks*, *Doctor Faustus*, and (recommended by Vinca Wiedemann) the four *Joseph and His Brothers* novels. Schepelern told him to read *The Magic Mountain* also, and that "some passages he found extremely difficult." As for *In Search of Lost Time*, von Trier "thought that he had read Proust's long novel years ago, but . . . discovered that he had left the bookmark in the middle of the first volume. . . . Now he read the entire work" with Wiedemann. Later, at Schepelern's recommendation, he read Georges Perec's *Life: A User's Manual*, Hermann Broch's *Death of Virgil* (which "may have influenced the Verge figure"), Robert Musil's *The Man Without Qualities*, Hermann Hesse's *The Glass Bead Game*, Louis Ferdinand Céline's *Journey to the End of the Night* and *Death on Credit*, and Jean-Paul Sartre's *The Roads to Freedom* trilogy.

24. Jenle Hallund, interview by the author, Copenhagen, June 12, 2019.

25. Thorsen, "Von Trier tørlagt."

26. Vinca Wiedemann, interview by the author, Skype, July 25, 2019.

27. Wiedemann, interview, 2019.

28. Wiedemann, interview, 2019. Emilie Spliid Pearce (interview by the author, Skype, August 15, 2019), von Trier's personal assistant on the film, also brought up von Trier "speaking a lot about what the novel could do and couldn't, or that he wanted to try out. Very much in relation to him reading Proust. . . . The way it's made is very much a try to emulate [the novel]."

29. Lars von Trier, *Nymphomaniac*, final shooting draft, January 2013, unpublished screenplay, 35–36, courtesy of Zentropa Productions.

30. The Vinteuil sonata allusion was important enough to von Trier that he asked Peter Schepelern whether there was an authentic piece of music that inspired it. Schepelern told him that there were several possibilities but recommended the first movement from Franck's *Sonata in A Major for Violin and Piano*. After von Trier listened to it on YouTube and "loved it," he used it in the film in a version for cello and piano. At the Copenhagen University ceremony where von Trier received the Sonning Prize on April 19, 2018, it was played by the cellist who performed in the film version. Schepelern, "Lars von Trier's Reading."

31. Von Trier, *Nymphomaniac*, final shooting draft, 64–65.

32. For many of the following examples, I thank Peter Schepelern, "Forget About Love: Sex and Detachment in Lars von Trier's *Nymphomaniac*," Kosmorama, no. 259, March 11, 2015, https://www.kosmorama.org/en/kosmorama/artikler/forget-about-love-sex-and-detachment-lars-von-triers-nymphomaniac.

33. Peter Schepelern, *Lars von Triers elementer* (Copenhagen: Rosinante, 1997), 247; Von Trier, *Nymphomaniac*, final shooting draft, 40.

34. Schepelern, "Forget About Love."

35. Hallund is the author of the novels *Mænd Bærer Min Kiste* (*Men Carry My Coffin*, People's Press, 2015) and *The Tip Toe Dancer* (in progress).

36. Hallund, interview, 2019.

37. Hallund, interview, 2019.

38. Working separately with von Trier, Wiedemann and Hallund played very different roles, with Wiedemann emphasizing that "I would never have in my wildest nightmares wanted to become his muse. . . . It was the opposite." Wiedemann, interview, 2019.

39. As documented in *The Five Obstructions* (2003), von Trier used similar techniques to bring depressed Danish filmmaker Jørgen Leth out of a creative slump.

40. Pearce (interview, 2019) said something quite similar: to the effect that von Trier was different from other directors she had worked with in knowing exactly what he wanted the film to be like.

41. Wiedemann, interview, 2019.

42. Wiedemann, interview, 2019.

43. Louise Vesth, interview by the author, Skype, September 12, 2019.

44. Gundula Kreutzer, *Curtain, Gong, Steam: Wagnerian Technologies of Nineteenth–Century Opera* (Oakland: University of California Press, 2018).

45. Yonca Talu, "Interview: Manuel Alberto Claro," *Film Comment*, January 23, 2019, https://www .filmcomment.com/blog/interview-manuel-alberto-claro/. Exteriors were shot in Cologne, Copenhagen, and primarily in Ghent, Belgium. The segments in the alley and Seligman's apartment, some two hours' worth, were shot on a soundstage in Cologne and given what Claro describes as a "heavy-handed" and "kind of theatrical feel" that announced that this was a narrative frame. Otherwise, the room was lit with practical lamps and shot simply: often with a two-shot, followed by two singles, and without the swish-pans and jump cuts common to von Trier's work since *Breaking the Waves* and including *Melancholia*. "You want this room to feel like a good place to come back to. . . . Solid, stable," Claro elaborates, so that "the chapters we cut to could be a little crazy and energetic. . . ." As for the film as a whole, it was to be a "punk marathon" (Silberg, "*Nymphomaniac*").

46. I thank Peter Schepelern ("Badley Nymphomaniac PS," email attachment, August 11, 2020) for this suggestion.

47. Anders Refn, interview by the author, Copenhagen, June 29, 2018.

48. Sophia Savage, "Lars von Trier Invites You to Interpret Six Artworks for 'Gesamt' Film Project," IndieWire, August 13, 2012, https://www.indiewire.com/2012/08/lars-von-trier-invites-you -to-interpret-six-artworks-for-gesamt-film-project-202184/.

49. Savage, "Lars von Trier Invites You."

50. Hallund quoted in Savage, "Lars von Trier Invites You."

51. Cecilie Høgsbro Østergaard, "In the Service of Good Taste," *Kunstkritikk*, December 11, 2012, https://kunstkritikk.no/in-the-service-of-good-taste/.

52. Østergaard, "Service of Good Taste."

53. Reviewer Østergaard begs to differ, arguing that "the relationship between the directors takes center stage, overshadowing the people's voice." If Hallund set out to represent the range of contributions, she "has also ruthlessly smashed them and combined them to form something new," having stated that the submissions were most often "stories about the decline in morals, about violence in the ever-lasting dance between the sexes, and about complex father-daughter relations. One really cannot help wonder whether this is actually Hallund's own

biased reading of the materials," adding that Hallund "fearlessly let the film begin with a quite remarkable text about the relationship between the two directors as regards von Trier's canon of works."

54. Vesth, interview, 2019. Hallund (interview, 2019) who is credited as cowriter of *The House That Jack Built*, and should, if anyone, know, put the issue similarly:

> When you work like this, you enter into a creative collaboration and Lars decides. I can tell him, I think that is the most stupid thing you can do, and I can argue and I can scream and we can discuss, but in the end you do whatever he does with it. But Lars is very generous, and he will if he likes how you think and he feels inspired, he'll just take whatever. So I can definitely . . . see myself [in the works] and that's fine, you know. But it is certainly Lars's films and Lars's artistry.

55. Claro, interview, 2018.

56. André Bazin, "Lettre de Siberia," in *Le cinéma français de la libération à lanouvelle vague 1945–1958*, *Cahiers du Cinéma* [1958] 1983: 178–81; quoted in Andrew Tracy, "The Essay Film," *Sight & Sound*, May 7, 2019, https://www.bfi.org.uk/news-opinion/sight-sound-magazine/features/deep-focus/essay-film.

57. Tracy, "Essay Film."

58. Quoted in Tracy.

59. Von Trier, "*Nymphomaniac*—Director's Comments."

60. Claro, interview, 2018.

61. Kenneth B. Lee, "Video Essay: The Essay Film—Some Thoughts of Discontent," *Sight & Sound*, May 22, 2017, https://www.bfi.org.uk/news-opinion/sight-sound-magazine/features/deep-focus/video-essay-essay-film-some-thoughts.

62. Lee, "Video Essay."

63. Bodil Marie Stavning Thomsen, *Lars von Trier's Renewal of Film, 1984–2014: Signal, Pixel, Diagram* (Arhus: Arhus University Press, 2018), 310–27.

64. Tracy, "Essay Film."

65. Timothy Corrigan, *The Essay Film: From Montaigne After Marker* (New York: Oxford University Press, 2011); Elizabeth Papazian and Caroline Eades, "Introduction: Dialogue, Politics, Utopia," in *The Essay Film: Dialogue/Politics/Utopia*, ed. Elizabeth Papazian and Caroline Eades (New York: Wallflower, 2016), 1–11.

66. Gilles Deleuze and Felix Guattari, *A Thousand Plateaus: Capitalism and Schizophrenia* (Minneapolis: University of Minnesota Press, 1987).

67. Bill Desowitz, "Cinematographer Manuel Claro Talks the Bearable Lightness of *Nymphomaniac*," IndieWire, April 3, 2014, https://www.indiewire.com/2014/04/cinematographer-manuel-claro-talks-the-bearable-lightness-of-nymphomaniac-192874/.

68. Søren Birkvad, "Hollywood Sin, Scandinavian Virtue: The 1967 Revolt of *I Am Curious* and *The Graduate*," *Film International* 50, no. 2 (2011): 42–54.

69. Corrigan, *Essay Film*, 81–204.

70. Papazian and Eades, "Introduction."

71. Lee, "Video Essay."

72. Papazian and Eades, "Introduction," 3.

73. Vesth, interview, 2019.

74. Wiedemann, interview, 2019.

75. Schepelern, "Forget About Love."

76. Wiedemann, interview, 2019. Von Trier's assistant Emilie Spliid Pearce (interview, 2019) kept the list of experts and remembers how important authenticity was to him, to the extent that twice, just before production and then again just before editing, "we invited everyone in that he'd spoken to, experts on fishing and a doctor, and sexologists, and all kinds of other stuff" to look through the script and "leave notes if there was anything . . . completely off."

77. Wiedemann, interview, 2019. Commenting on the Trier's fascination with the fin de siècle view of sexuality (according to Nietzsche, Wagner, Freud, Munch, and Strindberg) as obsessive and depraved, sexologist Christopher Graugaard pointed out to Trier that modern sexologists considered it outdated. Schepelern, "Forget About Love," 28.

78. Vinca Wiedemann, email message to author, August 31, 2019.

79. Hallund, interview, 2019. Peter Schepelern ("Forget About Love," 2015) agrees that, "though rooted in a realistic background, employing both academic and pragmatic sources, *Nymphomaniac* doesn't appear to be a realistic film. Von Trier's films have always turned away from realism and psychological causality. His specialty is the allegorical art film, a kind of fable filled with both didactic and ambiguously ironic statements, as well as augmented by quirkiness and meta-attitude."

80. Hallund, interview, 2019.

81. Hallund, interview, 2019.

82. Hallund, interview, 2019. Therapist Laila Tapholm, on the other hand, has said that watching the film was like living a flashback, and that the film was a nightmarishly accurate picture of sex addiction, which she had experienced for three years. Jakob Skov Jakobsen, "VIDEO: Laila var sexafhængig: Von Trier-film gav mig flashbacks," DR, December 18, 2013, http://www.dr.dk /Nyheder/Kultur/Film/2013/12/18/093010.htm.

83. Papazian and Eades, "Introduction," 6.

84. Von Trier, *Nymphomaniac*, final shooting draft, 115–16.

85. Jonathan Romney, "The Girl Can't Help It," *Film Comment*, March–April 2014, 29.

86. Schepelern, "Forget About Love."

87. Jack Stevenson, *Scandinavian Blue: The Erotic Cinema of Sweden and Denmark in the 1960s and 1970s* (Jefferson, NC: McFarland, 2010), 14.

88. Stevenson, *Scandinavian Blue*, 95.

89. Stevenson, 5.

90. Badley, *Lars von Trier*, 6–11; Peter Schepelern, "Lars von Trier and Cultural Liberalism," *Danish Film Institute*, January 30, 2014, 24–27, https://www.dfi.dk/en/english/lars-von-trier-and-cultural -liberalism. In fact, Denmark was the first country to abolish the censorship of pornography— of pornographic texts in 1967 and images in 1969, as well as film censorship for adults. Schepelern, "Lars von Trier and Cultural Liberalism."

91. Of these films, von Trier admits to having seen only *Summer with Monika* and *I Am Curious (Yellow)* and *(Blue)* (Schepelern, "Forget About Love"), although he is reputedly less than completely reliable where influences and sources are concerned, for reasons known only to himself. Jack Stevenson has argued that several of these once-controversial films and figures—especially *Jag är nyfiken* and Jens Jørgen Thorsen's *Stille Dage i Clichy* (1970)—influenced von Trier's earlier films and initiatives, most notably *Idioterne* and the concept of Dogme 95 (Stevenson, *Scandinavian Blue*, 30, 89, 90, 243). In 1981, as a student at the Danish Film School, von Trier testified on Thorsen's behalf in hearings over Thorsen's planned erotic film about the life of Jesus. Thorsen's street performances as a sexualized Christ also anticipated *Idioterne*'s central metaphor and mode (Stevenson, 243).

92. Stevenson, 256. That von Trier attempted (unsuccessfully) to contact Brøgger as a consultant suggests his interest in her ideas (Schepelern, "Forget About Love").

93. Schepelern.

94. Birkvad, "Hollywood Sin, Scandinavian Virtue," 44.

95. Birkvad, 47.

96. Stevenson, *Scandinavian Blue*, 89.

97. Marta Kuzma, "Whatever Happened to Sex in Scandinavia? *I Am Curious (Yellow)*," *Afterall: A Journal of Art, Context, and Enquiry* 17 (Spring 2008): 6.

98. Kevin Heffernan, "Prurient (Dis)Interest: The American Release and Reception of *I Am Curious (Yellow)*," in *Sex Scene: Media and the Sexual Revolution*, ed. Eric Schaefer (Durham, NC: Duke University Press, 2014), 117–22.

99. Elizabeth Björklund, *The Most Delicate Subject: A History of Sex Education Films in Sweden* (Lund: Centre for Languages and Literature, 2012), 55.

100. Stevenson, *Scandinavian Blue*, 2010, 134.

101. Elizabeth Björklund, " 'This is a dirty movie': *Taxi Driver* and 'Swedish Sin,' " *Journal of Scandinavian Cinema* 1, no. 2 (2011): 163–76. If, like art film, "sex education provided a legitimizing framework for showing sex on film," as Björklund explains, "the sincerity of this framework was distrusted" (*Most Delicate Subject*, 197).

102. Björklund, 192.

103. Mariah Larsson, "Practice Makes Perfect? The Production of the Swedish Sex Film in the 1970s," *Film International* 8, no. 6: (2010): 46.

104. Darragh O'Donoghue, "A Girl Named Joe: Nymphets, *Nymph()maniac*, and Lars von Trier," *Cineaste* 39, no. 3 (Summer 2014): 11.

105. Schepelern, "Forget About Love."

106. According to Stevenson (*Scandinavian Blue*, 206), Skarsgård also starred in Wickman's *Swedish Sex Games* (1975) and Sjöman's *Taboo* (1977).

107. Stevenson, 247–54.

108. Romney, "Girl Can't Help It," 30.

109. J. Hoberman, "Sex: The Terror and the Boredom," *New York Review of Books*, March 26, 2014, http://www.nybooks.com/daily/2014/03/26/nymphomaniac-sex-terror-boredom/. David Denby is similarly reminded of "illustrated seventeenth-century books of miscellaneous erudition, like *Angler* or Robert Burton's *Anatomy of Melancholy*, and of such eighteenth-century libertine texts as the Marquis d'Argens's *Thérèse Philosophe*—a volume in which the sexual 'education' of the heroine gets interrupted by discourses on the truth of philosophical materialism and the falsity of religion." Denby, "The Story of Joe," *New Yorker*, March 24, 2014, http://www.newyorker.com/magazine/2014/03/24/the-story-of-joe.

110. Thorsen, "Longing for the End."

111. Various scholars have treated Sadean "pornography" as a discourse, rhetoric, or poetics. See Roland Barthes, *Sade/Fourier/Loyola*, 1971, trans. Richard Miller (Berkeley: University of California Press, 1976); Marcel Hénaff, *Sade: The Invention of the Libertine Body*, trans. Xavier Callahan (Minneapolis: University of Minnesota Press, 1999); Dalia Judovitz, " 'Sex,' or the Misfortunes of Literature," in *Sade and the Narrative of Transgression*, ed. David B. Allison, Mark S. Roberts, and Allen S. Weiss (Cambridge: Cambridge University Press, 1995), 171–98; and Peter Michelson, *Speaking the Unspeakable: A Poetics of Obscenity* (Albany: State University of New York Press, 1993). David Denby, among other critics, asserts that "the emotional heart of *Nymphomaniac* isn't the sex scenes but the conversations between Joe and her

protector, which mix artful nonsense, curious semi-nonsense, and startling good sense in daunting profusion" ("Story of Joe").

112. Nick James, "The Story of ()," *Sight & Sound* 24, no. 3 (2014): 22–27.

113. Stig Björkman, ed., *Trier on von Trier*, trans. Neil Smith (London: Faber & Faber, 2003), 33.

114. Badley, *Lars von Trier*, 99–100.

115. See, for example, Paula Quigley, "The Spectacle of Suffering: The 'Woman's Film' and Lars von Trier," *Studies in European Cinema* 9, nos. 2–3 (2012): 155–68; Rosalind Galt, "The Suffering Spectator? Perversion and Complicity in *Antichrist* and *Nymphomaniac*," *Theory & Event* 18, no. 2 (2015): https://muse.jhu.edu/journals/theory_and_event/toc/tae.18.2.html; and Nicola Evans, "How to Make your Audience Suffer: Melodrama, Masochism, and Dead Time in Lars von Trier's *Dogville*," *Culture, Theory, and Critique* 55, no. 3 (2014): 365–82.

116. Badley, *Lars von Trier*, 124, 128–29.

117. Christian Braad Thomsen, "Control and Chaos," in *Lars von Trier: Interviews*, ed. Jan Lumholdt (Jackson: University of Mississippi Press, 2003), 110.

118. Marquis de Sade, *Justine, or Good Conduct Well Chastised*, in *The Marquis de Sade: Justine, Philosophy in the Bedroom, and Other Writings*, trans. Richard Seaver and Austryn Wainhouse (New York: Grove, 1965), 743.

119. Quoted in Austryn Wainhouse, "Foreword," in *Juliette*, by the Marquis de Sade, rev. ed., trans. Austryn Wainhouse (New York: Grove, 1968), ix.

120. Lowry Pressly, "*Nymphomaniac: Vol. 1*: Fishers of Men, Meaning," *Los Angeles Review of Books*, March 21, 2014, https://lareviewofbooks.org/essay/nymphomaniac-vol-1-fishers-men-meaning.

121. Schepelern, "Forget About Love."

122. Pressly, "*Nymphomaniac: Vol. 1*."

123. Sade, *Juliette*, quoted in Roland Barthes, *Sade/Fourier/Loyola*, trans. Richard Miller (Berkeley: University of California Press, [1971] 1976), 32n19.

124. Barthes, *Sade/Fourier/Loyola*, 32.

125. See Judovitz, "'Sex,' or The Misfortunes of Literature," 172.

126. Barthes, *Sade/Fourier/Loyola*; Hénaff, *Sade*.

127. Michelson, *Speaking the Unspeakable*.

128. Hénaff, *Sade*, 67.

129. Hénaff, 33.

130. Hénaff, 34.

131. Barthes, *Sade/Fourier/Loyola*, 33, 34.

132. Simone de Beauvoir, "Must We Burn Sade?" (1952), in *Simone de Beauvoir: Political Writings*, ed. Margaret A. Simons and Marybeth Timmermann (Urbana: University of Illinois Press, 2012), 73.

133. This made for a cumbersome process leading to anything but spontaneity or "chemistry": each shot had to be storyboarded, lined up precisely, matched, and performed by both sets of actors.

134. Hénaff, *Sade*, 24.

135. Hénaff, 23.

136. Hénaff, 24.

137. Hénaff covers the following five components: "Representation (the demystified body), the will to say everything, apathetic desire, the space of the masterly gaze, and a time made of repetitive sexual pleasure" (x–xii).

138. Sade, *Juliette*, 486.

139. Schepelern, "Forget About Love."

140. Hénaff, *Sade*, 32.

141. Jan Simons, *Playing the Waves: Lars von Trier's Game Cinema* (Amsterdam: Amsterdam University Press, 2007).

142. Von Trier may have chosen this piece in part as an homage to Tarkovsky's *Solaris* (1972), in which it is used.

143. Hénaff, *Sade*, 84–103.

144. See also Schepelern, "Forget About Love."

145. Evans, "How to Make your Audience Suffer."

146. Max Horkheimer and Theodor W. Adorno, "Excursus II: Juliette, or Enlightenment and Morality," in *Dialectic of Enlightenment: Philosophical Fragments*, ed. Gunzelin Schmid Noerr, trans. Edmond Jephcott (Stanford, CA: Stanford University Press, 2002), 68.

147. Horkheimer and Adorno, "Excursus II," 82.

148. Hénaff, *Sade*, 258.

149. Hénaff goes on to say, "The storyteller figure is never a man, and even if a man by chance happens to tell his story, the name *historien* is never bestowed on him" (258).

150. Barthes, *Sade/Fourier/Loyola*, 31.

151. Quoted in Wainhouse, "Foreword," ix.

152. Hallund, interview, 2019.

153. Beauvoir, "Must We Burn Sade?"

154. As Schepelern points out, Joe's attempt to be a maternal figure to P ends in a sexual relationship that goes more than sour and takes on overtones of child abuse and incest ("Forget About Love").

155. Angela Carter, *The Sadeian Woman and the Ideology of Pornography* (New York: Pantheon, 1978), 19–20.

156. Romney, "Girl Can't Help It," 29.

157. Oliver Lyttelton, "Stellan Skarsgård Says He 'Won't Get to Fuck' in Lars Von Trier's *The Nymphomaniac*, Will Go Full-Frontal," IndieWire, December 19, 2011, http://blogs.indiewire.com/theplaylist/stellan-skarsgard-says-he-wont-get-to-fuck-in-lars-von-triers-the-nymphomaniac-but-will-go-full-frontal.

158. Galt, "Suffering Spectator?" This shot might also, arguably, be a subversion of the publicity poster for *Mazurka På Sengekanten* (1970), from the popular "Beside" series.

159. Richard Brophy, "Lars von Trier's Joyless Sexual Tantrum," *New Yorker*, March 21, 2014, https://www.newyorker.com/culture/richard-brody/lars-von-triers-joyless-sexual-tantrum.

160. Judovitz, "'Sex,' or The Misfortunes of Literature," 158.

161. Galt, "Suffering Spectator?"

162. Peter Debruge, "With Shocking Abortion Scene Restored, *Nymph()maniac* Makes Venice Fest Most Daring," *Variety*, September 9, 2014, http://variety.com/2014/film/opinion/with-shocking-abortion-scene-restored-Snymphomaniac-makes-venice-fest-most-daring-1201301689/.

163. Schepelern, "Forget About Love."

164. According to Pearce (interview, 2019) the very clinical close-up images were added after the shoot was finished and editing had begun in Denmark.

165. Elena Del Rio, "Lars von Trier's *Nymph()maniac*: Polyphonic Anatomy of a Cruel Film," *Image and Narrative* 17, no. 5 (2016): 41–53.

166. Antonin Artaud, *The Theater and Its Double*, trans. Mary Caroline Richards (New York: Grove, 1958), 102.

167. Del Rio, "Lars von Trier's *Nymph()maniac*."

168. Jenle Hallund, Vinca Wiedemann, and Emilie Spliid Pearce were all exasperated with or furious at von Trier about the film's ending, which von Trier laughingly refused to justify.

169. Christine Evans, "Interpretation is a Fantasy: Truth, Interpretation, and Knowledge in *Nymph() maniac*," paper presented at Society for Cinema and Media Studies Conference, Montreal, Quebec, March 25, 2015.

170. Robert Sinnerbrink, "Provocation and Perversity: Lars von Trier's Cinematic Anti-Philosophy," in *The Global Auteur: The Politics of Authorship in Twenty-First Century Cinema*, ed. Sung-Hoon Jeong and Jermi Szaniawski (London: Bloomsbury, 2016), 95–114.

171. Schepelern, "Forget About Love."

172. Pasolini adapted this sort of rhetoric in *Salò*, a critique of fascism, consumerism, and nihilism, and a film that von Trier (together with Christian Braad Thomsen) reimported to Danish cinemas in 1999. Pasolini's libertines quote Nietzsche (while Pasolini quotes Dante's *Inferno* together with Sade). Notably, von Trier mentioned *Salò* to Pearce several times while making *Nymphomaniac* (Pearce, interview, 2019).

173. Lynne Huffer, "The Nymph Shoots Back: Agamben and the Feel of the Agon," *Theory & Event* 18, no. 2 (2015): https://muse.jhu.edu/journals/theory_and_event/toc/tae.18.2.html (accessed July 12, 2021).

174. The parallel parentheses are also an impishly self-reflexive allusion to the spelling of the title of *Antichrist* in the opening credits and publicity for the film with the woman symbol substituted for the final "t."

175. Pearce, interview, 2019. Pearce went on to describe how von Trier taught her bird calls and tested her on them with an app on his phone, and Wiedemann and Hallund also mentioned his knowledge of trees.

176. Wiedemann, interview, 2019.

177. Pearce, interview, 2019.

178. See also Thomsen, who notes how Joe's herbarium "creates connections between the leaves of the book, labia, and leaves on the tree" (*Renewal of Film*, 310–12). Ultimately, leaves, labia, sex, and her father are interwoven in an Oedipal connection. This begins when the pubescent Joe studies anatomical drawings of female body part in her father's medical books, and the film cuts to a scene in the forest in which her father tells her the story of the ash tree. It is picked up in *Volume II* in a sequence in which she takes up her herbarium after having given up sex temporarily but ends up being stimulated by it.

179. Hallund, interview, 2019.

180. Linda Badley, "*Antichrist*, Misogyny, and Witch Burning: The Nordic Cultural Contexts," *Journal of Scandinavian Cinema* 3, no. 1 (March 2013): 15–33.

181. Casper Sejersen and Ceilie Høgsbro, *Belongs to Joe: Book of Comfort for a Nymphomaniac* (London: Mack, 2015).

182. Del Rio, "Lars von Trier's *Nymph()maniac*," 47.

183. Del Rio, 47.

184. Von Trier quoted in Thorsen, "Von Trier tørlagt." Translated from the Danish: "Men i bund og grund er det jo en slavefilosofi, hvor man sådan flagellantisk skal underkaste sig og moralsk laves fuldstændig om. Og jeg kan meget godt lide mig, som jeg er."

185. Nikoline, quoted in Nicki Bruun, "Rap om kvindeligt begær på Ekko Shortlist," Ekko, June 12, 2020, https://www.ekkofilm.dk/artikler/rapper-udfolder-kvindeligt-begar/.

186. Nikoline, *Gourmet*, music video, 2020, https://www.nikolinemusic.com/videos (accessed July 16, 2021). Translated by Peter Schepelern. In the original Danish: "Jeg er ikk' kommet her for at please jer!. . . Som den nye Trier."

4. *THE HOUSE THAT JACK BUILT*

1. Lars von Trier, interview by the author, Copenhagen, June 28, 2018.

2. Jenle Hallund, interview by the author, Copenhagen, June 12, 2019.

3. Von Trier and Hallund continued their dialectical method of brainstorming concepts and allusions and writing dialogue, from their collaboration on *Nymphomaniac*, and to a lesser degree, *Melancholia*, with von Trier as Jack and Hallund as Verge and some of the female characters—for example, Simple (Hallund, interview by the author, 2019). This chapter reflects that fact by interweaving quotations from von Trier and Hallund throughout.

4. David Ehrlich, "Matt Dillon Says Lars von Trier Isn't Evil and That *The House That Jack Built* Is Art," IndieWire, December 14, 2018, https://www.indiewire.com/2018/12/matt-dillon-interview -lars-von-trier-the-house-that-jack-built-1202028057/.

5. Hallund, interview, 2019.

6. Von Trier, interview, 2018.

7. Quoted in John Gray, "A Point of View: Tom Ripley and the Meaning of Evil," BBC News, May 17, 2013, https://www.bbc.com/news/magazine-22551083.

8. Von Trier, interview, 2018. The coolly intelligent, charming, amoral Ripley, Highsmith's protagonist, would most likely be diagnosed with antisocial personality disorder. Unlike the psychopath, whose violence is sadistic, Ripley does not kill for enjoyment but out of rationality, to achieve personal goals.

9. Peter Schepelern, "Nine Questions for Lars von Trier Regarding *The House That Jack Built*," interview with Lars von Trier, *The House That Jack Built* (London: Artificial Eye, 2018), DVD.

10. Hallund, interview, 2019.

11. Jenle Hallund, interview by the author, FaceTime, October 9, 2020.

12. Schepelern, "Nine Questions."

13. David Jenkins, "Lars von Trier: 'I Know How to Kill,'" Little White Lies, December 13, 2018, https://lwlies.com/interviews/lars-von-trier-the-house-that-jack-built/.

14. Schepelern, "Nine Questions."

15. Hallund, interview, 2019. Manuel Alberto Claro (interview by the author, Copenhagen, June 28, 2018) confirms that "a lot of the hell [references] are from Blake's interpretation of Dante, no? I think Jenle Hallund has read Blake and that he and she sort of collaborated on that. But I'm not sure how much he's actually read. . . . I imagine she probably read a lot and Lars is like picking [her brain]."

16. Wendy Mitchell, "Lars Von Trier's *The House That Jack Built* Cuts Early Deals," Screen Daily, May 17, 2016, http://www.trustnordisk.com/content/exclusive-interview-louise-vesth-matt-dillon -bruno-ganz-star-von-trier-s-house-jack-built .

17. Hallund, interview, 2020.

18. Peter Schepelern, interview with Lars von Trier, University of Copenhagen, April 22, 2015.

19. Gary M. Kramer, "Matt Dillon on Playing Lars von Trier's Psychopath in Controversial *The House That Jack Built*," Salon, December 14, 2018, https://www.salon.com/2018/12/14/matt-dillon-on -playing-lars-von-triers-psychopath-in-controversial-the-house-that-jack-built/.

20. Hallund, interview, 2020.

21. Hallund.

22. François, Reumont, "Cinematographer Manuel Alberto Claro, DFF, Discusses *The House That Jack Built*," La Lettre AFC, May 17, 2018, https://www.afcinema.com/Cinematographer-Manuel-Alberto-Claro-DFF-discusses-Lars-Von-Trier-s-The-House-That-Jack-Built.html?lang=fr.

23. Schepelern, interview with Lars von Trier, 2015.

24. TrustNordisk presold the film in Latin America (California Filmes), Benelux (September), Poland (Gutek), Taiwan (Moviecloud), Former Yugoslavia (Cinemania), Czech Republic (Aero), and Romania (Independenta Film 97) (Mitchell, "Lars Von Trier").

25. Mike Fleming Jr., "Lars Von Trier Sets Matt Dillon, Bruno Ganz for *The House That Jack Built*," Deadline Hollywood, November, 2016, https://deadline.com/2016/11/lars-von-trier-matt-dillon-bruno-ganz-the-house-that-jack-built-1201846778/.

26. Scott Roxborough, "Berlin: Lars von Trier's *The House That Jack Built* Adds Riley Keough, Sofie Gråbøl (Exclusive)," *Hollywood Reporter*, February 11, 2017, https://www.hollywoodreporter.com/news/berlin-lars-von-triers-house-jack-built-adds-riley-keough-sofie-grabol-974732.

27. Elsa Keslassy, "Uma Thurman Joins Cast of Lars von Trier's *The House That Jack Built*," *Variety*, March 7, 2017, https://variety.com/2017/film/markets-festivals/uma-thurman-joins-cast-of-lars-von-triers-the-house-that-jack-built-1202003490/.

28. Catherine Shoard, "Lars von Trier Inspired by Donald Trump for New Serial-Killer Film," *Guardian* (February 14, 2017), https://www.theguardian.com/film/2017/feb/14/lars-von-trier-donald-trump-the-house-that-jack-built. The image also evokes the scythe-bearing character in the iconic "dance of death" at the end of Ingmar Bergman's *The Seventh Seal*.

29. Zack Sharf, "Lars von Trier Wants You to Know *The House That Jack Built* Will Be His Most Brutal Film Ever," IndieWire, January 2, 2017, http://www.trustnordisk.com/content/lars-von-trier-wants-you-know-house-jack-built-will-be-his-most-brutal-film-ever.

30. Zack Sharf, "*The House That Jack Built*: Uma Thurman Catches the Eye of a Serial Killer in New Look at Lars von Trier Film," IndieWire, April 26, 2018, https://www.indiewire.com/2018/04/the-house-that-jack-built-uma-thurman-first-look-lars-von-trier-1201957520/.

31. Eric Kohn, "Cannes Director: Lars von Trier Was 'a Victim of His Bad Jokes'—Exclusive," IndieWire, April 30, 2018, https://www.indiewire.com/2018/04/lars-von-trier-cannes-victim-the-house-that-jack-built-1201958902/.

32. Stephen Garrett, "Lars von Trier Film Triggers Outrage at Cannes . . . Or So Twitter Would Have You Believe," *Observer*, May 15, 2018, https://observer.com/2018/05/was-cannes-really-shocked-by-lars-von-trier-movie-the-house-that-jack-built/.

33. Zack Sharf, "PETA Defends Lars von Trier's *The House That Jack Built* Against Backlash Over Graphic Animal Mutilation Scene," IndieWire, May 27, 2018, https://www.indiewire.com/2018/05/peta-defends-lars-von-trier-the-house-that-jack-built-duck-mutilation-1201965931/.

34. Zack Sharf, "Lars Von Trier's *House That Jack Built* Baits Controversy with Shocking Posters of Characters Tied Up and Contorted," IndieWire, September 26, 2018, https://www.indiewire.com/2018/09/house-that-jack-built-posters-female-characters-tied-up-contorted-lars-von-trier-1202007137/.

35. Alicia Wilkinson, "Critics Called Lars von Trier's New Movie 'Repulsive.' It's Being Released Twice," Vox, December 14, 2018, https://www.vox.com/culture/2018/11/28/18113504/house-jack-built-lars-von-trier-unrated-r-rated-theater-streaming.

36. Michel Ciment and Hubert Niogret, "Entretien avec Lars von Trier," *Positif*, no. 288 (February 1985): 50; Peter Schepelern, "Nine Questions." The project was never completed, although he used parts of it in *Europa* (Schepelern, email to the author, August 28, 2020).

37. Schepelern, "Nine Questions."

38. Von Trier, interview, 2018.

39. Lars von Trier, *The House That Jack Built*, shooting draft, January 20, 2017, unpublished screenplay, courtesy of Zentropa Productions.

40. Armond White, "*The House That Jack Built* Takes On the Apocalypse," *National Review*, December 19, 2018, https://www.nationalreview.com/2018/12/movie-review-the-house-that-jack-built-dark-satire/.

41. Jan Kornum, Larsen, "A Conversation between Jan Kornum Larson and Lars von Trier," in *Lars von Trier: Interviews*, ed. Jan Lumholdt (Jackson: University Press of Mississippi, 2003), 39.

42. Harris's second novel, *The Silence of the Lambs*, and its A-list film adaptation, which won five Academy Awards in 1991, were responsible for the mainstreaming of the genre.

43. Nordic noir typically blends the police procedural with social and political commentary and family melodrama.

44. Lawrence Garcia, "*The House That Jack Built*: No Exit," Reverse Shot, December 14, 2018, http://www.reverseshot.org/reviews/entry/2515/jack_built.

45. Sharf, "Lars von Trier Wants You to Know."

46. Hallund, interview, 2019.

47. Sharf, "Lars von Trier Wants You to Know."

48. See chapter 2 of Philip L. Simpson, *Psycho Paths: Tracking the Serial Killer Through Contemporary American Film and Fiction* (Carbondale: Southern Illinois University Press, 2000), 70–112.

49. Through interviews with some of the most notorious serial killers of the 1970s and 1980s (including David Berkowitz, John Wayne Gacy, Bundy, and Manson), Douglas invented the now iconic method of psychological profiling, created and headed the FBI's Criminal Profiling Program, and wrote bestselling "true crime" studies such as *Mindhunter: Inside the FBI's Elite Crime Unit* (1995).

50. Simpson, *Psycho Paths*, 25.

51. David Schmidt, "Serial Killer Fiction: An Introduction," CrimeCulture, 2015, https://www.crimeculture.com/?page_id=1459 (accessed July 13, 2021).

52. Hallund, interview, 2020.

53. As early as scene 20, Verge asks, "And what about the police? I imagine they started coming around a lot?," calling attention to their absence.

54. Kyle Buchanan, "So, Just How Violent Is Lars von Trier's *The House That Jack Built*?," Vulture, November 28, 2018, https://www.vulture.com/2018/05/how-violent-is-the-house-that-jack-built-by-lars-von-trier.html.

55. As noted, an important source of inspiration, Highsmith's Ripley novels, were engineered to make readers empathize with an elegant, cold-blooded killer with the goal (much like Lecter's) of becoming an independently wealthy flaneur.

56. Von Trier, interview, 2018. Hallund (interview, 2020) confirmed that the film was Ridley Scott's *Hannibal* (2003).

57. Von Trier, interview, 2018.

58. Von Trier, interview, 2018. Von Trier apparently confused or blended *Saboteur* (1942), starring Robert Cummings, with *North by Northwest* (1959), starring Cary Grant, which have similar cliffhanger scenarios involving national monuments—the Statue of Liberty and Mount Rushmore, respectively.

59. Von Trier, interview, 2018.

60. Schepelern, "Nine Questions." In his "*The House That Jack Built* Director's Statement," July 1, 2016, unpublished document, courtesy of Zentropa Productions, von Trier wrote, "My aim is partly

to show Jack during the intervals, as an ordinary, likable (and very knowledgeable) human being who only in brief glimpses reveal his psychopathic nature, as opposed to the incidents, which are steeped in his psychopathy. The dream of becoming an artist is expressed in that way."

61. Von Trier, interview, 2018.

62. Von Trier, shooting draft, 126.

63. Von Trier, interview, 2018.

64. According to Hallund (interview, 2020), paraphrasing von Trier, as a child, he was impressed with a widely admired close relative of his mother who was an architect and dreamed of becoming one.

65. Nigel Andrews, "*The House That Jack Built*—Lars von Trier Returns to the Dark Corners of the Human Psyche," *Financial Times*, December 5, 2018, https://www.ft.com/content/70c2a718-f889 -11e8-af46-2022a0b02a6c.

66. Bret Easton Ellis, *American Psycho* (New York: Vintage, 1991), 1.

67. Like von Trier, Ellis became controversial by transgressing the boundaries of high and low culture, and hence also class. Ellis had been a "hot" young literary author after publishing best seller *Less Than Zero* (1988), so Simon & Schuster paid a $300,000 advance for *American Psycho*, but when passages were leaked to the press, complaints of violence and misogyny prompted the publishers to break the contract, in turn prompting Knopf to snatch it up for their Vintage Contemporary series. Then the National Organization for Women boycotted it for its graphic descriptions of violence against women, and reviewers applied labels such as "designer porn." The stir was unlike anything in thirty years.

As David Skal has suggested, what was okay for Stephen King or horror fiction was *not* okay for a "literary" author. King's reams of mayhem, gore, and brand name dropping were one thing; Ellis's reams of upscale gore sold under a literary imprint were another. Similarly, what was encouraged for a hardcore horror film was not acceptable for an art film. Skal, *The Monster Show: A Cultural History of the Horror Film* (New York: Farrar, Straus & Giroux, 2001), 376.

68. "*American Psycho* from Book to Screen," dir. Eric Saks, special feature, *American Psycho*, Killer Collector's Edition (Santa Monica, CA: Lionsgate Home Entertainment, 2005), DVD.

69. Hallund, interview, 2019.

70. Von Trier, shooting draft, 77.

71. Andrews, "*The House That Jack Built*," 2018.

72. Dostoevsky, quoted in Ellis, *American Psycho*, 2.

73. Mark Seltzer, *Serial Killers: Death and Life in America's Wound Culture* (London: Routledge, 1998).

74. Shoard, "Lars von Trier Inspired."

75. See especially Mary Trump, *Too Much and Never Enough: How My Family Created the World's Most Dangerous Man* (New York: Simon & Schuster, 2020).

76. Von Trier, *The House That Jack Built*, shooting draft, 80–81. Von Trier has often explained that he prefers working with women actors. To Peter Schepelern (interview with Lars von Trier, Copenhagen, April 22, 2015) he said: "They let themselves be better pushed out of a place where they cannot bottom, once you have agreed on what the purpose of the whole exercise is . . . and the men . . . can't release control . . . they think that they as actors can control a movie. . . . which is completely wrong, they can't. I'm asking for a palette of different colors, taking the scenes in different ways, and I have a hard time getting that from male actors." Translated by Peter Schepelern.

77. Hallund, interview, 2019. Hallund added, "[But] . . . I thought it could've been so much fun if he had had more of a conflict in the beginning with Lady #1. Lars and I had some discussions

about this because it could have built more of Jack's character had we seen a proper confrontation, [if] we could see how he was triggered, and . . . had we seen more ethical side to Jack. . . . But that was the only window for a different kind of female portrait."

78. Hallund, interview, 2019.

79. Hallund, interview, 2019.

80. Hallund, interview, 2019. That rage, like that of some real and many fictional serial killers such as Norman Bates (based on the notorious Ed Gein), may have originated in his relationship with the powerful and manipulative mother who turned him into a kind of eugenics experiment.

81. Hallund, interview, 2019.

82. *American Psycho from Book to Screen*.

83. Hallund, interview, 2019.

84. Stephen Barber, *The Anatomy of Cruelty: Antonin Artaud's Life and Works* (London: SunVision, 2013), 6.

85. Angelos Koutsourakis, "The Dialectics of Cruelty: Rethinking Artaudian Cinema." *Cinema Journal* 55, no. 3 (Spring 2016): 67.

86. Haneke's second theatrical feature, *Benny's Video*, is about a teenager who progresses from filming a pig slaughter to filming his killing of a girl and which employs Haneke's signature method of presenting the action through the killer's "home movies": the viewer watches the footage only to find that they are watching *with* Benny, its director and eventual murderer.

87. Von Trier, *The House That Jack Built*, shooting draft, 6.

88. Tom Beasley, "*Painted Bird* Star Stellan Skarsgård: The Violence Is Truthful, and That's Horrible," Yahoo Movies, September 7, 2020, https://autos.yahoo.com/painted-bird-stellan-skarsgard-violence-090306294.html.

89. Originally, Haneke wanted his film set in the United States and has claimed that he intended the film as a message targeting American audiences of Hollywood genre films that turn violence into entertainment. When a 2007 American remake was broached, he opted to direct it frame for frame, and spoke in interviews of violence as an American cultural phenomenon produced and consumed through the entertainment industry.

90. Schepelern, "Nine Questions."

91. Von Trier, "Director's Statement." Wendy Mitchell ("Lars Von Trier") quotes producer Louise Vesth as saying that von Trier "planned to split the shoot into two parts" so he could "change something [for the second half of the shoot] if he wants to," and that "for the cast it will also be really exciting, they can work together to change things." However, in a later email message to the author, Vesth explained that Lars "changed his mind and we shot everything together. So the process ended up being quite traditional" (Louise Vesth, email message to the author, October 22, 2020).

92. Von Trier, "Director's Statement."

93. Lawrence Garcia, "*The House That Jack Built* (review)," Letterboxd, May 15, 2018, https://letterboxd.com/lgarcia/film/the-house-that-jack-built-2018/. "No mere exercise in sadism (or masochism), *The House That Jack Built* is an anguished attempt to stare into the pits of hell, to look at the most inhumane acts that mankind has ever produced and locate, if not beauty, then the source of suffering, or just some glimpse of understanding in the form of 'extravagant art,'" Garcia adds.

94. "Lars von Trier Nazi Comments at Cannes 2011," YouTube, 4:26, May 18, 2011, https://www.youtube.com/watch?v=CHKojTI-pNM.

95. Evidently a few fans of YouTube *Downfall* parodies recognized von Trier's reference, and within days after the press conference a parody featured Ganz as Hitler enraged about missing a planned "meet and greet" with von Trier at Cannes after the latter's disgrace. Pounding his heart, the Führer rants, "Von Trier is the only movie director, the only one, the only one. . . . who truly speaks to my inner self." Greg Kilday, "In New *Downfall* Parody, Hitler Is Outraged by Cannes' Film Festival's Ban of Lars von Trier," IndieWire, May 21, 2011, https://www.hollywoodreporter.com/news/new-downfall-parody-hitler-is-190888.

96. David Ansen, "Trapped in a Viper's Nest," *Newsweek*, February 20, 2005, https://www.newsweek.com/trapped-vipers-nest-122099.

97. As Manuel Claro (interview, 2018) speculated, "That press conference, or that whole thing after *Melancholia* inspired this movie. What he was referring to, I think, was Hitler in the movie *Der Untergang* [*Downfall*, 2004]. It was like, 'I sympathize with that guy that I watched for two hours.' You know, because if you spend enough time, even though you know he's the most evil person in the world, you sympathize with him, and that's the thing he's testing with this movie." However, Anders Refn claims to have recommended Ganz to von Trier for the role after editing British auteur Sally Potter's *The Party* (2017), in which Ganz played Gottfried, the German boyfriend of Patricia Clarkson's April. Von Trier and Refn invited Ganz to lunch, whereupon "Lars said, 'Heil Hitler' to him, and he was totally stone-faced," Refn noted (interview, 2018).

98. Von Trier, interview, 2018.

99. Robert Sinnerbrink, "Provocation and Perversity: Lars von Trier's Cinematic Anti-Philosophy," in *The Global Auteur: The Politics of Authorship in Twenty-First Century Cinema*, ed. Sung-Hoon Jeong and Jermi Szaniawski (London: Bloomsbury, 2016), 95–114.

100. Hallund, interview, 2019.

101. Hallund, interview, 2020.

102. Hallund, interview, 2020.

103. Von Trier, "Director's Statement."

104. Per Juul Carlsen, "The Only Redeeming Factor Is the World Ending," FILM #72, Danish Film Institute, May 4, 2011, https://www.dfi.dk/en/english/only-redeeming-factor-world-ending.

105. Von Trier, interview, 2018.

106. Von Trier, interview, 2018.

107. Sami Saif, "*Dogville* Confessions," *Dogville*, directed by Lars von Trier, disc 2 (Copenhagen: Nordisk, 2003), DVD.

108. Von Trier, *The House That Jack Built*, shooting draft, 82.

109. Von Trier, 71.

110. Joel Black, *The Aesthetics of Murder: A Study in Romantic Literature and Contemporary Culture* (Baltimore, MD: Johns Hopkins University Press, 1991), 39.

111. Thomas De Quincey, *On Murder Considered as One of the Fine Arts* (1827, 1829, 1854) (London: Oneworld Classics, 2010), 35.

112. Steven Jay Schneider, "Murder as Art/The Art of Murder: Aestheticizing Violence in Modern Cinematic Horror," *Intensities: The Journal of Cult Media*, no. 3 (Spring 2003): https://intensitiescultmedia.files.wordpress.com/2012/12/schneider-murder-as-art.pdf (accessed July 13, 2021).

113. Schneider, "Murder as Art."

114. Richard Dyer, "Kill and Kill Again," *Sight and Sound* 7, no. 9 (September 1997): 14.

115. He also records his exploits in a massive ledger modeled on William Blake's illuminated manuscripts.

116. Maria Ionita, "Longform Televisual Narrative and Operatic Structure in Brian Fuller's *Hannibal*," *CineAction* Issue 94 (2014): 23–28, https://www.thefreelibrary.com/Long-form+televisual+narrative+and+operatic+structure+in+Bryan . . . -a0385797952.

117. Similarly, in *Dexter* (2006–2013), the eponymous blood pattern analyst (Michael T. Hall) is both a profiler and vigilante serial killer whose aesthetic includes Jackson Pollock-style blood spatter on white walls, three-dimensional red string maps, trophies encased in pristine glass slides, or bloodless victims that resemble sectioned Barbie dolls.

118. Kristian Eidnes Andersen, interview by the author, Zoom, February 2, 2021.

119. Stig Björkman, "An Interview About *Kingdom*," Reocities, June 1997 (link discontinued).

120. Hallund, interview, 2020.

121. Bodil Marie Stavning Thomsen, "The Demonic Quality of Darkness in *The House That Jack Built*: Haptic Transmedial Affects Throughout the Works of Lars von Trier," in *Transmedia Directors: Artistry, Industry, and New Audiovisual Aesthetics*, ed. Carol Vernallis, Holly Rogers, and Lisa Perrott (London: Bloomsbury, 2020), 368.

122. Hallund, interview, 2019.

123. Von Trier, *The House That Jack Built*, shooting draft, 92.

124. Frederic Spotts, *Hitler and the Power of Aesthetics* (New York: Overlook, 2004), back cover.

125. As Hallund, von Trier's source for the Blake references, puts it, "Jack uses [Blake's ideas] in a very twisted and. . . . psychopathic way to excuse his own actions" (interview, 2019).

126. Spotts, *Hitler and the Power of Aesthetics*, 123–26.

127. Spotts, 311–20.

128. I thank William J. Simmons for this reference.

129. Von Trier, "Director's Statement."

130. Friedrich Nietzsche, *Beyond Good and Evil: Prelude to a Philosophy of the Future*, trans. Helen Zimmern, in *The Complete Works of Friedrich Nietzsche (1909–1913)*, ed. Dr. Oscar Levy, vol. 5 (London: T. N. Foulis, [1886] 1909), 96.

131. Von Trier, *The House That Jack Built*, shooting draft, 111.

132. Hallund, interview, 2019.

133. Von Trier, *The House That Jack Built*, shooting draft, 107.

134. Although Swiss, Ganz was known for his iconic performances in German film and television.

135. In his association with German roles and his knowledge of German literature and culture including the history of the Third Reich, Ganz may also allude to Thomas Mann's *Doktor Faustus: Das Leben des deutschen Tonsetzers Adrian Leverkühn, erzählt von einem Freunde* (*Doctor Faustus: The Life of the German Composer Adrian Leverkühn, Told by a Friend*, 1947), which von Trier claims to have read (interview, 2018), a novel whose Faustian protagonist, a composer, chooses to contract syphilitic madness in order to achieve unparalleled creativity. Based loosely on the life of Nietzsche while alluding to Schoenberg's invention of the twelve-tone system, Mann's novel is interpreted by some to compare Leverkühn's selling of his soul with that of the German people who chose Hitler.

136. Von Trier, interview, 2018.

137. Hallund, interview, 2019.

138. Von Trier, *The House That Jack Built*, shooting draft, 122. Assistant director Anders Refn, who filmed the sequence in Italy, said that it was a difficult shoot because the village men were so old that they could not keep a rhythm: "I was screaming, 'Ono. Due. Ono. Due'" (interview, 2018).

139. Von Trier, *The House That Jack Built*, shooting draft, 37.

140. William Blake, "And Did Those Feet in Ancient Time" (1808), in *The Complete Poetry and Prose of William Blake*, ed. David V. Erdmann with commentary by Harold Bloom, 1965 (New York: Anchor, 1988), 95.

141. About the mill, von Trier said, "I haven't read Blake but I talked to people who said that there was this thing with the mill. Doesn't say if it was a water mill or what kind of mill it was. But as I like water that runs, then, it was obvious to get a mill. And . . . it's something you don't expect to find in hell . . . in a small forest in in a cave" (interview, 2018).

142. Von Trier, *The House That Jack Built*, shooting draft, 1.

143. Von Trier, 114.

144. Andersen, interview, 2021.

145. Von Trier, *The House That Jack Built*, shooting draft, 111.

146. Von Trier, 120.

147. Von Trier, "Director's Statement."

148. Hallund, interview, 2020.

149. Manuel Alberto Claro, interview by the author, Copenhagen, June 13, 2019.

150. Von Trier, *The House That Jack Built*, shooting draft, 2017, 89.

151. Von Trier, 111.

152. The Delacroix painting was suggested by Per Kirkeby. Hallund, interview, 2019.

153. Von Trier, *The House That Jack Built*, shooting draft, 125.

154. John Milton, *Paradise Lost* (1667), book 1, l.63, https://www.dartmouth.edu/~milton/reading_room/pl/book_1/text.shtml (accessed July 13, 2021). More completely, Milton's line, from *Paradise Lost*, is "A dungeon horrible, on all sides round, / As one great furnace flamed, / yet from these flames / No light, but rather darkness visible."

155. Thomsen, "Demonic Quality of Darkness," 370.

156. Carl G. Jung, *The Integration of the Personality*, in *Collected Works of C. G. Jung*, ed. and trans. Gerhard Adler and R. F. C. Hull (Princeton, NJ: Princeton University Press, [1939] 1970), 17.

157. Von Trier, *The House That Jack Built*, shooting draft, 47–48.

158. Carl J. Jung, *Psychology and Religion: West and East*, in *Collected Works of C. G. Jung*, ed. and trans. Gerhard Adler and R. F. C. Hull (Princeton: Princeton University Press, [1938] 1970), 11.

159. Stig Björkman, ed., *Trier on von Trier*, trans. Neil Smith (London: Faber & Faber, 2003), 7.

160. Von Trier, *The House That Jack Built*, shooting draft, 94.

161. Von Trier, 4.

CODA

1. Lars von Trier and Niels Vørsel, "The Kingdom III: EXODUS. Treatment, Summary," Synopses, Notes, and Letters to Zentropa Employees for "Kingdom III," n.d., T I, D:8, Lars von Trier Collection, Danish Film Institute. Although the document is undated, Peter Schepelern places it in the year 2000 in his chronology of von Trier's career. See Schepelern, ed., *Lars von Trier: Det Gode Med Det Onde*, Brandts Museum of Art and Visual Culture (Copenhagen: Strandberg, 2017), 37.

2. Christian Lund, "Lars von Trier: The Burden from Donald Duck," interview with Lars von Trier, Louisiana Channel, Louisiana Museum of Modern Art, November 2020, https://channel.louisiana.dk/video/lars-von-trierthe-burden-from-donald-duck (accessed July 15, 2021).

3. Von Trier's reference is probably to the final part of Proust's *In Search of Lost Time*, vol. 1.

4. Ole Michelsen, "Passion Is the Lifeblood of Cinema" (1982), in *Lars von Trier: Interviews*, ed. Jan Lumholdt (Jackson: University of Mississippi Press, 2003), 10.

APPENDIX

1. Lars von Trier, "*Antichrist* Action Sketch," August 15, 2006, "'Antichrist' materialer," n.d., Lars von Trier Collection, Danish Film Institute. Ellipses in original.
2. Lars von Trier, "*Antichrist* Handlingsskitse," August 15, 2006, "'Antichrist' materialer," Lars von Trier Collection, Danish Film Institute.

FILMOGRAPHY

Turen til Squashland (*A Trip to Squashland*), animation, 1 min., 1968

Hvorfor flygte fra det du ved du ikke kan flygte fra? Fordi du er en kujon (*Why Try to Escape from That Which You Know You Can't Escape From? Because You Are a Coward*), 7 min., 1970

En blomst (*A Flower*), 7.49 min., 1971

Orchidégartneren (*The Orchid Gardener*), 37 min., 1978

Menthe la bienheureuse, 31 min., 1979

Nocturne, 8 min., 1980

Den sidste detalje (*The Last Detail*), 31 min., 1981

Befrielsesbilleder (*Images of Liberation*), 57 min., 1982

The Element of Crime/Forbrydelsens Element, 103 min., 1984

Epidemic, 106 min., 1987

Medea, television film, 75 min., 1988

Europa (*Zentropa*), 113 min., 1991

Riget (*The Kingdom*), television miniseries, episodes 1–4, 63, 65, 69, 75 min., 1994

Breaking the Waves, 158 min., 1996

Riget II (*The Kingdom*), television miniseries, episodes 1–4, 63, 79, 76, 78 min., 1997

Dogme #2: Idioterne (*Dogme #2: The Idiots*), 111 min., 1998

D-dag (*D-Day*), television film, 70 min., 1999

Dancer in the Dark, 139 min., 2000

Dogville, 178 min., 2003

De fem benspænd (*The Five Obstructions*), with Jørgen Leth, 90 min., 2003

Dear Wendy, filmscript, directed by Thomas Vinterberg, 105 min., 2004

Manderlay, 139 min., 2005

Direktøren for det hele (*The Boss of It All*), 99 min., 2006

Occupations, episode, *Chacun son cinéma*, 3 min., 2007

De unge år: Nietzsche sagaen 1 (*The Early Years: Erik Nietzsche Part 1*), filmscript, directed by Jacob Thuesen, 91 min., 2007

Antichrist, 108 min., 2009

Dimension, fragment of feature film, recorded 1991–1997, 27 min., 2010

Melancholia, 135 min., 2011

Nymphomaniac: Vol. I and *Vol. II*, 117 min. and 123 min., 2013

Nymphomaniac: The Director's Cut, 325 min., 2014

The House That Jack Built, 152 min., 2018

BIBLIOGRAPHY

Abram, Christopher. *Evergreen Ash: Ecology and Catastrophe in Old Norse Myth and Literature*. Charlottesville: University of Virginia Press, 2019.

Ackbar, Abbas. "Junk Space, *Dogville*, and Poor Theory." Lecture, Film Theory and Visual Culture Seminar, Vanderbilt University, December 6, 2013.

Adorno, Theodor. *The Culture Industry*. New York: Routledge, [1972, 1976] 2001.

Aftab, Kaleem. "Lars von Trier—'It's Good that People Boo.'" *Independent*, May 29, 2009. https://www .independent.co.uk/arts-entertainment/films/features/lars-von-trier-it-s-good-people-boo -1692406.html.

Alling, Thomas. "Sightseeing with the Holy Ghost." In *Lars von Trier: Interviews*, ed. Jan Lumholdt, 26–27. Jackson: University Press of Mississippi, 2003.

Andersen, Kristian Eidnes. Interview by the author, Facetime, February 1, 2021.

——. Interview by the author, Zoom, February 2, 2021.

Andrews, Nigel. "Beauty and the Unspeakable." *Financial Times*, July 22, 2009. https://amp.ft.com/content /c5d21ac4-76dc-11de-b23c-00144feabdco.

——. "*The House That Jack Built*—Lars von Trier Returns to the Dark Corners of the Human Psyche." *Financial Times*, December 5, 2018. https://www.ft.com/content/70c2a718-f889-11e8-af46-2022a0 b02a6c.

Anker, Elizabeth S., and Rita Felski. "Introduction." In *Critique and Postcritique*, ed. Elizabeth S. Anker and Rita Felski, 1–28. Durham, NC: Duke University Press, 2017.

Ansen, David. "Trapped in a Viper's Nest." *Newsweek*, February 20, 2005. https://www.newsweek.com /trapped-vipers-nest-122099.

Antonova, Natalia. "The Touch of Your Hand Behind a Closed Door." Global Comment, April 1, 2020. http://globalcomment.com/the-touch-of-your-hand-behind-a-closed-door/

"A Remarkable Castle." Tjolöholms Slott, January 5, 2014. http://www.Tjolöholm.se/in-english/the -castleas-history?jglmid=162.

Artaud, Antonin. *The Theater and Its Double*. Trans. Mary Caroline Richards. New York: Grove, 1958.

ArtyFarty. Season 1, episode 4, "Er Von Trier Okay?" (Is Von Trier OK?). Aired August 9, 2020. https:// www.dr.dk/drtv/se/artyfarty_-er-von-trier-okay_201018 . Trans. Peter Schepelern.

Badley, Linda. "*Antichrist*, Misogyny, and Witch Burning: The Nordic Cultural Contexts." *Journal of Scandinavian Cinema* 3, no. 1 (March 1, 2013): 15–33.

——. "'Fill All My Holes': *Nymphomaniac*, Sade, and the (Female) Libertine Body." In "Cinema as Provocation," special issue, *Ekphrasis: Images, Cinema, Media, Theory* 14, no. 2 (2015): 21–38.

——. *Lars von Trier*. Urbana: University of Illinois Press, 2011.

——. "*Nymphomaniac* as Retro Scandinavian Blue." In "Sexuality and Scandinavian Cinema," special issue, *Journal of Scandinavian Cinema* 5, no. 2 (2015): 191–204.

——. "Tag det gode med det onde." In *Lars von Trier Det God Med Det Onde*, ed. Peter Schepelern, 99–110. Brandts Museum of Art and Visual Culture, Copenhagen: Strandberg, 2017.

Badt, Karin. "Most Hated Director at Cannes: Lars von Trier as Antichrist or Shaman?" Huffington Post, May 29, 2009. http://www.huffingtonpost.com/.

Bainbridge, Caroline. "'Cinematic Screaming' or 'All About My Mother': Lars von Trier's Cinematic Extremism as Therapeutic Encounter." In *Media and the Inner World: Psycho-cultural Perspectives on Emotion, Media, and Popular Culture*, ed. Carolyne Bainbridge and C. Yates, 53–68. Basingstoke: Palgrave Macmillan, 2014.

——. "On the Experience of a Melancholic Gaze." *British Journal of Psychotherapy* 35, no. 1 (2019): 142–55.

Barber, Stephen. *The Anatomy of Cruelty: Antonin Artaud's Life and Works*. London: SunVision, 2013.

Barthes, Roland. *Sade/Fourier/Loyola*. Trans Richard Miller. Berkeley: University of California Press, [1971] 1976.

Bataille, Georges. *Eroticism: Death and Sensuality*. Trans. Mary Dalwood. San Francisco: City Lights, [1957] 1986.

Beasley, Tom. "*Painted Bird* Star Stellan Skarsgård: The Violence Is Truthful, and That's Horrible." Yahoo Movies, September 7, 2020. https://autos.yahoo.com/painted-bird-stellan-skarsgard-violence-090306294.html.

Beauvoir, Simone de. "Must We Burn Sade?" (1952). *Simone de Beauvoir: Political Writings*, ed. Margaret A. Simons and Marybeth Timmermann, 44–101. Urbana: University of Illinois Press, 2012.

Berkowitz, Joe. "Danish Film Critics Do Their Best *Nymphomaniac* Face in Spoof Posters." Fast Company, December 18, 2013. https://www.fastcompany.com/3023568/danish-film-critics-do-their-best-nymphomaniac-face-in-spoof-posters

Birkvad, Søren. "Hollywood Sin, Scandinavian Virtue: The 1967 Revolt of *I Am Curious* and *The Graduate*." *Film International* 50, no. 2 (2011): 42–54.

Björklund, Elizabeth. "'This is a dirty movie': *Taxi Driver* and 'Swedish Sin.'" *Journal of Scandinavian Cinema* 1, no. 2 (2011): 163–76.

——. *The Most Delicate Subject: A History of Sex Education Films in Sweden*. Lund: Centre for Languages and Literature, 2012.

Björkman, Stig. "An Interview About *Kingdom*." Reocities, June 1997. Link discontinued.

——. "Making the Waves." *Sight and Sound* 19, no. 8 (2009): 16–19.

Björkman, Stig, ed. *Trier on von Trier*. Trans. Neil Smith. London: Faber & Faber, 2003.

Black, Joel. *The Aesthetics of Murder: A Study in Romantic Literature and Contemporary Culture*. Baltimore, MD: Johns Hopkins University Press, 1991.

Blake, William. "And did those feet in ancient time" (1808). In *The Complete Poetry and Prose of William Blake*, by William Blake, ed. David V. Erdmann with commentary by Harold Bloom, 95. New York: Anchor, [1965] 1988.

Bo, Michael. "De overlevede Antikrist—og von Trier." *Politiken*, May 23, 2009. http://politiken.dk/.

Boatwright, Kirsten L. "Constraining Lars von Trier: Issues of Censorship, Creativity, and Provocation." PhD diss., Middle Tennessee State University, December 2011.

Bondebjerg, Ib. "Lars von Trier." In *The Danish Directors*, ed. Mette Hjort and Ib Bondebjerg, 208–23. London: Intellect, 2001.

Bordwell, David. "Cinema in the World's Happiest Place." Observations on Film Art: David Bordwell's Website on Cinema, July 2, 2009. http://www.davidbordwell.net/blog/2009/07/02/cinema-in-the -worlds-happiest-place/.

Bradshaw, Peter. "*Melancholia*—Review." *Guardian*, September 29, 2011. https://www.theguardian.com /film/2011/sep/29/melancholia-film-review.

Brassier, Ray. *Nihil Unbound: Enlightenment and Extinction*. New York: Palgrave Macmillan, 2007.

Brereton, Pat. *Environmental Ethics and Film*. London: Routledge, 2016.

Broch, Hermann. "Notes on the Problem of Kitsch" (1950). In *Kitsch: The World of Bad Taste*, ed. Gillo Dorfles, 49–76. New York: Universe, 1969.

Brøgger, Suzanne. *Fri os fra kærlighen*. Copenhagen: Gyldendal, 1973.

Brooks, Xan. "*Antichrist*: A Work of Genius or the Sickest Film in the History of Cinema?" *Guardian*, July 16, 2009. http://www.guardian.co.uk/film.

——. "Cannes 2011 Diary: The End of the Festival Is Nigh." *Guardian*, May 18, 2011. https://www .theguardian.com/film/2011/may/18/cannes-film-festival-2011-diary-melancholia.

——. "Lars von Trier on Filmmaking and Fear: 'Sometimes, alcohol is the only thing that will help.'" *Guardian*, December 3, 2018. https://www.theguardian.com/film/2018/dec/03/lars-von-trier-on -filmmaking-and-fear-sometimes-alcohol-is-the-only-thing-that-will-help.

——. "Mangy Foxes and Fake Firs: The Reel Chaos of the Cannes Film Festival." *Guardian*, May 18, 2009. https://www.theguardian.com/film/2009/may/18/cannes-film-festival-antichrist-lars-von-trier.

Brophy, Richard. "Lars von Trier's Joyless Sexual Tantrum." *New Yorker*, March 21, 2014. https://www .newyorker.com/culture/richard-brody/lars-von-triers-joyless-sexual-tantrum.

Buchanan, Kyle. "So, Just How Violent Is Lars von Trier's *The House That Jack Built*?" Vulture, November 28, 2018. https://www.vulture.com/2018/05/how-violent-is-the-house-that-jack-built-by-lars-von -trier.html.

Burke, Edmond. *A Philosophical Enquiry Into the Origin of Our Ideas of the Sublime and Beautiful* (1757). London: Cambridge University Press, 2014.

Bruun, Nicki. "Rap om kvindeligt begær på Ekko Shortlist." Ekko, June 12, 2020. https://www.ekkofilm .dk/artikler/rapper-udfolder-kvindeligt-begar/.

BWW News Desk. "Opera Philadelphia Triumphs with *Breaking the Waves*." *Broadway World*, September 28, 2016. https://wwwbroadwayworld.com/philadelphia/article/Opera- Philadelphia-Triumphs-With-BREAKING-THE-WAVES-20160928.

Calinescu, Matei. *Five Phases of Modernity: Modernism, Avant-Garde, Decadence, Kitsch, Postmodernism*. Durham, NC: Duke University Press, 1987.

Carlsen, Per Juul. "The Only Redeeming Factor Is the World Ending." *FILM* #72. Danish Film Institute, May 4, 2011. https://www.dfi.dk/en/english/only-redeeming-factor-world-ending.

Carnegy, Patrick. *Wagner and the Art of the Theatre*. New Haven, CT: Yale University Press, 2006.

Carter, Angela. *The Sadeian Woman and the Ideology of Pornography*. New York: Pantheon, 1978.

Child, Ben. "Shia La Beouf Sent Sex Tapes to Win Part in Lars von Trier's *Nymphomaniac*." *Guardian*, August 31, 2012. https://www.theguardian.com/film/2012/aug/31/shia-labeouf-sex-tape-von-trier -nymphomaniac.

Ciment, Michel, and Hubert Niogret. "Entretien avec Lars von Trier." *Positif*, no. 288 (February 1985): 47–50.

Ciment, Michel, and Phillipe Rouyer. "A Conversation with Lars von Trier" (1988). In *Lars von Trier: Interviews*, ed. Jan Lumholdt, 59–62. Jackson: University of Mississippi Press, 2003.

Clark, Brian. "First Poster for Lars von Trier's *Nymphomaniac* Gives New Meaning to the Word 'Teaser.'"
Screen Anarchy, May 2, 2013. https://screenanarchy.com/2013/05/first-poster-for-lars-von-triers
-nymphomaniac-gives-new-meaning-to-teaser.html.

Claro, Manuel Alberto. Interview by the author, Copenhagen, June 13, 2019.

——. Interview by the author, Copenhagen, June 28, 2018.

——. Interview by the author, Skype, November 22, 2013.

——. Interview by the author, telephone, October 5, 2013.

Corrigan, Timothy. *The Essay Film: From Montaigne, After Marker*. New York: Oxford University Press,
2011.

——. "Essayism and Contemporary Film Narrative." In *The Essay Film: Dialogue/Politics/Utopia*, ed. Elizabeth A. Papazian and Caroline Eades, 15–27. New York: Wallflower, 2016.

Coulthard, Lisa, and Chelsea Birks. "Desublimating Monstrous Desire: The Horror of Gender in New
Extremist Cinema." *Journal of Gender Studies* 25, no. 4 (2016): 461–76.

Dargis, Manohla. "This Is How the End Begins." *New York Times*, December 30, 2011. http://www.nytimes
.com/2012/01/01/movies/awardsseason/manohla-dargis-looks-at-the-overture-to-melancholia
.html.

Davidson, H. R. Ellis. *Gods and Myths of Northern Europe*. London: Penguin, 1990.

Davis, Jason. "Not Knowing Serial Killers with Hannibal Lecktor." *Hannibal Lecter and Philosophy: The
Heart of the Matter*, ed. Joseph Westfall, 109–21. Chicago: Open Court, 2016.

Debruge, Peter. "With Shocking Abortion Scene Restored, *Nymph()maniac* Makes Venice Fest Most
Daring." *Variety*, September 9, 2014. http://variety.com/2014/film/opinion/with-shocking-abortion
-scene-restored-Snymphomaniac-makes-venice-fest-most-daring-1201301689/.

Deleuze, Gilles, and Felix Guattari. *A Thousand Plateaus: Capitalism and Schizophrenia*. Minneapolis: University of Minnesota Press, 1987.

Del Rio, Elena. "Lars von Trier's *Nymph()maniac*: Polyphonic Anatomy of a Cruel Film." *Image and Narrative* 17, no. 5 (2016): 41–53.

Denby, David. "The Story of Joe." *New Yorker*, March 24, 2014. http://www.newyorker.com/magazine
/2014/03/24/the-story-of-joe.

Deppman, Jed, Daniel Ferrer, and Michael Groden, eds. *Genetic Criticism: Texts and Avant-textes*. Philadelphia: University of Pennsylvania Press, 2004.

De Quincey, Thomas. *On Murder Considered as One of the Fine Arts* (1827, 1829, 1854). London: Oneworld
Classics, 2010.

Desowitz, Bill. "Cinematographer Manuel Claro Talks the Bearable Lightness of *Nymphomaniac*."
IndieWire, April 3, 2014. https://www.indiewire.com/2014/04/cinematographer-manuel-claro-talks
-the-bearable-lightness-of-nymphomaniac-192874/.

Ditlev Jensen, Kristian. "Nordic Nonsense." Nordisk Film and TV Fond, n.d. www.nordiskfilmogtvfond
.com/managed . . . /lars_eng_version.doc (accessed November 12, 2012).

Douglas, John E., and Mark Olshaker. *Mindhunter: Inside the FBI's Elite Serial Crime Unit*. 1995. New York:
Simon & Schuster, 2017.

Dyer, Richard. "Kill and Kill Again." *Sight and Sound* 7, no. 9 (September 1997): 14–17.

Ebert, Roger. "Cannes #5, 'For Even Now Already It Is in the World.'" *Chicago Sun-Times*, May 17, 2009.
http://blogs.suntimes.com/ebert/.

——. "Cannes #6, A Devil's Advocate for *Antichrist*." *Chicago Sun-Times*, May 19, 2009. http://blogs
.suntimes.com/ebert/.

——. "Cannes #10, 'And, at Last, the Winners Are . . .'" *Chicago Sun-Times*, May 24, 2009. http://blogs
.suntimes.com/ebert/.

——. "I See It Coming, I Will Face It, I Will Not Turn Away." November 9, 2011. https://www
.rogerebert.com/reviews/melancholia-2011.

Ehrlich, David. "Matt Dillon Says Lars von Trier Isn't Evil and That *The House That Jack Built* Is Art."
IndieWire, December 14, 2018. https://www.indiewire.com/2018/12/matt-dillon-interview-lars-von
-trier-the-house-that-jack-built-1202028057/.

Ellis, Bret Easton. *American Psycho*. New York: Vintage, 1991.

Ellis, Hilda Roderick. *The Road to Hel: A Study of the Conception of the Dead in Old Norse Literature*. Westport, CT: Greenwood, 1968.

Elsaesser, Thomas. "Black Suns and a Bright Planet: *Melancholia* as Thought Experiment." In *Politics,
Theory, and Film: Critical Encounters with Lars von Trier*, ed. Bonnie Honig and Lori J. Marso, 305–35.
Oxford: Oxford University Press, 2016.

——. *European Cinema and Continental Philosophy: Film as Thought Experiment*. London: Bloomsbury, 2019.

——. "The Global Author: Control, Creative Constraints, and Performative Self-Contradiction." In
The Global Auteur: The Politics of Authorship in Twenty-First Century Cinema, ed. Sung-Hoon Jeong and
Jermi Szaniawski, 21–41. London: Bloomsbury, 2016.

Evans, Christine. "Interpretation Is a Fantasy: Truth, Interpretation, and Knowledge in *Nymph()maniac*."
Paper presented at Society for Cinema and Media Studies Conference, Montreal, Quebec, March 25,
2015.

Evans, Nicola. "How to Make Your Audience Suffer: Melodrama, Masochism, and Dead Time in Lars
von Trier's *Dogville*." *Culture, Theory, and Critique* 55, no. 3 (2014): 365–82.

Fanning, Evan. "*Antichrist* was Lars' 'Fun' Way of Treating Depression." *Independent*, July 26, 2009. https://
www.independent.ie/entertainment/movies/antichrist-was-lars-fun-way-of-treating-depression
-26553823.html.

Feinstein, Howard. "Lars von Trier: 'I will never do a press conference again.'" IndieWire, May 20, 2011.
https://www.indiewire.com/2011/05/lars-von-trier-i-will-never-do-a-press-conference-again-54069/.

Fleming, Mike, Jr. "Lars Von Trier Sets Matt Dillon, Bruno Ganz for *The House That Jack Built*." Deadline Hollywood, November 2016, https://deadline.com/2016/11/lars-von-trier-matt-dillon-bruno
-ganz-the-house-that-jack-built-1201846778/ (accessed July 15, 2021).

Foucault, Michel. *The Birth of the Clinic: An Archeology of Medical Perception*. New York: Vintage, [1973]
1994.

——. *Discipline and Punish: The Birth of the Prison*. New York: Vintage, [1975] 1995.

Friedländer, Saul. *Reflections of Nazism: An Essay on Kitsch and Death*. Trans. Thomas Weyr. New York:
Harper & Row, 1982.

French, Philip. "*Melancholia*—Review." *Observer*, October 2, 2011. https://www.theguardian.com/film
/2011/oct/02/melancholia-lars-von-trier-review.

French, Sarah, and Zoë Shacklock. "The Affective Sublime in Lars von Trier's *Melancholia* and Terrence
Malick's *The Tree of Life*." *New Review of Film and Television Studies* 12, no. 4 (2014): 339–56.

Freud, Sigmund. "Mourning and Melancholia" (1917). In *The Standard Edition of the Complete Psychological Works of Sigmund Freud*, ed. James Strachey, 239–60. Vol. 14. London: Hogarth, 1957.

Frey, Mattias. *Extreme Cinema: The Transgressive Rhetoric of Today's Art Film Culture*. New Brunswick, NJ:
Rutgers University Press, 2016.

Galt, Rosalind. "The Suffering Spectator? Perversion and Complicity in *Antichrist* and *Nymphomaniac*."
Theory & Event 18, no. 2 (2015): https://muse.jhu.edu/journals/theory_and_event/toc/tae.18.2.html
(accessed July 15, 2021).

Garcia, Lawrence. "*The House That Jack Built* (Review)." Letterboxd, May 15, 2018. https://letterboxd.com
/lgarcia/film/the-house-that-jack-built-2018/.

——. "*The House That Jack Built*: No Exit." Reverse Shot, December 14, 2018. http://www.reverseshot.org /reviews/entry/2515/jack_built.

Garrett, Stephen. "Lars von Trier Film Triggers Outrage at Cannes . . . Or So Twitter Would Have You Believe." *Observer*, May 15, 2018. https://observer.com/2018/05/was-cannes-really-shocked-by -lars-von-trier-movie-the-house-that-jack-built/.

Gray, John. "A Point of View: Tom Ripley and the Meaning of Evil." BBC News, May 17, 2013. https:// www.bbc.com/news/magazine-22551083.

Greenberg, Clement. *Art and Culture*. Boston: Beacon, 1978.

Grey, Thomas. "The Idea of Nature in Wagner's *Ring*." In *The Cambridge Companion to Wagner's Ring of the Nibelung*, ed. Mark Berry and Nicholas Vazsonyi, 205–31. London: Cambridge University Press, 2020.

——. "Wagner's *Ring* as Eco-Parable." In *Music Theater as Global Culture: Wagner's Legacy Today*, ed. Anno Mungen, Nicholas Vazsonyi, Julie Hubbert, Ivana Rentsch, and Arne Stolberg, 183–98. Würzburg: Königshausen & Neumann, 2017.

Grodal, Torben. "Frozen Style and Strong Emotions of Panic and Separation: Trier's Prologues to *Antichrist* and *Melancholia*." *Journal of Scandinavian Cinema* 2, no. 1 (2012): 47–53.

Grusin, Richard. "Post-Cinematic Atavism." Post-Cinema: Theorizing Twenty-First-Century Century Film, 2016. https://reframe.sussex.ac.uk/post-cinema/5-3-grusin/ (accessed July 15, 2021).

Gullestad, Siri Erika. "Crippled Feet: Sadism in Lars von Trier's *Antichrist*." *Scandinavian Psychoanalytic Review* 34, n. 2 (2011): 79–84.

Hallund, Jenle. Interview by the author, Copenhagen, June 12, 2019.

——. Interview by the author, Facetime, October 9, 2020.

Hanna, Beth. "Everyone's Orgasming in New Character Posters for Lars von Trier's *Nymphomaniac*." IndieWire, October 10, 2013. https://www.indiewire.com/2013/10/everyones-orgasming-in-new -character-posters-for-lars-von-triers-nymphomaniac-195647/.

Heath, Chris. "Lars Attacks!" *GQ*, October 2011, https://www.gq.com/story/lars-von-trier-gq-interview -october-2011 (accessed July 15, 2021).

Heffernan, Kevin. "Prurient (Dis)Interest: The American Release and Reception of *I Am Curious (Yellow)*." In *Sex Scene: Media and the Sexual Revolution*, ed. Eric Schaefer, 105–25. Durham, NC: Duke University Press, 2014.

Heise, Ursula K. *Sense of Place and Sense of Planet: The Environmental Imagination of the Global*. Oxford: Oxford University Press, 2008.

Hénaff, Marcel. *Sade: The Invention of the Libertine Body*. Trans. Xavier Callahan. Minneapolis: University of Minnesota Press, 1999.

Hird, Myra. "Waste, Landfills, and an Environmental Ethic of Vulnerability." *Ethics and the Environment* 18, no. 1 (2013): 105–24.

Hobbs, Simon. *Cultivating Extreme Cinema: Text, Paratext, and Home Video Culture*. Edinburgh: Edinburgh University Press, 2020.

Hoberman, J. "Cannes 2011: Lars von Trier's *Melancholia*. Wow." VoiceFilm, May 18, 2011. http://www .voicefilm.com/2011/05/cannes_2011_lars_von_triers_melancholia_wow.php.

——. "Sex: The Terror and the Boredom." *New York Review of Books*, March 26, 2014, http://www .nybooks.com/daily/2014/03/26/nymphomaniac-sex-terror-boredom/.

Holm, Siv [Agnethe Thomsen]. *Jeg—en kvinde*. Copenhagen: Stig Vendelkærs Forlag, 1961.

Honig, B., and L. J. Marso, ed. *Politics, Theory, and Film: Critical Encounters with Lars von Trier*. London: Oxford University Press, 2016.

Hopper, Jessica. "In Which Nature Is Lars von Trier's Satanic Church." This Recording, October 27, 2009. http://thisrecording.com/.

Horeck, Tanya, and Tina Kendall, ed. *The New Extremism in Cinema: From France to Europe*. Edinburgh: Edinburgh University Press, 2011.

Horkheimer, Max, and Theodor W. Adorno. "Excursus II: Juliette, or Enlightenment and Morality." In *Dialectic of Enlightenment: Philosophical Fragments*, ed. Gunzelin Schmid Noerr, trans. Edmond Jephcott, 63–93. Stanford, CA: Stanford University Press, 2002.

Hübner, Laura. "Her Defiant Stare: Dreams of Another World in *Summer with Monika*." *Studies in European Cinema* 2, no. 2 (2005): 103–13.

Huffer, Lynne. "The Nymph Shoots Back: Agamben and the Feel of the Agon." *Theory & Event* 18, no. 2 (2015): https://muse.jhu.edu/journals/theory_and_event/toc/tae.18.2.html (accessed July 15, 2021).

Ionita, Maria. "Longform Televisual Narrative and Operatic Structure in Brian Fuller's *Hannibal*." *Cine-Action*, no. 94 (2014): 23–28.

Jakobsen, Jakob Skov. "Laila var sexafhængig: Von Trier-film gav mig flashbacks." DR, December 18, 2013. http://www.dr.dk/Nyheder/Kultur/Film/2013/12/18/093010.htm.

Jagernauth, Kevin. "Lars Von Trier Gets Gagged, Reveals Chapter Titles for *Nymphomaniac* and Introduces New Film Genre." The Playlist, May 31, 2013. https://theplaylist.net/lars-von-trier-gets-gagged-reveals-chapter-titles-for-nymphomaniac-introduces-new-film-genre-20130531/.

James, Nick. "The Story of ()." *Sight & Sound*, 24, no. 3 (2014): 22–27.

Jenkins, David. "Lars von Trier: 'I Know How to Kill.'" Little White Lies, December 13, 2018. https://lwlies.com/interviews/lars-von-trier-the-house-that-jack-built/.

Jensen, Anders Thomas. *Antichrist. Efter idé af Lars von Trier, Skrevet af Anders Thomas Jensen*. Lars von Trier Collection, Danish Film Institute, n.d.

Judovitz, Dalia. "'Sex,' or The Misfortunes of Literature." In *Sade and the Narrative of Transgression*, ed. David B. Allison, Mark S. Roberts, and Allen S. Weiss, 171–98. Cambridge: Cambridge University Press, 1995.

Jung, Carl G. *The Integration of the Personality*. In *Collected Works of C. G. Jung*, ed. and trans. Gerhard Adler and R. F. C. Hull. Vol. 17. Princeton, NJ: Princeton University Press, [1939] 1970.

——. *Psychology and Religion: West and East*. In *Collected Works of C .G. Jung*, ed. and trans. Gerhard Adler and R. F. C. Hull. Vol. 11. Princeton, NJ: Princeton University Press, [1938] 1970.

Kara, Selmin. "Anthropocenema: Cinema in the Age of Mass Extinctions." In *Post-Cinema: Theorizing Twenty-First-Century Film*, ed. Shane Denson and Julia Leyda. Falmer: REFRAME, 2016, https://reframe.sussex.ac.uk/post-cinema/6-2-kara/ (accessed August 9, 2021).

Kastrup, Kim. "Trier-dramatiker giver sig selv mundkurv på i tre år." *Ekstra Bladet*, April 14, 2015. https://ekstrabladet.dk/underholdning/kultur/trier-dramatiker-giver-sig-selv-mundkurv-paa-i-tre-aar/5521978.

Kerner, Aaron Michael, and Jonathan L. Knapp. *Extreme Cinema: Affective Strategies in Transnational Media*. Edinburgh: Edinburgh University Press, 2016.

Keslassy, Elsa. "Uma Thurman Joins Cast of Lars von Trier's *The House That Jack Built*." *Variety*, March 7, 2017. https://variety.com/2017/film/markets-festivals/uma-thurman-joins-cast-of-lars-von-triers-the-house-that-jack-built-1202003490/.

Kilday, Greg. "In New *Downfall* Parody, Hitler Is Outraged by Cannes' Film Festival's Ban of Lars von Trier." IndieWire, May 21, 2011. https://www.hollywoodreporter.com/news/new-downfall-parody-hitler-is-190888.

Killeen, Ger. "Grace Without Gravity: Lars von Trier's Prologue to *Antichrist*." Headlandia: Words from the Edge of the World, 2014. http://headlandia.blogspot.com/2014/02/gravity-without-grace-prologue-to-lars.html (accessed July 15, 2021).

"Kirsten Dunst Talks Rehab, Depression To British ELLE." Huffington Post, August 2, 2011. https://www.huffpost.com/entry/kirsten-dunst-talks-rehab_n_915931.

Kittler, Friedrich. "World-Breath: On Wagner's Media Technology." In Opera Through Other Eyes, ed. David J. Levin, 215–35. Stanford, CA: Stanford University Press. 1994.

"Kitsch." Urban Dictionary, March 10, 2014. http://www.urbandictionary.com/.

Knegt, Peter. "Stensgard and von Trier." FILM: Danish Films Digital Issue (Fall 2015): http://www.dfi-film.dk/nymphomaniac-long (accessed July 15, 2021).

Kohn, Eric. "Cannes Director: Lars von Trier Was 'A Victim of His Bad Jokes'—Exclusive." IndieWire, April 30, 2018. https://www.indiewire.com/2018/04/lars-von-trier-cannes-victim-the-house-that-jack-built-1201958902/.

Koolhaas, Rem. "Junkspace." 2001. http://www.cavvia.net/junkspace/ (accessed July 15, 2021).

Koster, Ole. Interview with Lars von Trier. Cannes, May 23, 2003, TV2. Dogville, directed by Lars Von Trier. Disc 2. Copenhagen: Nordisk, 2003. DVD.

Koutsourakis, Angelos. "The Dialectics of Cruelty: Rethinking Artaudian Cinema." Cinema Journal 55, no. 3 (Spring 2016): 65–89.

——. Politics as Form in Lars von Trier: A Post-Brechtian Reading. London: Bloomsbury, 2013.

Kramer, Gary M. "Matt Dillon on Playing Lars von Trier's Psychopath in Controversial The House That Jack Built." Salon, December 14, 2018. https://www.salon.com/2018/12/14/matt-dillon-on-playing-lars-von-triers-psychopath-in-controversial-the-house-that-jack-built/.

Kreutzer, Gundula. Curtain, Gong, Steam: Wagnerian Technologies of Nineteenth-Century Opera. Oakland: University of California Press, 2018.

Kuzma, Marta. "Whatever Happened to Sex in Scandinavia? I Am Curious (Yellow)." Afterall: A Journal of Art, Context, and Enquiry, no. 17 (Spring 2008): 5–19.

Lagercrantz, Olof. August Strindberg. Stockholm: Wahlstrøm & Widstrand, 1979.

Lapin, Andrew. "In Grisly, Sadistic The House That Jack Built, Lars von Trier Deconstructs Himself." NPR, December 13, 2018. https://www.npr.org/2018/12/13/675254118/in-grisly-sadistic-the-house-that-jack-built-lars-von-trier-deconstructs-himself/.

Larkin, David. "'Indulging in Romance with Wagner': Tristan in Lars von Trier's Melancholia." Music and the Moving Image 9, no. 1 (Spring 2016): 38–58.

"Lars von Trier Nazi Comments at Cannes 2011." YouTube, 4:26, May 18, 2011. https://www.youtube.com/watch?v=CHKojTI-pNM.

Larsen, Jan Kornum. "A Conversation Between Jan Kornum Larson and Lars von Trier." In Lars von Trier: Interviews, ed. Jan Lumholdt, 32–46. Jackson: University Press of Mississippi, 2003.

Larsson, Mariah. "Practice Makes Perfect? The Production of the Swedish Sex Film in the 1970s." Film International 8, no. 6 (2010): 40–49.

Lee, Kenneth B. "Video Essay: The Essay Film—Some Thoughts of Discontent." Sight & Sound, May 22, 2017. https://www.bfi.org.uk/news-opinion/sight-sound-magazine/features/deep-focus/video-essay-essay-film-some-thoughts.

Link, Trevor. "Depression, Melancholia, and Me: Lars von Trier's Politics of Displeasure." Occupied Territories, November 21, 2011. https://occupiedterritories.tumblr.com/post/13114178124/depression-melancholia-and-me-lars-von-triers.

Love, Catherine. "The Maids Review: Jean Genet's Would-be Murderers Set Pulses Racing." Guardian, November 23, 2018. https://www.theguardian.com/stage/2018/nov/23/the-maids-review-home-manchester.

Lübecker, Nikolaj. The Feel-Bad Film. Edinburgh: Edinburgh University Press, 2015.

Lund, Christian. "Lars von Trier: The Burden from Donald Duck." *Louisiana Channel*, Louisiana Museum of Modern Art, November 2020. https://channel.louisiana.dk/video/lars-von-trierthe-burden-from-donald-duck (accessed July 15, 2021).

Lyttelton, Oliver. "Stellan Skarsgård Says He 'Won't Get To Fuck' In Lars Von Trier's *The Nymphomaniac*, Will Go Full-Frontal." The Playlist, December 19, 2011. http://blogs.indiewire.com/theplaylist/stellan-skarsgard-says-he-wont-get-to-fuck-in-lars-von-triers-the-nymphomaniac-but-will-go-full-frontal.

Magee, Brian. *The Tristan Chord: Wagner and Philosophy*. New York: Henry Holt, 2000.

Menninghaus, Winfried. "On the Vital Significance of 'Kitsch': Walter Benjamin's Politics of 'Bad Taste.'" In *Walter Benjamin and the Architecture of Modernity*, ed. Andrew Benjamin, 29–58. New York: Charles Rice, 2009.

Michelsen, Ole. "Passion Is the Lifeblood of Cinema" (1982). In *Lars von Trier: Interviews*, ed. Jan Lumholdt, 5–12. Jackson: University of Mississippi Press, 2003.

Michelson, Peter. *Speaking the Unspeakable: A Poetics of Obscenity*. Albany: State University of New York Press, 1993.

Milton, John. *Paradise Lost* (1667). Book 1. https://www.dartmouth.edu/~milton/reading_room/pl/book_1/text.shtml (accessed July 15, 2021).

Minor, Ryan. "Introduction to Lars von Trier's *Deed of Conveyance*." *Opera Quarterly* 23, nos. 2–3 (Spring–Summer 2007): 338–40.

Mitchell, Wendy. "Lars Von Trier's *The House That Jack Built* Cuts Early Deals." Screen Daily, May 17, 2016. http://www.trustnordisk.com/content/exclusive-interview-louise-vesth-matt-dillon-bruno-ganz-star-von-trier-s-house-jack-built.

Morton, Timothy. *Dark Ecology: For a Logic of Future Coexistence*. New York: Columbia University Press, [2016] 2018.

——. *The Ecological Thought*. Cambridge, MA: Harvard University Press, 2010.

"Music and Sound Design." *The Making of Antichrist/Antichrist*. New York: Criterion Collection, 2010. DVD.

National Staff. "Lars von Trier Turns to Crowdsourcing for New Film." The National News, August 29, 2012, https://www.thenational.ae/arts-culture/lars-von-trier-turns-to-crowdsourcing-for-new-film-1.408914.

Nietzsche, Friedrich. *Beyond Good and Evil: Prelude to a Philosophy of the Future* (1886). Trans. Helen Zimmern. In *The Complete Works of Friedrich Nietzsche (1909–1913)*, ed. Dr. Oscar Levy. Apophthemgms and Interludes 146, 96. Vol. 5. London: T. N. Foulis, 1909.

Nikoline. *Gourmet*. Music video. 2020. https://www.nikolinemusic.com/videos (accessed July 16, 2021).

Noheden, Kristoffer. "Hypnotic Ecologies: Environmental Melancholia in Lars von Trier's Films." *Journal of Scandinavian Cinema* 8, no. 2 (2018): 135–48.

Nordic Council Film Prize Jury. "Prize Winner 2009." Nordic Co-operation, HYPERLINK "https://www.norden.org/en/nominee/prize-winner-2009-0" https://www.norden.org/en/nominee/prize-winner-2009-0 (accessed August 9, 2021).

O'Donoghue, Darragh. "A Girl Named Joe: Nymphets, *Nymph()maniac*, and Lars von Trier." *Cineaste* 39, no. 3 (Summer 2014): 10–15.

O'Hehir, Andrew. "Lars von Trier: 'I Don't Want to be an Adult.'" Salon, May 21, 2011. https://www.salon.com/2011/05/21/lars_von_trier_interview/.

——. "Pick of the Week: Lars von Trier's Spectacular *Melancholia*." Salon, November 10, 2011. http://www.salon.com/2011/11/11/pick_of_the_week_lars_von_triers_spectacular_melancholia/.

Olesen, Elisabeth. *Adventure Guide to Sweden*. Edison, NJ: Hunter, 2005.

Østergaard, Cecilie Høgsbro. "In the Service of Good Taste." *Kunstkritikk*, December 11, 2012, https://kunstkritikk.no/in-the-service-of-good-taste/.

Page, Nicholas. "Her Dark Materials: *Antichrist*'s "Mysogyny [sic] Consultant" Interviewed." The Big Picture, August 6, 2009. http://www.thebigpicturemagazine.com/.

Page, Tim. "Filmmaker's Audacious Teaming of His *Melancholia* with Wagner's Music." *Washington Post*, December 23, 2011. https://www.washingtonpost.com/lifestyle/style/filmmakers-audacious-teaming-of-his-melancholia-with-wagners-music/2011/12/15/gIQAWRpgDP_story.html.

Papazian, Elizabeth, and Caroline Eades. "Introduction: Dialogue, Politics, Utopia." In *The Essay Film: Dialogue/Politics/Utopia*, ed. Elizabeth Papazian and Caroline Eades, 1–11. New York: Wallflower, 2016.

Pearce, Emilie Spliid. Interview by the author, Skype, August 15, 2019.

Piil, Morten. "Kindred Spirits." *FILM #66*. Danish Film Institute, June 2, 2009. http://www.dfi.dk/.

Powell, Dilys. Review of *The Seventh Seal*. *Sunday Times*, March 9, 1958.

Pressly, Lowry. "*Nymphomaniac: Vol. 1*: Fishers of Men, Meaning." *Los Angeles Review of Books*, March 21, 2014. https://lareviewofbooks.org/essay/nymphomaniac-vol-1-fishers-men-meaning.

Proust, Marcel. *In Search of Lost Time* (1913–1927). Vol. 5, *The Captive*. Trans. C. K. Scott Moncrieff and Terence Gilmartin. Rev. trans. D. J. Enright, 205–6. New York: Modern Library, 2003.

Quigley, Paula. "The Spectacle of Suffering: The 'Woman's Film' and Lars von Trier." *Studies in European Cinema* 9, nos. 2–3 (2012): 155–68.

Ravn, Dorthe. " 'Von Trier vil lave Satan-film.' " *Berlingske Tidende*, October 20, 2004, https://www.berlingske.dk/kultur/von-trier-vil-lave-satan-film.

Rao, Mallika. "The *Melancholia* Postulate." *Atlantic*, May 9, 2020. https://www.theatlantic.com/culture/archive/2020/05/watching-melancholia-during-pandemic/611383/.

Read, Rupert. "An Allegory of a 'Therapeutic' Reading of a Film: Of *Melancholia*." *Sequence One: Planet Melancholia* 1, no. 2 (2014): https://reframe.sussex.ac.uk/sequence1/1-2-an-allegory-of-a-therapeutic-reading/ (accessed July 15, 2021).

Refn, Anders. Interview by the author, Copenhagen, June 29, 2018.

Rehlin, Gunnar. "Filmen är mitt inferno." Fokus, May 15, 2009. https://www.fokus.se/2009/05/filmen-ar-mitt-inferno/.

Reumont, François. "Cinematographer Manuel Alberto Claro, DFF, Discusses *The House That Jack Built*." La Lettre AFC, May 17, 2018. https://www.afcinema.com/Cinematographer-Manuel-Alberto-Claro-DFF-discusses-Lars-Von-Trier-s-The-House-That-Jack-Built.html?lang=fr.

Ricoeur, Paul. *Freud and Philosophy*. Trans. Denis Savage. New Haven, CT: Yale University Press, 1970.

Rockwell, John. *The Idiots*. London: British Film Institute, 2003.

——. "REVERBERATIONS; Maybe Lars von Trier's Vision Was Just What Wagner Needed." *New York Times*, June 11, 2004. HYPERLINK "https://www.nytimes.com/2004/06/11/movies/reverberations-maybe-lars-von-trier-s-vision-was-just-what-wagner-needed.html" https://www.nytimes.com/2004/06/11/movies/reverberations-maybe-lars-von-trier-s-vision-was-just-what-wagner-needed.html.

——. "Von Trier and Wagner, a Bond Sealed in Emotion." *New York Times*, April 8, 2001. https://www.nytimes.com/2001/04/08/movies/film-von-trier-and-wagner-a-bond-sealed-in-emotion.html.

Romer, Knud. "A Hearse Heading Home." *FILM* #66. Danish Film Institute, May 2009, https://www.dfi.dk/files/docs/2018-02/FILM66%5B1%5D%20%281%29.pdf (accessed August 9, 2021).

Romney, Jonathan. "The Girl Can't Help It." *Film Comment*, March–April 2014, 27–31.

Jonathan Romney, "*Melancholia*, Lars von Trier, 130 Mins." *Independent*, October 22, 2011. https://www.independent.co.uk/arts-entertainment/films/reviews/melancholia-lars-von-trier-130-mins-15-2364172.html.

Ross, Alex. "Melancholia, Bile." Alex Ross: The Rest Is Noise, November 19, 2011. https://www
.therestisnoise.com/2011/11/melancholia-bile.html.

Roxborough, Scott. "Berlin: Lars von Trier's *The House That Jack Built* Adds Riley Keough, Sofie Gråbøl
(Exclusive)." *Hollywood Reporter*, February 11, 2017. https://www.hollywoodreporter.com/news/berlin
-lars-von-triers-house-jack-built-adds-riley-keough-sofie-grabol-974732.

——. "Lars von Trier Admits to Being a Nazi, Understanding Hitler (Cannes 2011)." *Hollywood Reporter*,
May 18, 2011. https://www.hollywoodreporter.com/news/lars-von-trier-admits-being-189747.

——. "Lars von Trier Imposes Voluntary Gag Order on Himself after Police Questioning." *Hollywood Reporter*, October 5, 2011. https://www.hollywoodreporter.com/news/lars-von-trier-police
-questioning-244514.

——. "Lars von Trier Speared Over *Antichrist*." *Hollywood Reporter*, May 18, 2009. https://www
.hollywoodreporter.com/news/lars-von-trier-speared-antichrist-84190.

Roxborough, Scott, and Stuart Kemp. "Lars von Trier Named Persona Non Grata in Cannes After
Hitler Remarks." *Hollywood Reporter*, May 19, 2011. https://www.hollywoodreporter.com/news/lars
-von-trier-named-persona-190227.

Ryzik, Melena. "Lars von Trier Kicks Up a Cannes Controversy." *New York Times*, May 18, 2011. https://
artsbeat.blogs.nytimes.com/2011/05/18/lars-von-trier-kicks-ups-a-cannes-controvery/,

Sade, Marquis de. *Juliette* (1797–1801). Rev. ed. Trans. Austryn Wainhouse. New York: Grove, 1968.

——. *Justine, or Good Conduct Well Chastised* (1791). In *The Marquis de Sade: Justine, Philosophy in the Bedroom,
and Other Writings*. Trans. Richard Seaver and Austryn Wainhouse, 447–743. New York: Grove, 1965.

Safranski, Rüdiger. *Schopenhauer and the Wild Years of Philosophy*. Trans. Ewald Osers London: Weiden-
feld & Nicholson, 1989.

Saif, Sami. "*Dogville* Confessions." *Dogville*, directed by Lars von Trier. Disc 2. Copenhagen: Nordisk,
2003. DVD.

Saks, Eric, dir. *American Psycho: From Book to Screen*. *American Psycho*. Killer Collector's Edition. Santa
Monica, CA: Lionsgate Home Entertainment, 2005. DVD.

Savage, Sophia. "Lars von Trier Invites You to Interpret Six Artworks for *Gesamt* Film Project."
IndieWire, August 13, 2012. https://www.indiewire.com/2012/08/lars-von-trier-invites-you-to
-interpret-six-artworks-for-gesamt-film-project-202184/.

Schepelern, Peter. "After the Fall: Sex and Evil in Lars von Trier's *Antichrist*." In *Bridges Across Cultures*.
Perugia, Italy, 2013. Published in collaboration with *Voces del Caribe*, 2013: 5–13. https://img1.wsimg
.com/blobby/go/17d75147-ba5c-4e83-bc9f-efc947767190/BAC2013.pdf (accessed August 9, 2021).

——. *Antichrist I–V*. Unpublished manuscript. Lars von Trier Collection, Danish Film Institute, 2015.

——. "BADLEY: ANTICHRIST CHAPTER." Email file attachment addressed to author, March 20, 2020.

——. "Drillepinden." *Ekko Filmmagasinet*, August 23, 2005, https://www.ekkofilm.dk/artikler
/drillepinden/.

——. Email message to the author, August 11, 2020.

——. Email message to the author, August 28, 2020.

——. Email message to the author, March 24, 2015.

——. "Forget About Love: Sex and Detachment in Lars von Trier's *Nymphomaniac*." Kosmorama,
March 11, 2015. https://www.kosmorama.org/en/kosmorama/artikler/forget-about-love-sex-and
-detachment-lars-von-triers-nymphomaniac.

——. "Hvisken og råb." *Ekko Filmmagasinet*, May 17, 2009, https://www.ekkofilm.dk/artikler/hvisken
-og-rab/.

——. Interview with Lars von Trier, University of Copenhagen, April 22, 2015. English translation by
Peter Schepelern.

——. "Lars von Trier and Cultural Liberalism." *FILM*, Danish Film Institute, January 30, 2014, 24–27, https://www.dfi.dk/en/english/lars-von-trier-and-cultural-liberalism.

——. *Lars von Triers elementer*. Copenhagen: Rosinante, 1997.

——. "Linda Badley: *Melancholia*." Email file attachment addressed to the author, June 10, 2020.

——. *Lars von Triers film: Tvang og befrielse*. Copenhagen: Rosinante [2000], 2018.

——. "The Making of an Auteur: Notes on the Auteur Theory and Lars von Trier." In *Visual Authorship: Creativity and Intentionality in Media*, ed. Torben Grodal, Bente Larsen, and Iben Thorving Laursen, 103–27. Copenhagen: University of Copenhagen/ Museum Tusculanum, 2005.

——. "Nine Questions for Lars von Trier Regarding *The House That Jack Built*." *The House That Jack Built*, directed by Lars von Trier. London: Artificial Eye, 2018. DVD.

Schepelern, Peter, ed. *Lars von Trier Det God Med Det Onde*. Copenhagen: Strandberg, 2017.

Schmidt, David. "Serial Killer Fiction: An Introduction." CrimeCulture, 2015, https://www.crimeculture.com/?page_id=1459 (accessed July 15, 2021).

Schneider, Steven Jay. "Murder as Art/The Art of Murder: Aestheticizing Violence in Modern Cinematic Horror." *Intensities: The Journal of Cult Media*, no. 3 (Spring 2003): https://intensitiescultmedia.files.wordpress.com/2012/12/schneider-murder-as-art.pdf (accessed July 15, 2021).

Schopenhauer, Arthur. *Aesthetics, Book III: The World as Will and Representation* (1818). Vol. 1. Trans. Judith Norman, Alistair Welchman, and Christopher Janaway. Cambridge: Cambridge University Press, 2014.

——. *Ethics, Book IV: The World as Will and Representation* (1818). Vol. 1. Trans. Judith Norman, Alistair Welchman, and Christopher Janaway. Cambridge: Cambridge University Press, 2014.

Schwarzbaum, Lisa. "Cannes Film Festival: Lars von Trier's Stunning *Melancholia*—the End of the World (and a Challenge to *The Tree of Life*)." *Entertainment Weekly*, May 18, 201l. https://ew.com/article/2011/05/18/cannes-film-festival-lars-von-trier-melancholia-terrence-malick/.

Sejersen, Casper, and Ceilie Høgsbro. *Belongs to Joe: Book of Comfort for a Nymphomaniac*. London: Mack, 2015.

Seltzer, Mark. *Serial Killers: Death and Life in America's Wound Culture*. London: Routledge, 1998.

Sharf, Zack. "Cannes 2011 Jury Preferred *Melancholia* Over *Tree of Life*, but Wouldn't Award von Trier." IndieWire, May 29, 2020. https://www.indiewire.com/2020/05/cannes-jury-melancholia-palme-dor-tree-of-life-1202234293/.

——. "*The House That Jack Built*: Uma Thurman Catches the Eye of a Serial Killer in New Look at Lars von Trier Film." IndieWire, April 26, 2018. https://www.indiewire.com/2018/04/the-house-that-jack-built-uma-thurman-first-look-lars-von-trier-1201957520/.

——. "Lars von Trier Wants You to Know *The House That Jack Built* Will Be His Most Brutal Film Ever." IndieWire, January 2, 2017. http://www.trustnordisk.com/content/lars-von-trier-wants-you-know-house-jack-built-will-be-his-most-brutal-film-ever/.

——. "Lars Von Trier's *House That Jack Built* Baits Controversy with Shocking Posters of Characters Tied Up and Contorted." IndieWire, September 26, 2018. https://www.indiewire.com/2018/09/house-that-jack-built-posters-female-characters-tied-up-contorted-lars-von-trier-1202007137/.

——. "PETA Defends Lars von Trier's *The House That Jack Built* Against Backlash over Graphic Animal Mutilation Scene." IndieWire, May 27, 2018. https://www.indiewire.com/2018/05/peta-defends-lars-von-trier-the-house-that-jack-built-duck-mutilation-1201965931/.

Shaviro, Steven. "*Melancholia*: Or The Anti-Sublime." In *Sequence One: Planet Melancholia* 1.1, 2012. https://reframe.sussex.ac.uk/sequence/files/2012/12/MELANCHOLIA-or-The-Romantic-Anti-Sublime-SEQUENCE-1.1-2012-Steven-Shaviro.pdf (accessed July 15, 2021).

Shoard, Catherine. "Lars von Trier Inspired by Donald Trump for New Serial-Killer Film." *Guardian*, February 14, 2017. https://www.theguardian.com/film/2017/feb/14/lars-von-trier-donald-trump-the -house-that-jack-built.

——. "Lars von Trier Makes Vow of Silence After Cannes Furore." *Guardian*, October 5, 2011. http:// www.theguardian.com/film/2011/oct/05/lars-von-trier-cannes.

Shone, Tom. "*Nymphomaniac*, *The Wolf of Wall Street*, and Cinema's Bad Sex Renaissance." *Guardian*, March 19, 2014. https://www.theguardian.com/film/2014/mar/19/nymphomaniac-wolf-wall-street -cinemas-bad-sex-renaissance.

Siegal, Nina. "Lars von Trier Wants to Turn All His Films into Diamonds." *New York Times*, February 11, 2019. https://www.nytimes.com/2019/02/11/arts/design/lars-von-trier-diamond-melancholia .html.

Silberg, John. "*Nymphomaniac*: How Cinematographer Manuel Alberto Claro Brought Lars von Trier's Vision to Life." Creative Planet Network, March 26, 2014. https://www.creativeplanetnetwork.com /news/nymphomaniac-how-cinematographer-manuel-alberto-claro-brought-lars-von-triers -vision-life-338397.

Simons, Jan. *Playing the Waves: Lars von Trier's Game Cinema*. Amsterdam: Amsterdam University Press, 2007.

Simpson, Philip L. *Psycho Paths: Tracking the Serial Killer Through Contemporary American Film and Fiction*. Carbondale: Southern Illinois University Press, 2000.

Sinnerbrink, Robert. *New Philosophies of Film: Thinking Images*. New York: Continuum, 2011.

——. "Provocation and Perversity: Lars von Trier's Cinematic Anti-Philosophy." In *The Global Auteur: The Politics of Authorship in Twenty-First-Century Cinema*, ed. Sung-Hoon Jeong and Jermi Szaniawski, 95–114. London: Bloomsbury, 2016.

Skal, David. *The Monster Show: A Cultural History of the Horror Film*. New York: Farrar, Straus & Giroux, 2001.

Sollers, Philippe. *Sade's Way*. Video documentary. ParisLike, 2013. http://www.parislike.com/EN/snoopy -philippe-sollers-video.php (accessed July 16, 2021).

Soper, Kate. *What Is Nature? Culture, Politics, and the Non-human*. Oxford: Blackwell,1995.

Spotts, Frederic. *Hitler and the Power of Aesthetics*. 2002. New York: Overlook, 2004.

Stefanski, Emma. "The Most Messed-up Serial Killer Film in Years Keeps Finding Ways to Piss People Off." Thrillist, September, 16, 2018. https://www.thrillist.com/entertainment/nation/the-house-that -jack-built-posters-lars-von-trier.

Stevenson, Jack. *Lars von Trier*. London: British Film Institute, 2002.

——. *Scandinavian Blue: The Erotic Cinema of Sweden and Denmark on the 1960s and 1970s*. Jefferson, NC: McFarland, 2010.

Stoler, Ann Laura. *Along the Archival Grain: Epistemic Anxieties and Colonial Common Sense*. Princeton, NJ: Princeton University Press, 2010.

Strindberg, August. "The Battle of the Brains" (1887). In *Selected Essays by August Strindberg*, ed. and trans. Michael Robinson, 25–46. Cambridge: Cambridge University Press, 1996.

——. *A Dream Play* (1901). In *Miss Julie and Other Plays*, ed. and trans. Michael Robinson, 175–247. Oxford: Oxford University Press, 1998.

——. *The Father* (1887). In *Miss Julie and Other Plays*, ed., trans. Michael Robinson, 1–53. Oxford: Oxford University Press, 1998.

——. *Han och hon: En själs utvecklingshistoria, 1875–76*. In *Salmlade Skrifter*, ed. John Landquist. Vol. 55. Stockholm: Bonniers, 1919.

——. *A Madman's Defense* (1895). Trans. Evert Springchorn. New York: Doubleday, 1967.

——. *Miss Julie* (1888). In *Miss Julie and Other Plays*, ed. and trans. Michael Robinson, 55–110. Oxford: Oxford University Press, 1998.

——. "Soul Murder (*Apropos Rosmersholm*)" (1887). In *Selected Essays by August Strindberg*, ed. and trans. Michael Robinson, 64–72. Cambridge: Cambridge University Press, 1996.

——. *The Stronger* (1889). In *Pre-Inferno Plays*, ed. and trans. Walter Johnson, 189–98. Seattle: University of Washington Press, 1970.

——. *A Witch* (1890). Trans. Mary Sandberg. Venice, CA: Lapis, 1990.

Sumner, Anne. *Tjolöholm: A Woman's Achievement*. Trans. Alan Crozier. Fjärås: Tjolöholm Foundation, 2001.

Tapper, Michael. "A Romance in Decomposition." In *Lars von Trier: Interviews*, ed. Jan Lumhold, 71–80. Jackson: University of Mississippi Press, 2003.

Taubin, Amy. "All Movies Great and Small." *Film Comment*, July-August, 2011, https://www.filmcomment .com/article/cannes-2011-report-1/ (accessed July 15, 2021).

Talu, Yonca. "Interview: Manuel Alberto Claro." *Film Comment*, January 23, 2019, https://www .filmcomment.com/blog/interview-manuel-alberto-claro/ (accessed July 15, 2021).

Thomsen, Bodil Marie Stavning. "The Demonic Quality of Darkness in *The House That Jack Built*: Haptic Transmedial Affects Throughout the Works of Lars von Trier." In *Transmedia Directors: Artistry, Industry, and New Audiovisual Aesthetics*, ed. Carol Vernallis, Holly Rogers, and Lisa Perrott, 362–77. London: Bloomsbury, 2020.

——. *Lars von Trier's Renewal of Film, 1984–2014: Signal, Pixel, Diagram*. Arhus: Arhus University Press, 2018.

Thomsen, Christian Braad. "Control and Chaos" (1996). In *Lars von Trier: Interviews*, ed. Jan Lumholdt, 106–16. Jackson: University of Mississippi Press, 2003.

Thomsen, Torsten Bøgh. "Foggy Signs: Dark Ecological Queerings in Lars von Trier's *Antichrist*." *Journal of Scandinavian Cinema* 8, no. 2 (2018): 123–34.

Thorsen, Nils. *Geniet—Lars von Triers liv, film og fobier*. Copenhagen: Politiken, 2011.

——. "Longing for the End of All." Production notes, press kit, *Melancholia* official website, Magnolia Films, 2011. http://www.magpictures.com/presskit.aspx?id=bbcb733d-8d0e-495a-ba6d-be9a79453 d1czzzzzz (accessed July 15, 2021).

——. "Von Trier tørlagt, nøgen og på røven." *Politiken*, November 29, 2014, https://politiken.dk /magasinet/interview/art5555223/Von-Trier-tørlagt-nøgen-og-på-røven.

Tjolöholms Slott. 2020. http://www.Tjolöholm.se/ (accessed July 15, 2021).

Tracy, Andrew. "The Essay Film." *Sight & Sound*, May 7, 2019. https://www.bfi.org.uk/news-opinion/sight -sound-magazine/features/deep-focus/essay-film.

Trust Film Sales. "Lars von Trier Shoots Antichrist in Eden." August 18, 2008, http://www.trust-film .dk/.

Umland, Rebecca A., and Samuel J. Umland. "Burn, Witch, Burn: A First Look at the Scandinavian Horror Film." In *Horror International*, ed. Steven Jay Schneider and Tony Williams, 290–314. Detroit, MI: Wayne State University Press, 2005.

Valsson, Pétur. "Elevating the Ugly: Lars von Trier's Anti-Aesthetic." Paper presented at the Society for the Advancement of Scandinavian Studies, New Orleans, Louisiana, April 28, 2016.

Van Hoeij. "Selling Lars von Trier's *Nymphomaniac*: How to Create a Sexy, Controversial Hit." IndieWire, December 12, 2013. https://www.indiewire.com/2013/12/selling-lars-von-triers-nymphomaniac-how -to-create-a-sexy-controversial-hit-241390/.

Vaughan, William. *German Romantic Painting*. New Haven, CT: Yale University Press, 1980.

Vesth, Louise. Email message to the author, October 22, 2020.

——. Interview by the author, Skype, September 12, 2019.

Von Trier, Lars. "*Antichrist* Final Script." July 2008. Unpublished screenplay. Courtesy of Zentropa Productions.

——. "'Antichrist' materialer." Lars von Trier Collection, Danish Film Institute, n.d.

——. *Bag fornedrelsens porte* [Behind the gates of debasement]. 1975. Unpublished manuscript. December 9, 2012.

——. "*Deed of Conveyance*: Lars Von Trier on the Nibelungen Ring—The Enriched Darkness." Mostly Opera, October 4, 2007. https://mostlyopera.blogspot.com/2007/10/lars-von-trier-on-nibelungen-ring.html.

——. "Director's Confession." *Antichrist* official website, May 18, 2009. http://www.antichristthemovie.com.

——. "Directors [*sic*] Intentions: *Melancholia*." Copenhagen, March 2010. Unpublished document. Courtesy of Zentropa Productions.

——. "Director's Statement." Production notes, press kit, *Melancholia* official website, Magnolia Pictures, 2011. http://www.magpictures.com/presskit.aspx?id=bbcb733d-8d0e-495a-ba6d-be9a79453d1c (accessed July 15, 2021).

——. "Eliza eller Den lille bog om det dejlige og det tarvelige" [Eliza, or The little book about the delightful and the vulgar]. Unpublished manuscript, 1976. "Trier Eliza-roman renskhrift." Lars von Trier Collection, Danish Film Institute.

——. Interview by the author, Copenhagen, June 28, 2018.

——. "Interview with Lars von Trier." 2011. "Extras/The Making of *Melancholia*/The Visual Style." *Melancholia*, directed by Lars von Trier. London: Curzon Artificial Eye, 2012. DVD.

——. ' "I Understand Hitler." ' YouTube, 4:26, May 18, 2011. https://www.youtube.com/watch?v=QpUqpLhoiRw.

——. "Lars von Trier noter til Die Walküre." Lars von Trier Collection, Danish Film Institute, 2003.

——. "*Melancholia*." 2nd and final draft, March 4, 2010. Rev. by VW [Vinca Wiedemann], July 5, 2010. Unpublished screenplay. Courtesy of Zentropa Productions.

——. "*Nymphomaniac*—Director's Comments." Copenhagen, April 2012. Unpublished document. Courtesy of Zentropa Productions.

——. "*Nymphomaniac*." Final shooting draft. January 2013. Unpublished screenplay. Courtesy of Zentropa Productions.

——. Public acceptance statement, n.d. T VII 80, Lars von Trier Collection, Danish Film Institute.

——. "Scenesynopsis, Act II." n.d., T V 55, Lars von Trier Collection, Danish Film Institute.

——. "*The House That Jack Built* Director's Statement." July 1, 2016. Unpublished document. Courtesy of Zentropa Productions.

——. "*The House That Jack Built*." Shooting draft. January 20, 2017. Unpublished screenplay. Courtesy of Zentropa Productions.

——. "Turnbook, Notes, Drawings, and Research from the opera project 'Nibelungens Ring.'" n.d. T VII, 55, Lars von Trier Collection, Danish Film Institute.

Von Trier, Lars, and Jens Albinus. Commentary. *The Idiots (Idioterne)*. Dogme Kollektion 1–4. Disc 2. ES: Copenhagen, DK: Electric Parc, 2005. DVD.

Von Trier, Lars, and Murray Smith. Audio commentary. *Antichrist*, dir. Lars von Trier. New York: Criterion Collection, 2009. DVD.

Von Trier, Lars, and Niels Vorsel. "The Kingdom III: EXODUS. Treatment, Summary." Synopses, Notes and Letters to Zentropa Employees for "Kingdom III." n.d., TI, D:8, Lars von Trier Collection, Danish Film Institute.

Von Trier, Lars, and Peter Schepelern. Audio commentary. *Melancholia*, dir. Lars von Trier. London: Artificial Eye, 2012. Blu-ray.

Wachthausen, Jean-Luc. "Lars von Trier: '*Antichrist* est ma thérapie.'" *Le Figaro*, May 18, 2009. http://www.lefigaro.fr/.

Waddell, Calum. "Lars von Trier: Satanic Scandals." Total Sci Fi Online, 2009, http://totalscifionline.com/interviews/3756-lars-von-trier-satanic-scandals (link unavailable).

Wainhouse, Austryn. "Foreword." In *Juliette* (1797–1801), by the Marquis de Sade, rev. ed., trans. Austryn Wainhouse, xii–x. New York: Grove, 1968.

Weis, Jakob. *Von Trier—Persona non grata*. Copenhagen: SAGA Edgmont, 2020.

White, Armond. "*The House That Jack Built* Takes On the Apocalypse." *National Review*, December 19, 2018. https://www.nationalreview.com/2018/12/movie-review-the-house-that-jack-built-dark-satire/.

White, Rob. "Interview with Manuel Alberto Claro." *Film Quarterly* 65, no. 4 (Summer 2012): https://filmquarterly.org/2012/07/11/interview-with-manuel-alberto-claro/ (accessed July 15, 2021).

Wiedemann, Vinca. Email message to the author, August 31, 2019.

——. Interview by the author, Skype, July 25, 2019.

Wilkinson, Alicia. "Critics Called Lars von Trier's New Movie 'Repulsive.' It's Being Released Twice." *Vox*, December 14, 2018. https://www.vox.com/culture/2018/11/28/18113504/house-jack-built-lars-von-trier-unrated-r-rated-theater-streaming.

Yau, John. "Eric Frischl's Privileged Bubble." Hyperallergic, November 14, 2020, https://hyperallergic.com/600691/eric-fischls-privileged-bubble/.

Zacharek, Stephanie. "Best Movies 2011: Why I Loved *Melancholia*, and Why *Tree of Life* Left Me Cold." Slate, January 2, 2012. https://slate.com/culture/2012/01/best-movies-2011-why-i-loved-melancholia-and-why-tree-of-life-left-me-cold.html.

Zuckerman, Esther. "Please Don't Let Personalized *Nymphomaniac* Posters Happen." Yahoo News, February 4, 2014. https://tinyurl.com/ysyj2356).

Zylinska, Joanna. *Minimal Ethics for the Anthropocene*. London: Open Humanities, 2014.

INDEX